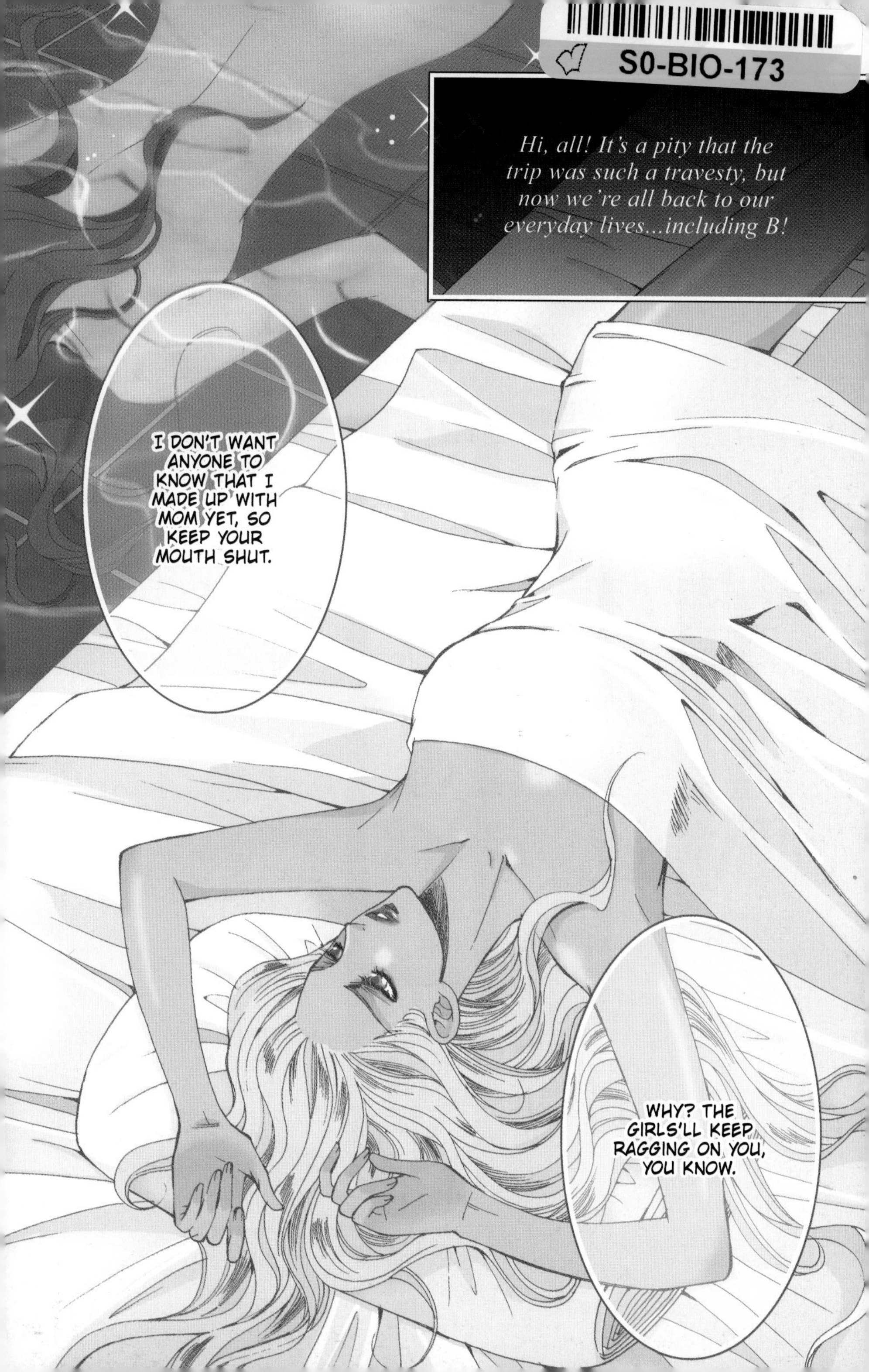
Hi, all! It's a pity that the trip was such a travesty, but now we're all back to our everyday lives...including B!
I DON'T WANT ANYONE TO KNOW THAT I MADE UP WITH MOM YET, SO KEEP YOUR MOUTH SHUT.
WHY? THE GIRLS'LL KEEP RAGGING ON YOU, YOU KNOW.

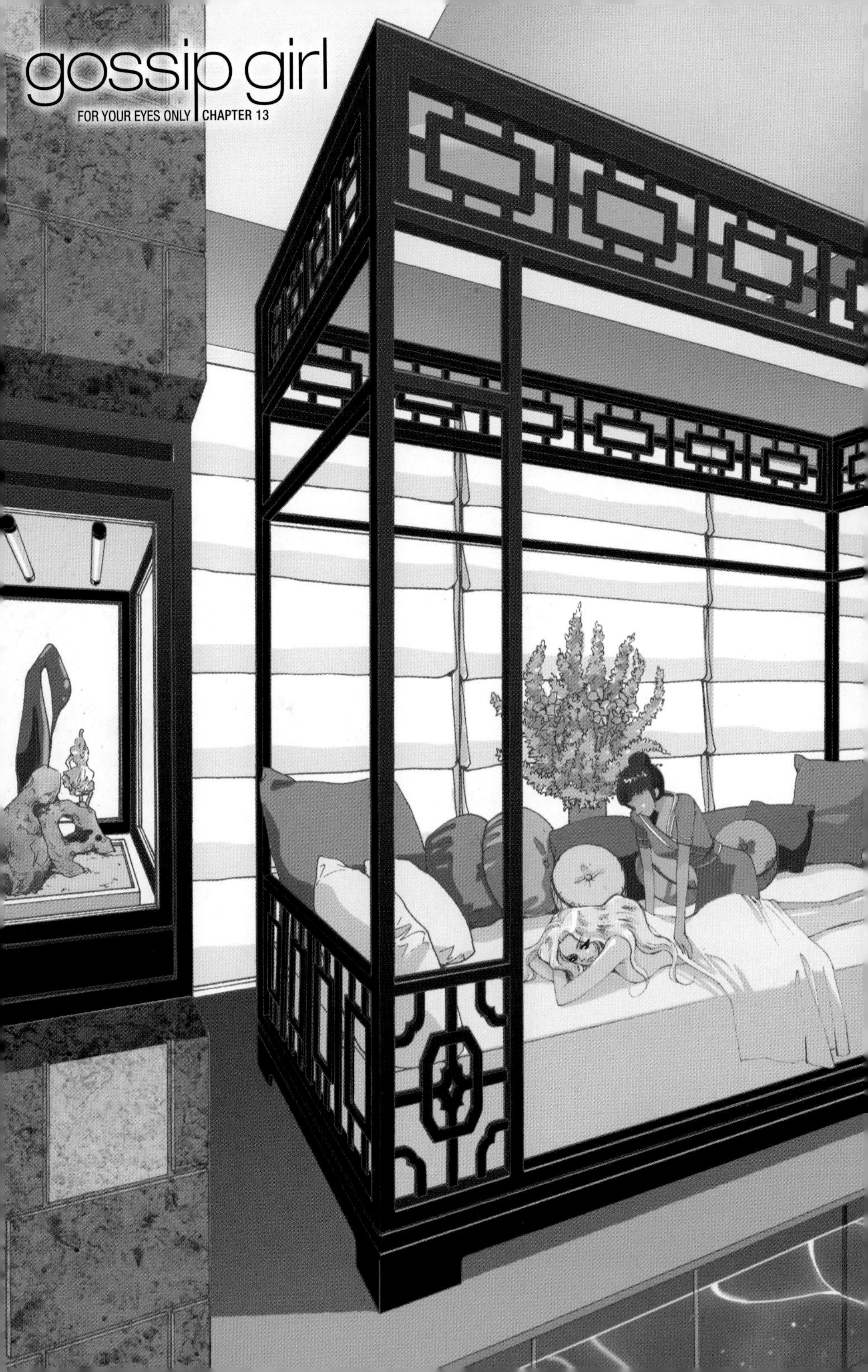
gossip girl
FOR YOUR EYES ONLY | CHAPTER 13

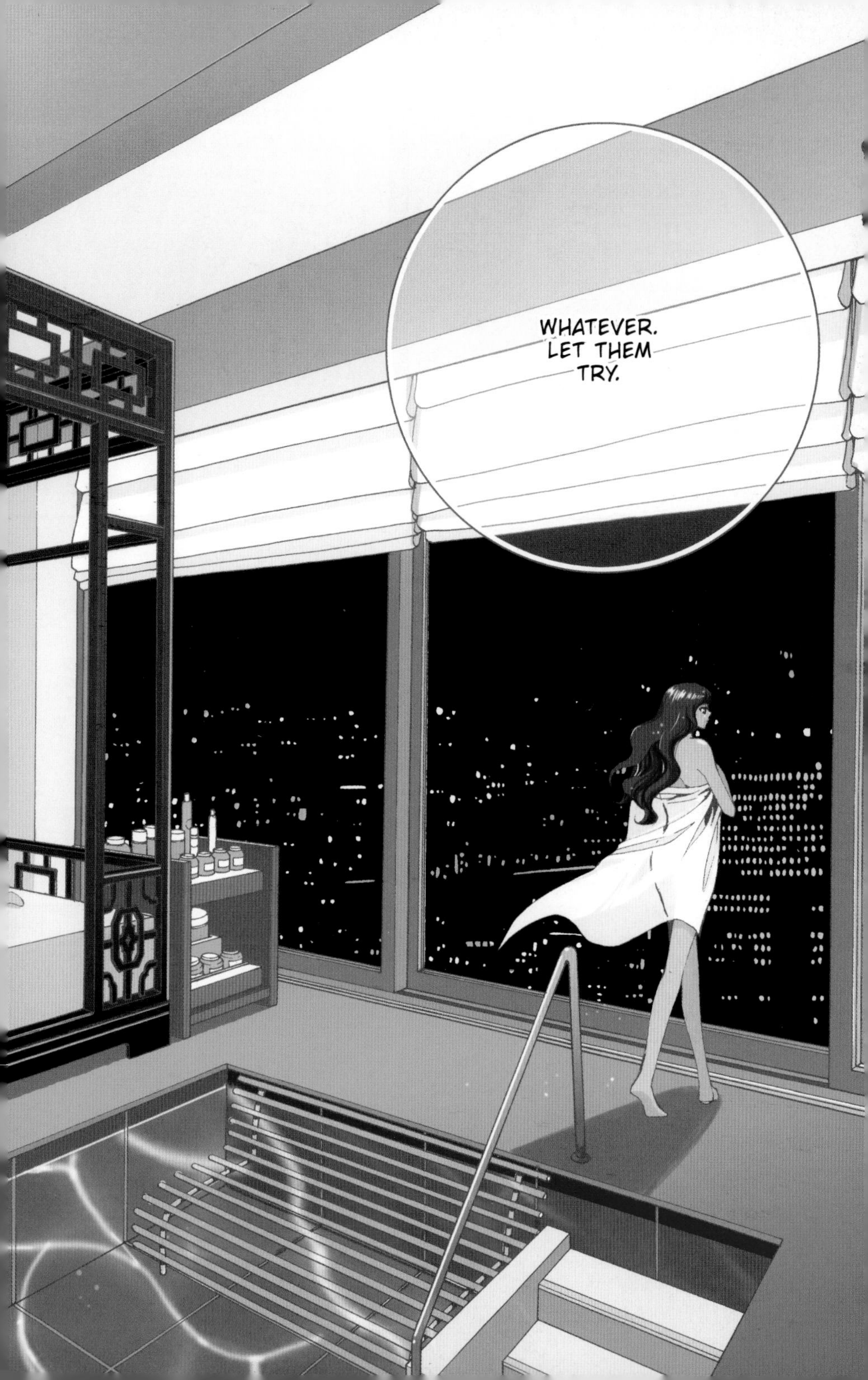
WHATEVER. LET THEM TRY.

I'M GOING TO LET THAT LITTLE J GET COMFORTABLE, AND WHEN I DO MAKE MY MOVE, SHE'LL NEVER SEE ME COMING.

BESIDES, WHY ON EARTH WOULD I BE AFRAID OF THE GIRLS?

WHO DO YOU THINK TAUGHT THEM HOW TO GET IT DONE?

AH-HA-HA! SO SPILL, HOW IS IT DONE?

YOU NEED TO MAKE SURE YOU PUT THE RIGHT KIND OF SCREWS TO THE PERSON YOU WANT TO GET RID OF.

LIKE A CUSTOM-MADE SUIT!

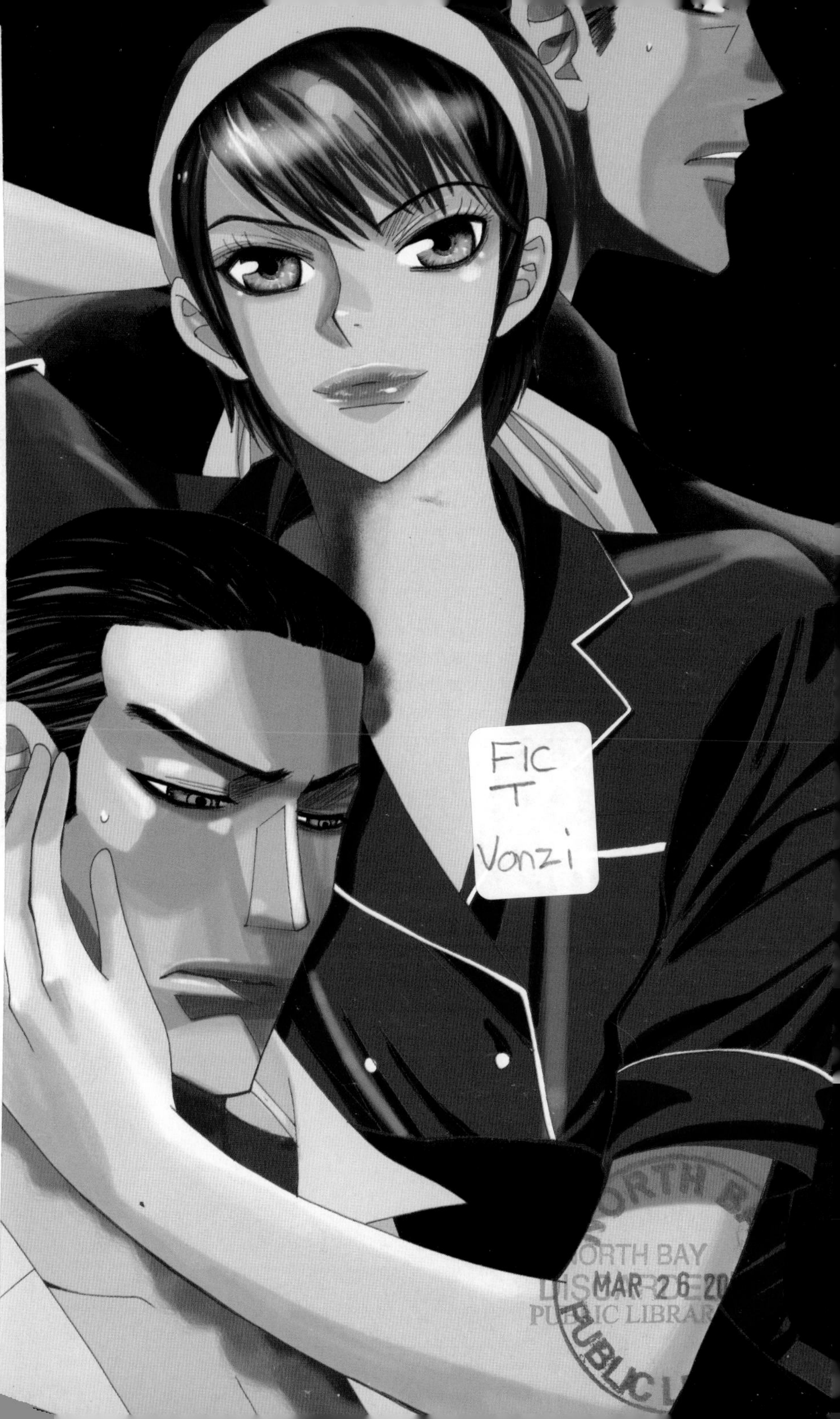

gossip girl

FOR YOUR EYES ONLY

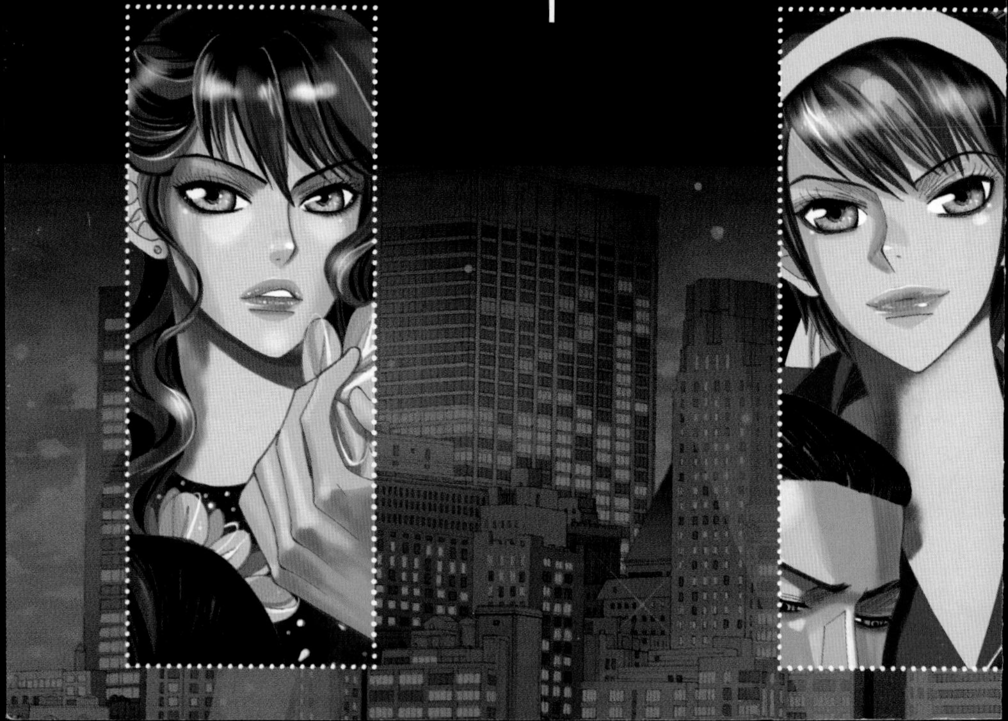

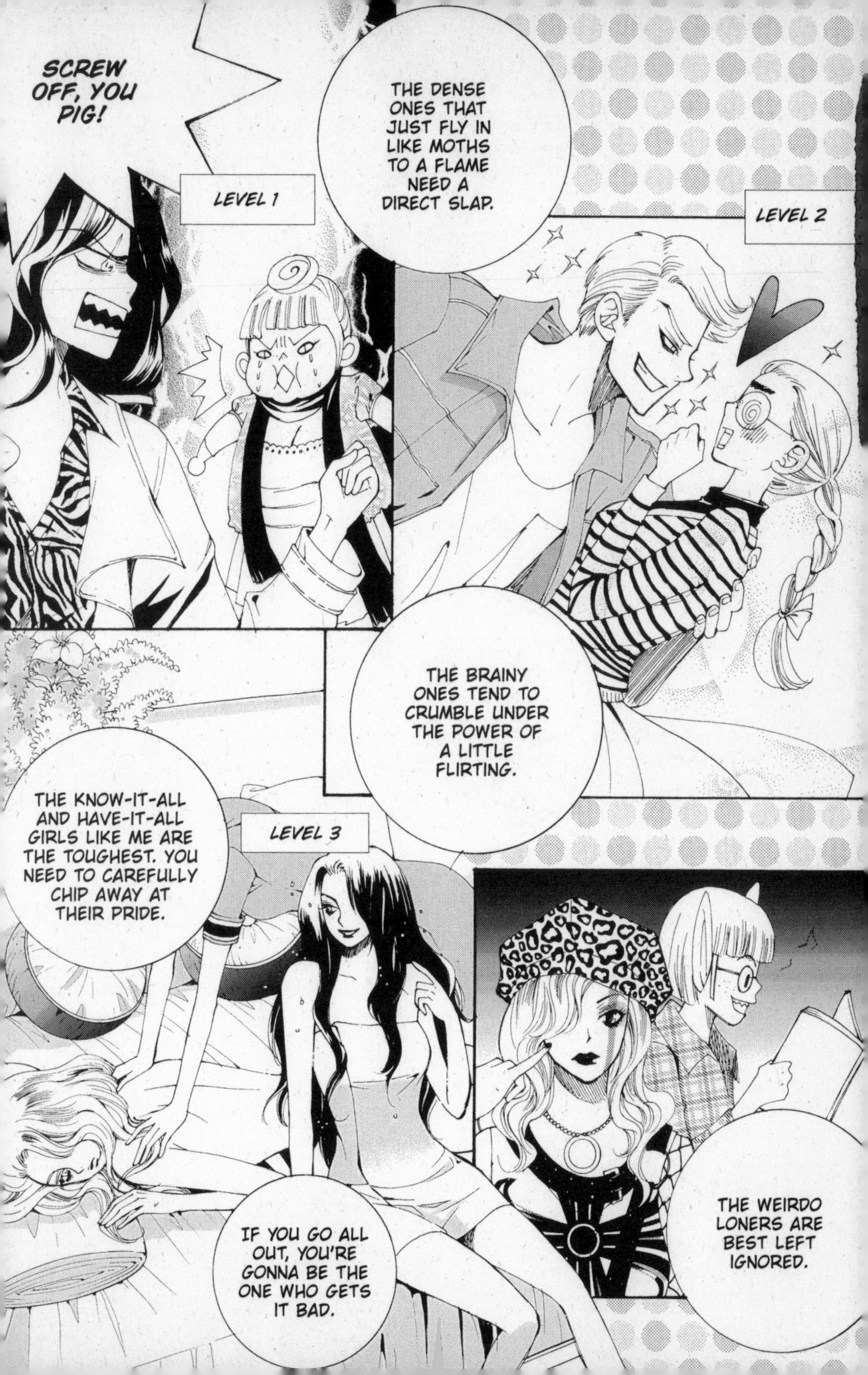
SCREW OFF, YOU PIG!
LEVEL 1
THE DENSE ONES THAT JUST FLY IN LIKE MOTHS TO A FLAME NEED A DIRECT SLAP.
LEVEL 2
THE BRAINY ONES TEND TO CRUMBLE UNDER THE POWER OF A LITTLE FLIRTING.
THE KNOW-IT-ALL AND HAVE-IT-ALL GIRLS LIKE ME ARE THE TOUGHEST. YOU NEED TO CAREFULLY CHIP AWAY AT THEIR PRIDE.
LEVEL 3
IF YOU GO ALL OUT, YOU'RE GONNA BE THE ONE WHO GETS IT BAD.
THE WEIRDO LONERS ARE BEST LEFT IGNORED.

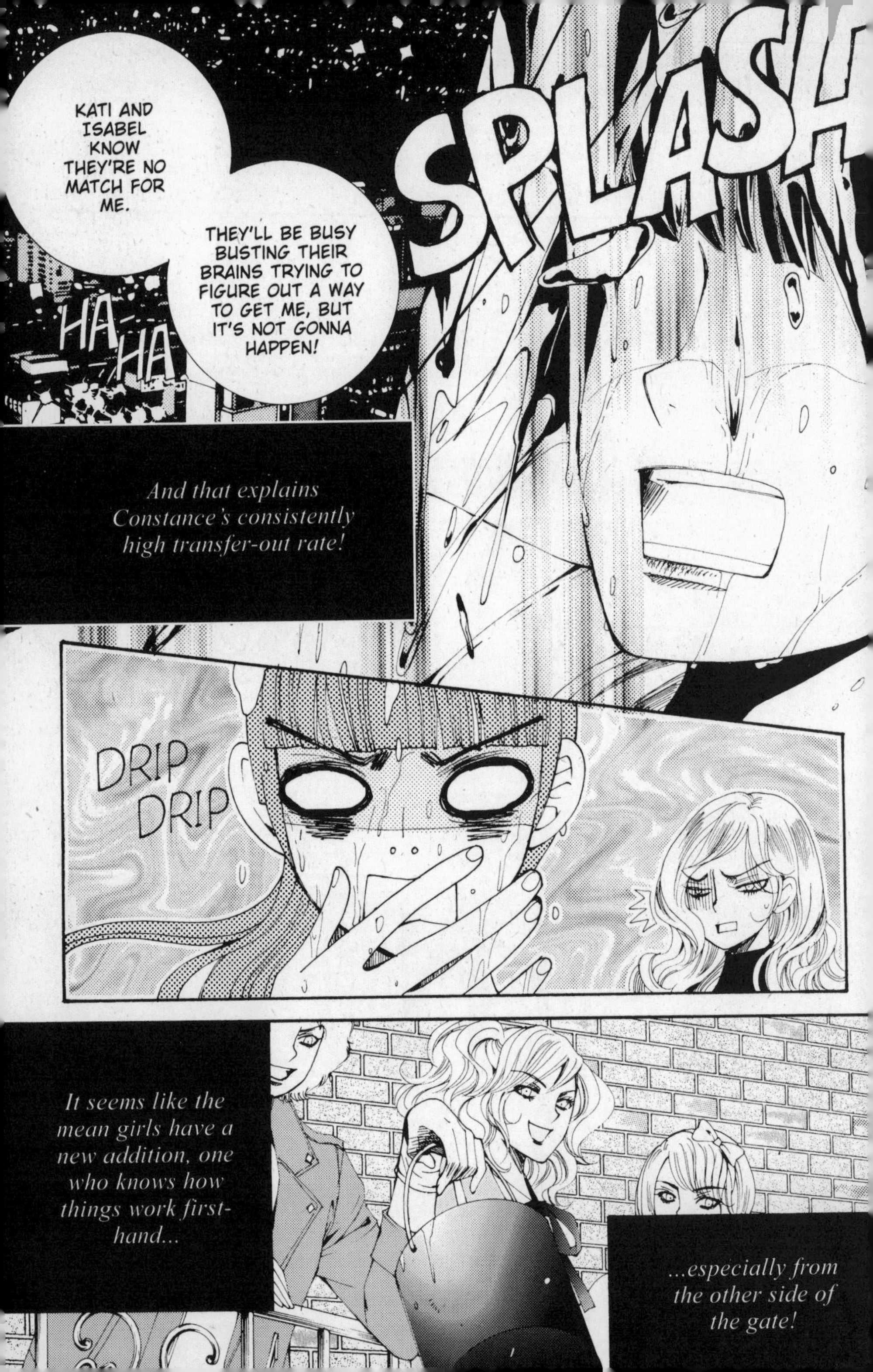
KATI AND ISABEL KNOW THEY'RE NO MATCH FOR ME.
THEY'LL BE BUSY BUSTING THEIR BRAINS TRYING TO FIGURE OUT A WAY TO GET ME, BUT IT'S NOT GONNA HAPPEN!
HA HA
SPLASH
And that explains Constance's consistently high transfer-out rate!
DRIP DRIP
It seems like the mean girls have a new addition, one who knows how things work first-hand...
...especially from the other side of the gate!

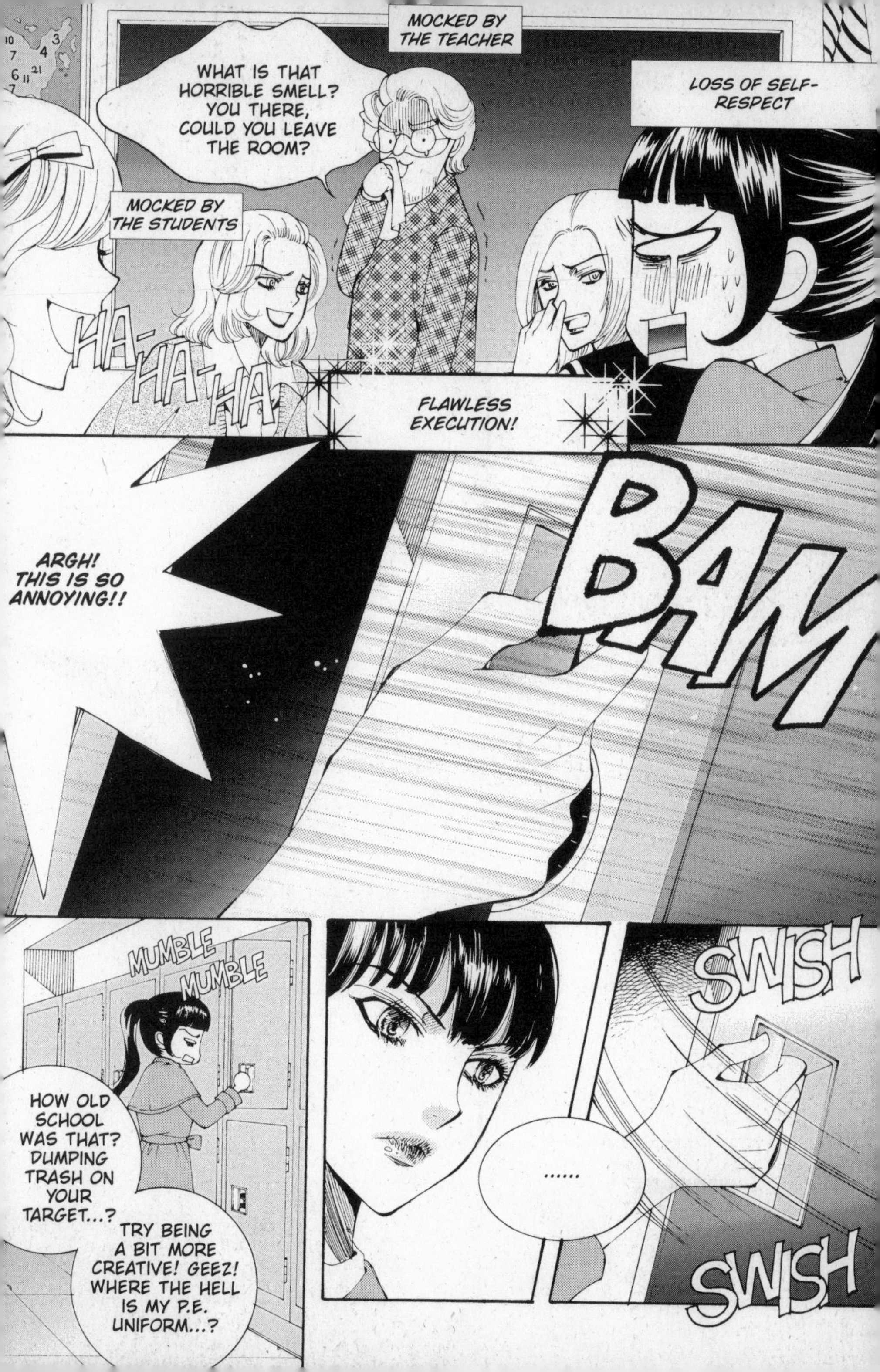
WHAT IS THAT HORRIBLE SMELL? YOU THERE, COULD YOU LEAVE THE ROOM?
MOCKED BY THE TEACHER
LOSS OF SELF-RESPECT
MOCKED BY THE STUDENTS
HA-HA-HA
FLAWLESS EXECUTION!
ARGH! THIS IS SO ANNOYING!!
BAM
MUMBLE MUMBLE
HOW OLD SCHOOL WAS THAT? DUMPING TRASH ON YOUR TARGET...?
TRY BEING A BIT MORE CREATIVE! GEEZ! WHERE THE HELL IS MY P.E. UNIFORM...?
......
SWISH
SWISH

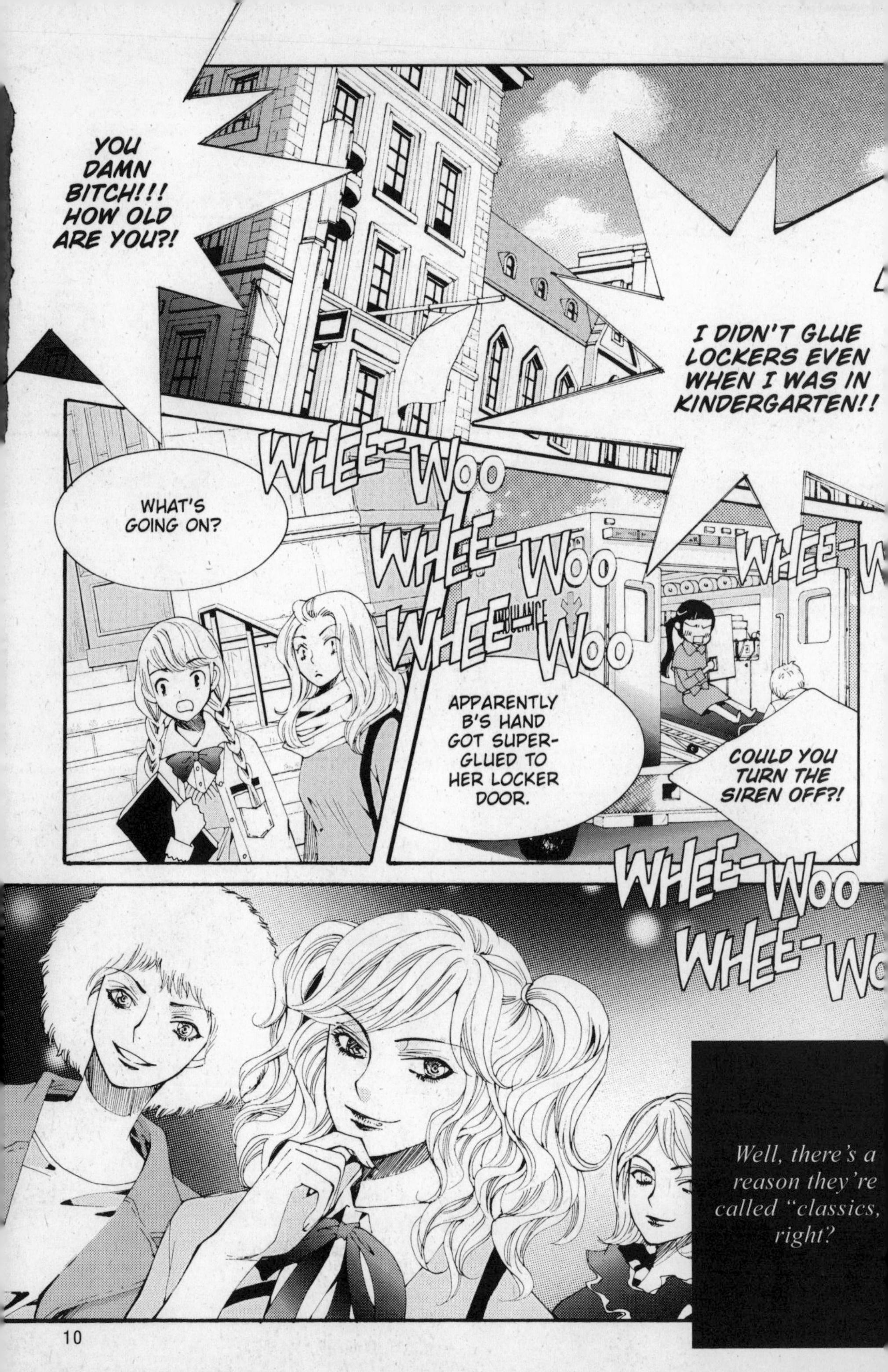
YOU DAMN BITCH!!! HOW OLD ARE YOU?!
I DIDN'T GLUE LOCKERS EVEN WHEN I WAS IN KINDERGARTEN!!
WHAT'S GOING ON?
WHEE-WOO
WHEE-WOO
WHEE-WOO
WHEE-W
AMBULANCE
APPARENTLY B'S HAND GOT SUPER-GLUED TO HER LOCKER DOOR.
COULD YOU TURN THE SIREN OFF?!
WHEE-WOO
WHEE-WO
Well, there's a reason they're called "classics, right?

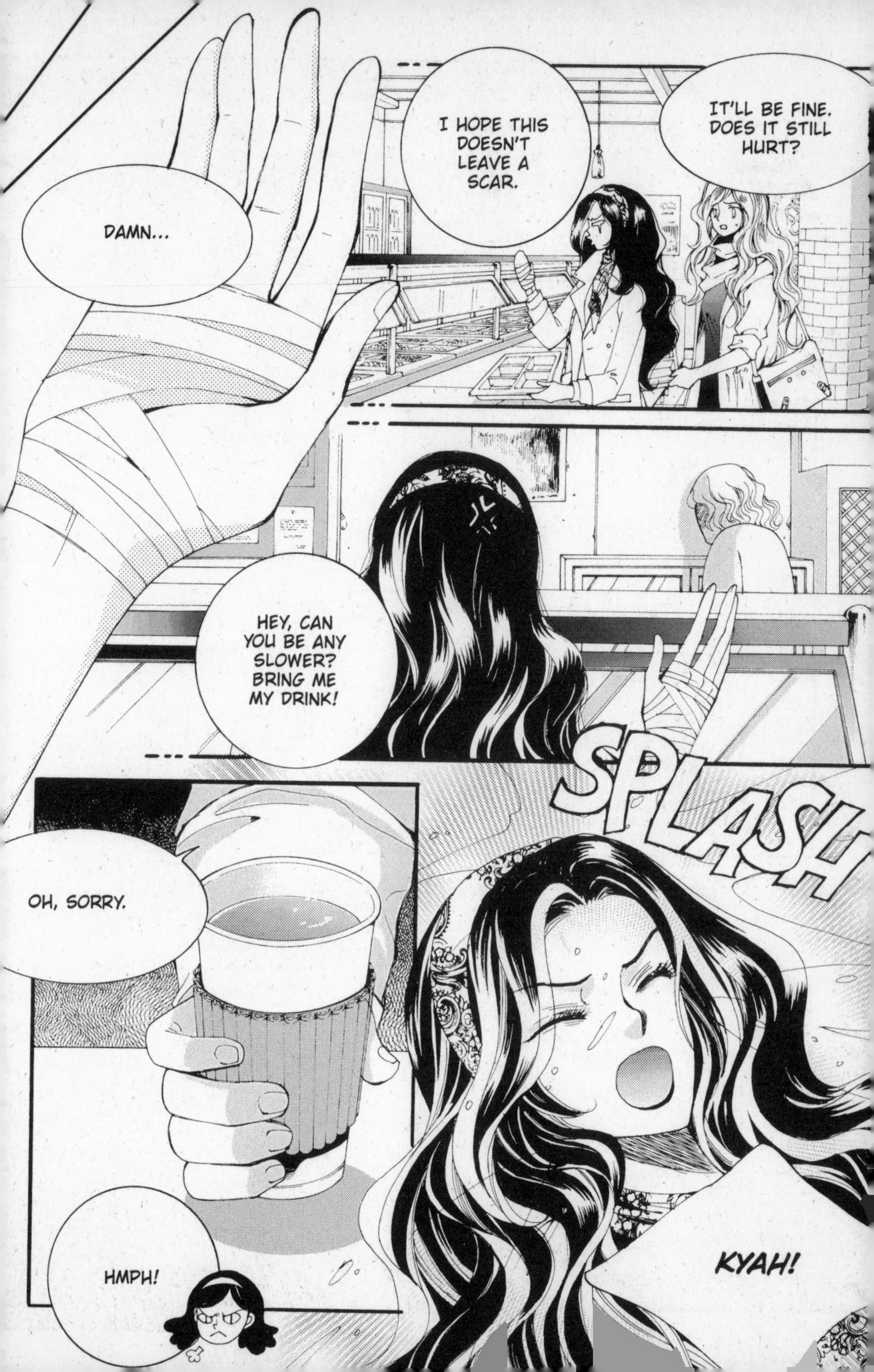
DAMN...
I HOPE THIS DOESN'T LEAVE A SCAR.
IT'LL BE FINE. DOES IT STILL HURT?
HEY, CAN YOU BE ANY SLOWER? BRING ME MY DRINK!
OH, SORRY.
HMPH!
SPLASH
KYAH!

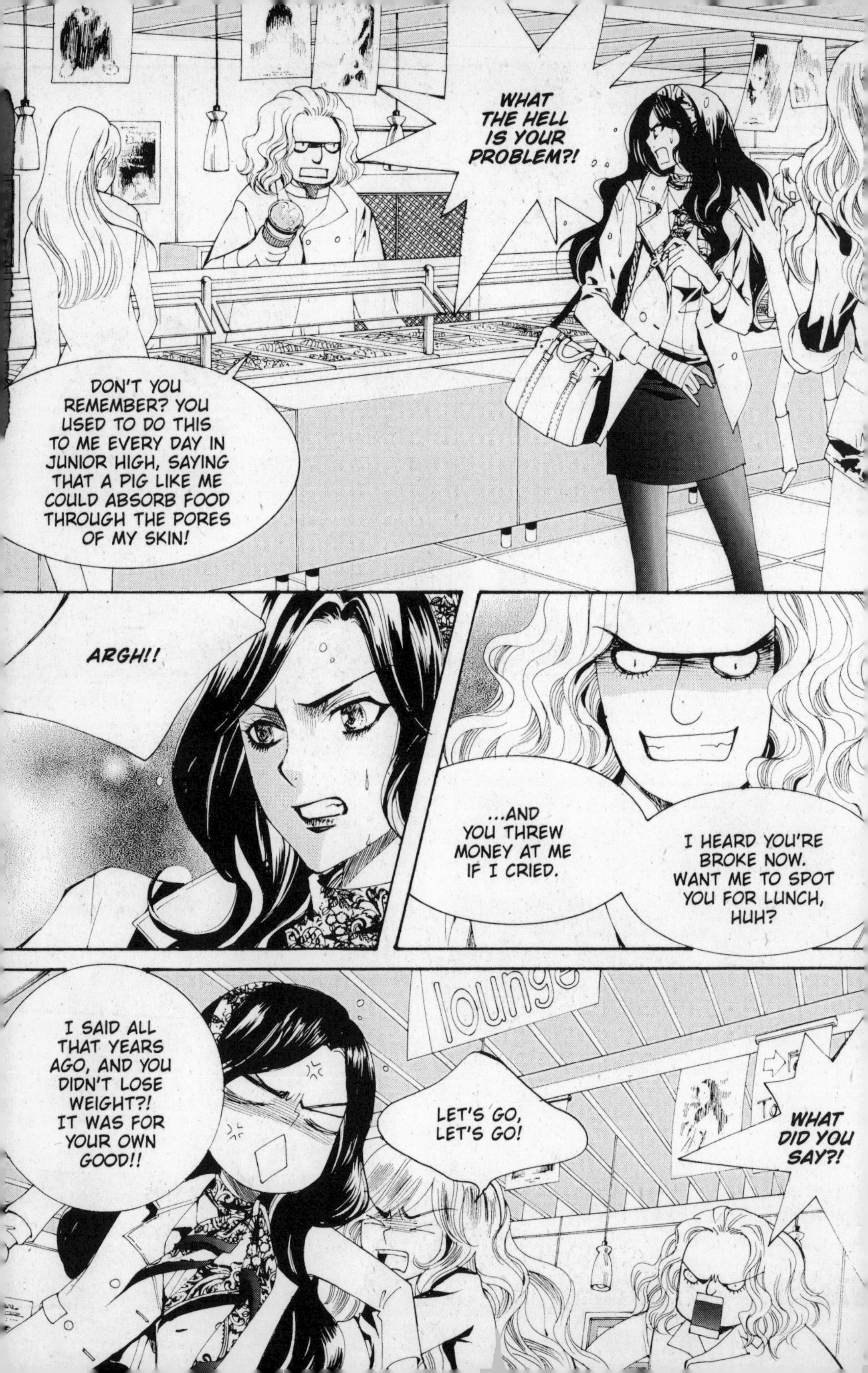
WHAT THE HELL IS YOUR PROBLEM?!
DON'T YOU REMEMBER? YOU USED TO DO THIS TO ME EVERY DAY IN JUNIOR HIGH, SAYING THAT A PIG LIKE ME COULD ABSORB FOOD THROUGH THE PORES OF MY SKIN!
ARGH!!
...AND YOU THREW MONEY AT ME IF I CRIED.
I HEARD YOU'RE BROKE NOW. WANT ME TO SPOT YOU FOR LUNCH, HUH?
I SAID ALL THAT YEARS AGO, AND YOU DIDN'T LOSE WEIGHT?! IT WAS FOR YOUR OWN GOOD!!
lounge
LET'S GO, LET'S GO!
WHAT DID YOU SAY?!

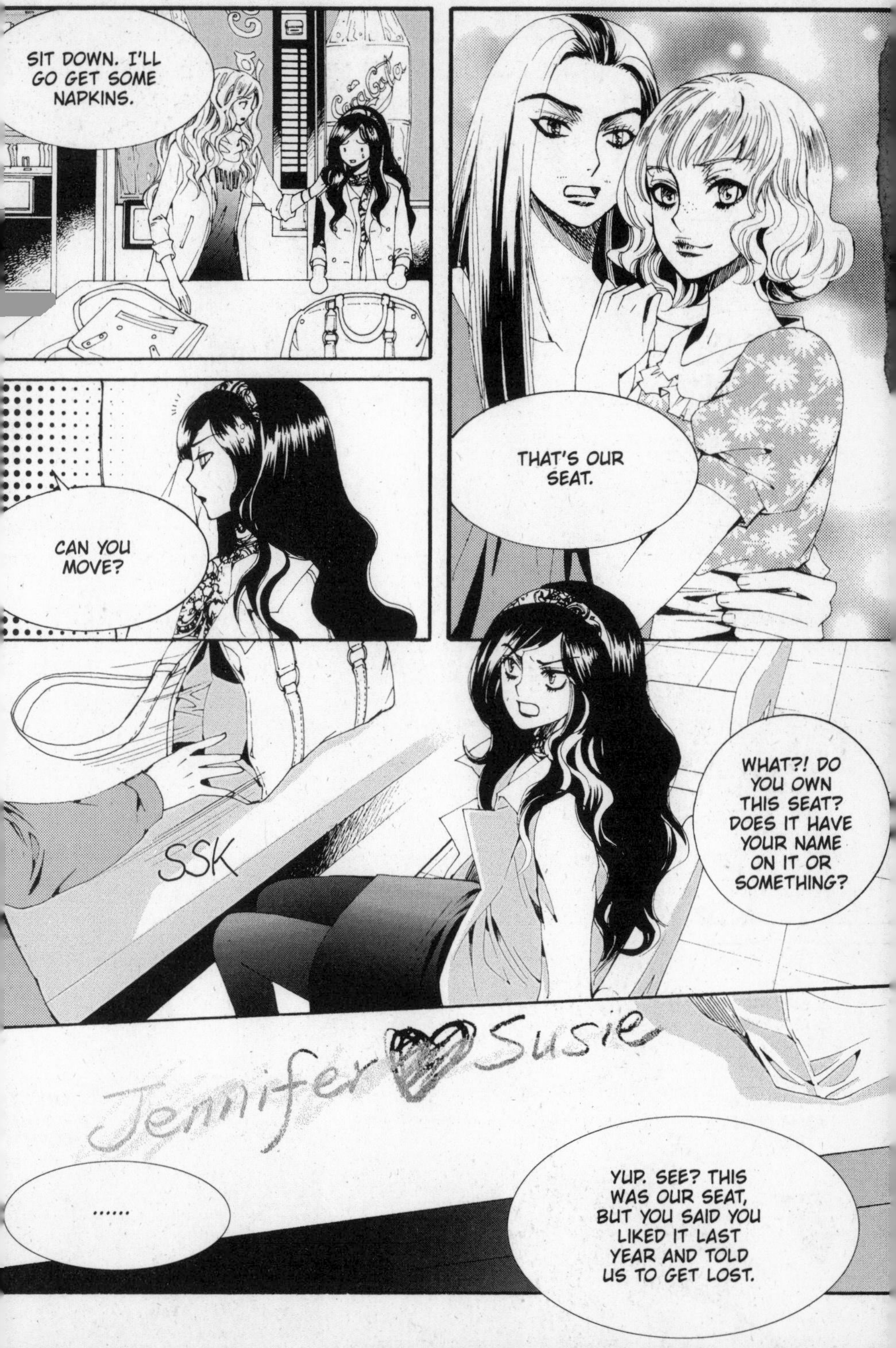
SIT DOWN. I'LL GO GET SOME NAPKINS.
THAT'S OUR SEAT.
CAN YOU MOVE?
SSK
WHAT?! DO YOU OWN THIS SEAT? DOES IT HAVE YOUR NAME ON IT OR SOMETHING?
Jennifer ♥ Susie
......
YUP. SEE? THIS WAS OUR SEAT, BUT YOU SAID YOU LIKED IT LAST YEAR AND TOLD US TO GET LOST.

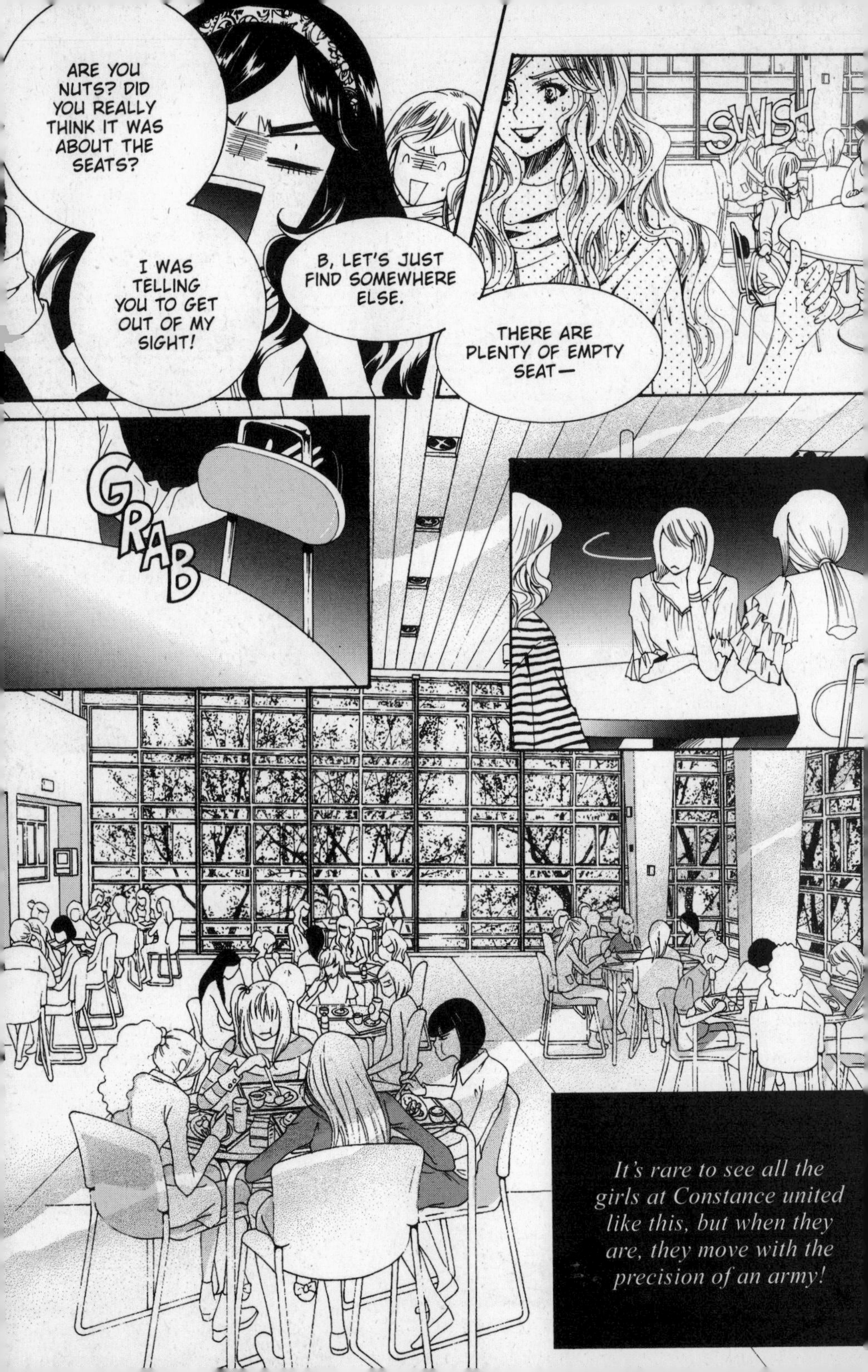
ARE YOU NUTS? DID YOU REALLY THINK IT WAS ABOUT THE SEATS?
I WAS TELLING YOU TO GET OUT OF MY SIGHT!
B, LET'S JUST FIND SOMEWHERE ELSE.
SWISH
THERE ARE PLENTY OF EMPTY SEAT—
GRAB
It's rare to see all the girls at Constance united like this, but when they are, they move with the precision of an army!

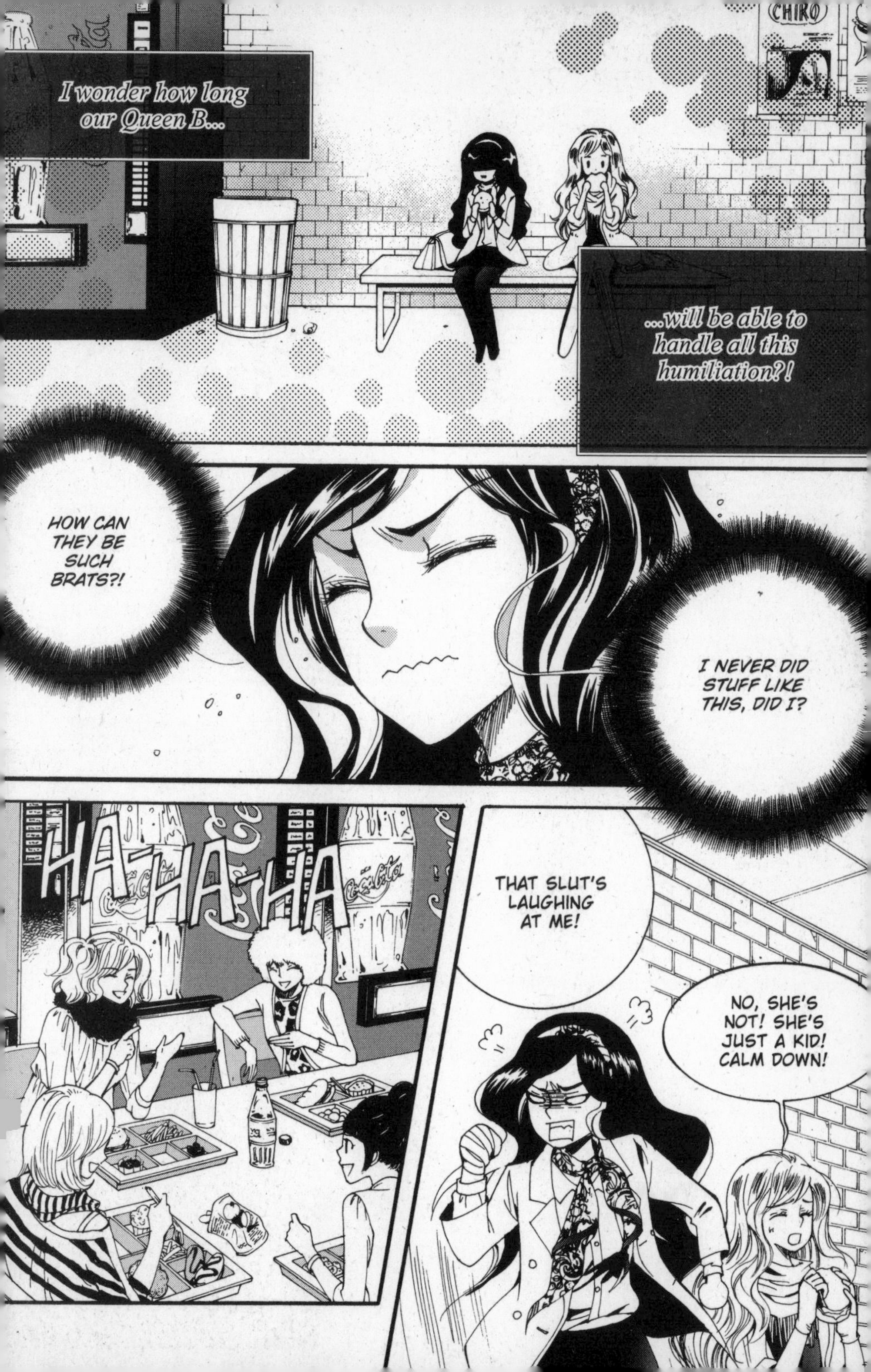
I wonder how long our Queen B...
...will be able to handle all this humiliation?!
HOW CAN THEY BE SUCH BRATS?!
I NEVER DID STUFF LIKE THIS, DID I?
HA-HA-HA
THAT SLUT'S LAUGHING AT ME!
NO, SHE'S NOT! SHE'S JUST A KID! CALM DOWN!

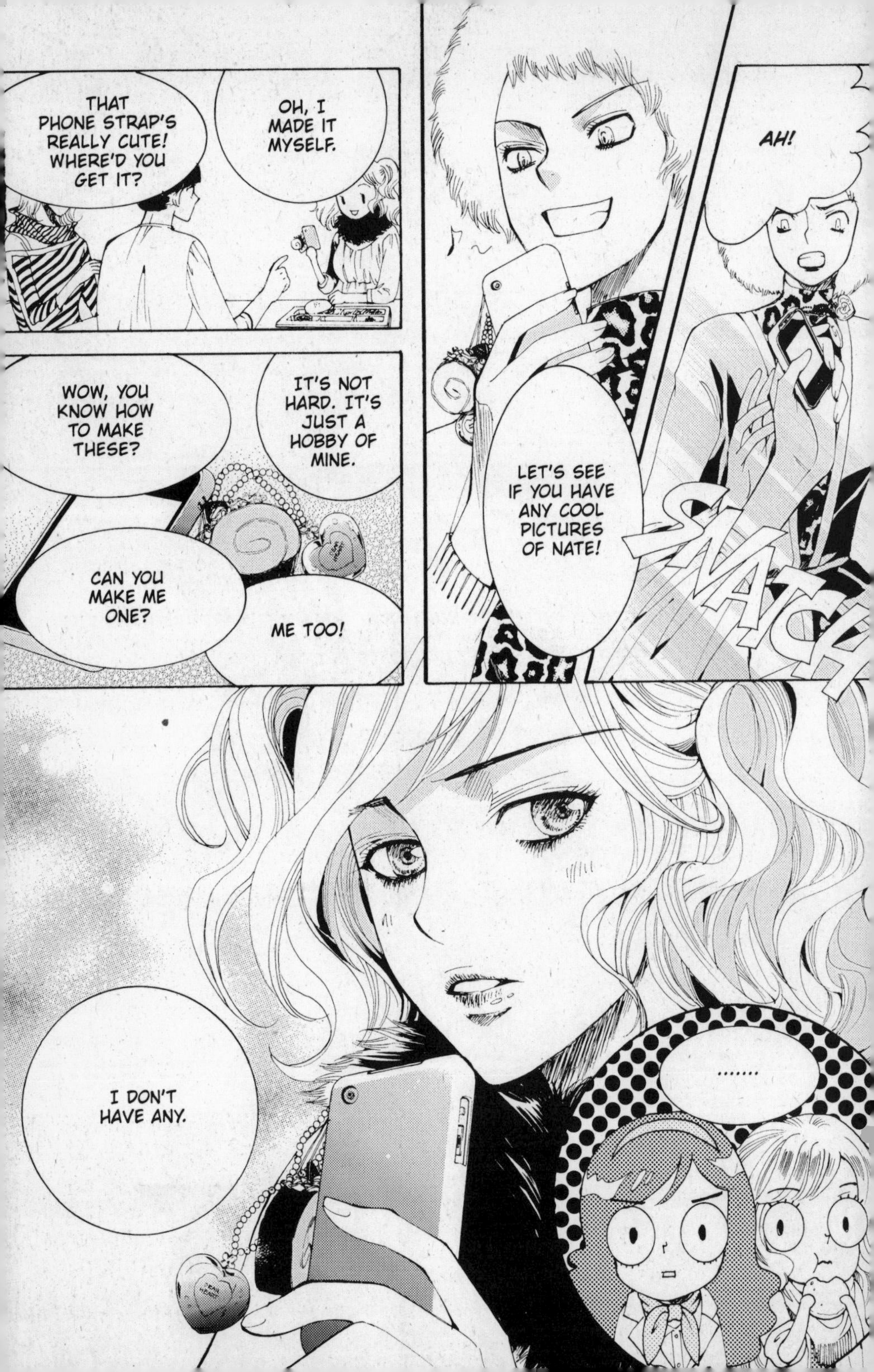
THAT PHONE STRAP'S REALLY CUTE! WHERE'D YOU GET IT?
OH, I MADE IT MYSELF.
WOW, YOU KNOW HOW TO MAKE THESE?
IT'S NOT HARD. IT'S JUST A HOBBY OF MINE.
CAN YOU MAKE ME ONE?
ME TOO!
LET'S SEE IF YOU HAVE ANY COOL PICTURES OF NATE!
AH!
SNATCH
I DON'T HAVE ANY.
....

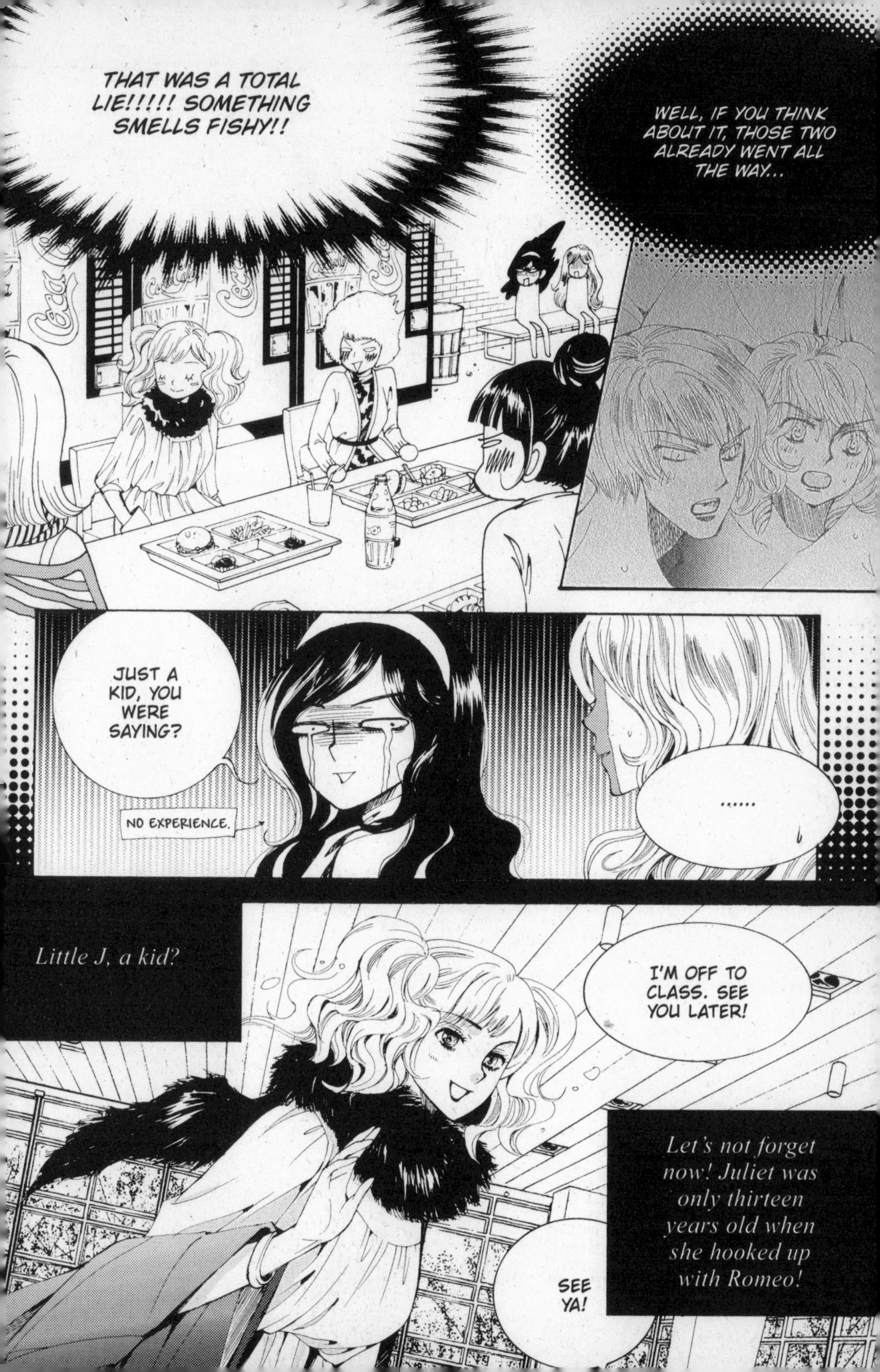
THAT WAS A TOTAL LIE!!!!! SOMETHING SMELLS FISHY!!
WELL, IF YOU THINK ABOUT IT, THOSE TWO ALREADY WENT ALL THE WAY...
JUST A KID, YOU WERE SAYING?
NO EXPERIENCE.
......
Little J, a kid?
I'M OFF TO CLASS. SEE YOU LATER!
Let's not forget now! Juliet was only thirteen years old when she hooked up with Romeo!
SEE YA!

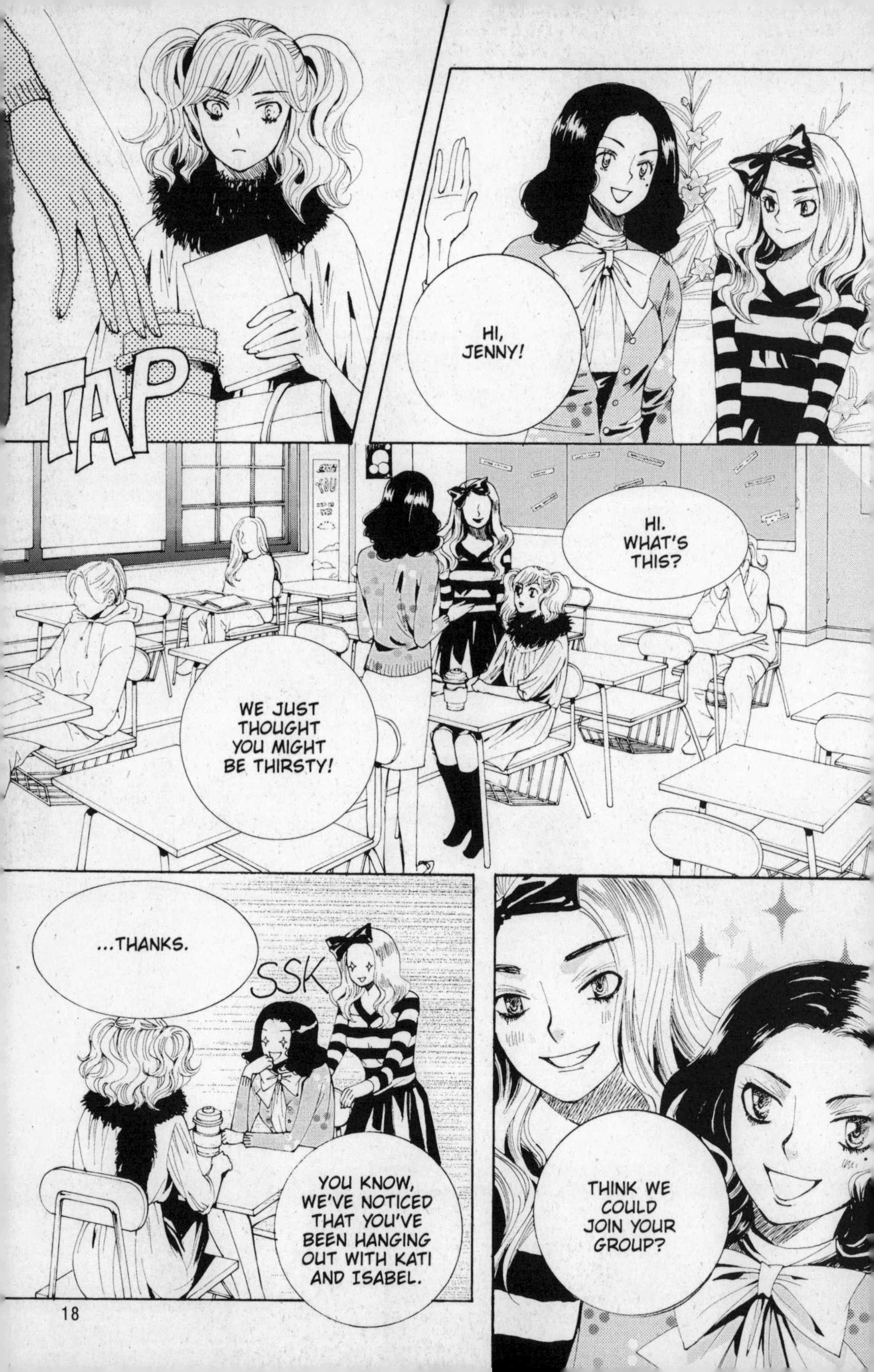
TAP
HI, JENNY!
HI. WHAT'S THIS?
WE JUST THOUGHT YOU MIGHT BE THIRSTY!
...THANKS.
SSK
YOU KNOW, WE'VE NOTICED THAT YOU'VE BEEN HANGING OUT WITH KATI AND ISABEL.
THINK WE COULD JOIN YOUR GROUP?

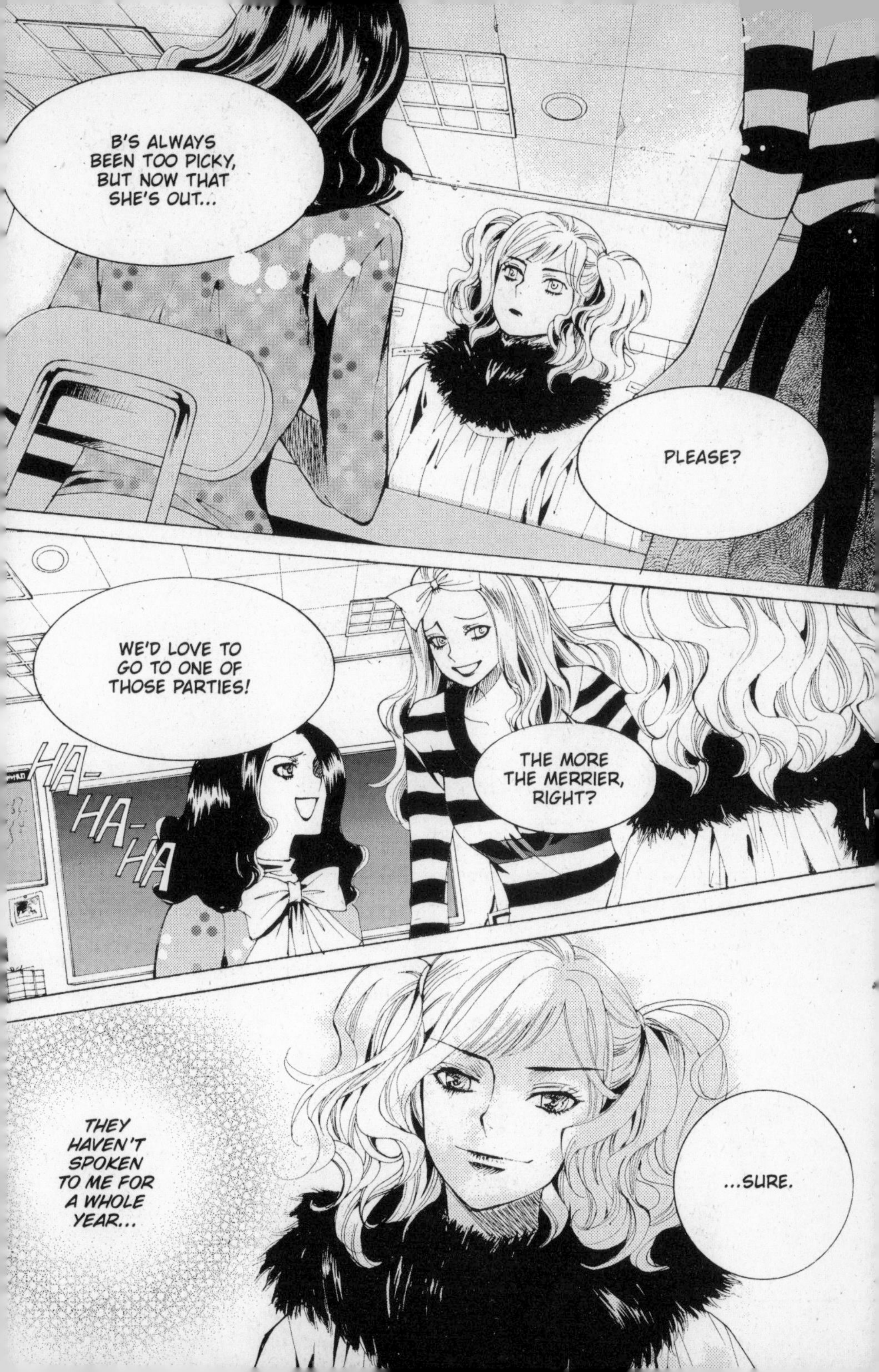
B'S ALWAYS BEEN TOO PICKY, BUT NOW THAT SHE'S OUT...
PLEASE?
WE'D LOVE TO GO TO ONE OF THOSE PARTIES!
HA-HA-HA
THE MORE THE MERRIER, RIGHT?
THEY HAVEN'T SPOKEN TO ME FOR A WHOLE YEAR...
...SURE.

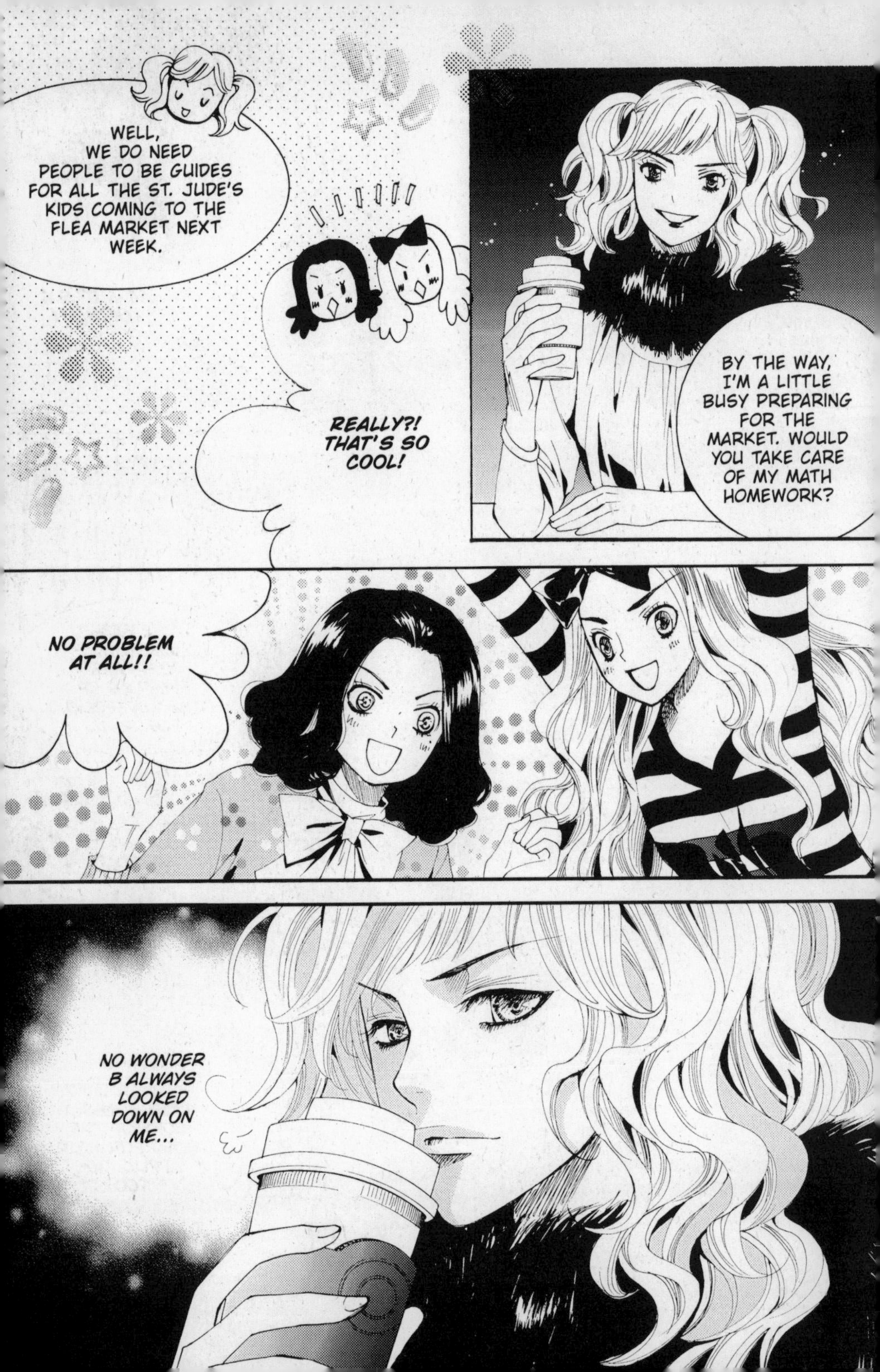
WELL, WE DO NEED PEOPLE TO BE GUIDES FOR ALL THE ST. JUDE'S KIDS COMING TO THE FLEA MARKET NEXT WEEK.
REALLY?! THAT'S SO COOL!
BY THE WAY, I'M A LITTLE BUSY PREPARING FOR THE MARKET. WOULD YOU TAKE CARE OF MY MATH HOMEWORK?
NO PROBLEM AT ALL!!
NO WONDER B ALWAYS LOOKED DOWN ON ME...

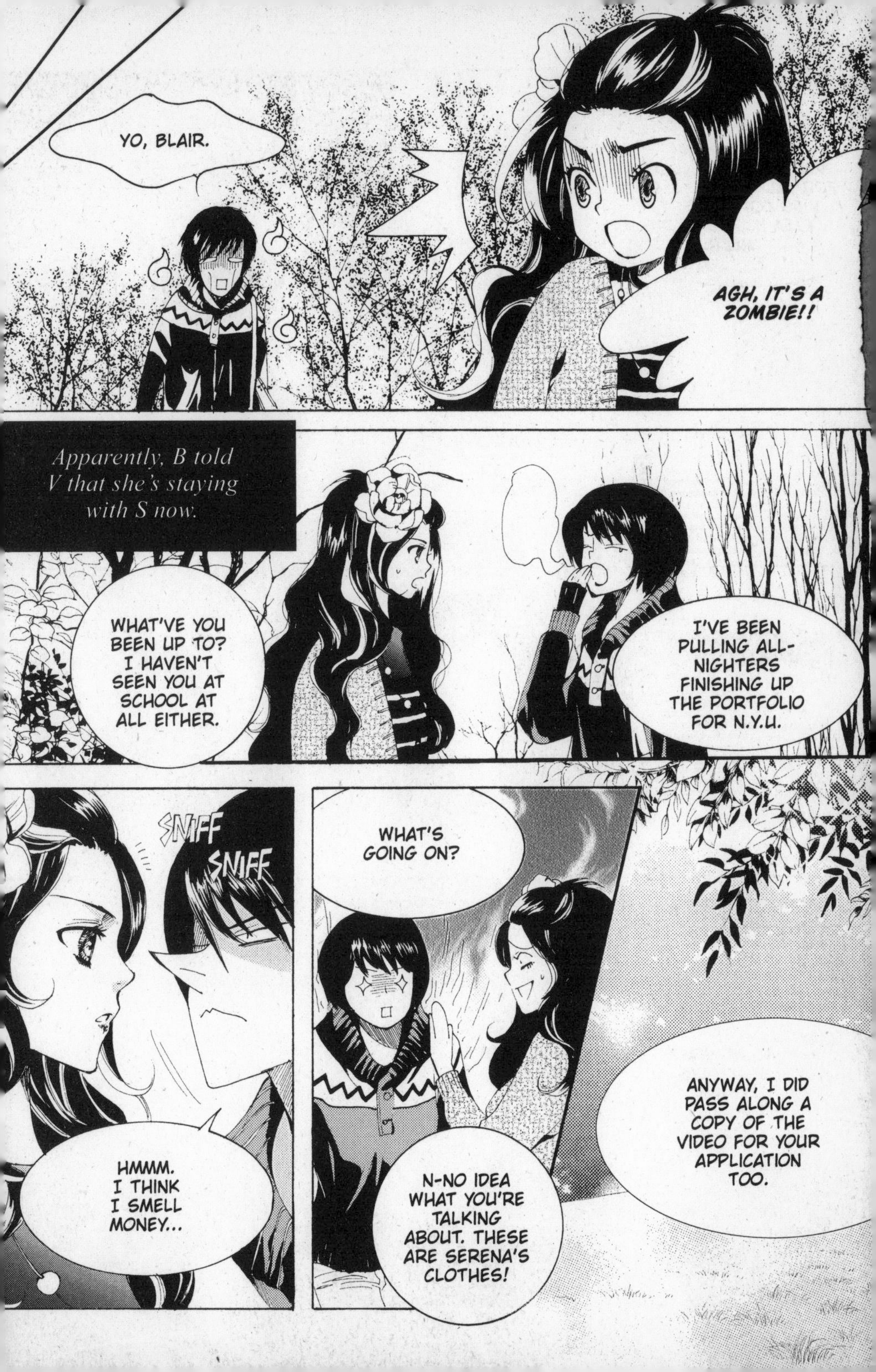
YO, BLAIR.
AGH, IT'S A ZOMBIE!!
Apparently, B told V that she's staying with S now.
WHAT'VE YOU BEEN UP TO? I HAVEN'T SEEN YOU AT SCHOOL AT ALL EITHER.
I'VE BEEN PULLING ALL-NIGHTERS FINISHING UP THE PORTFOLIO FOR N.Y.U.
SNIFF
SNIFF
HMMM. I THINK I SMELL MONEY...
WHAT'S GOING ON?
N-NO IDEA WHAT YOU'RE TALKING ABOUT. THESE ARE SERENA'S CLOTHES!
ANYWAY, I DID PASS ALONG A COPY OF THE VIDEO FOR YOUR APPLICATION TOO.

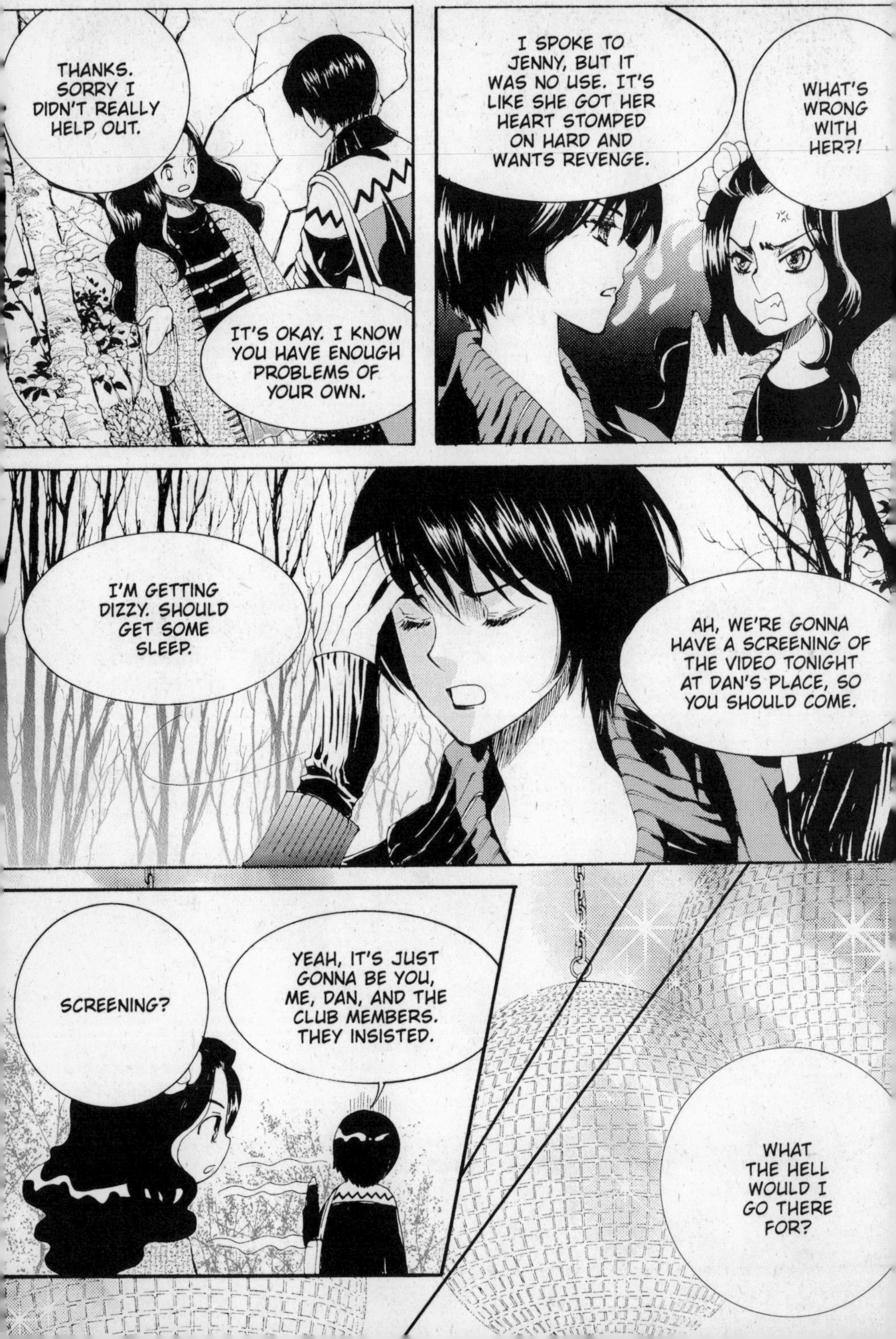
THANKS. SORRY I DIDN'T REALLY HELP OUT.
IT'S OKAY. I KNOW YOU HAVE ENOUGH PROBLEMS OF YOUR OWN.
I SPOKE TO JENNY, BUT IT WAS NO USE. IT'S LIKE SHE GOT HER HEART STOMPED ON HARD AND WANTS REVENGE.
WHAT'S WRONG WITH HER?!
I'M GETTING DIZZY. SHOULD GET SOME SLEEP.
AH, WE'RE GONNA HAVE A SCREENING OF THE VIDEO TONIGHT AT DAN'S PLACE, SO YOU SHOULD COME.
SCREENING?
YEAH, IT'S JUST GONNA BE YOU, ME, DAN, AND THE CLUB MEMBERS. THEY INSISTED.
WHAT THE HELL WOULD I GO THERE FOR?

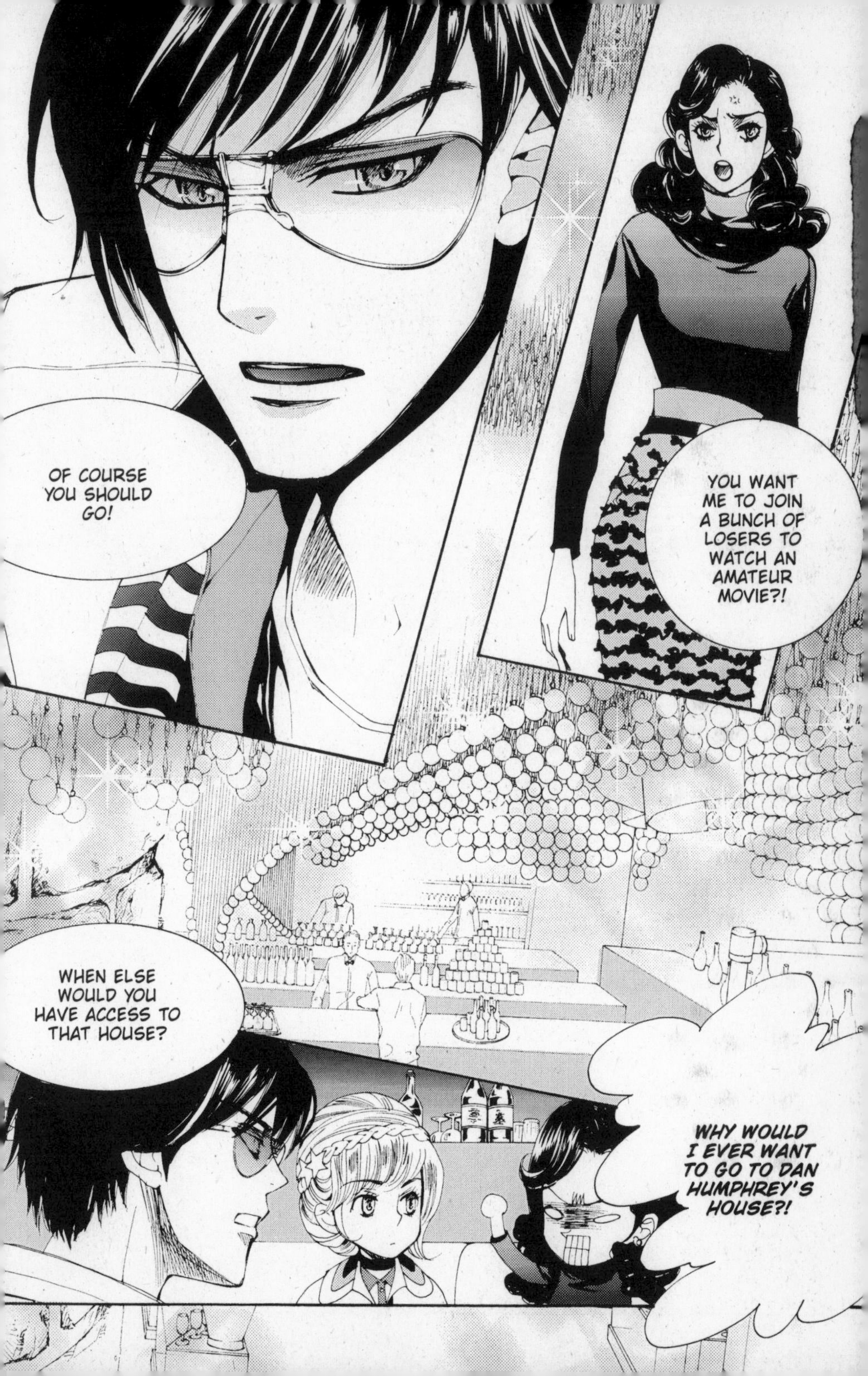
OF COURSE YOU SHOULD GO!
YOU WANT ME TO JOIN A BUNCH OF LOSERS TO WATCH AN AMATEUR MOVIE?!
WHEN ELSE WOULD YOU HAVE ACCESS TO THAT HOUSE?
WHY WOULD I EVER WANT TO GO TO DAN HUMPHREY'S HOUSE?!

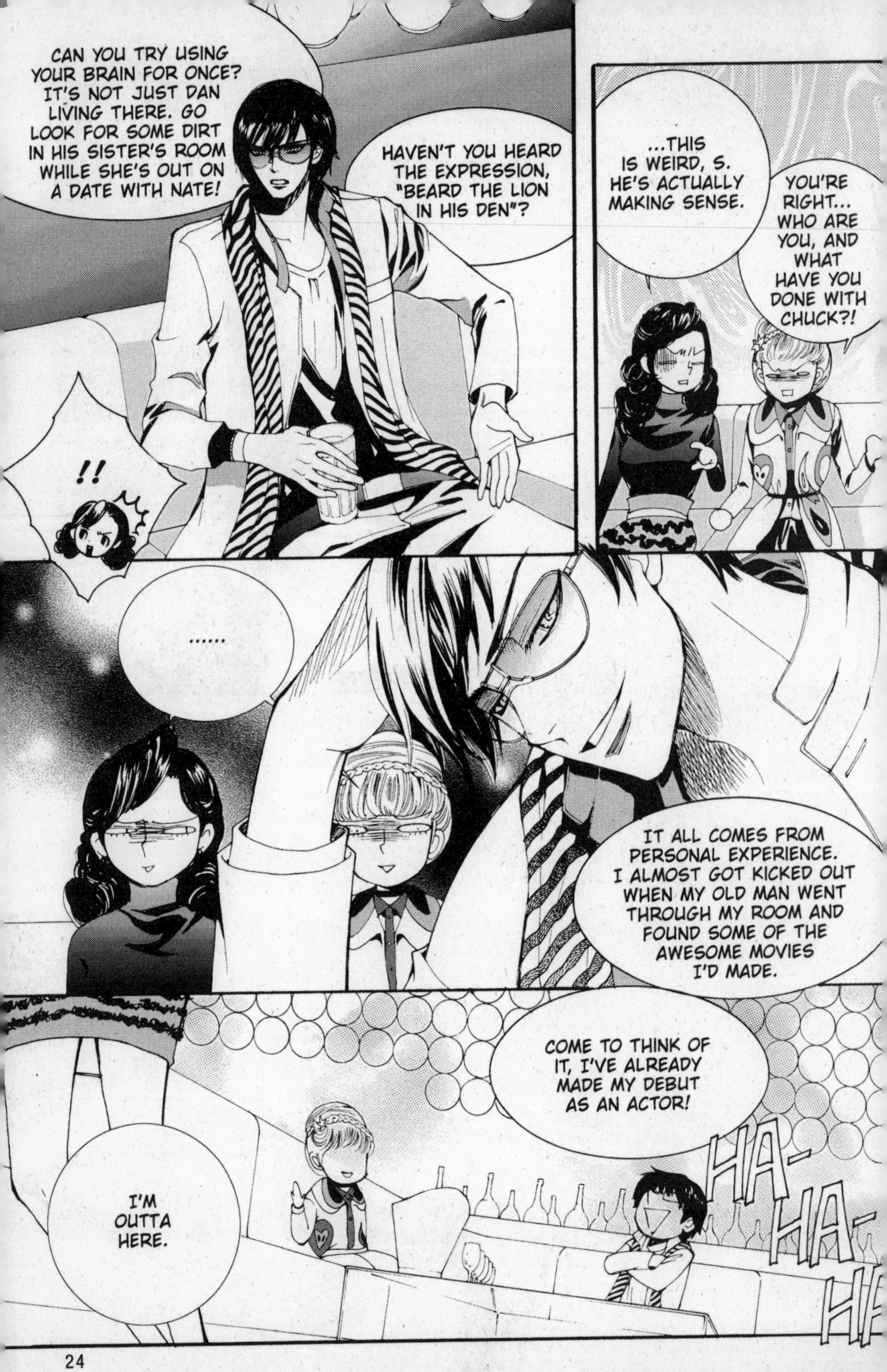

CAN YOU TRY USING YOUR BRAIN FOR ONCE? IT'S NOT JUST DAN LIVING THERE. GO LOOK FOR SOME DIRT IN HIS SISTER'S ROOM WHILE SHE'S OUT ON A DATE WITH NATE!
HAVEN'T YOU HEARD THE EXPRESSION, "BEARD THE LION IN HIS DEN"?
!!
...THIS IS WEIRD, S. HE'S ACTUALLY MAKING SENSE.
YOU'RE RIGHT... WHO ARE YOU, AND WHAT HAVE YOU DONE WITH CHUCK?!
......
IT ALL COMES FROM PERSONAL EXPERIENCE. I ALMOST GOT KICKED OUT WHEN MY OLD MAN WENT THROUGH MY ROOM AND FOUND SOME OF THE AWESOME MOVIES I'D MADE.
COME TO THINK OF IT, I'VE ALREADY MADE MY DEBUT AS AN ACTOR!
I'M OUTTA HERE.
HA-HA-HA

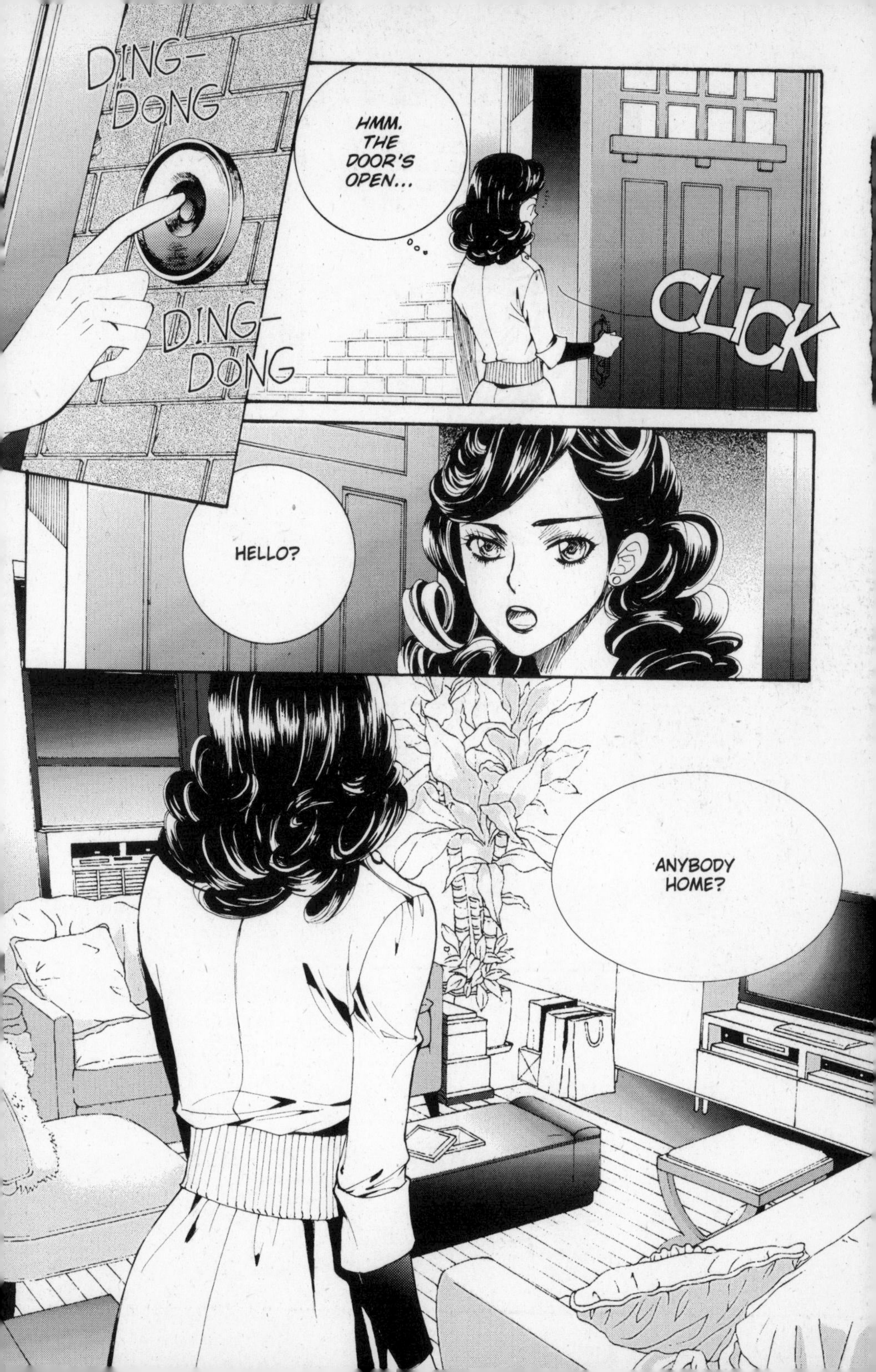
DING-DONG
DING-DONG
HMM. THE DOOR'S OPEN...
CLICK
HELLO?
ANYBODY HOME?

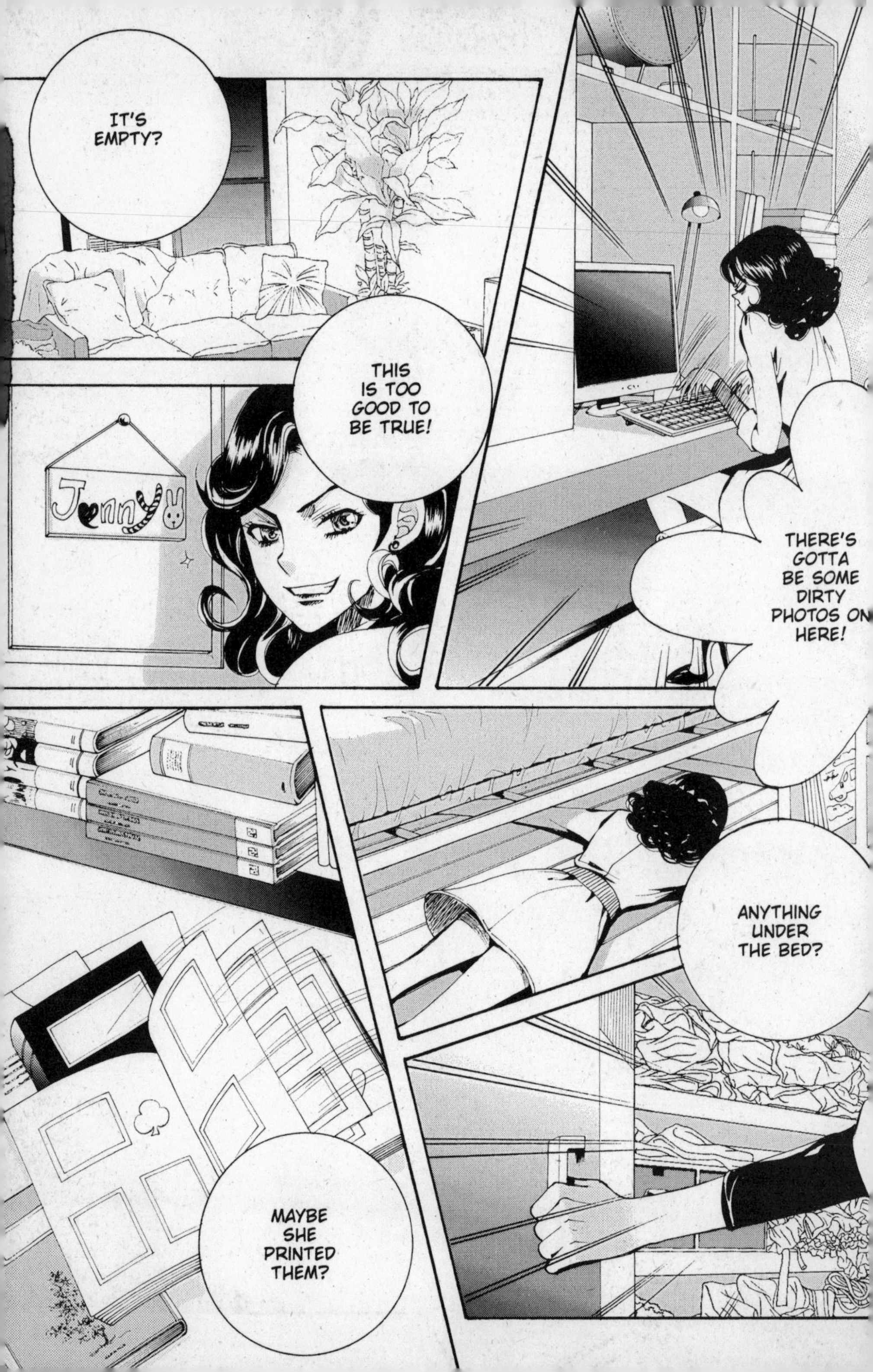
IT'S EMPTY?
THIS IS TOO GOOD TO BE TRUE!
THERE'S GOTTA BE SOME DIRTY PHOTOS ON HERE!
MAYBE SHE PRINTED THEM?
ANYTHING UNDER THE BED?

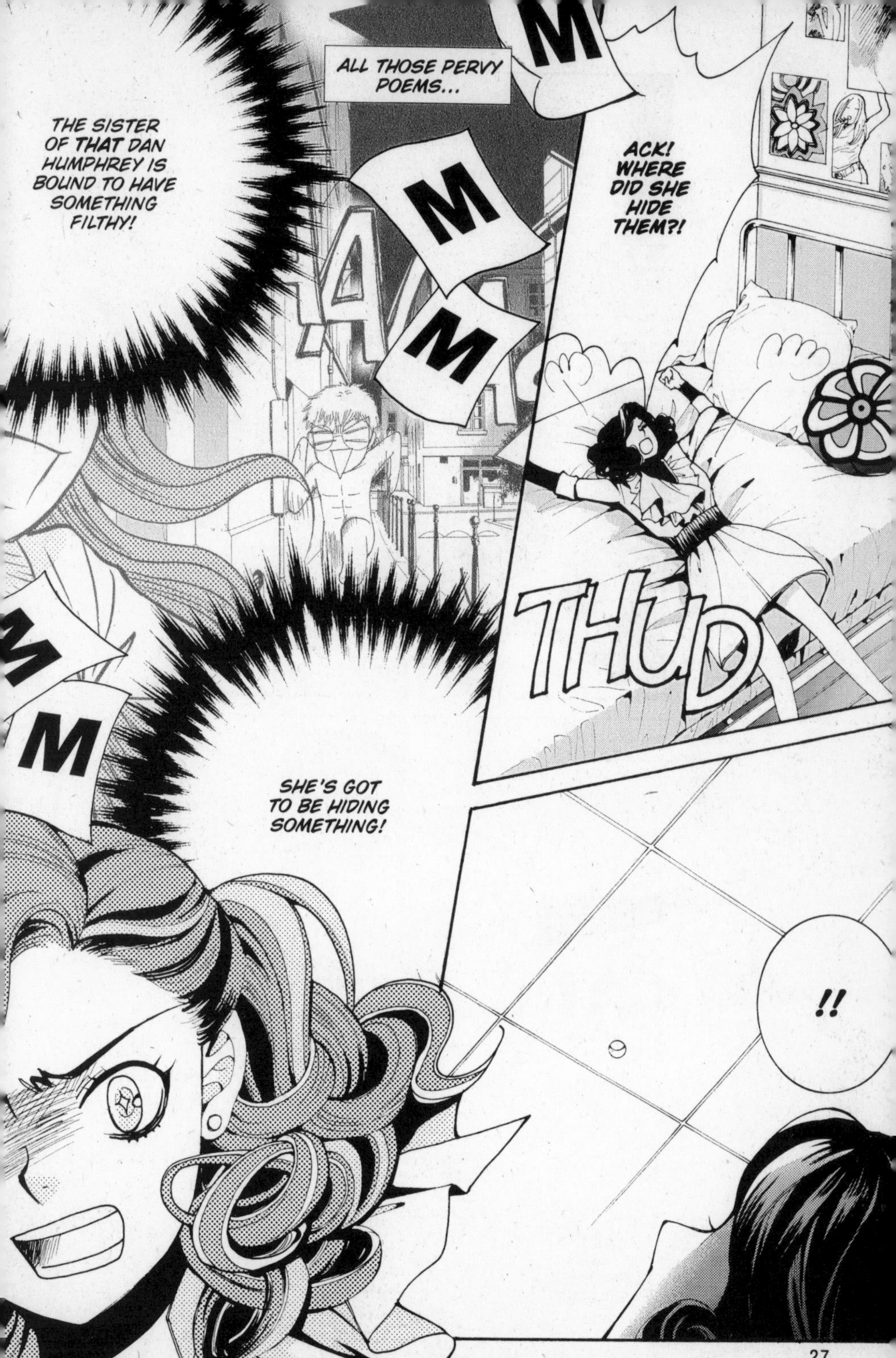
THE SISTER OF THAT DAN HUMPHREY IS BOUND TO HAVE SOMETHING FILTHY!
ALL THOSE PERVY POEMS...
M
M
M
M
M
M
SHE'S GOT TO BE HIDING SOMETHING!
ACK! WHERE DID SHE HIDE THEM?!
THUD
!!

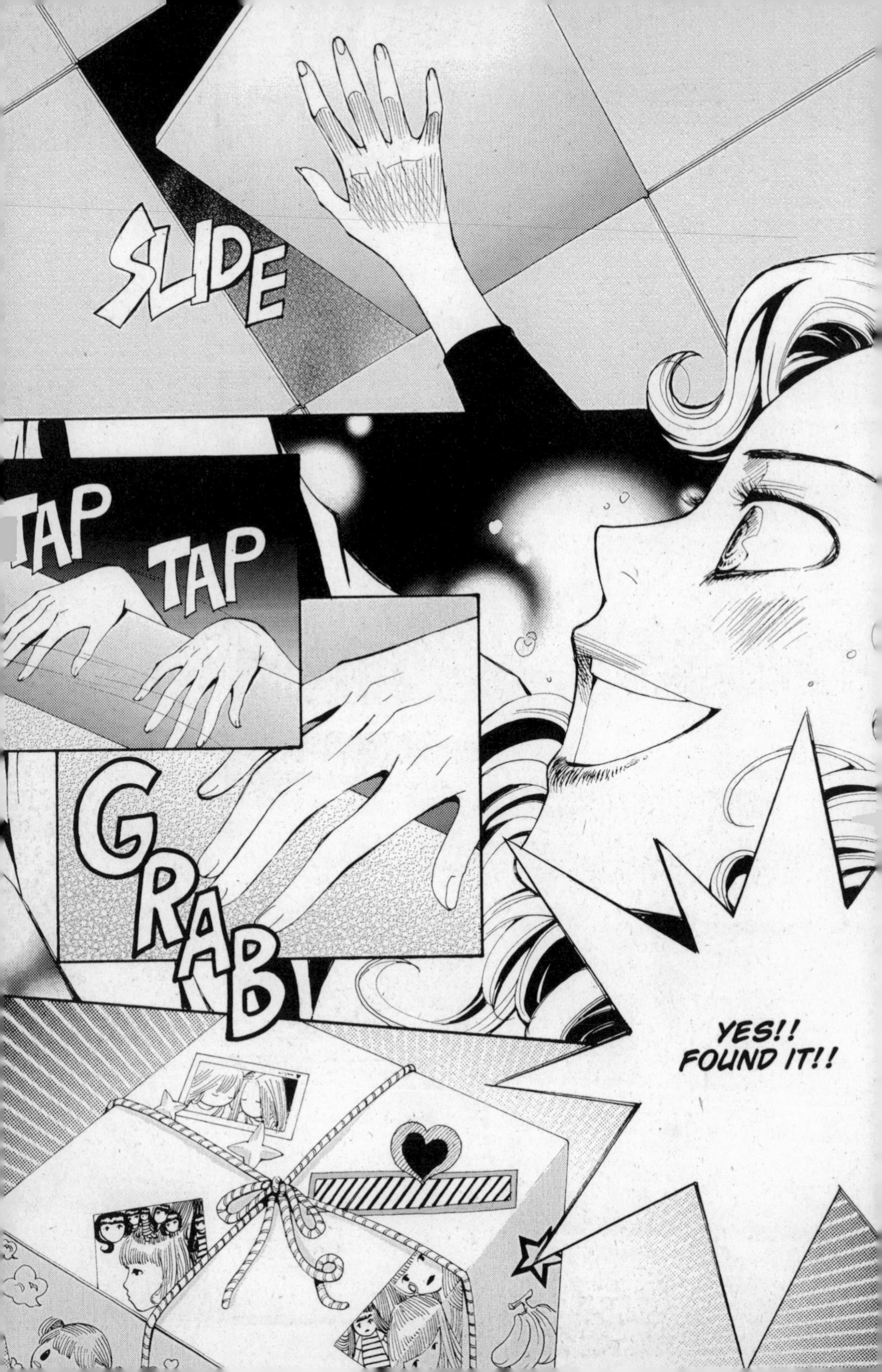
SLIDE
TAP
TAP
GRAB
YES!! FOUND IT!!

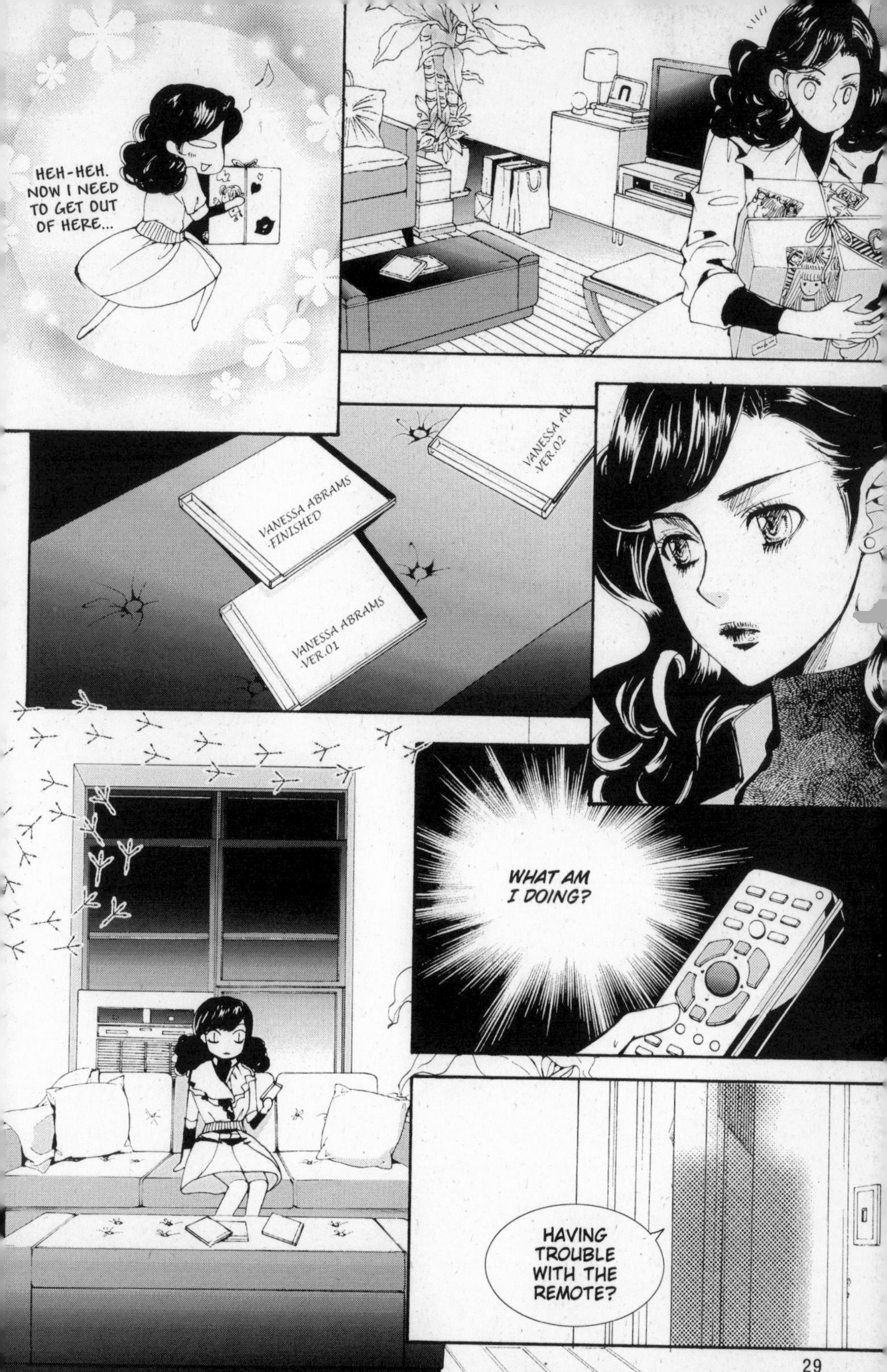
HEH-HEH. NOW I NEED TO GET OUT OF HERE...
VANESSA ABRAMS :FINISHED
VANESSA ABRAMS :VER.01
VANESSA AB :VER.02
WHAT AM I DOING?
HAVING TROUBLE WITH THE REMOTE?

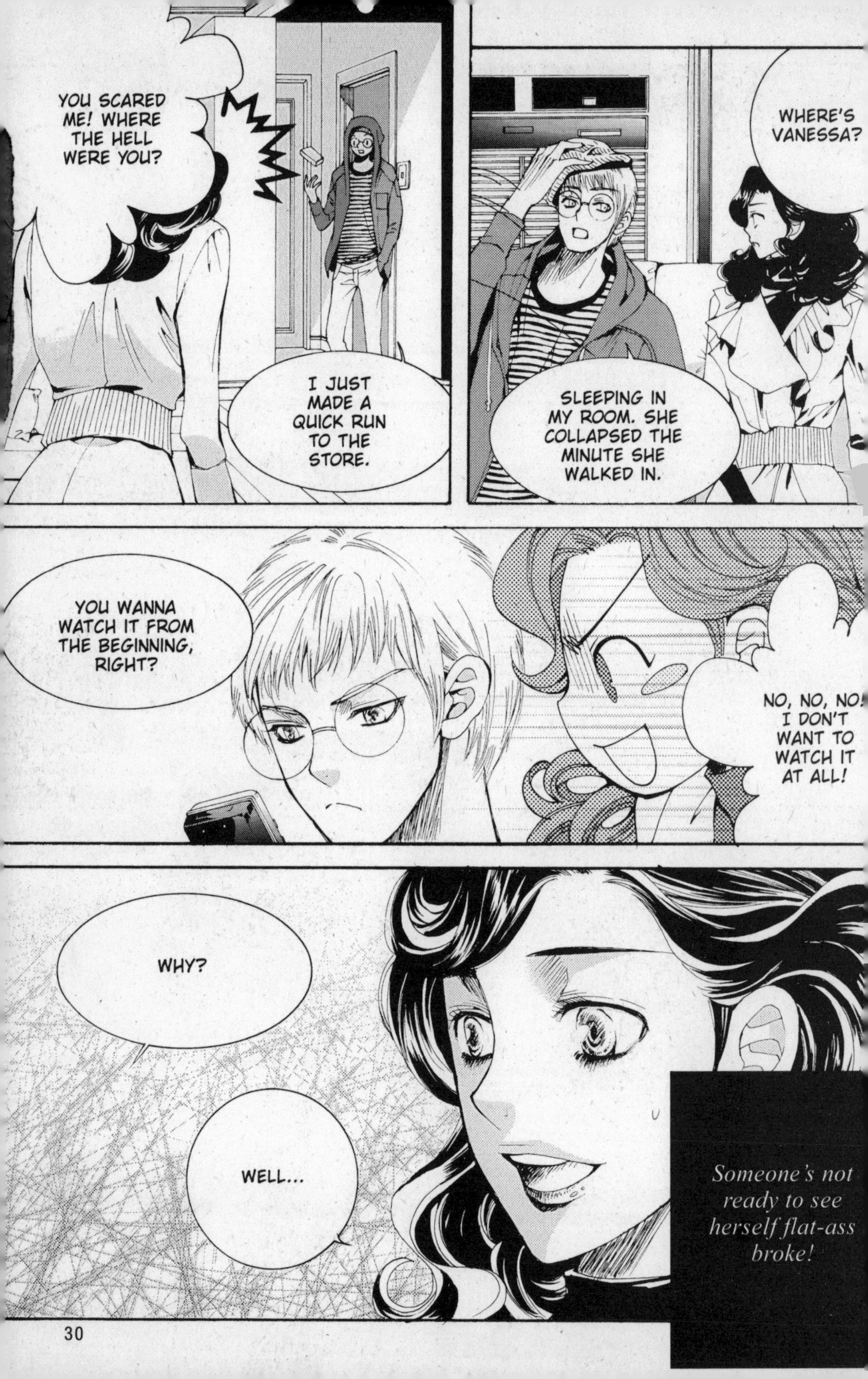
YOU SCARED ME! WHERE THE HELL WERE YOU?
I JUST MADE A QUICK RUN TO THE STORE.
WHERE'S VANESSA?
SLEEPING IN MY ROOM. SHE COLLAPSED THE MINUTE SHE WALKED IN.
YOU WANNA WATCH IT FROM THE BEGINNING, RIGHT?
NO, NO, NO! I DON'T WANT TO WATCH IT AT ALL!
WHY?
WELL...
Someone's not ready to see herself flat-ass broke!

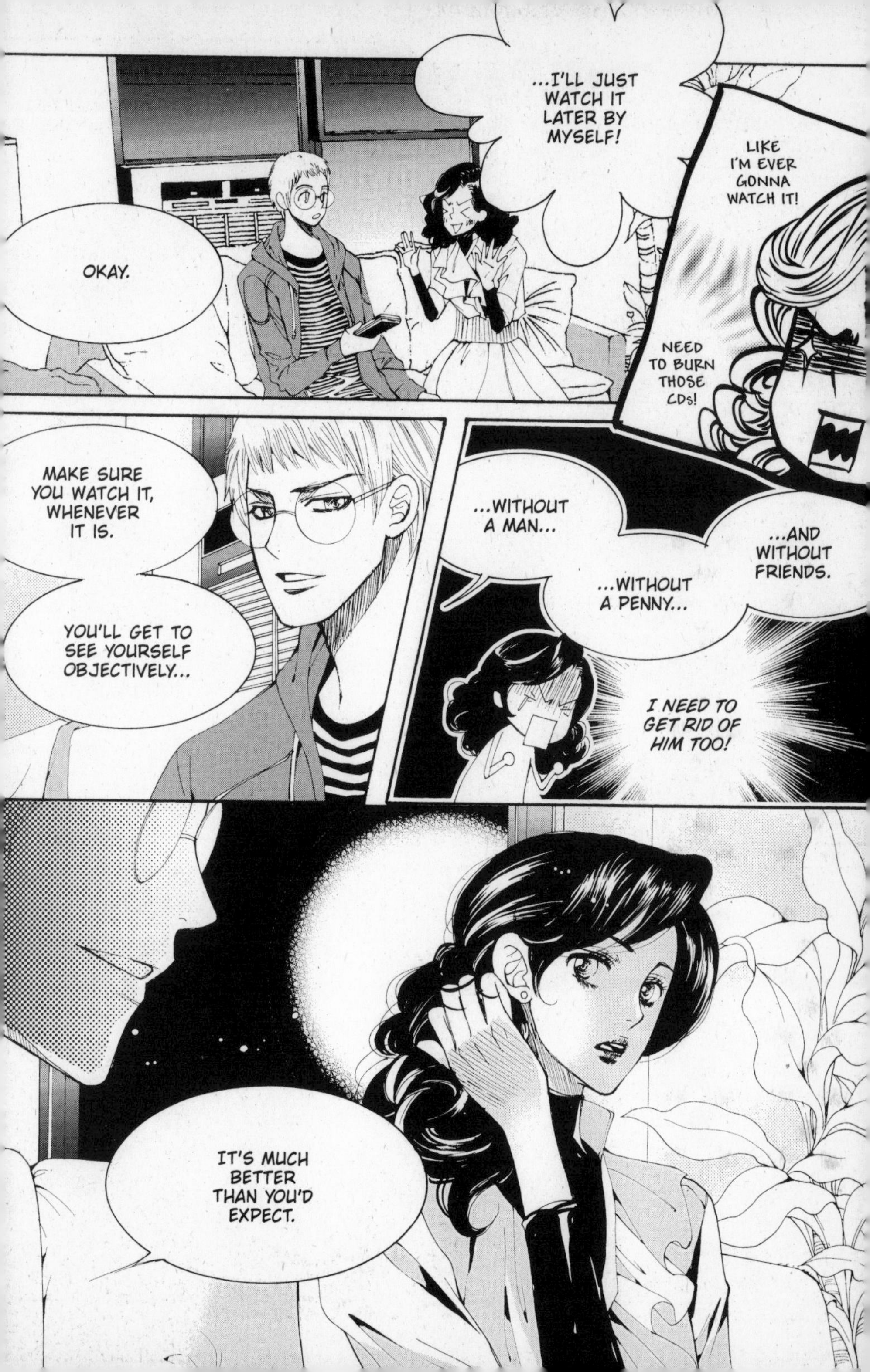
...I'LL JUST WATCH IT LATER BY MYSELF!
OKAY.
LIKE I'M EVER GONNA WATCH IT!
NEED TO BURN THOSE CDs!
MAKE SURE YOU WATCH IT, WHENEVER IT IS.
YOU'LL GET TO SEE YOURSELF OBJECTIVELY...
...WITHOUT A MAN...
...WITHOUT A PENNY...
...AND WITHOUT FRIENDS.
I NEED TO GET RID OF HIM TOO!
IT'S MUCH BETTER THAN YOU'D EXPECT.

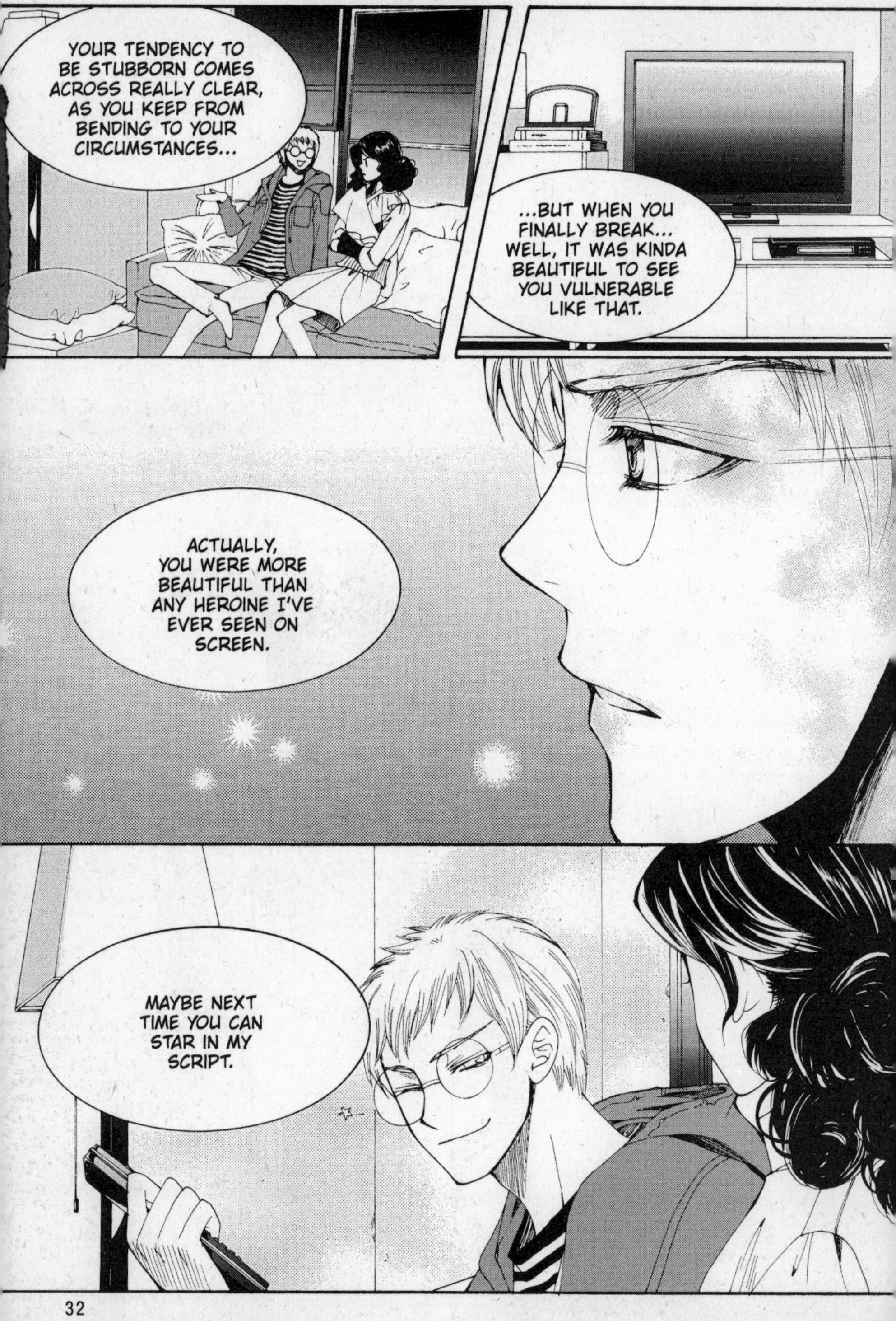
YOUR TENDENCY TO BE STUBBORN COMES ACROSS REALLY CLEAR, AS YOU KEEP FROM BENDING TO YOUR CIRCUMSTANCES...
...BUT WHEN YOU FINALLY BREAK... WELL, IT WAS KINDA BEAUTIFUL TO SEE YOU VULNERABLE LIKE THAT.
ACTUALLY, YOU WERE MORE BEAUTIFUL THAN ANY HEROINE I'VE EVER SEEN ON SCREEN.
MAYBE NEXT TIME YOU CAN STAR IN MY SCRIPT.

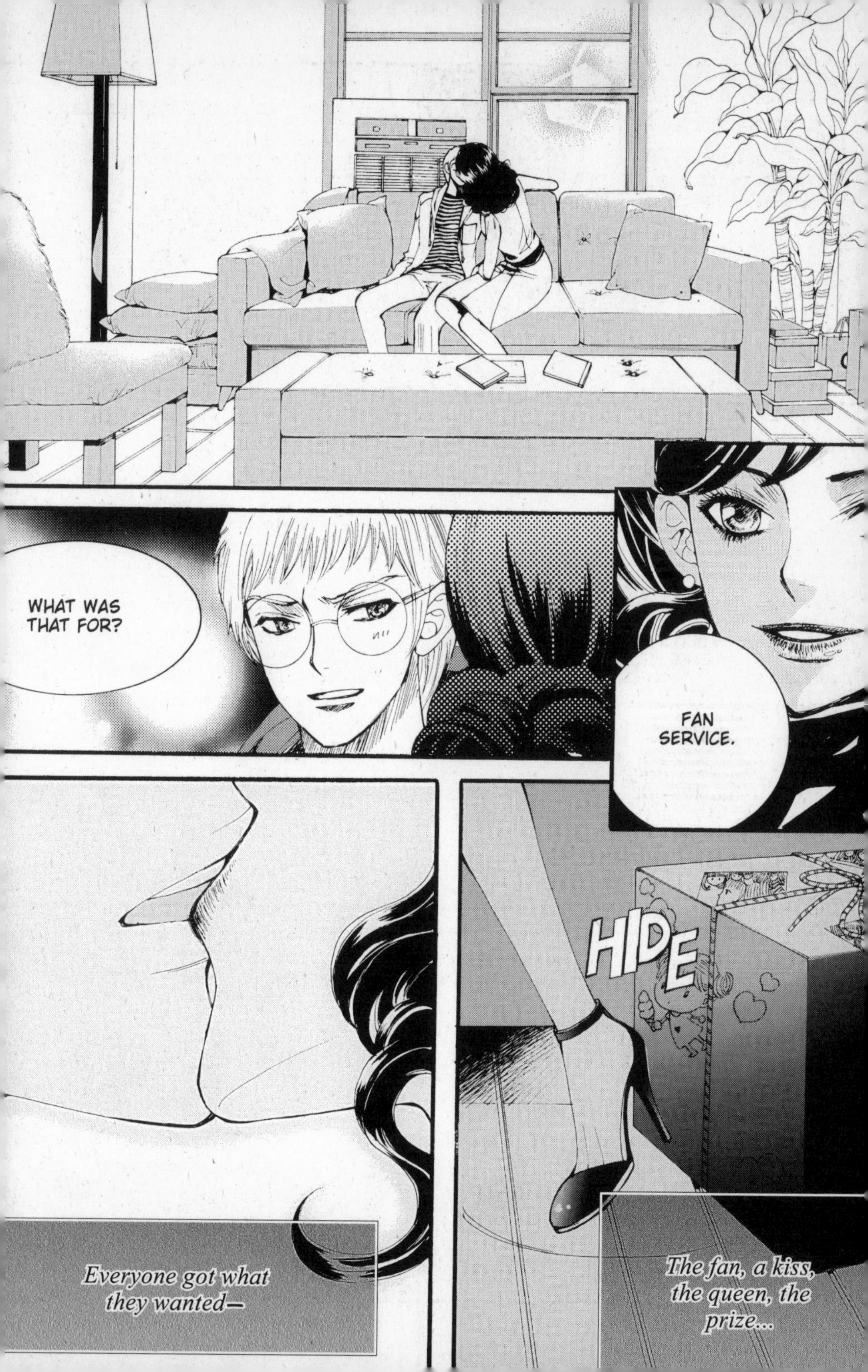
WHAT WAS THAT FOR?
FAN SERVICE.
Everyone got what they wanted—
HIDE
The fan, a kiss, the queen, the prize...

...and the artist, a tortured soul.

DAN! WAKE UP! BREAKFAST'S READY!!

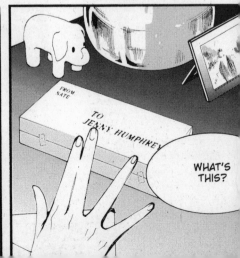

FROM NATE

TO JENNY HUMPHREY

WHAT'S THIS?

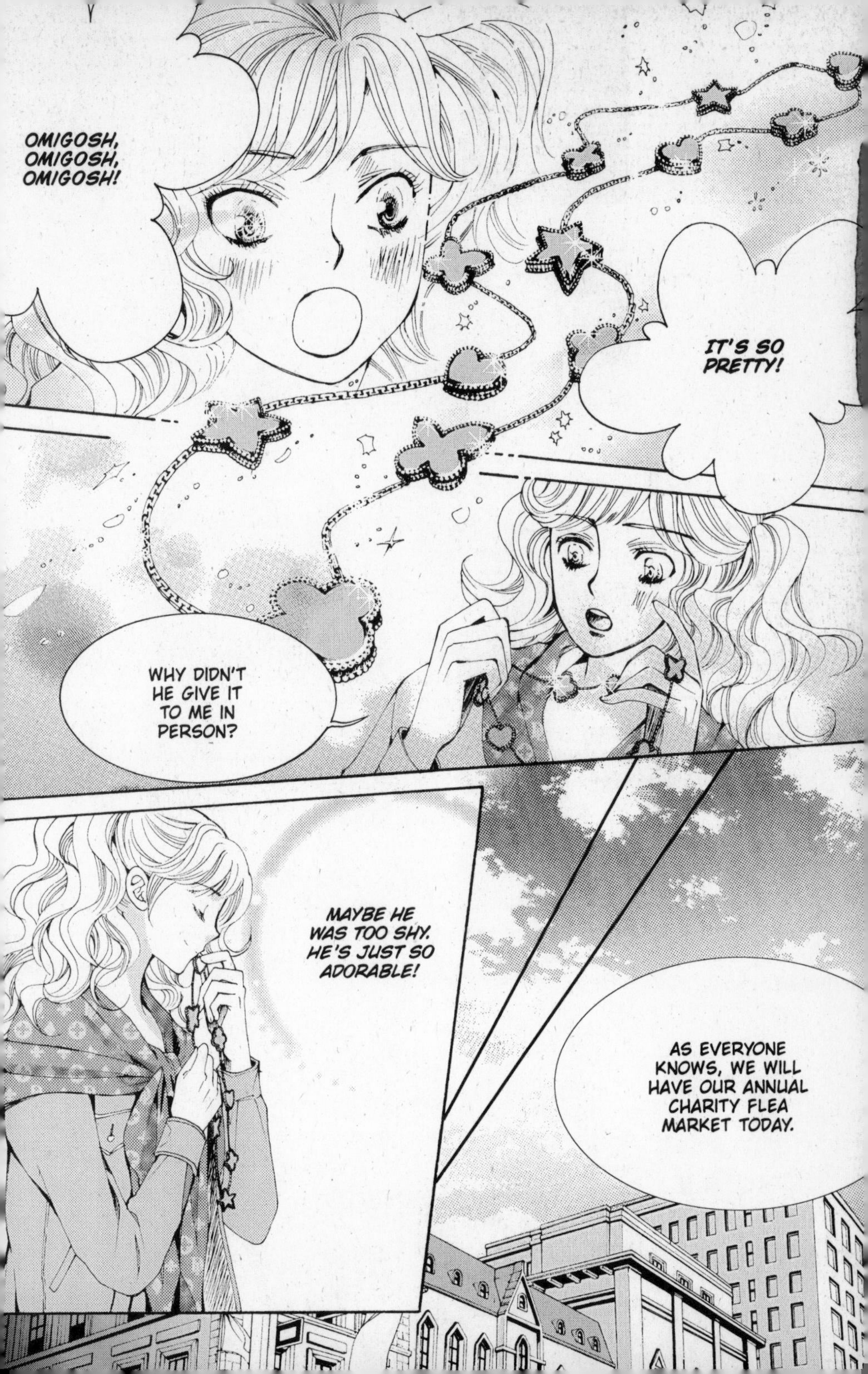
OMIGOSH, OMIGOSH, OMIGOSH!
IT'S SO PRETTY!
WHY DIDN'T HE GIVE IT TO ME IN PERSON?
MAYBE HE WAS TOO SHY. HE'S JUST SO ADORABLE!
AS EVERYONE KNOWS, WE WILL HAVE OUR ANNUAL CHARITY FLEA MARKET TODAY.

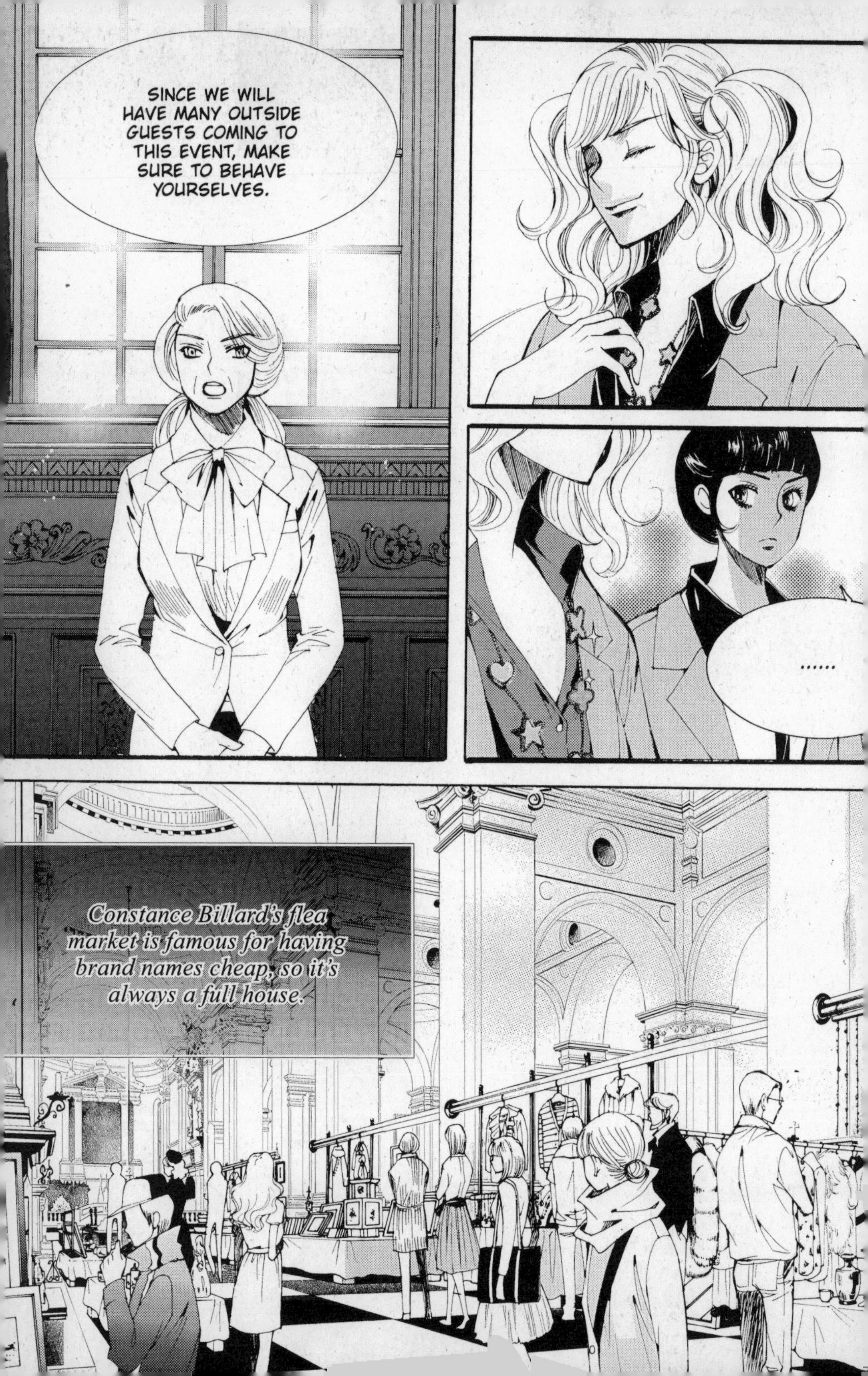
SINCE WE WILL HAVE MANY OUTSIDE GUESTS COMING TO THIS EVENT, MAKE SURE TO BEHAVE YOURSELVES.
......
Constance Billard's flea market is famous for having brand names cheap, so it's always a full house.

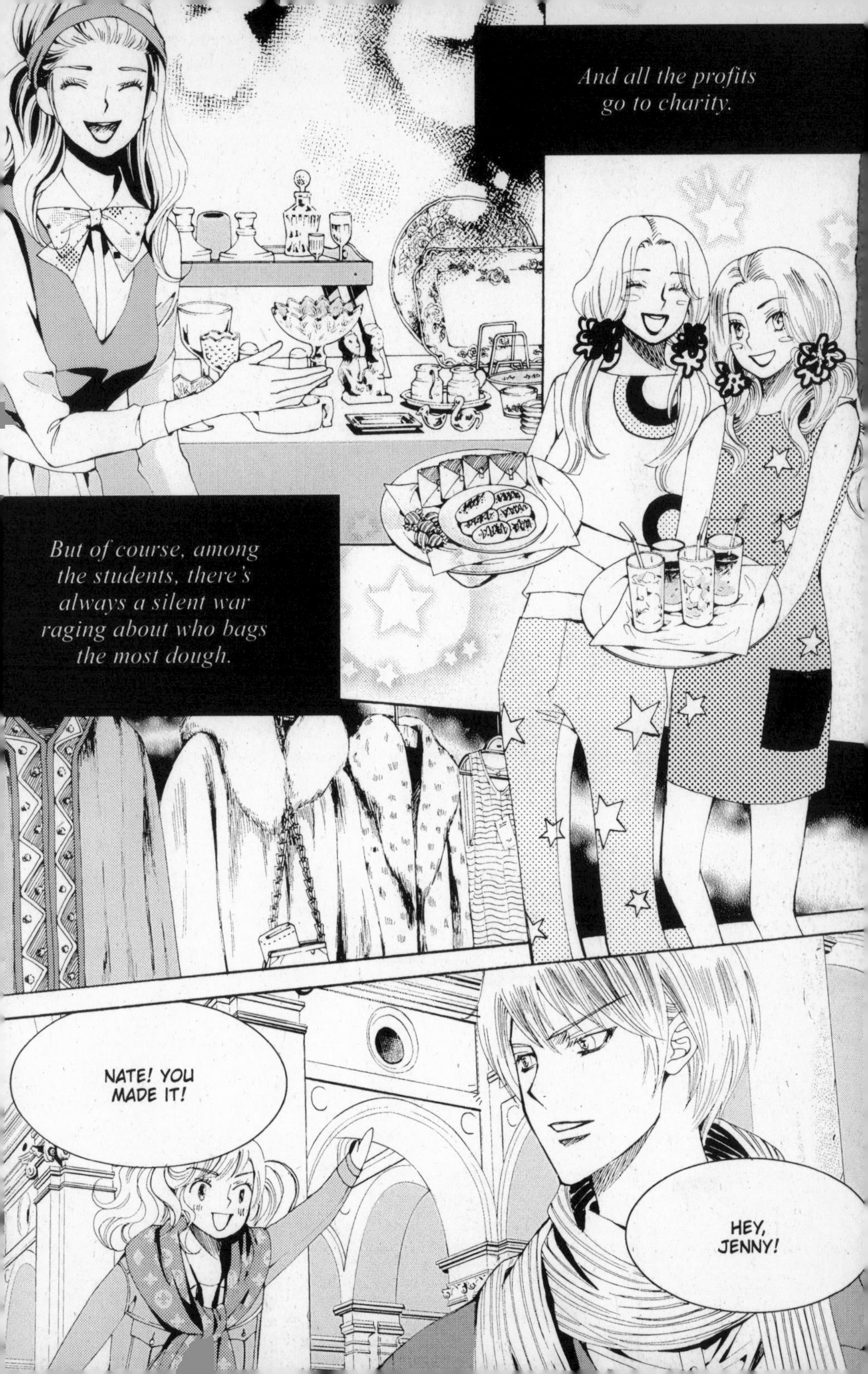
And all the profits go to charity.
But of course, among the students, there's always a silent war raging about who bags the most dough.
NATE! YOU MADE IT!
HEY, JENNY!

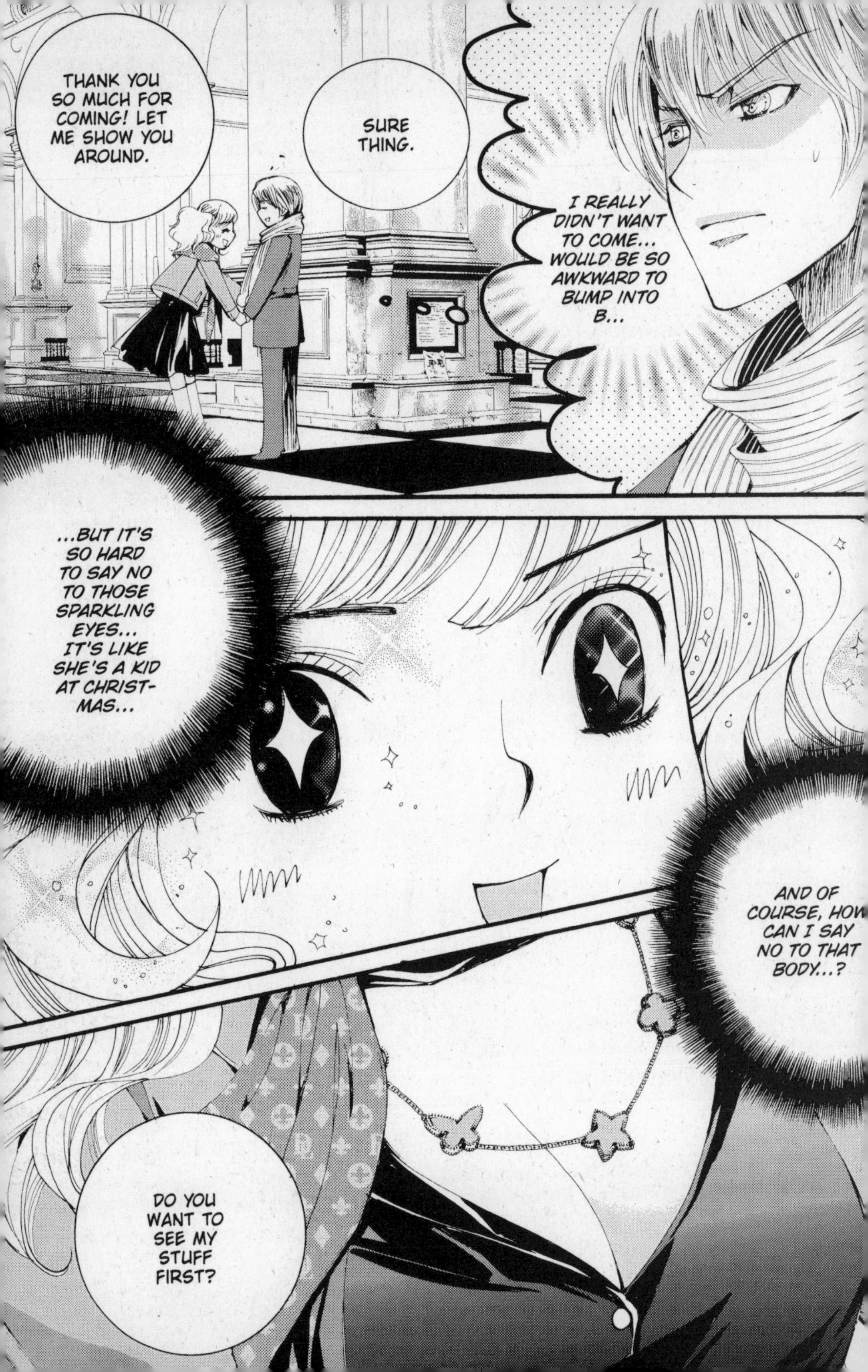
THANK YOU SO MUCH FOR COMING! LET ME SHOW YOU AROUND.
SURE THING.
I REALLY DIDN'T WANT TO COME... WOULD BE SO AWKWARD TO BUMP INTO B...
...BUT IT'S SO HARD TO SAY NO TO THOSE SPARKLING EYES... IT'S LIKE SHE'S A KID AT CHRIST-MAS...
AND OF COURSE, HOW CAN I SAY NO TO THAT BODY...?
DO YOU WANT TO SEE MY STUFF FIRST?

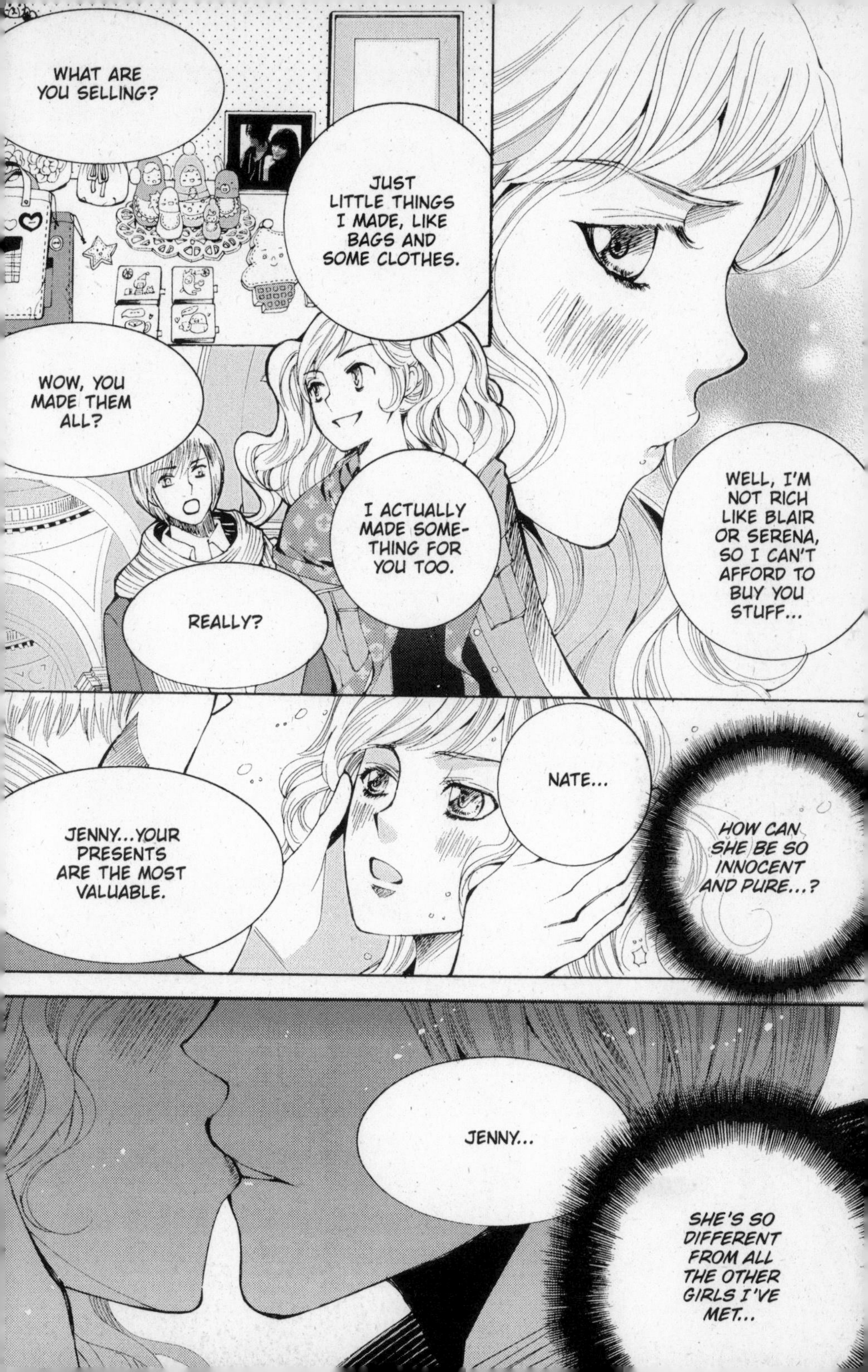
WHAT ARE YOU SELLING?
JUST LITTLE THINGS I MADE, LIKE BAGS AND SOME CLOTHES.
WOW, YOU MADE THEM ALL?
I ACTUALLY MADE SOME-THING FOR YOU TOO.
REALLY?
WELL, I'M NOT RICH LIKE BLAIR OR SERENA, SO I CAN'T AFFORD TO BUY YOU STUFF...
JENNY...YOUR PRESENTS ARE THE MOST VALUABLE.
NATE...
HOW CAN SHE BE SO INNOCENT AND PURE...?
JENNY...
SHE'S SO DIFFERENT FROM ALL THE OTHER GIRLS I'VE MET...

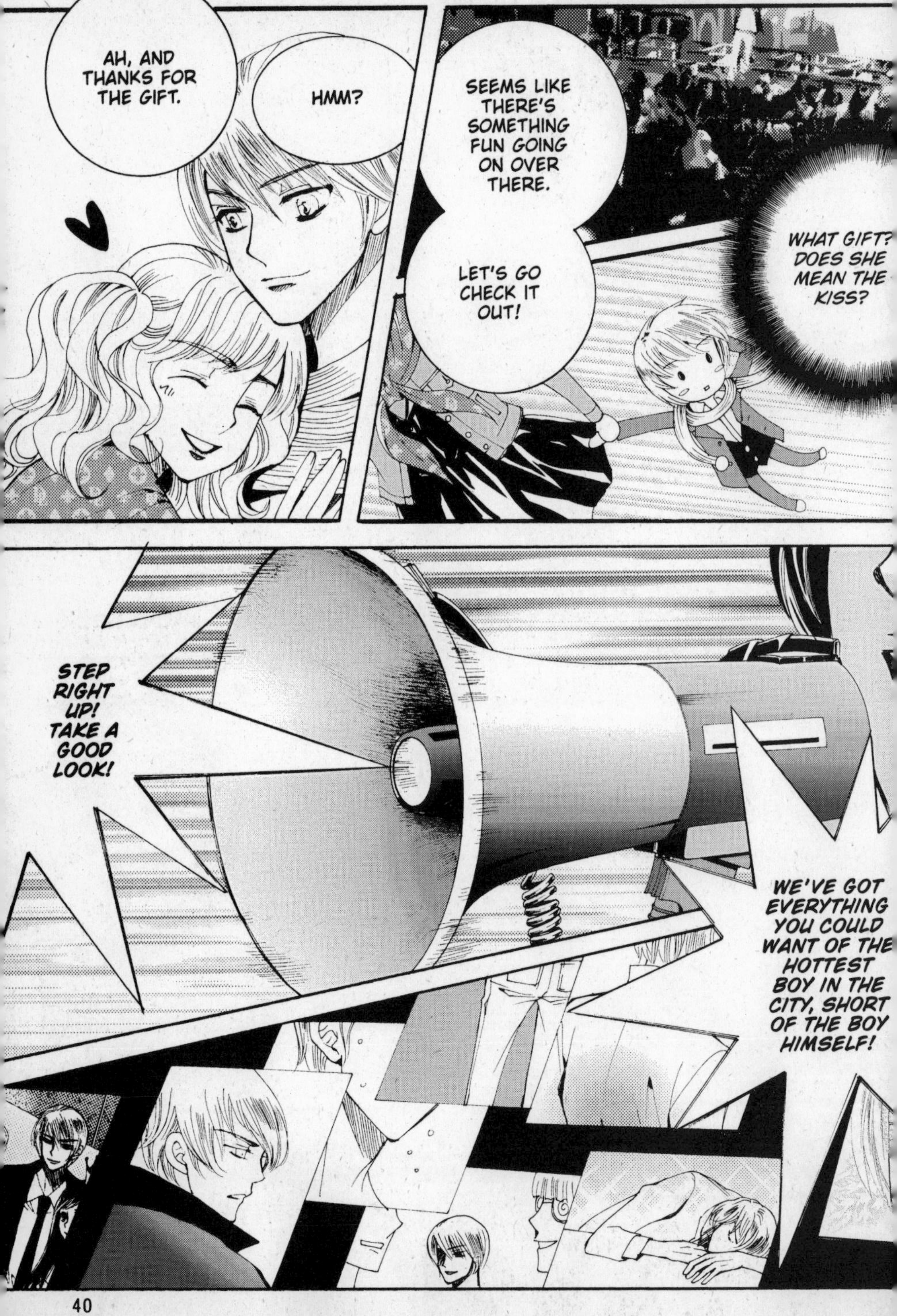
AH, AND THANKS FOR THE GIFT.
HMM?
SEEMS LIKE THERE'S SOMETHING FUN GOING ON OVER THERE.
LET'S GO CHECK IT OUT!
WHAT GIFT? DOES SHE MEAN THE KISS?
STEP RIGHT UP! TAKE A GOOD LOOK!
WE'VE GOT EVERYTHING YOU COULD WANT OF THE HOTTEST BOY IN THE CITY, SHORT OF THE BOY HIMSELF!

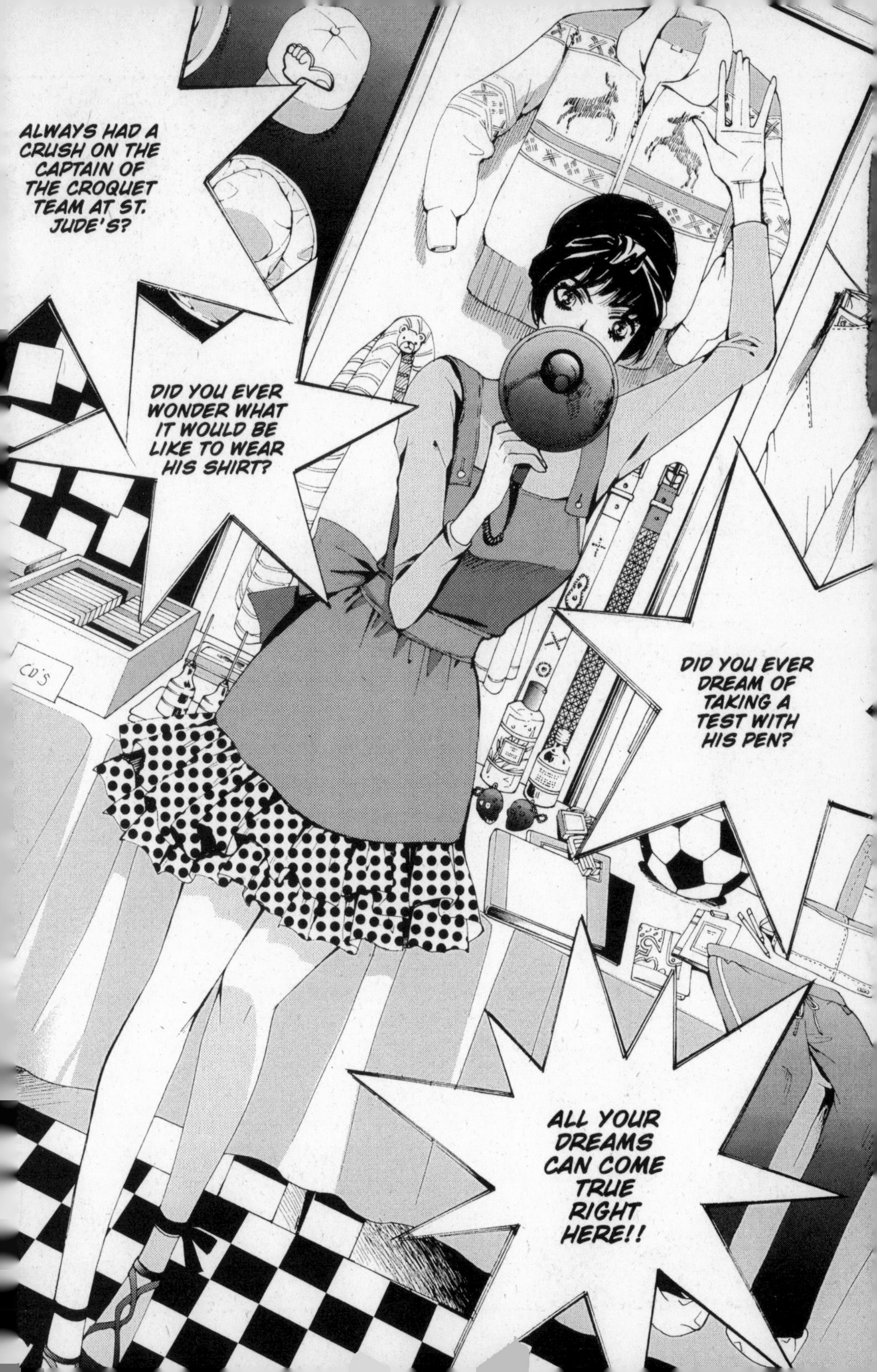
ALWAYS HAD A CRUSH ON THE CAPTAIN OF THE CROQUET TEAM AT ST. JUDE'S?
DID YOU EVER WONDER WHAT IT WOULD BE LIKE TO WEAR HIS SHIRT?
DID YOU EVER DREAM OF TAKING A TEST WITH HIS PEN?
ALL YOUR DREAMS CAN COME TRUE RIGHT HERE!!
CD'S

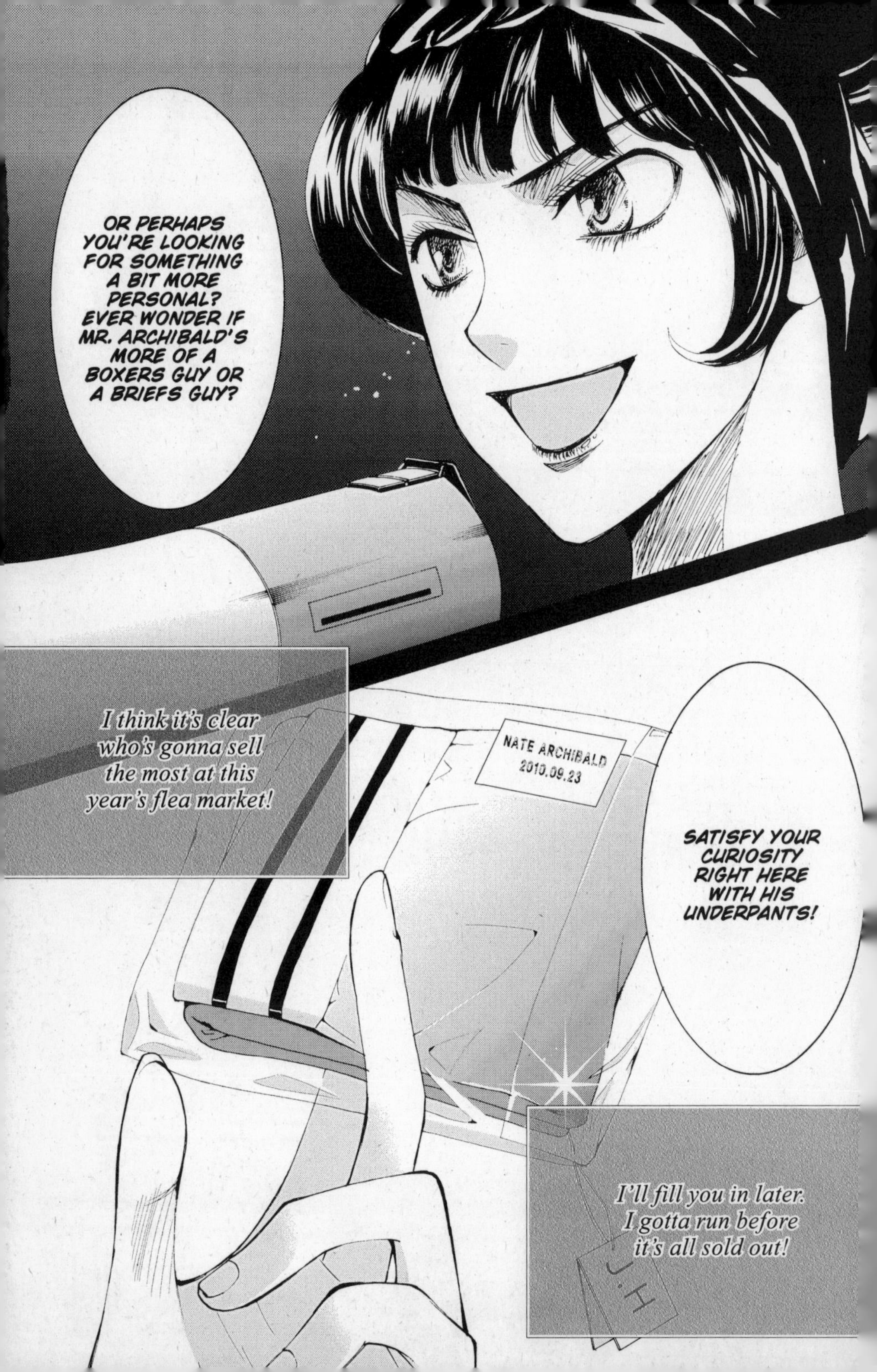
OR PERHAPS YOU'RE LOOKING FOR SOMETHING A BIT MORE PERSONAL? EVER WONDER IF MR. ARCHIBALD'S MORE OF A BOXERS GUY OR A BRIEFS GUY?
I think it's clear who's gonna sell the most at this year's flea market!
NATE ARCHIBALD 2010.09.23
SATISFY YOUR CURIOSITY RIGHT HERE WITH HIS UNDERPANTS!
I'll fill you in later. I gotta run before it's all sold out!
J.H

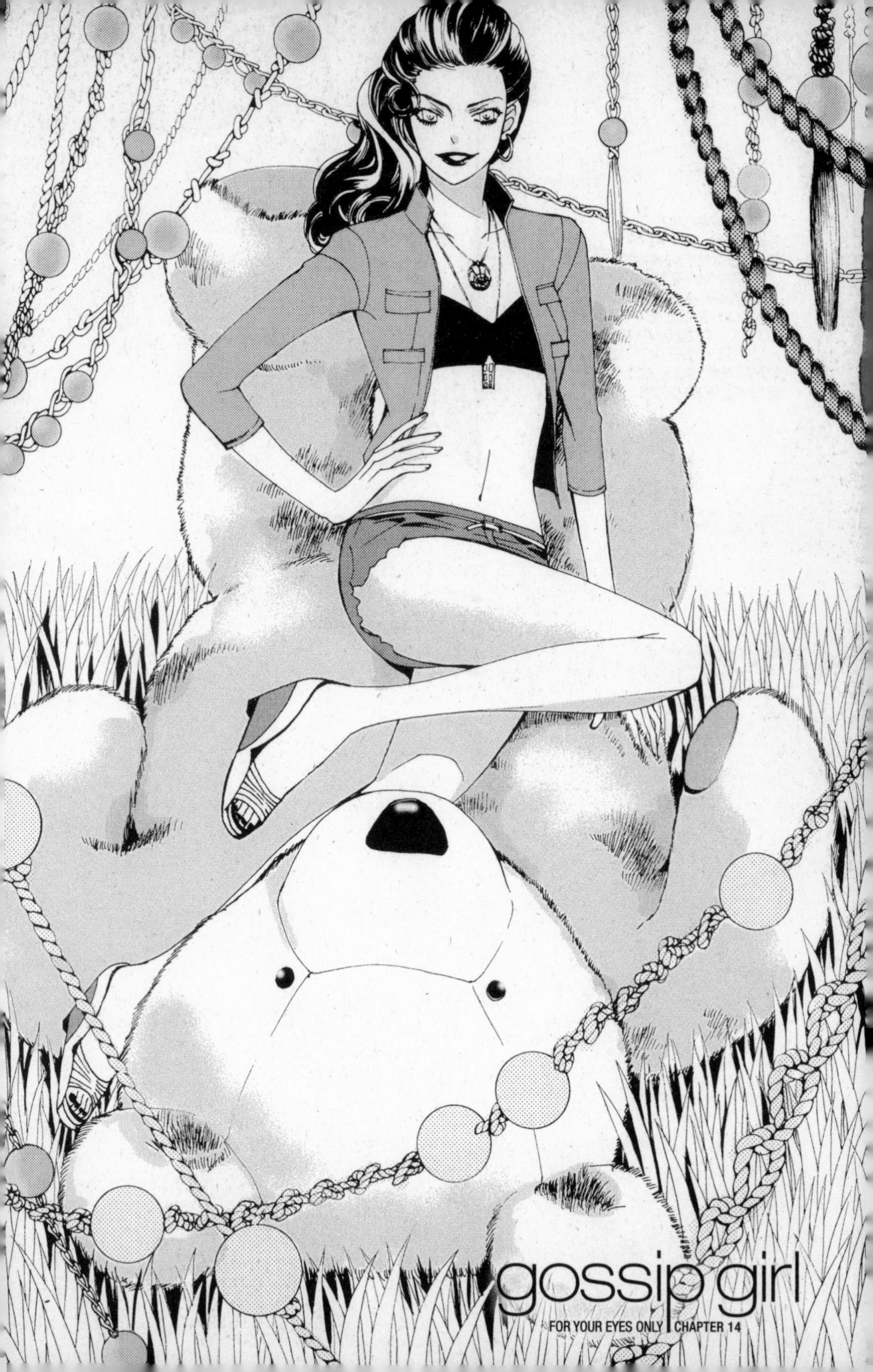
gossip girl
FOR YOUR EYES ONLY | CHAPTER 14

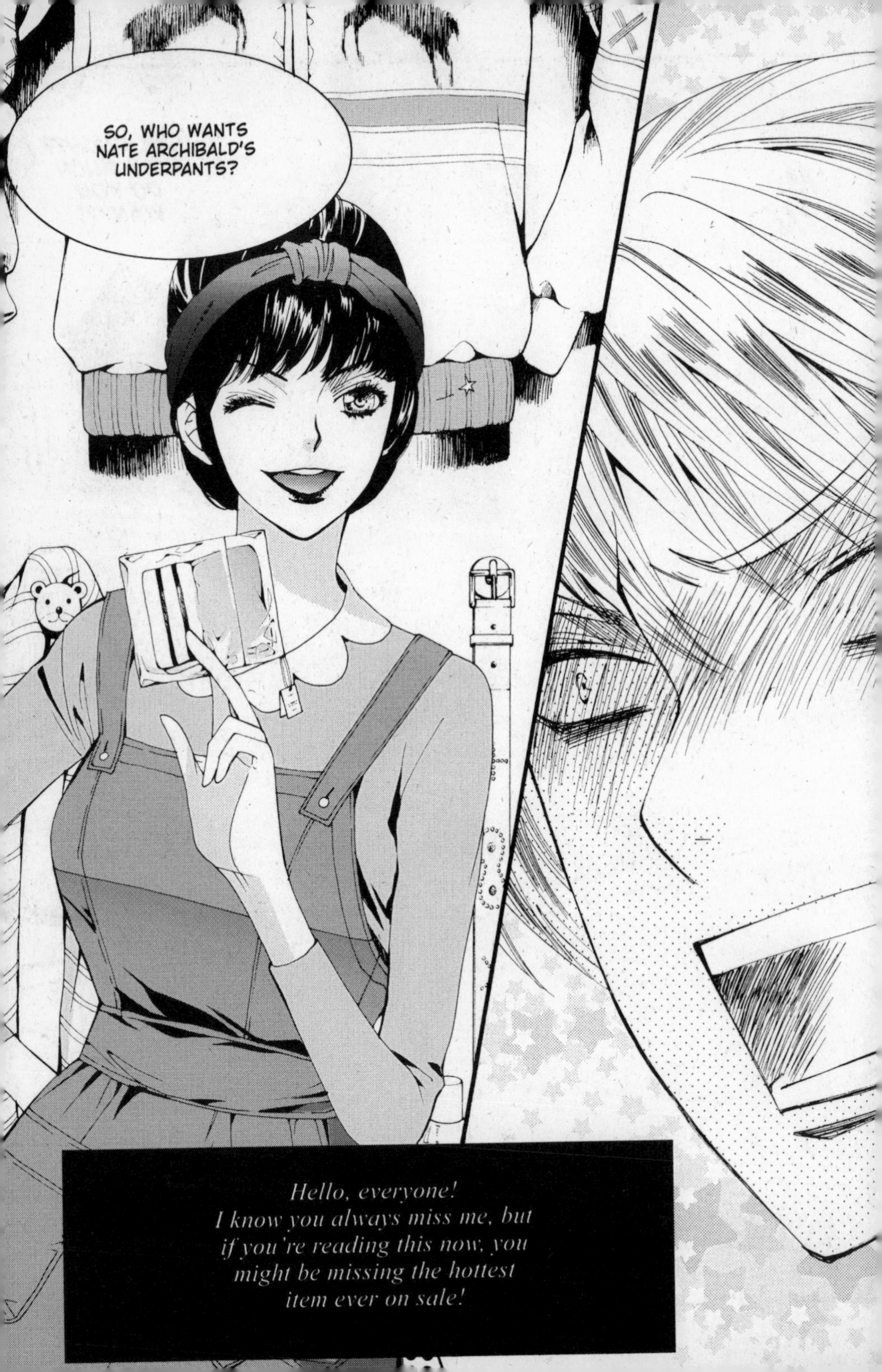
SO, WHO WANTS NATE ARCHIBALD'S UNDERPANTS?
Hello, everyone! I know you always miss me, but if you're reading this now, you might be missing the hottest item ever on sale!

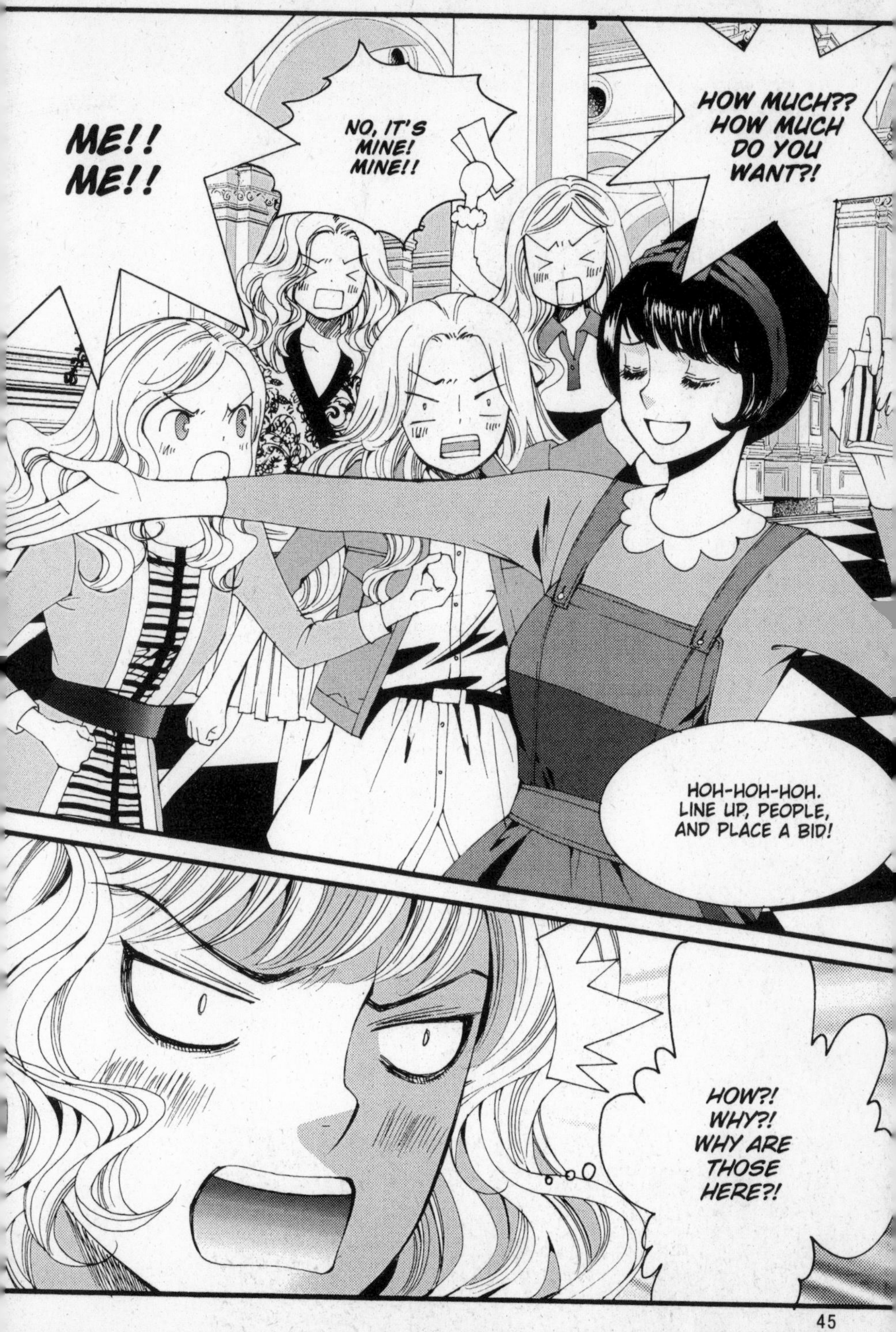
ME!! ME!!
NO, IT'S MINE! MINE!!
HOW MUCH?? HOW MUCH DO YOU WANT?!
HOH-HOH-HOH. LINE UP, PEOPLE, AND PLACE A BID!
HOW?! WHY?! WHY ARE THOSE HERE?!

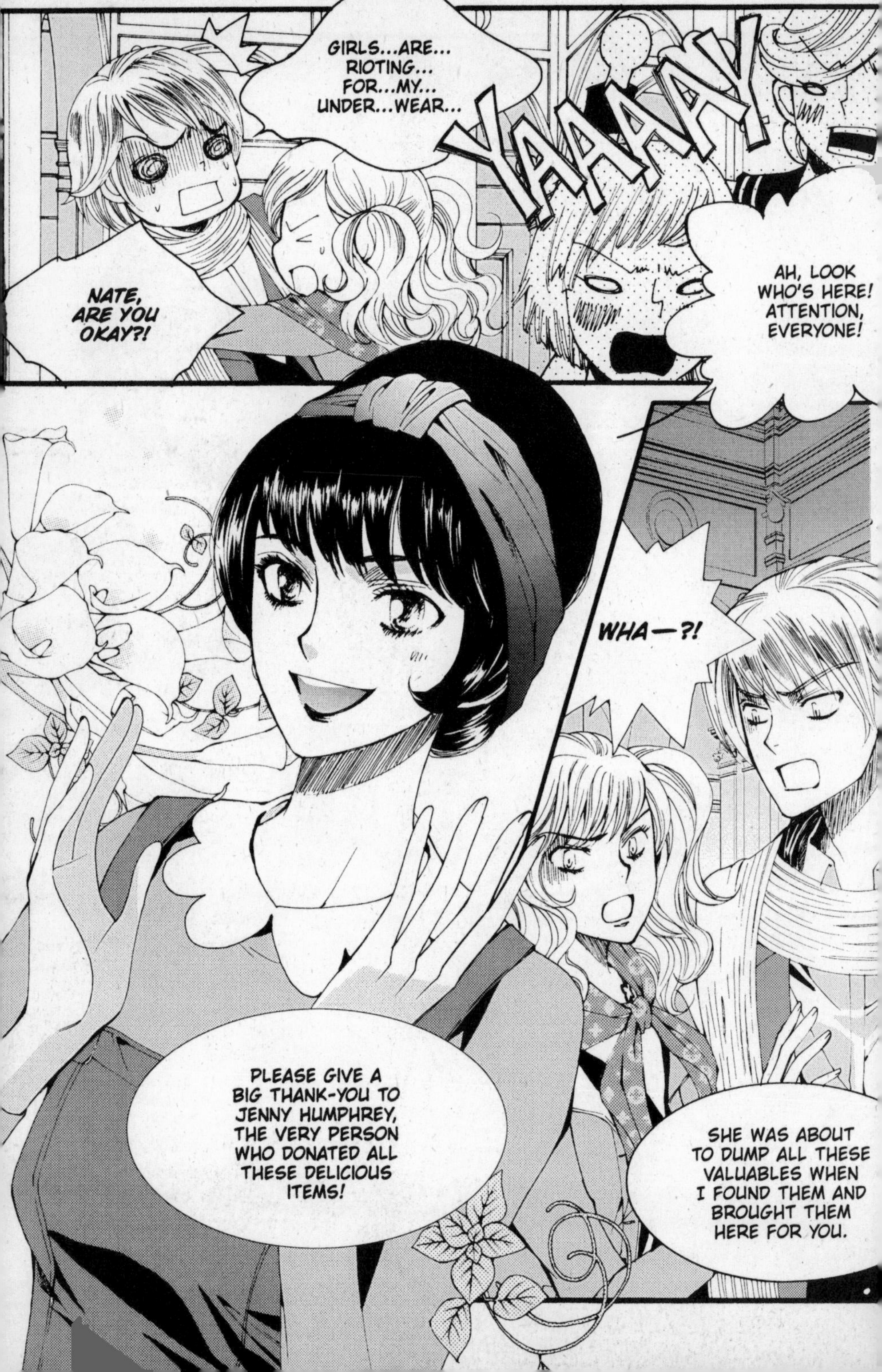
GIRLS...ARE... RIOTING... FOR...MY... UNDER...WEAR...
YAAAAY
NATE, ARE YOU OKAY?!
AH, LOOK WHO'S HERE! ATTENTION, EVERYONE!
PLEASE GIVE A BIG THANK-YOU TO JENNY HUMPHREY, THE VERY PERSON WHO DONATED ALL THESE DELICIOUS ITEMS!
WHA—?!
SHE WAS ABOUT TO DUMP ALL THESE VALUABLES WHEN I FOUND THEM AND BROUGHT THEM HERE FOR YOU.

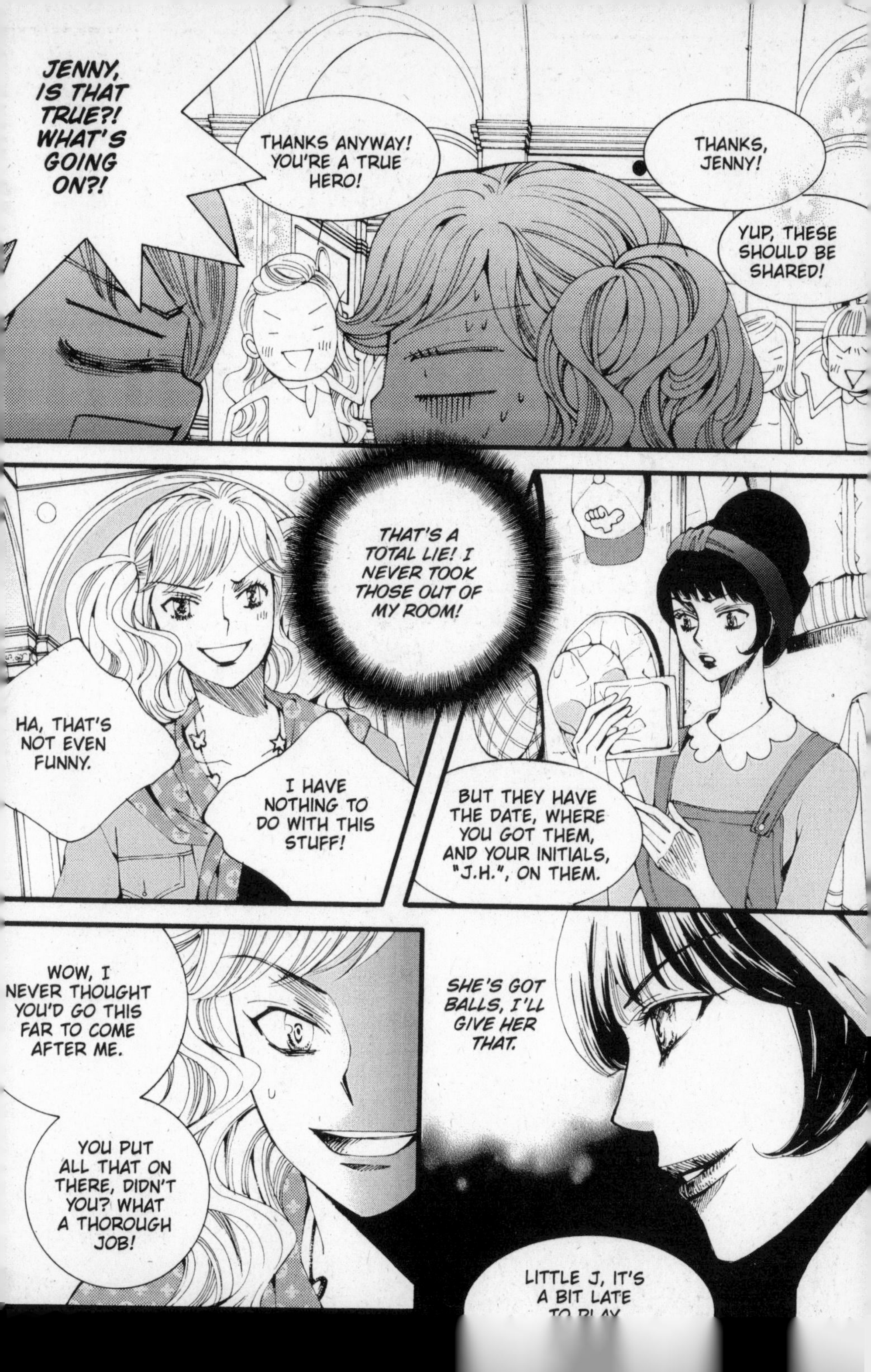
JENNY, IS THAT TRUE?! WHAT'S GOING ON?!
THANKS ANYWAY! YOU'RE A TRUE HERO!
THANKS, JENNY!
YUP, THESE SHOULD BE SHARED!
THAT'S A TOTAL LIE! I NEVER TOOK THOSE OUT OF MY ROOM!
HA, THAT'S NOT EVEN FUNNY.
I HAVE NOTHING TO DO WITH THIS STUFF!
BUT THEY HAVE THE DATE, WHERE YOU GOT THEM, AND YOUR INITIALS, "J.H.", ON THEM.
WOW, I NEVER THOUGHT YOU'D GO THIS FAR TO COME AFTER ME.
YOU PUT ALL THAT ON THERE, DIDN'T YOU? WHAT A THOROUGH JOB!
SHE'S GOT BALLS, I'LL GIVE HER THAT.
LITTLE J, IT'S A BIT LATE

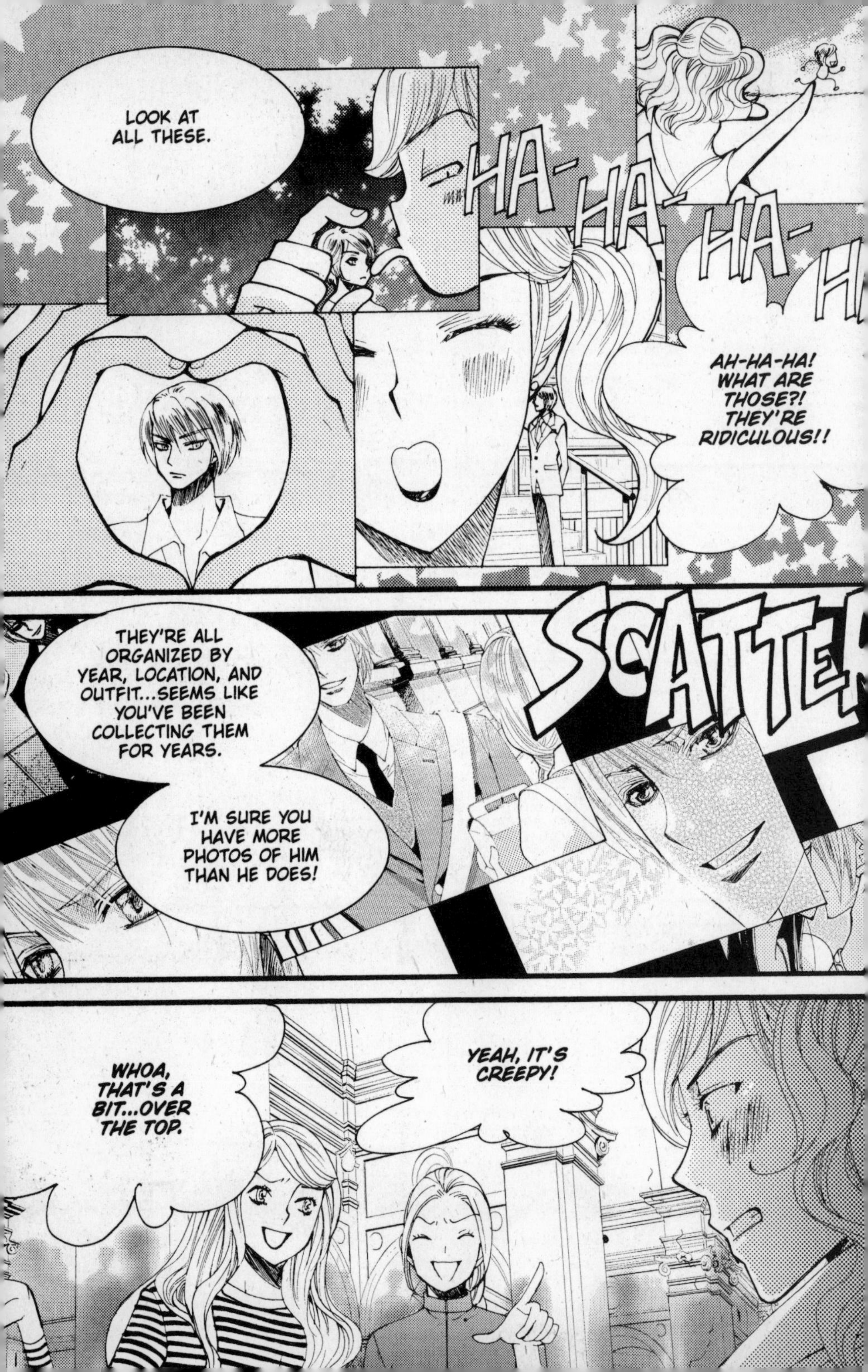
LOOK AT ALL THESE.
HA-HA-
HA-HA-
HA-H
AH-HA-HA! WHAT ARE THOSE?! THEY'RE RIDICULOUS!!
THEY'RE ALL ORGANIZED BY YEAR, LOCATION, AND OUTFIT...SEEMS LIKE YOU'VE BEEN COLLECTING THEM FOR YEARS.
I'M SURE YOU HAVE MORE PHOTOS OF HIM THAN HE DOES!
SCATTE
WHOA, THAT'S A BIT...OVER THE TOP.
YEAH, IT'S CREEPY!

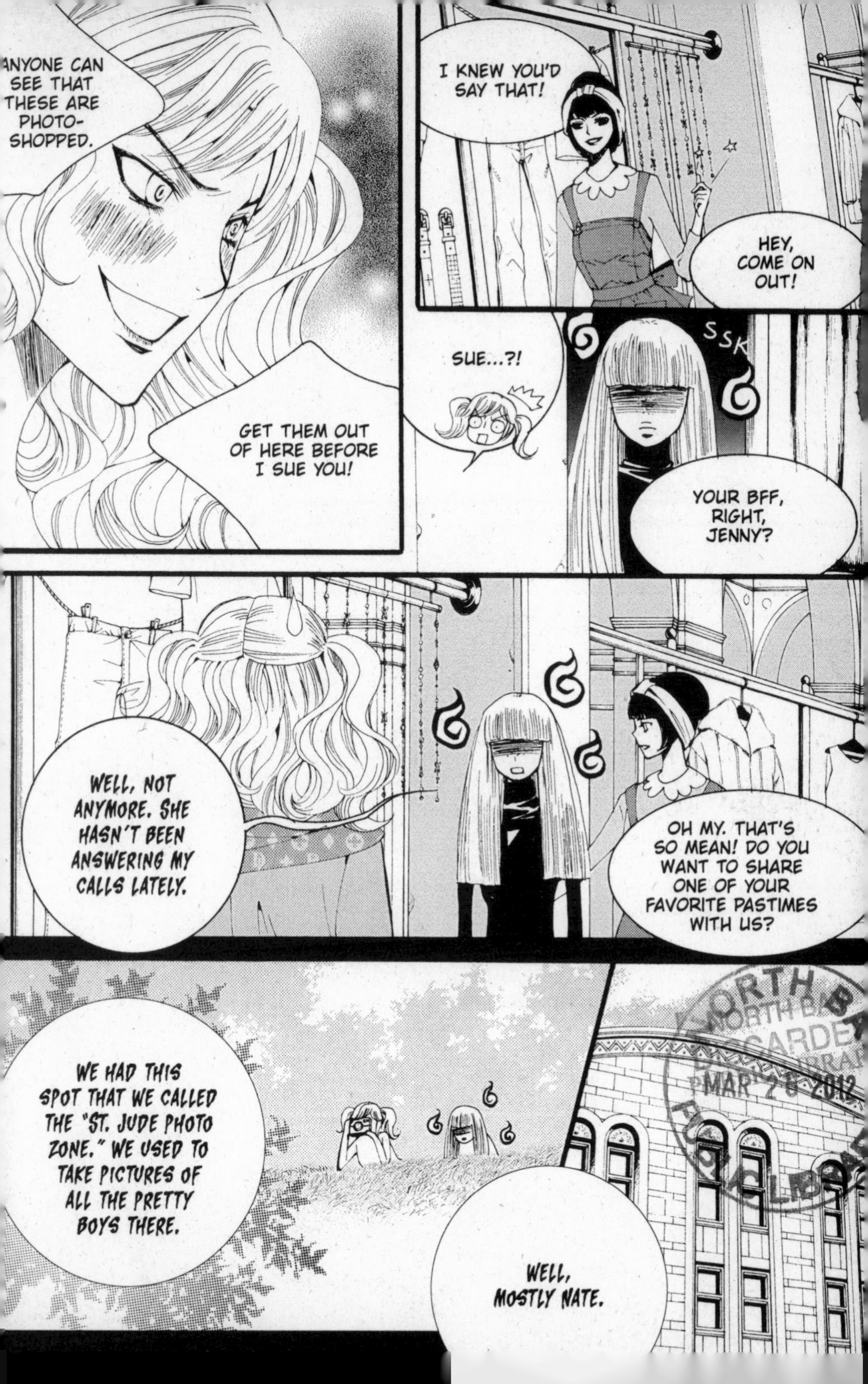
ANYONE CAN SEE THAT THESE ARE PHOTO-SHOPPED.
GET THEM OUT OF HERE BEFORE I SUE YOU!
I KNEW YOU'D SAY THAT!
HEY, COME ON OUT!
SUE...?!
SSK
YOUR BFF, RIGHT, JENNY?
WELL, NOT ANYMORE. SHE HASN'T BEEN ANSWERING MY CALLS LATELY.
OH MY. THAT'S SO MEAN! DO YOU WANT TO SHARE ONE OF YOUR FAVORITE PASTIMES WITH US?
WE HAD THIS SPOT THAT WE CALLED THE "ST. JUDE PHOTO ZONE." WE USED TO TAKE PICTURES OF ALL THE PRETTY BOYS THERE.
WELL, MOSTLY NATE.

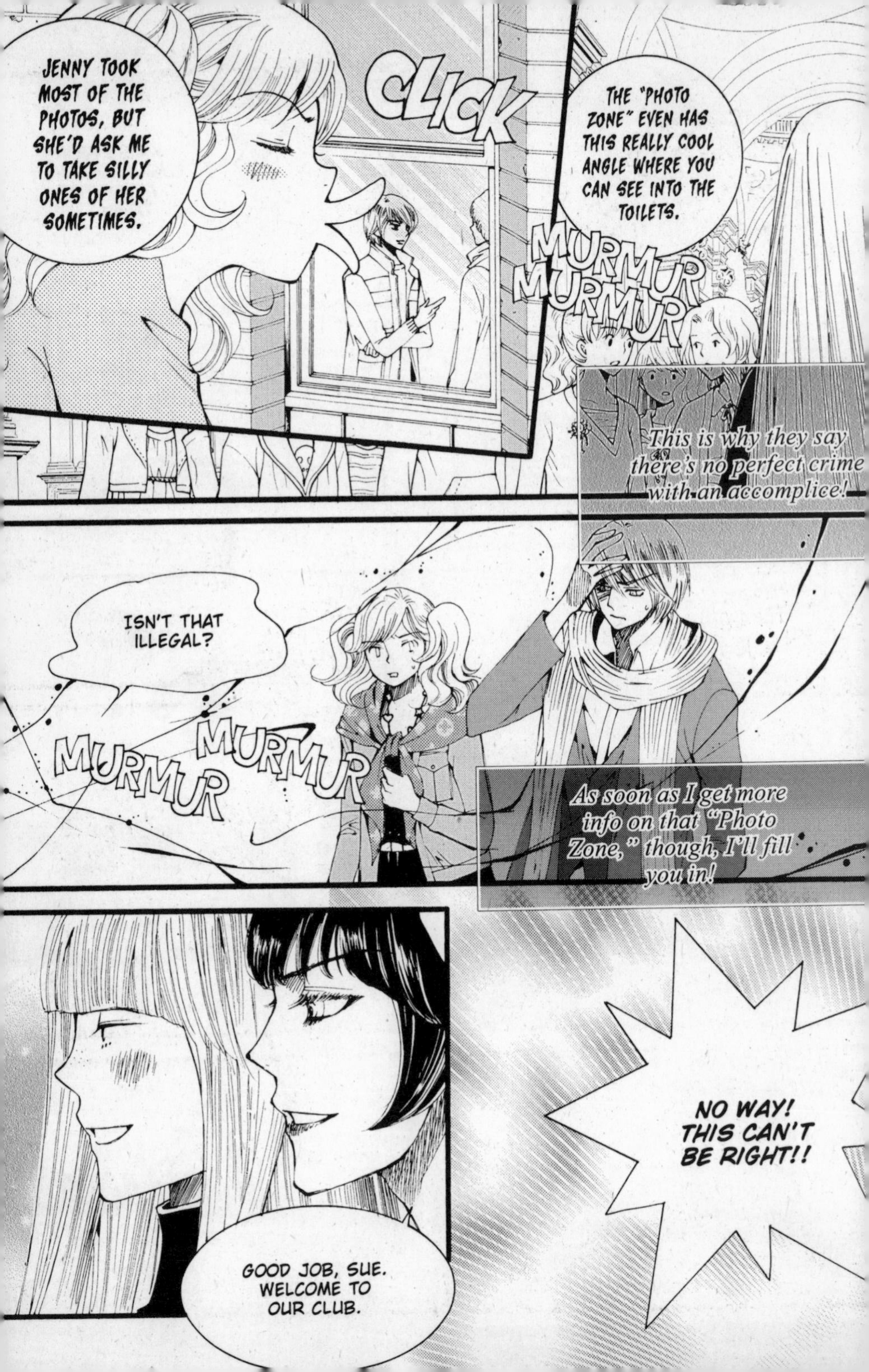
JENNY TOOK MOST OF THE PHOTOS, BUT SHE'D ASK ME TO TAKE SILLY ONES OF HER SOMETIMES.
CLICK
THE "PHOTO ZONE" EVEN HAS THIS REALLY COOL ANGLE WHERE YOU CAN SEE INTO THE TOILETS.
MURMUR MURMUR
This is why they say there's no perfect crime with an accomplice!
ISN'T THAT ILLEGAL?
MURMUR MURMUR
As soon as I get more info on that "Photo Zone," though, I'll fill you in!
GOOD JOB, SUE. WELCOME TO OUR CLUB.
NO WAY! THIS CAN'T BE RIGHT!!

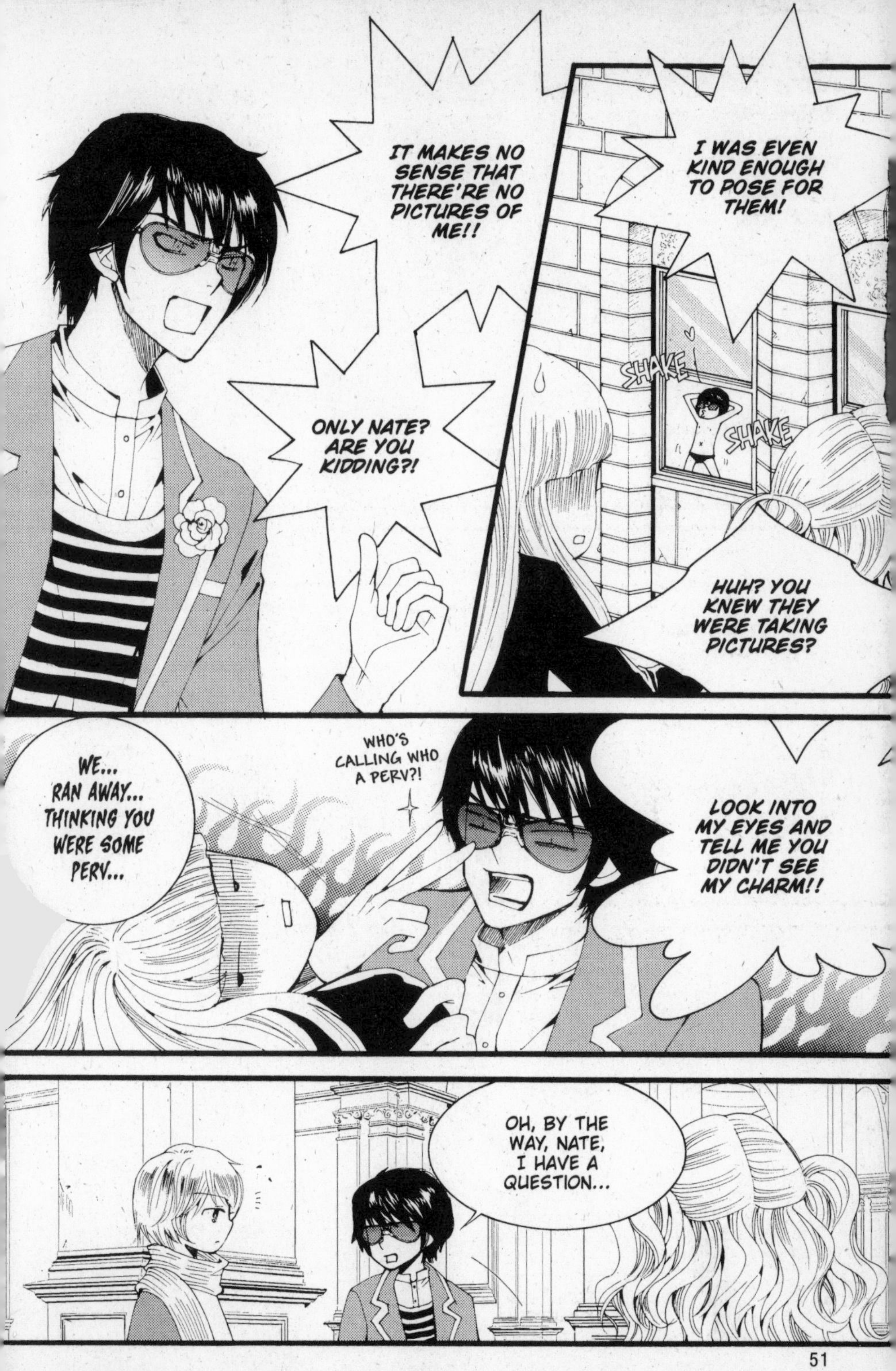
IT MAKES NO SENSE THAT THERE'RE NO PICTURES OF ME!!
ONLY NATE? ARE YOU KIDDING?!
I WAS EVEN KIND ENOUGH TO POSE FOR THEM!
SHAKE
SHAKE
HUH? YOU KNEW THEY WERE TAKING PICTURES?
WE... RAN AWAY... THINKING YOU WERE SOME PERV...
WHO'S CALLING WHO A PERV?!
LOOK INTO MY EYES AND TELL ME YOU DIDN'T SEE MY CHARM!!
OH, BY THE WAY, NATE, I HAVE A QUESTION...

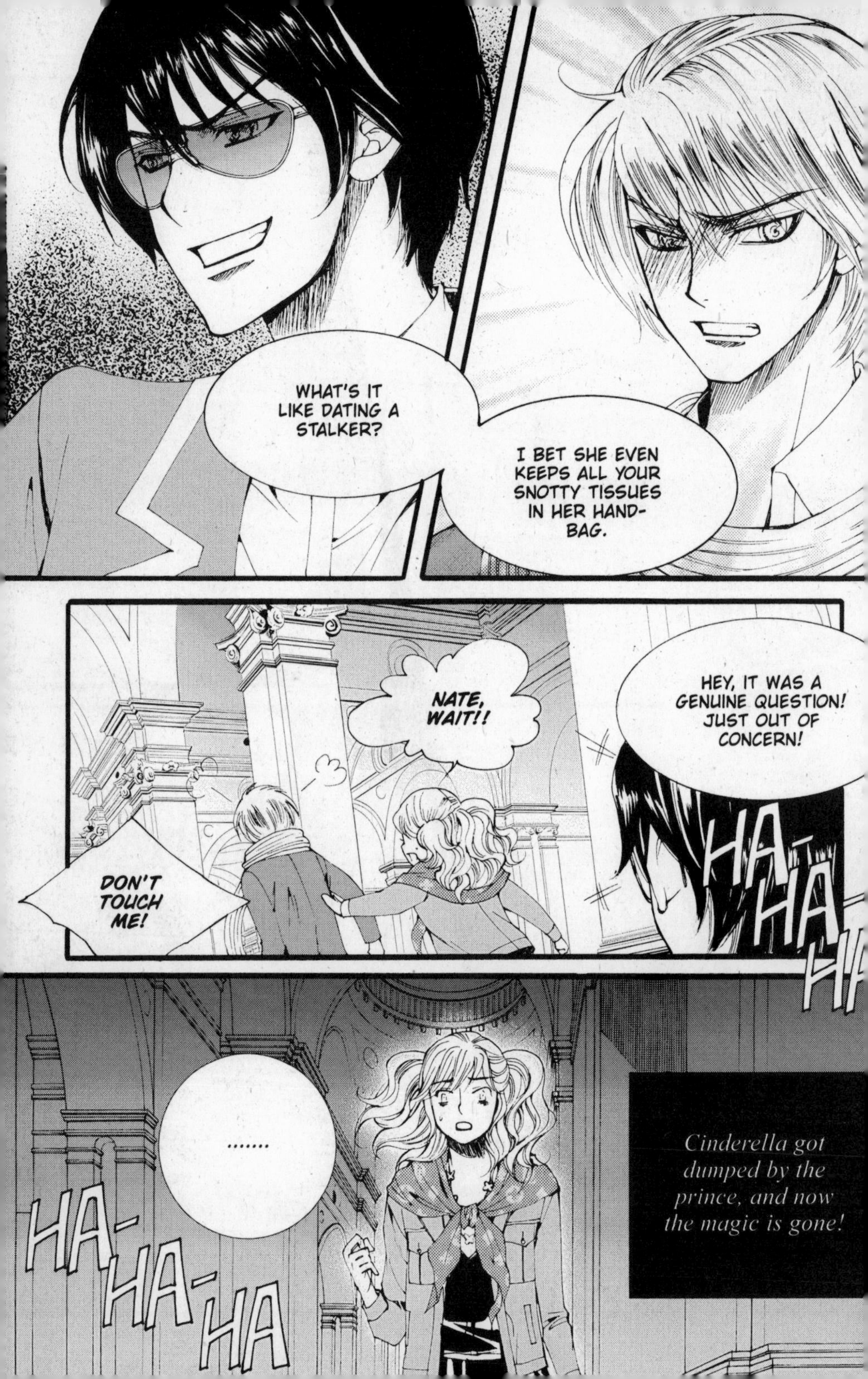
WHAT'S IT LIKE DATING A STALKER?
I BET SHE EVEN KEEPS ALL YOUR SNOTTY TISSUES IN HER HAND-BAG.
DON'T TOUCH ME!
NATE, WAIT!!
HEY, IT WAS A GENUINE QUESTION! JUST OUT OF CONCERN!
HA-HA-HA
....
HA-HA-HA
Cinderella got dumped by the prince, and now the magic is gone!

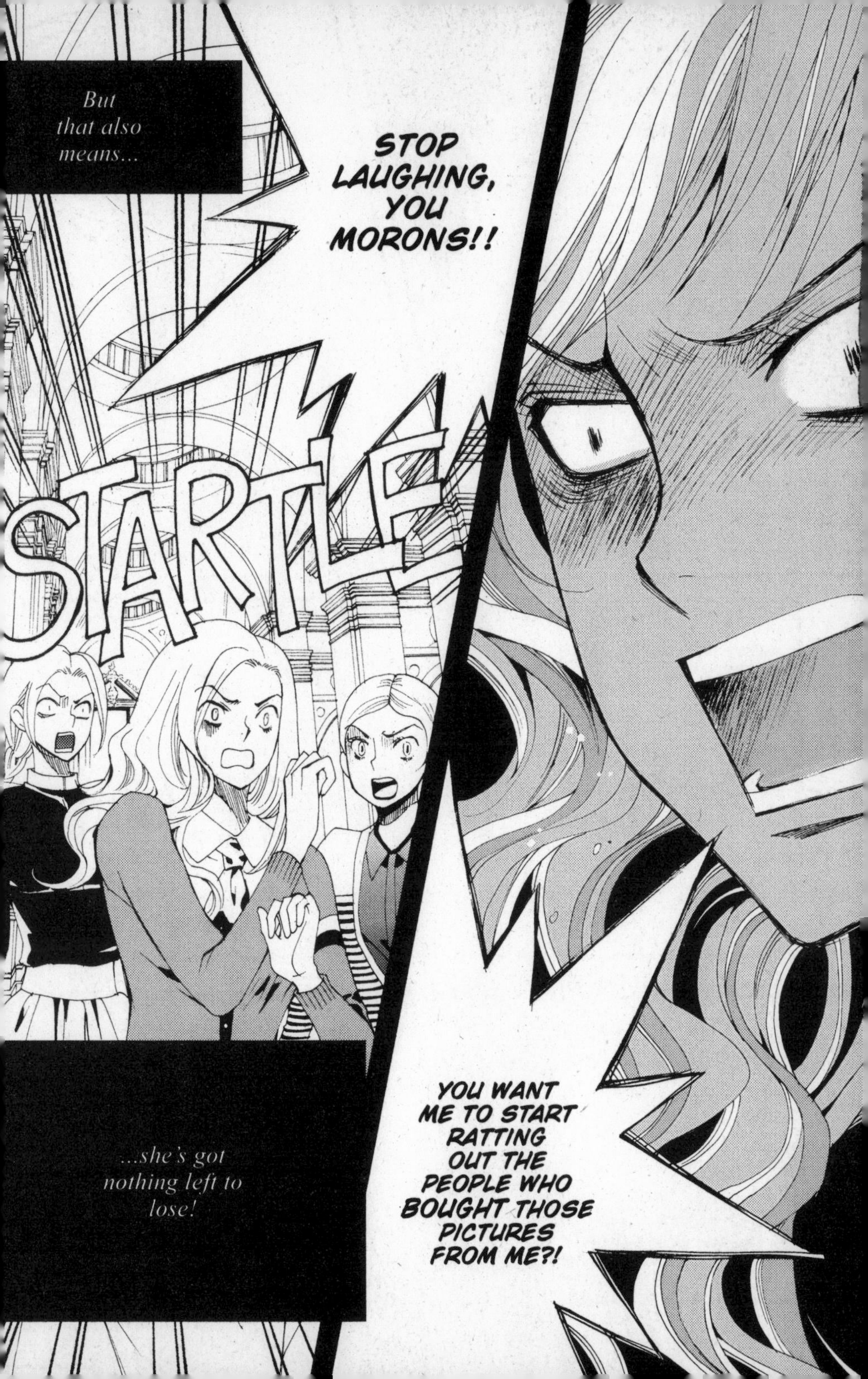
But that also means...
STOP LAUGHING, YOU MORONS!!
STARTLE
...she's got nothing left to lose!
YOU WANT ME TO START RATTING OUT THE PEOPLE WHO BOUGHT THOSE PICTURES FROM ME?!

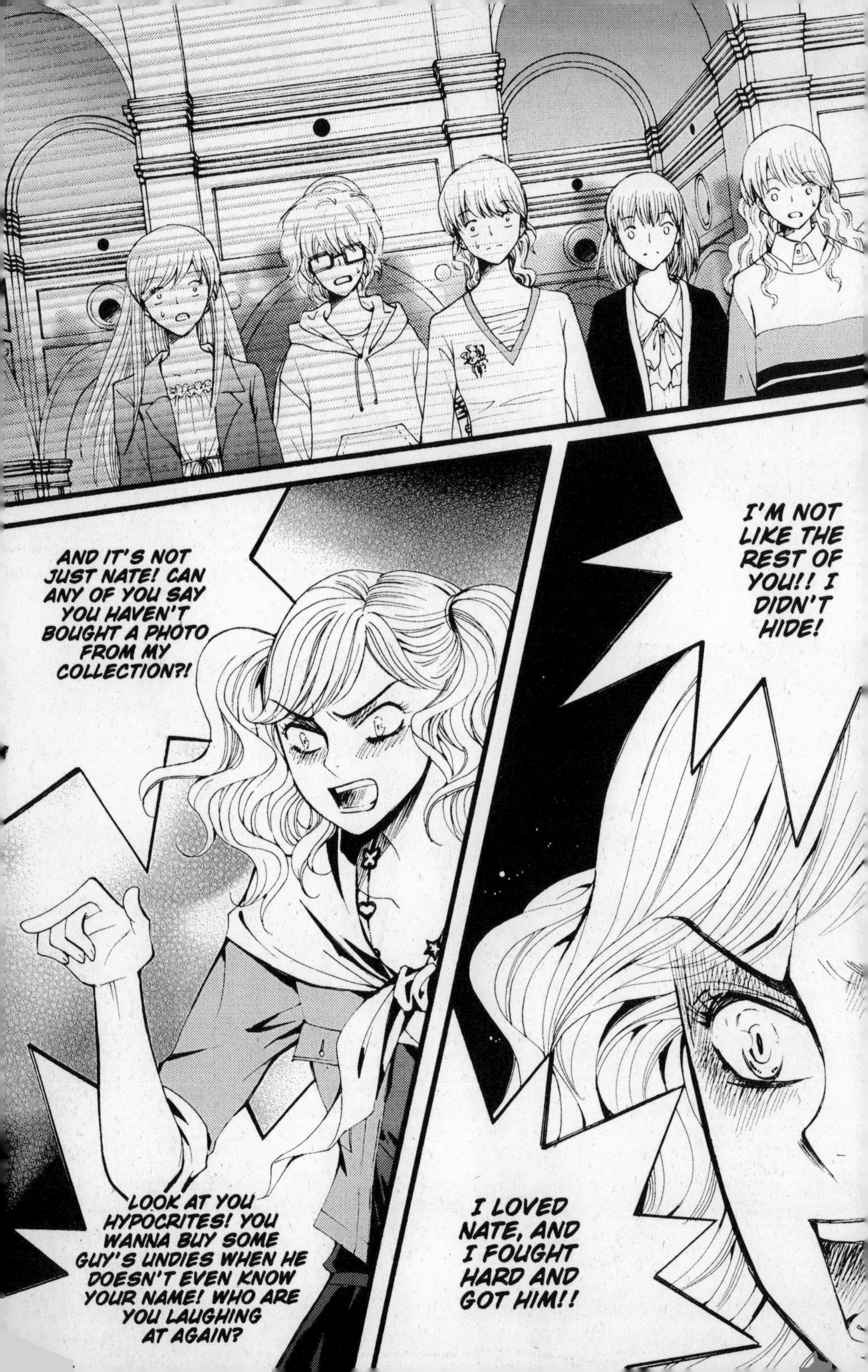
I'M NOT LIKE THE REST OF YOU!! I DIDN'T HIDE!
I LOVED NATE, AND I FOUGHT HARD AND GOT HIM!!
AND IT'S NOT JUST NATE! CAN ANY OF YOU SAY YOU HAVEN'T BOUGHT A PHOTO FROM MY COLLECTION?!
LOOK AT YOU HYPOCRITES! YOU WANNA BUY SOME GUY'S UNDIES WHEN HE DOESN'T EVEN KNOW YOUR NAME! WHO ARE YOU LAUGHING AT AGAIN?

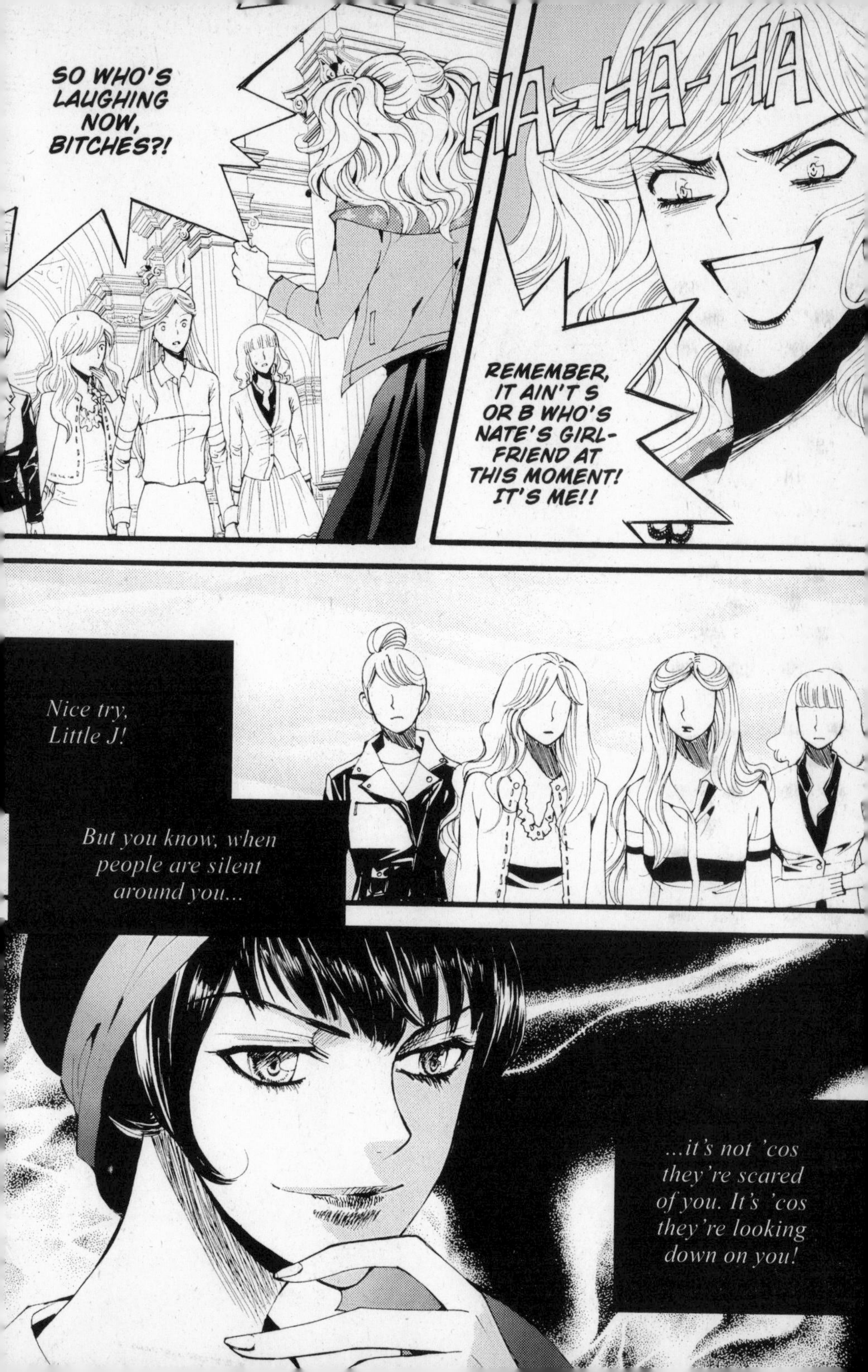
SO WHO'S LAUGHING NOW, BITCHES?!
HA-HA-HA
REMEMBER, IT AIN'T S OR B WHO'S NATE'S GIRL-FRIEND AT THIS MOMENT! IT'S ME!!
Nice try, Little J!
But you know, when people are silent around you...
...it's not 'cos they're scared of you. It's 'cos they're looking down on you!

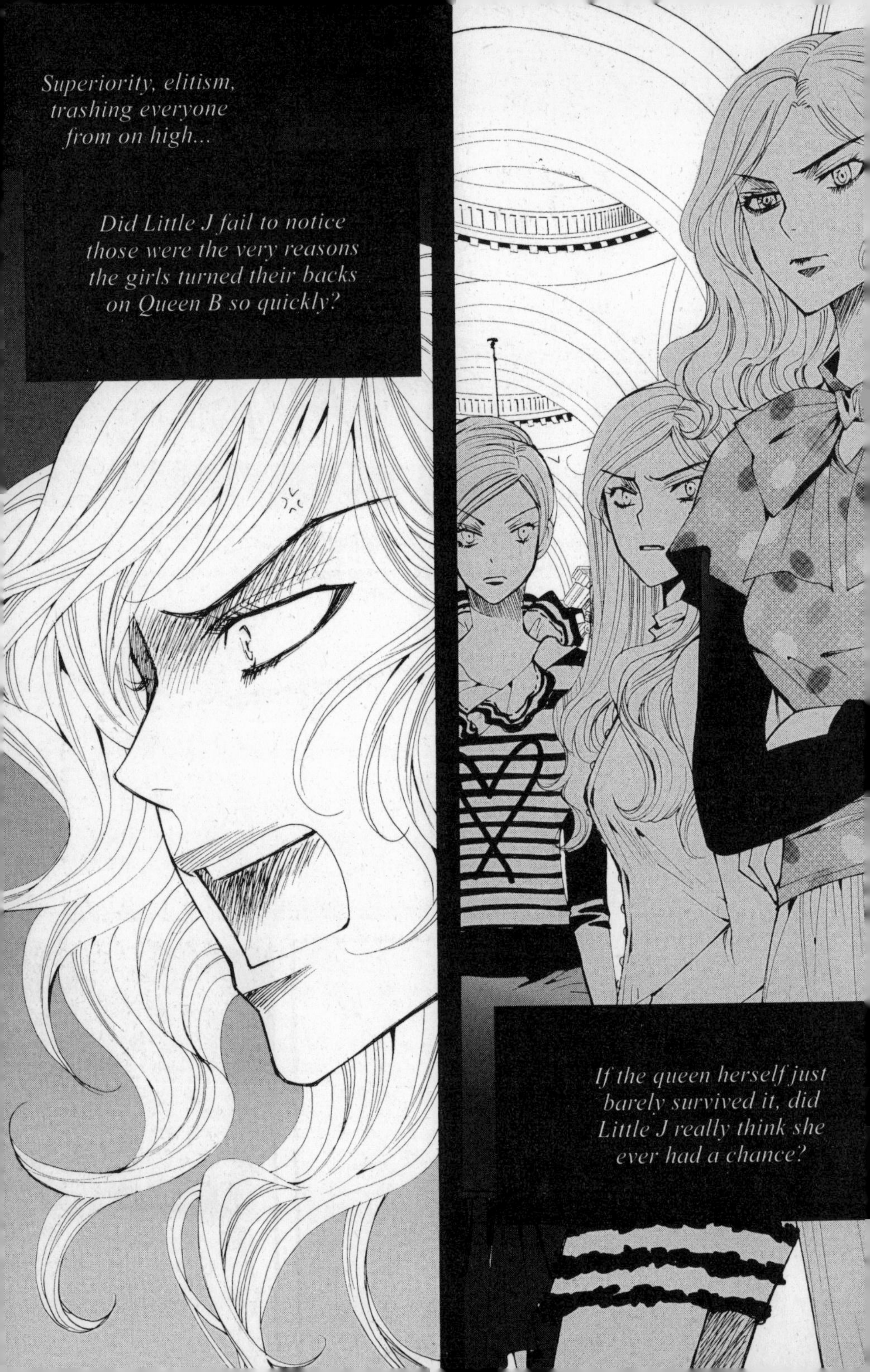
Superiority, elitism, trashing everyone from on high...
Did Little J fail to notice those were the very reasons the girls turned their backs on Queen B so quickly?
If the queen herself just barely survived it, did Little J really think she ever had a chance?

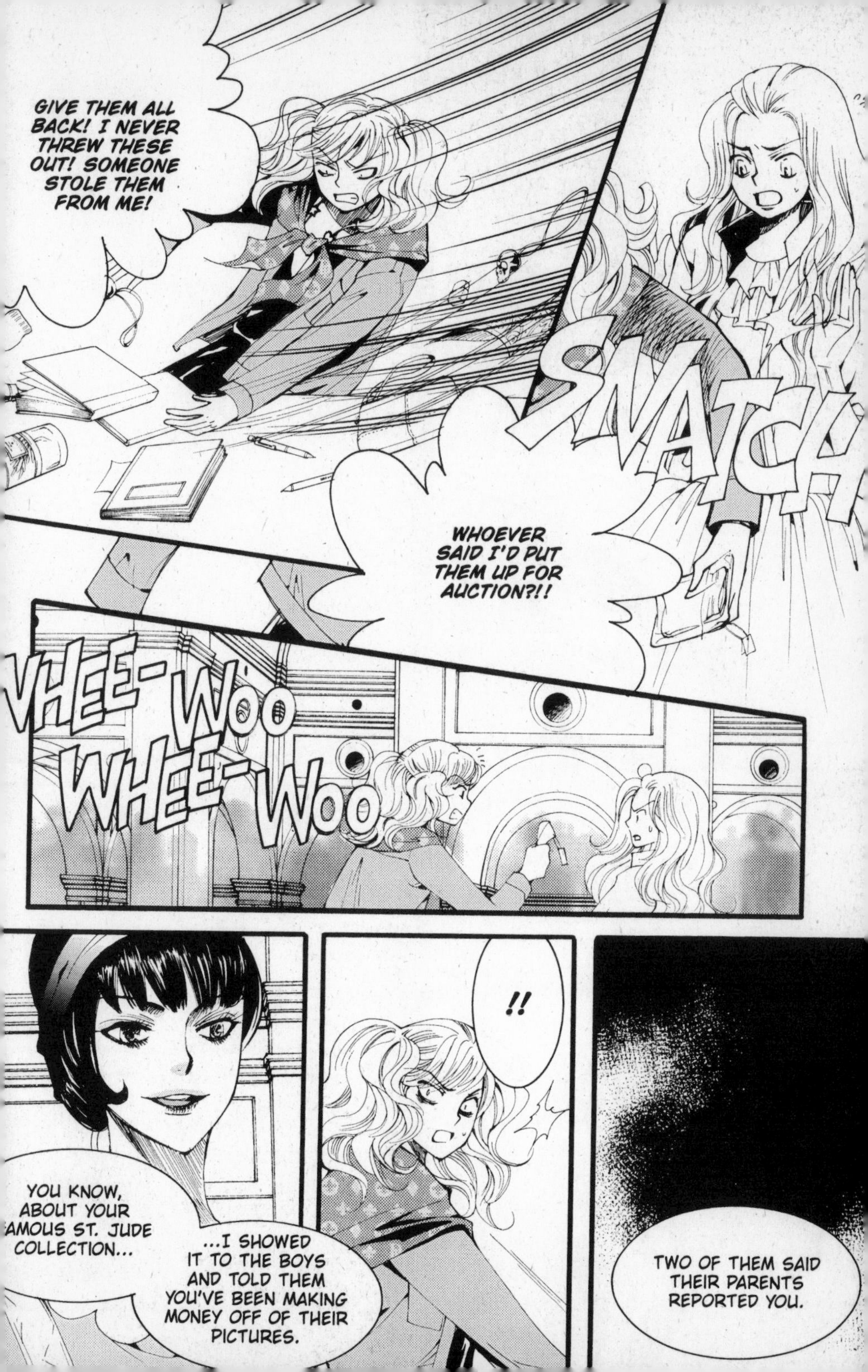
GIVE THEM ALL BACK! I NEVER THREW THESE OUT! SOMEONE STOLE THEM FROM ME!
SNATCH
WHOEVER SAID I'D PUT THEM UP FOR AUCTION?!!
WHEE-WOO WHEE-WOO
YOU KNOW, ABOUT YOUR FAMOUS ST. JUDE COLLECTION...
...I SHOWED IT TO THE BOYS AND TOLD THEM YOU'VE BEEN MAKING MONEY OFF OF THEIR PICTURES.
!!
TWO OF THEM SAID THEIR PARENTS REPORTED YOU.

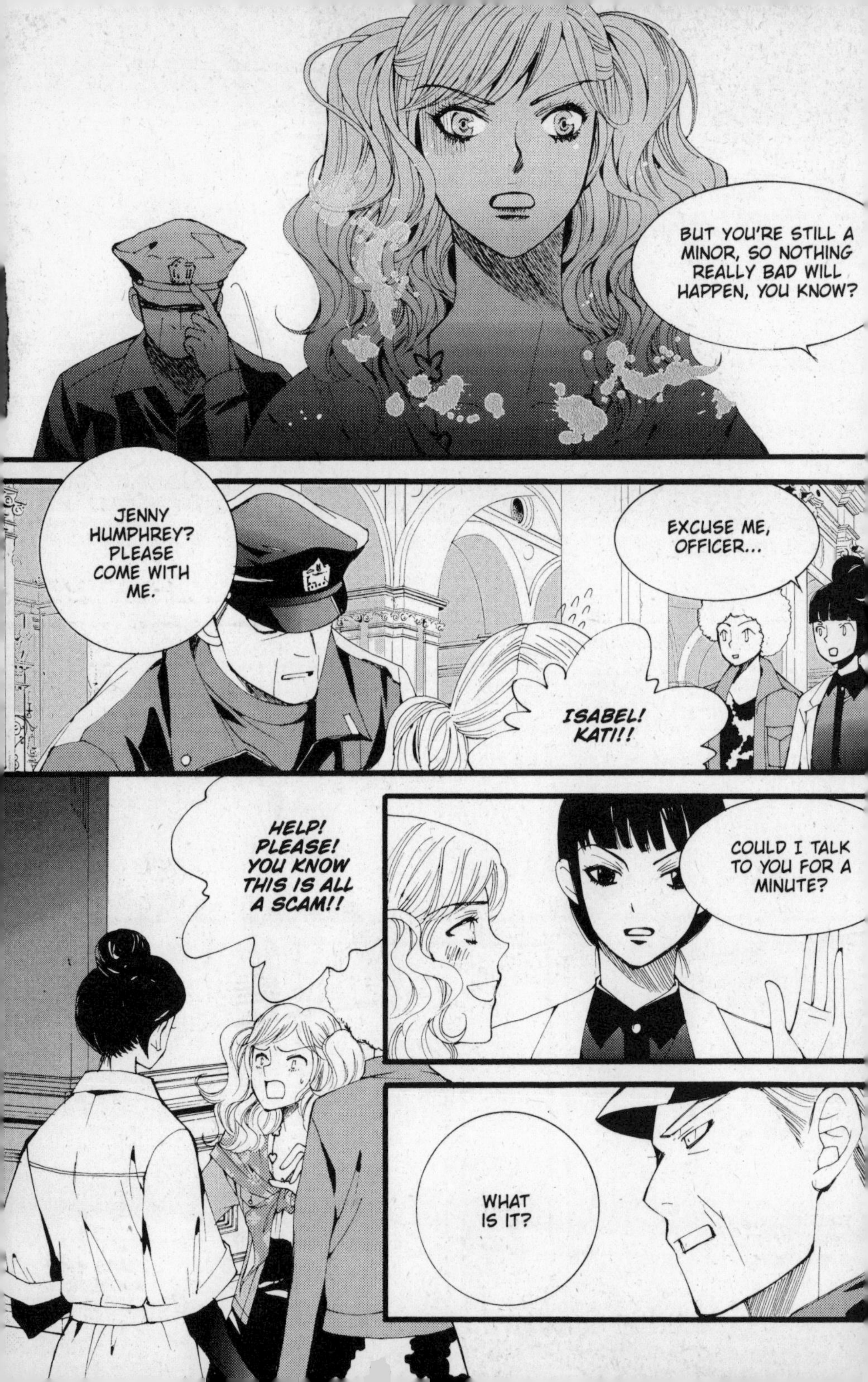
BUT YOU'RE STILL A MINOR, SO NOTHING REALLY BAD WILL HAPPEN, YOU KNOW?
JENNY HUMPHREY? PLEASE COME WITH ME.
EXCUSE ME, OFFICER...
ISABEL! KATI!!
HELP! PLEASE! YOU KNOW THIS IS ALL A SCAM!!
COULD I TALK TO YOU FOR A MINUTE?
WHAT IS IT?

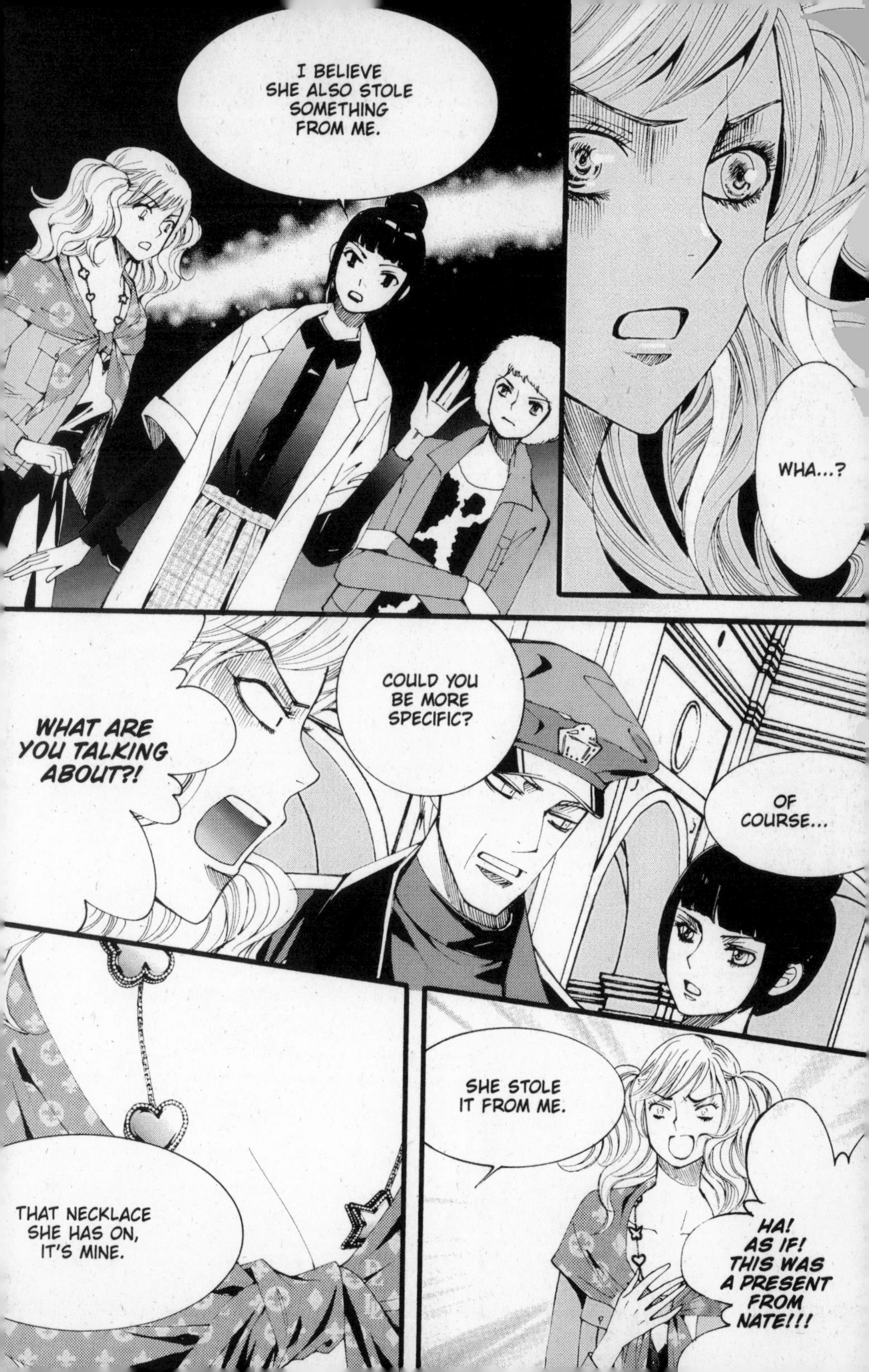
I BELIEVE SHE ALSO STOLE SOMETHING FROM ME.
WHA...?
WHAT ARE YOU TALKING ABOUT?!
COULD YOU BE MORE SPECIFIC?
OF COURSE...
THAT NECKLACE SHE HAS ON, IT'S MINE.
SHE STOLE IT FROM ME.
HA! AS IF! THIS WAS A PRESENT FROM NATE!!!

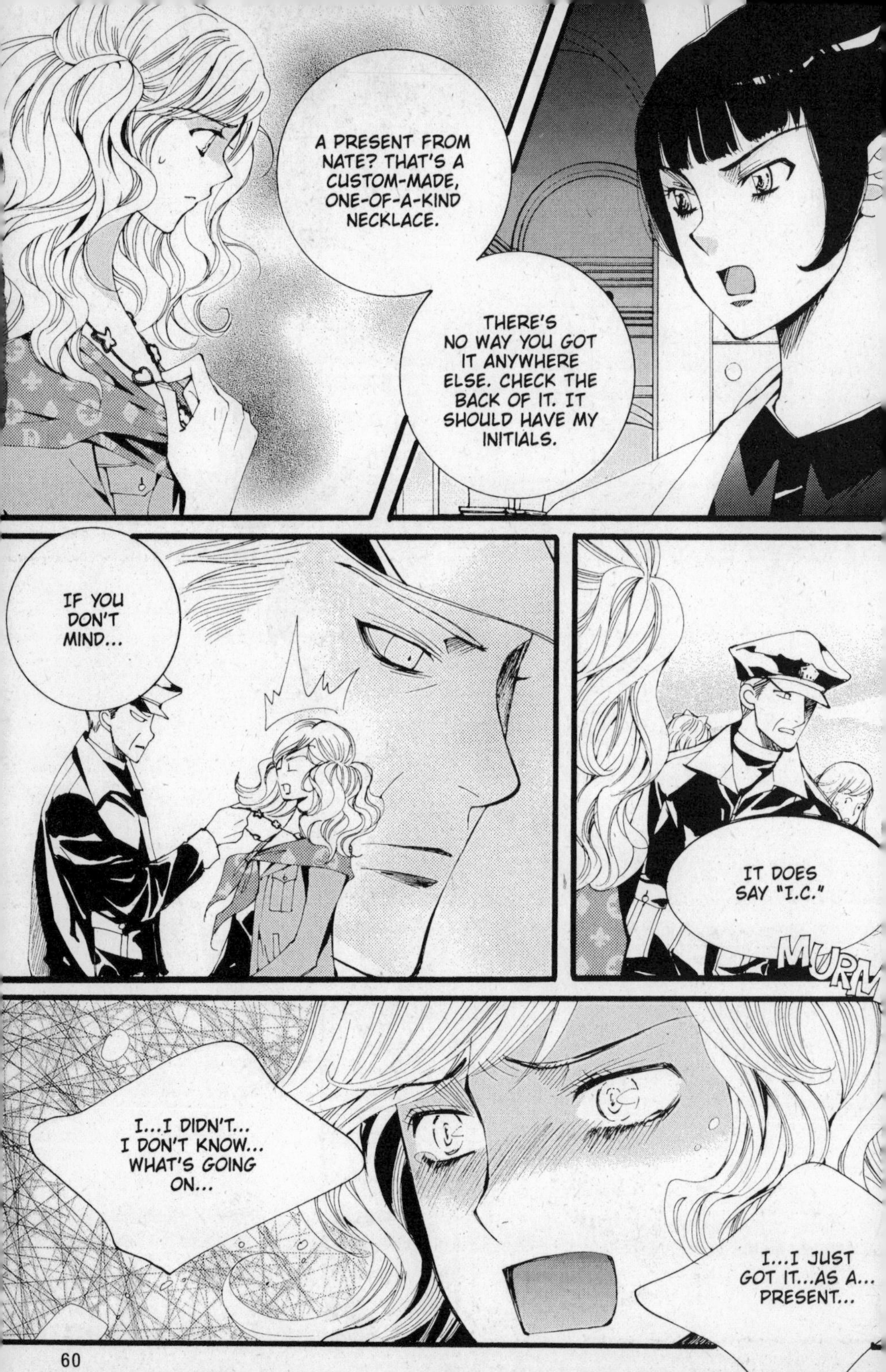
A PRESENT FROM NATE? THAT'S A CUSTOM-MADE, ONE-OF-A-KIND NECKLACE.
THERE'S NO WAY YOU GOT IT ANYWHERE ELSE. CHECK THE BACK OF IT. IT SHOULD HAVE MY INITIALS.
IF YOU DON'T MIND...
IT DOES SAY "I.C."
MURM
I...I DIDN'T... I DON'T KNOW... WHAT'S GOING ON...
I...I JUST GOT IT...AS A... PRESENT...

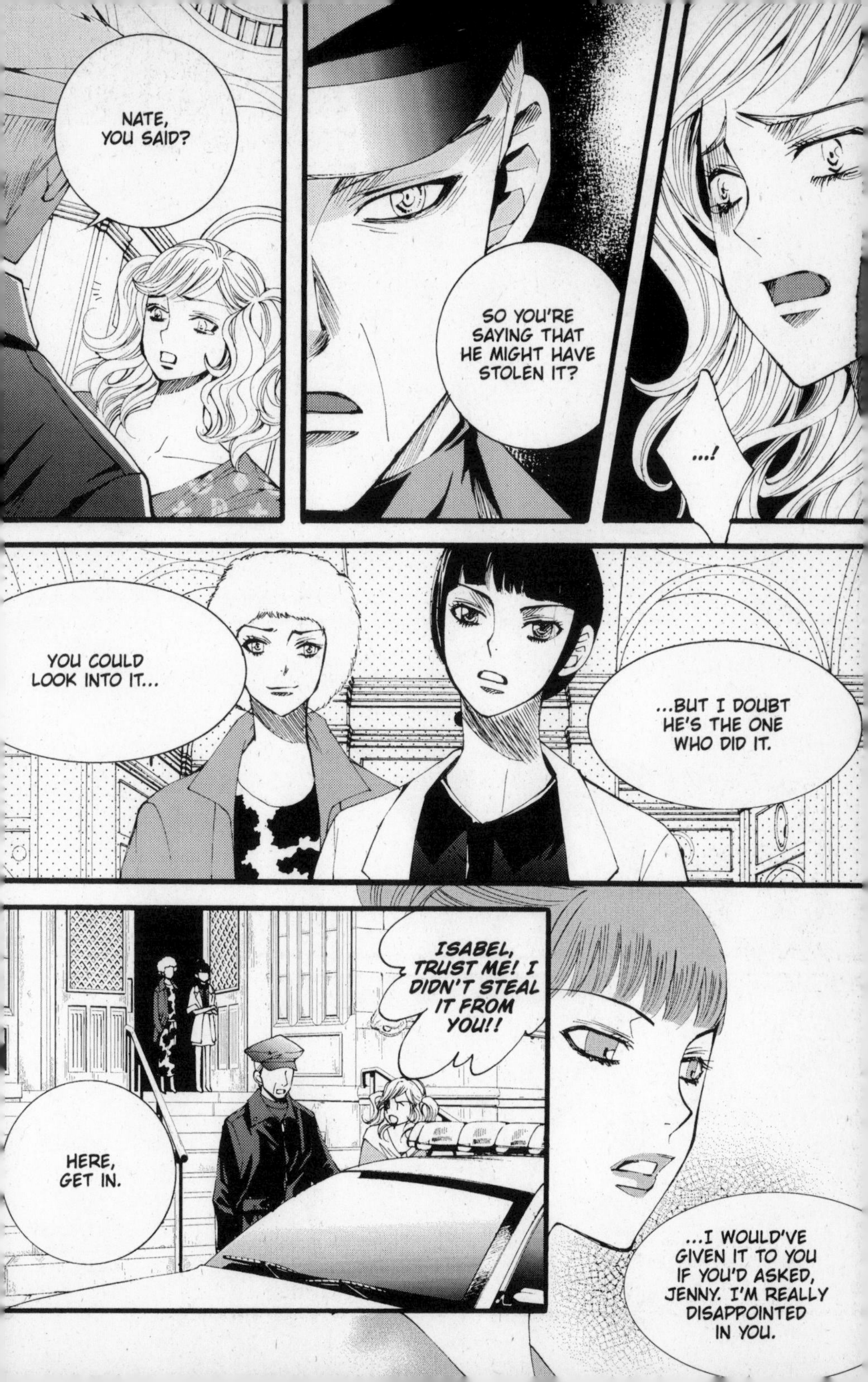
NATE, YOU SAID?
SO YOU'RE SAYING THAT HE MIGHT HAVE STOLEN IT?
...!
YOU COULD LOOK INTO IT...
...BUT I DOUBT HE'S THE ONE WHO DID IT.
HERE, GET IN.
ISABEL, TRUST ME! I DIDN'T STEAL IT FROM YOU!!
...I WOULD'VE GIVEN IT TO YOU IF YOU'D ASKED, JENNY. I'M REALLY DISAPPOINTED IN YOU.

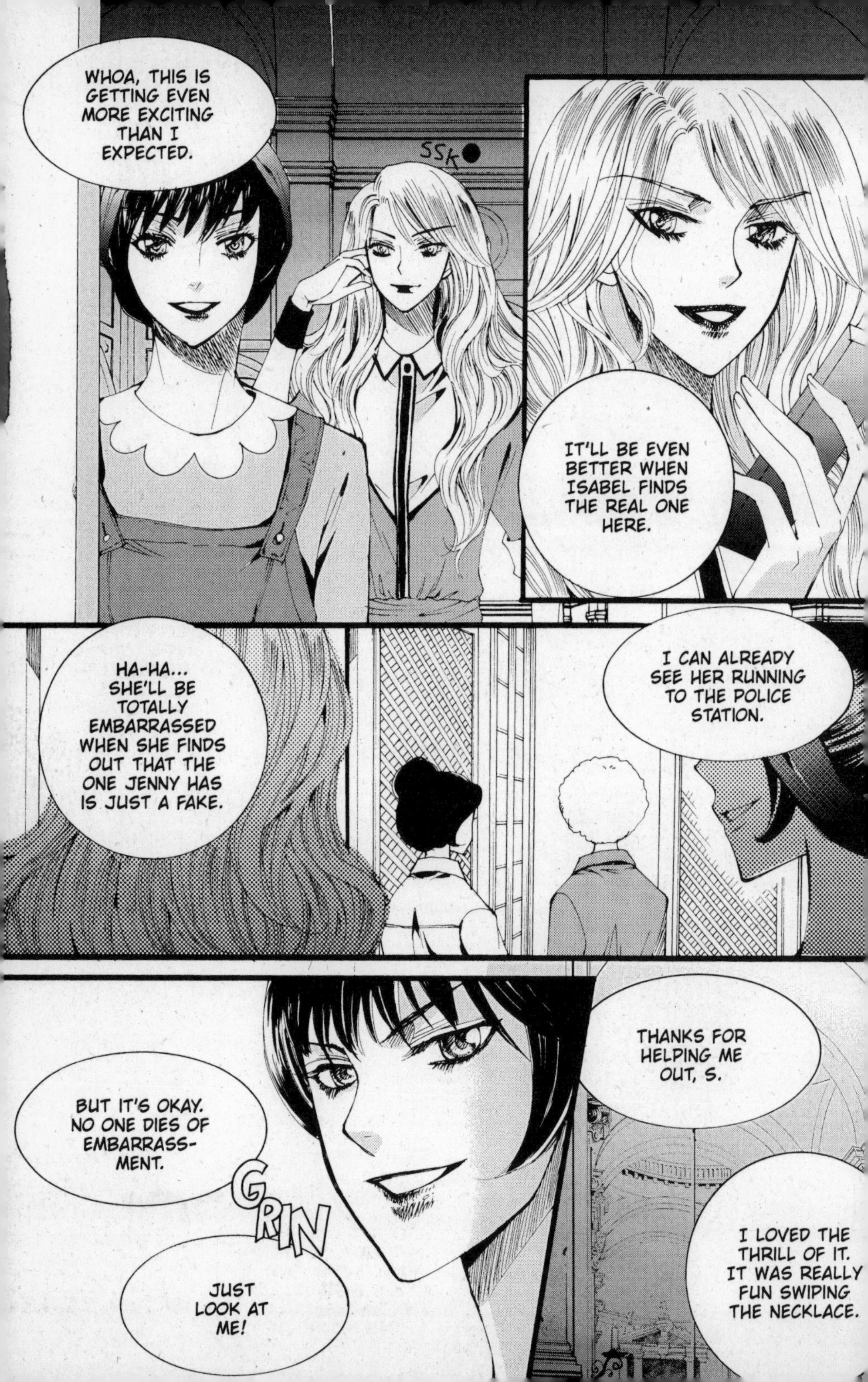
WHOA, THIS IS GETTING EVEN MORE EXCITING THAN I EXPECTED.
SSK
IT'LL BE EVEN BETTER WHEN ISABEL FINDS THE REAL ONE HERE.
HA-HA... SHE'LL BE TOTALLY EMBARRASSED WHEN SHE FINDS OUT THAT THE ONE JENNY HAS IS JUST A FAKE.
I CAN ALREADY SEE HER RUNNING TO THE POLICE STATION.
BUT IT'S OKAY. NO ONE DIES OF EMBARRASS-MENT.
GRIN
JUST LOOK AT ME!
THANKS FOR HELPING ME OUT, S.
I LOVED THE THRILL OF IT. IT WAS REALLY FUN SWIPING THE NECKLACE.

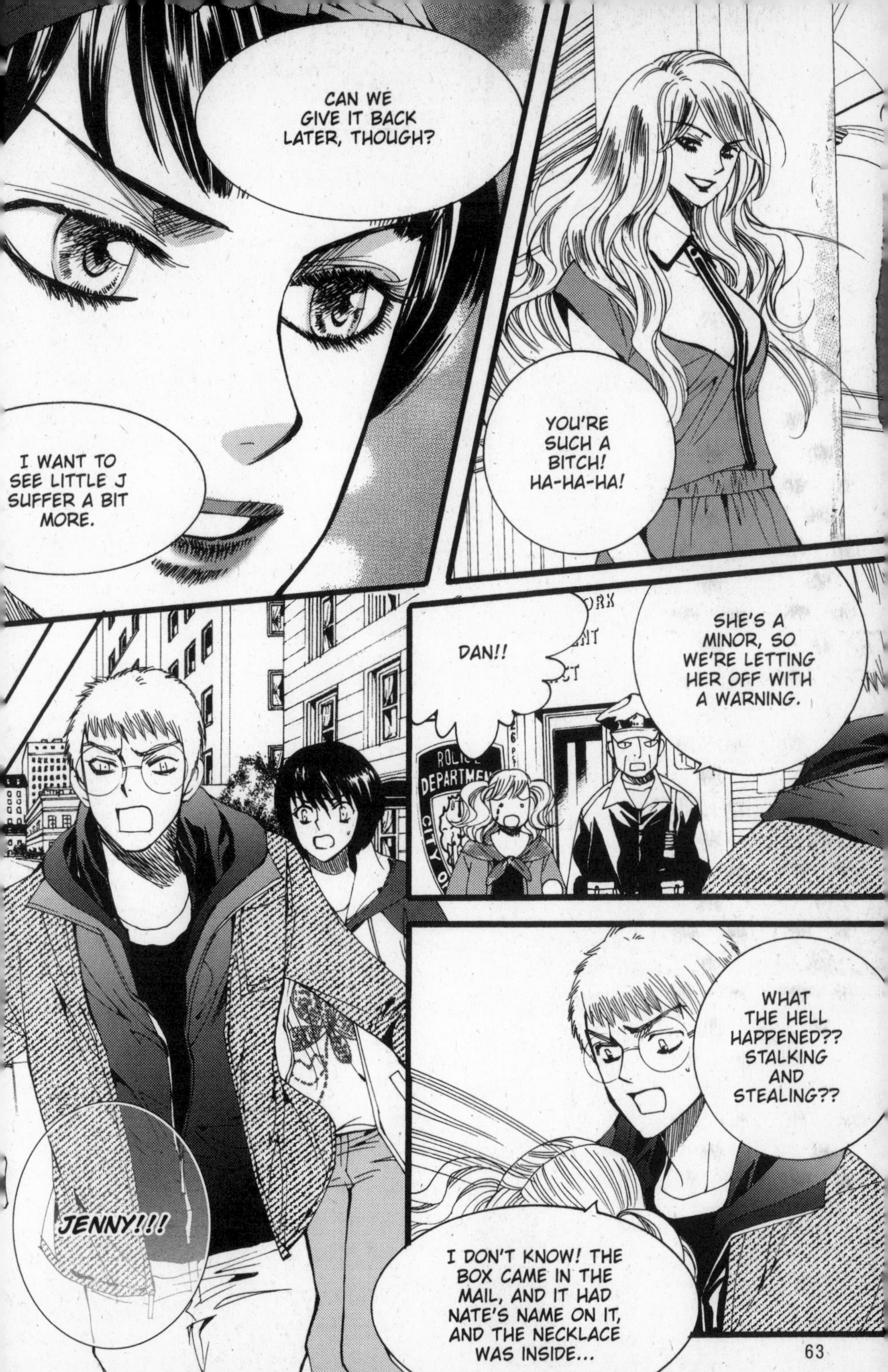
CAN WE GIVE IT BACK LATER, THOUGH?
I WANT TO SEE LITTLE J SUFFER A BIT MORE.
YOU'RE SUCH A BITCH! HA-HA-HA!
JENNY!!!
DAN!!
SHE'S A MINOR, SO WE'RE LETTING HER OFF WITH A WARNING.
WHAT THE HELL HAPPENED?? STALKING AND STEALING??
I DON'T KNOW! THE BOX CAME IN THE MAIL, AND IT HAD NATE'S NAME ON IT, AND THE NECKLACE WAS INSIDE...

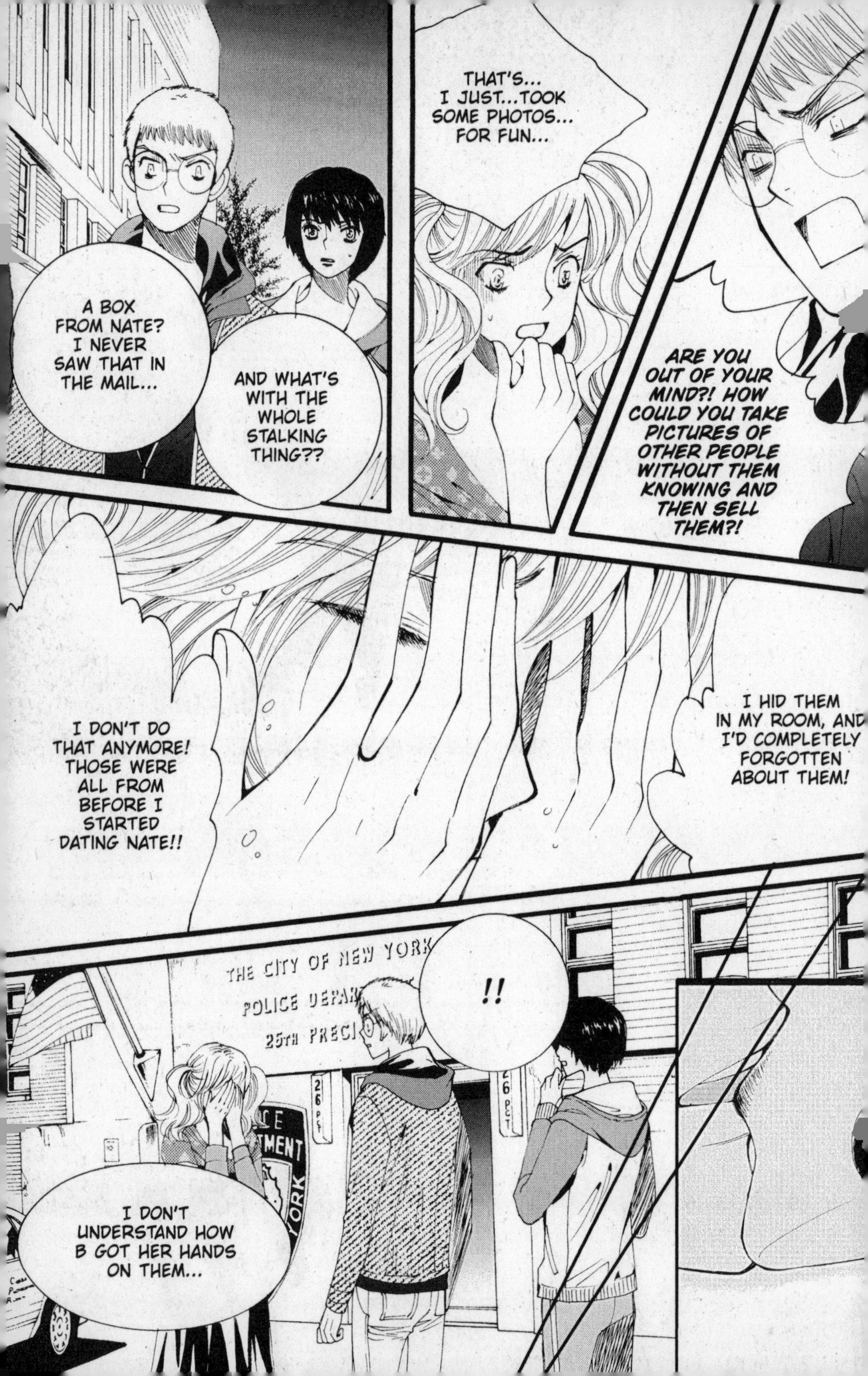
A BOX FROM NATE? I NEVER SAW THAT IN THE MAIL...
AND WHAT'S WITH THE WHOLE STALKING THING??
THAT'S... I JUST...TOOK SOME PHOTOS... FOR FUN...
ARE YOU OUT OF YOUR MIND?! HOW COULD YOU TAKE PICTURES OF OTHER PEOPLE WITHOUT THEM KNOWING AND THEN SELL THEM?!
I DON'T DO THAT ANYMORE! THOSE WERE ALL FROM BEFORE I STARTED DATING NATE!!
I HID THEM IN MY ROOM, AND I'D COMPLETELY FORGOTTEN ABOUT THEM!
THE CITY OF NEW YORK
POLICE DEPAR
25TH PRECI
!!
I DON'T UNDERSTAND HOW B GOT HER HANDS ON THEM...

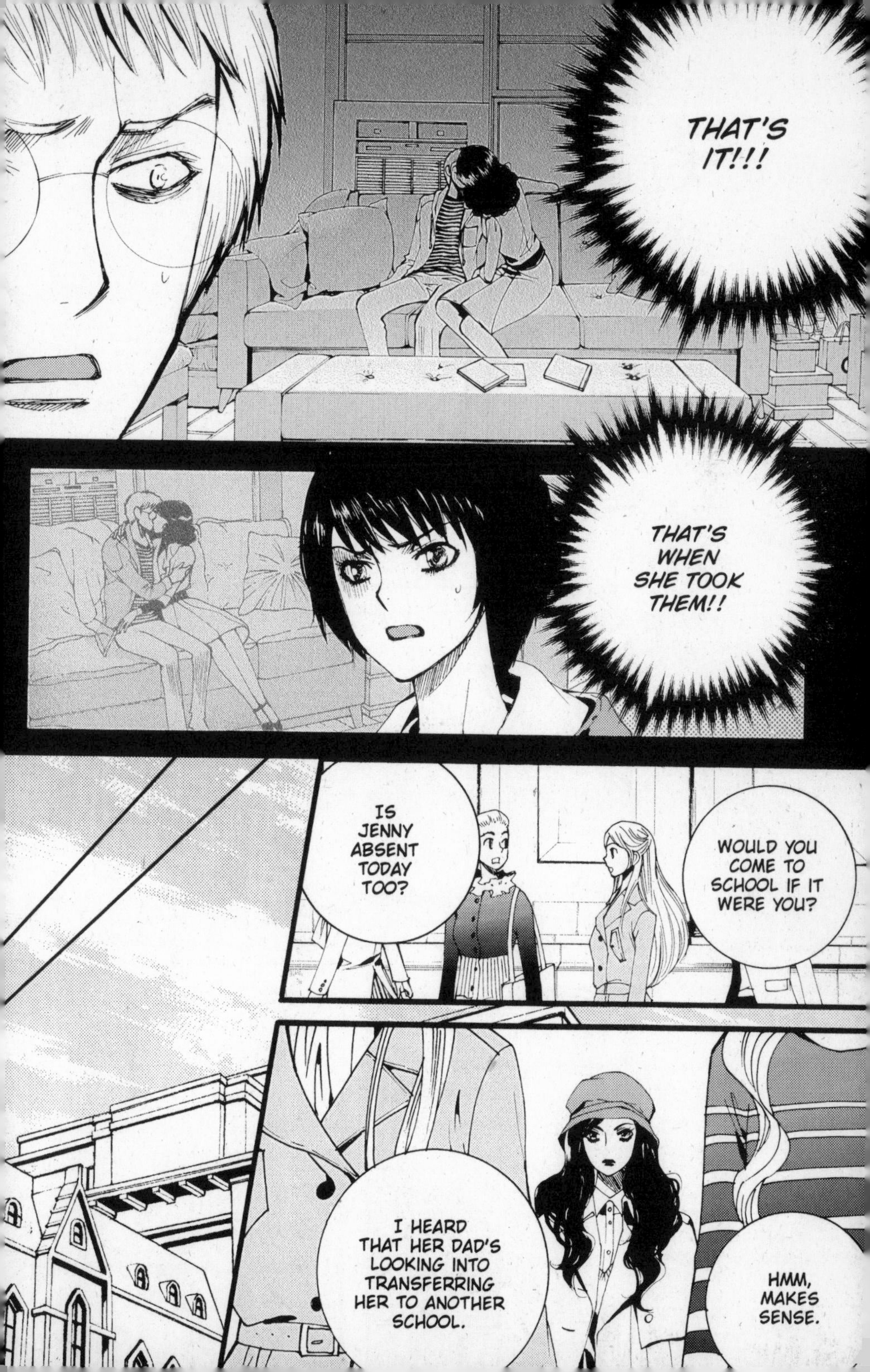
THAT'S IT!!!
THAT'S WHEN SHE TOOK THEM!!
IS JENNY ABSENT TODAY TOO?
WOULD YOU COME TO SCHOOL IF IT WERE YOU?
I HEARD THAT HER DAD'S LOOKING INTO TRANSFERRING HER TO ANOTHER SCHOOL.
HMM, MAKES SENSE.

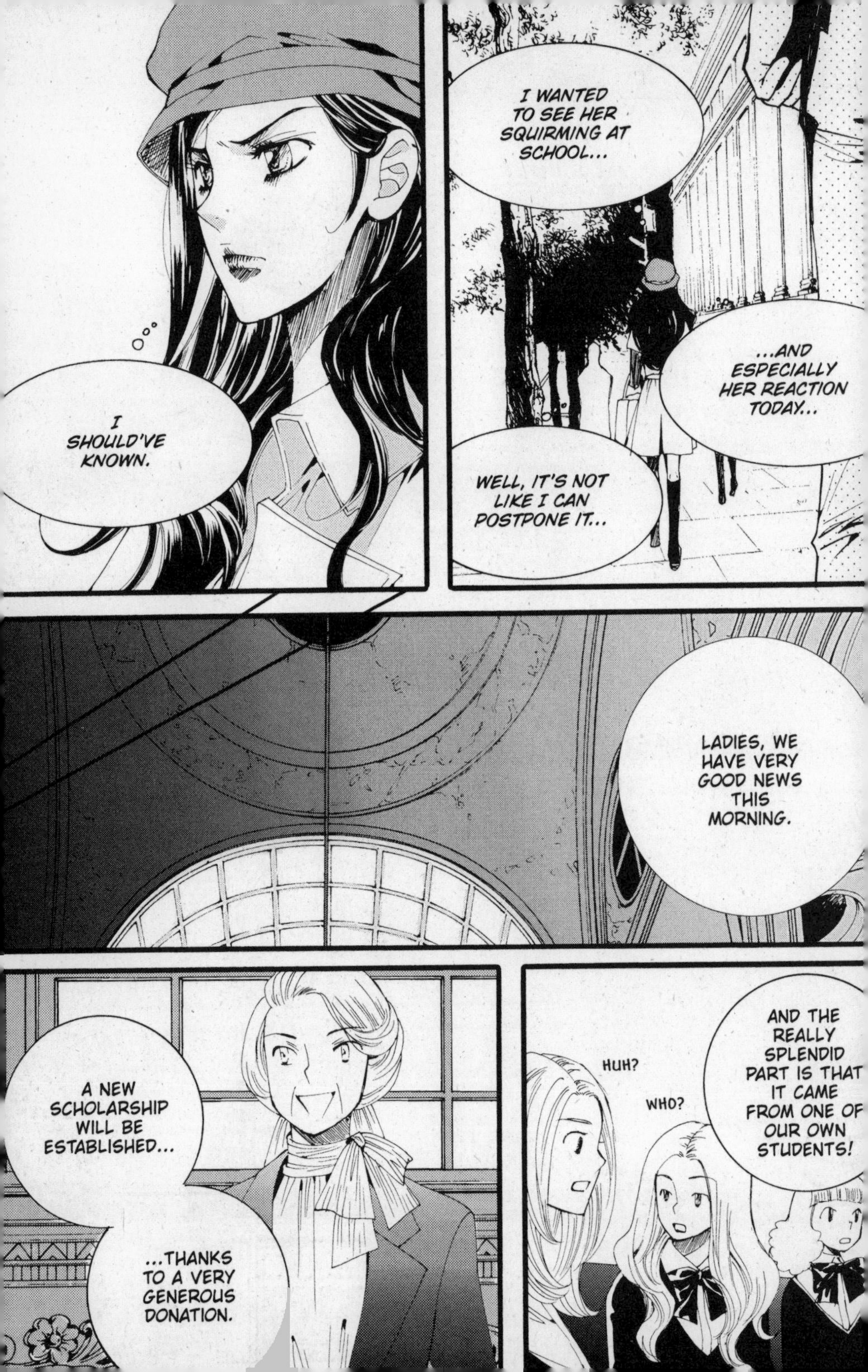
I SHOULD'VE KNOWN.
I WANTED TO SEE HER SQUIRMING AT SCHOOL...
...AND ESPECIALLY HER REACTION TODAY...
WELL, IT'S NOT LIKE I CAN POSTPONE IT...
LADIES, WE HAVE VERY GOOD NEWS THIS MORNING.
A NEW SCHOLARSHIP WILL BE ESTABLISHED...
...THANKS TO A VERY GENEROUS DONATION.
HUH?
WHO?
AND THE REALLY SPLENDID PART IS THAT IT CAME FROM ONE OF OUR OWN STUDENTS!

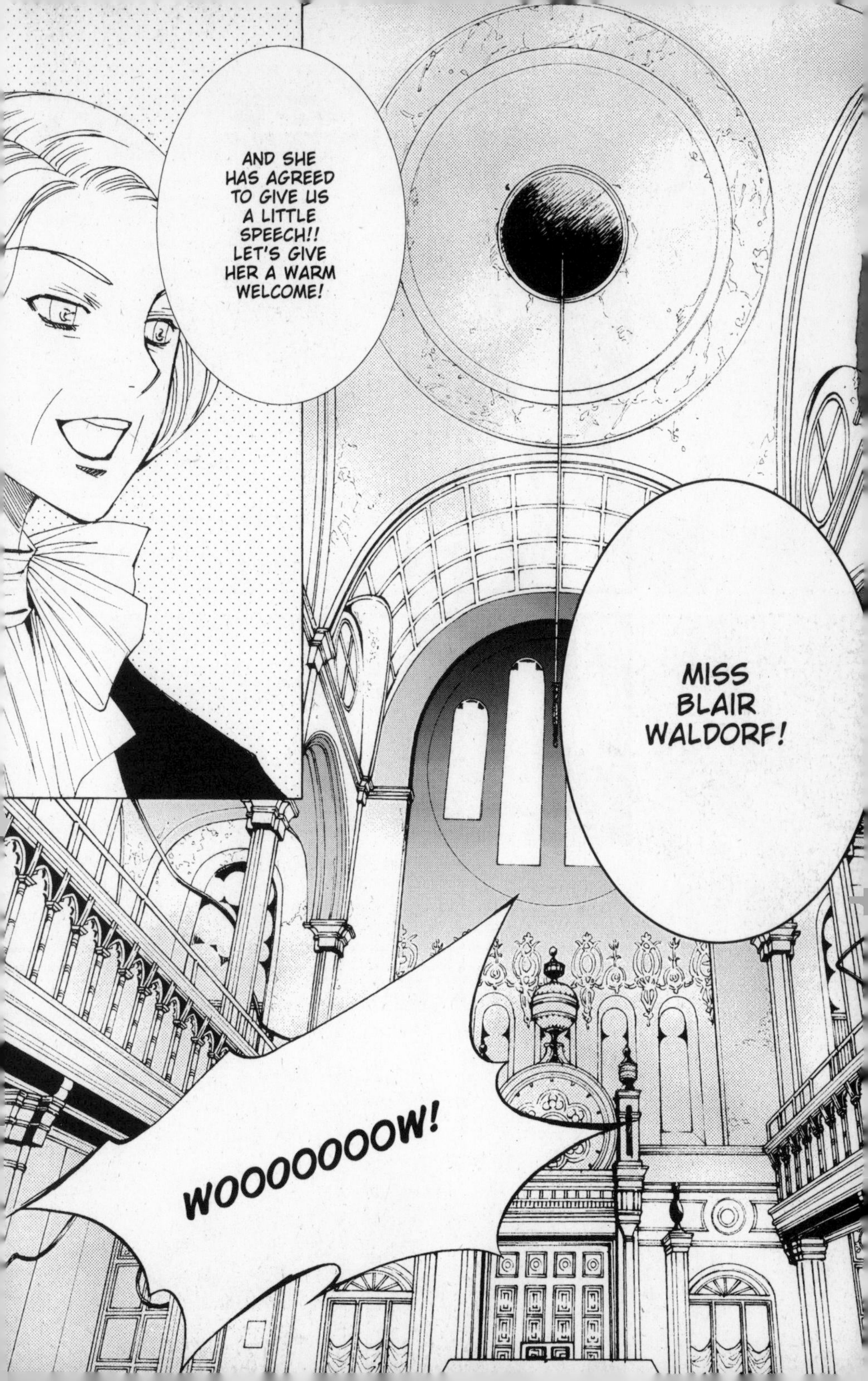
AND SHE HAS AGREED TO GIVE US A LITTLE SPEECH!! LET'S GIVE HER A WARM WELCOME!
MISS BLAIR WALDORF!
WOOOOOOOW!

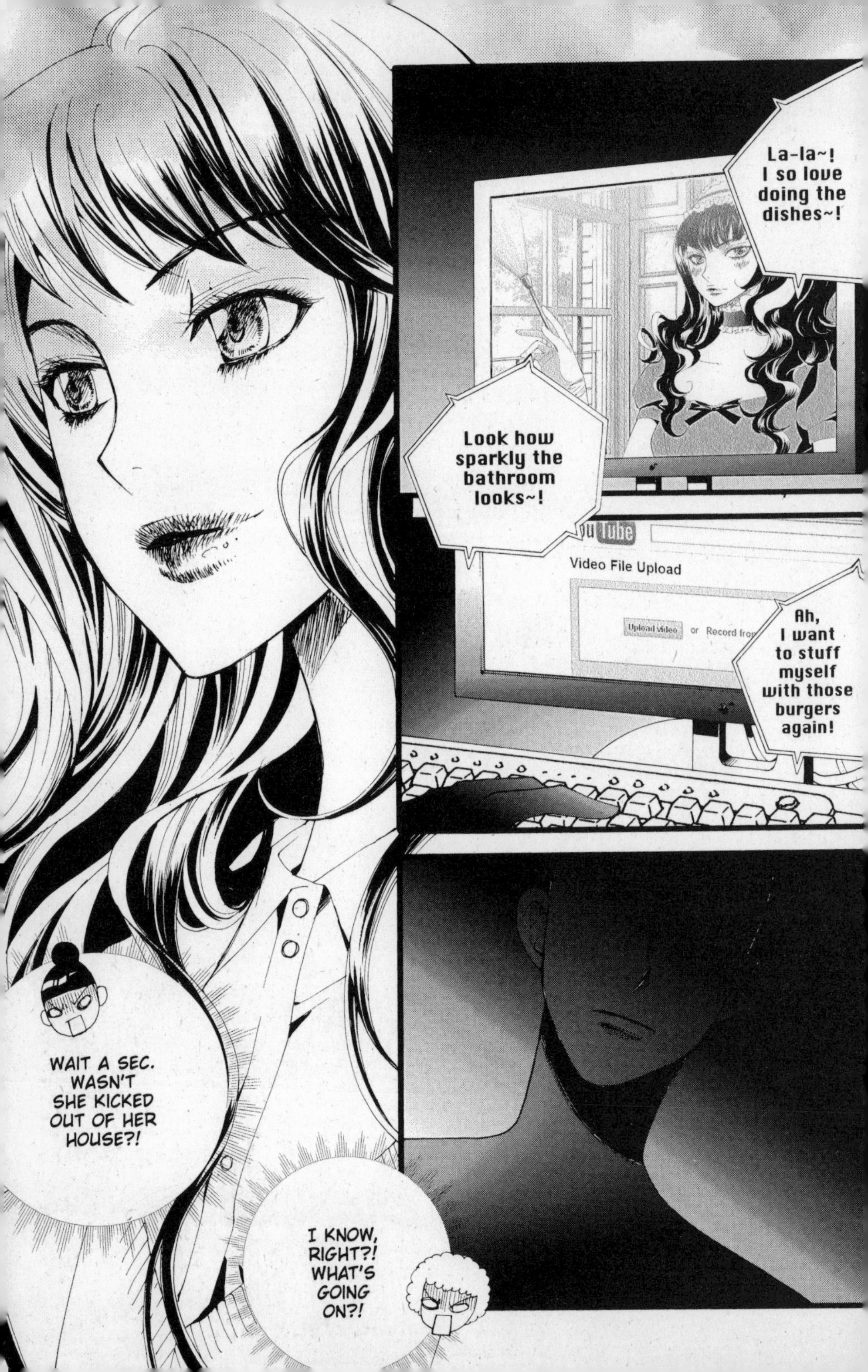
WAIT A SEC. WASN'T SHE KICKED OUT OF HER HOUSE?!
I KNOW, RIGHT?! WHAT'S GOING ON?!
La-la~! I so love doing the dishes~!
Look how sparkly the bathroom looks~!
Video File Upload
Upload video
or
Record from
Ah, I want to stuff myself with those burgers again!

gossip girl

FOR YOUR EYES ONLY

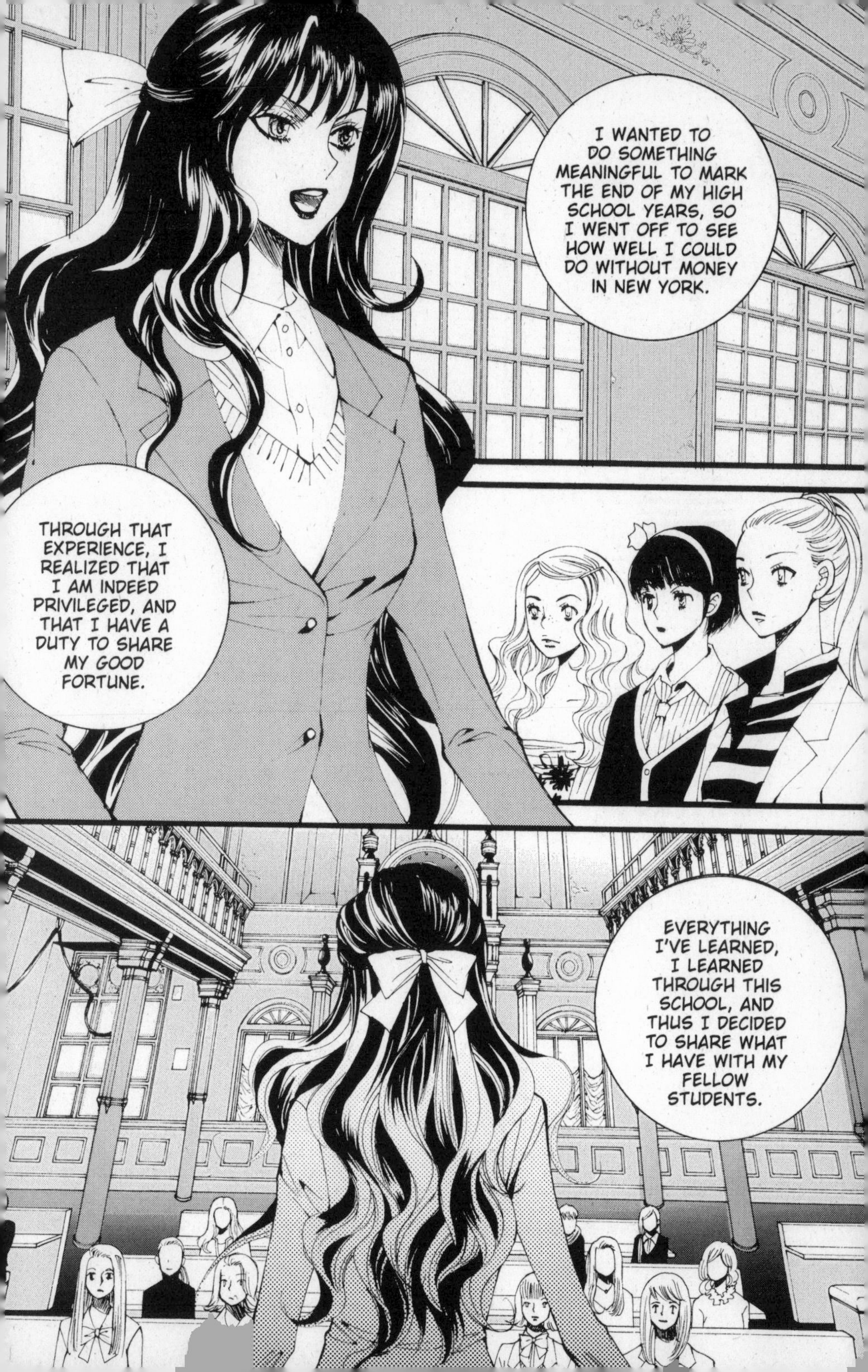
I WANTED TO DO SOMETHING MEANINGFUL TO MARK THE END OF MY HIGH SCHOOL YEARS, SO I WENT OFF TO SEE HOW WELL I COULD DO WITHOUT MONEY IN NEW YORK.
THROUGH THAT EXPERIENCE, I REALIZED THAT I AM INDEED PRIVILEGED, AND THAT I HAVE A DUTY TO SHARE MY GOOD FORTUNE.
EVERYTHING I'VE LEARNED, I LEARNED THROUGH THIS SCHOOL, AND THUS I DECIDED TO SHARE WHAT I HAVE WITH MY FELLOW STUDENTS.

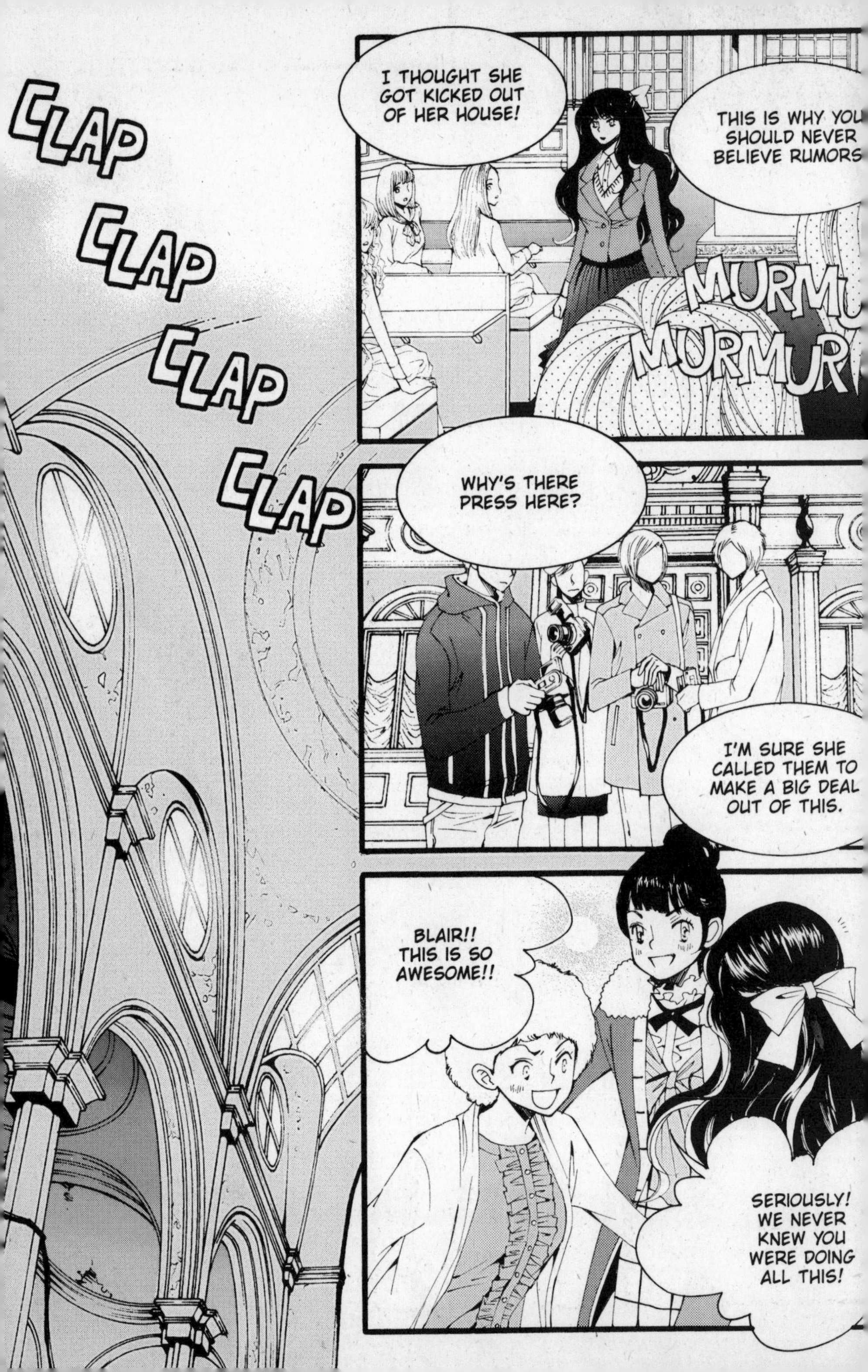
CLAP
CLAP
CLAP
CLAP
I THOUGHT SHE GOT KICKED OUT OF HER HOUSE!
THIS IS WHY YOU SHOULD NEVER BELIEVE RUMORS
MURMU
MURMUR
WHY'S THERE PRESS HERE?
I'M SURE SHE CALLED THEM TO MAKE A BIG DEAL OUT OF THIS.
BLAIR!! THIS IS SO AWESOME!!
SERIOUSLY! WE NEVER KNEW YOU WERE DOING ALL THIS!

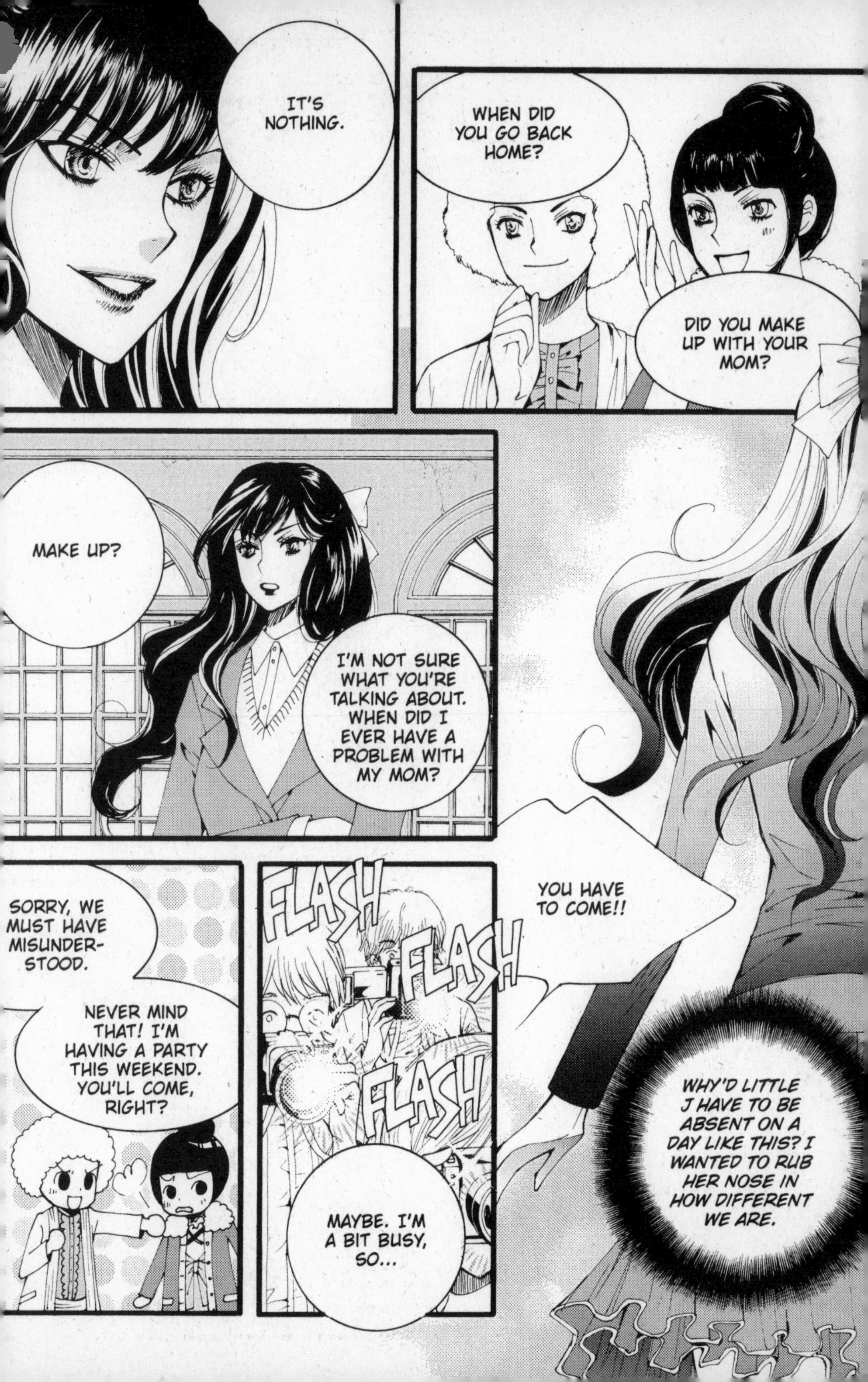
IT'S NOTHING.
WHEN DID YOU GO BACK HOME?
DID YOU MAKE UP WITH YOUR MOM?
MAKE UP?
I'M NOT SURE WHAT YOU'RE TALKING ABOUT. WHEN DID I EVER HAVE A PROBLEM WITH MY MOM?
SORRY, WE MUST HAVE MISUNDER-STOOD.
NEVER MIND THAT! I'M HAVING A PARTY THIS WEEKEND. YOU'LL COME, RIGHT?
FLASH
FLASH
FLASH
MAYBE. I'M A BIT BUSY, SO...
YOU HAVE TO COME!!
WHY'D LITTLE J HAVE TO BE ABSENT ON A DAY LIKE THIS? I WANTED TO RUB HER NOSE IN HOW DIFFERENT WE ARE.

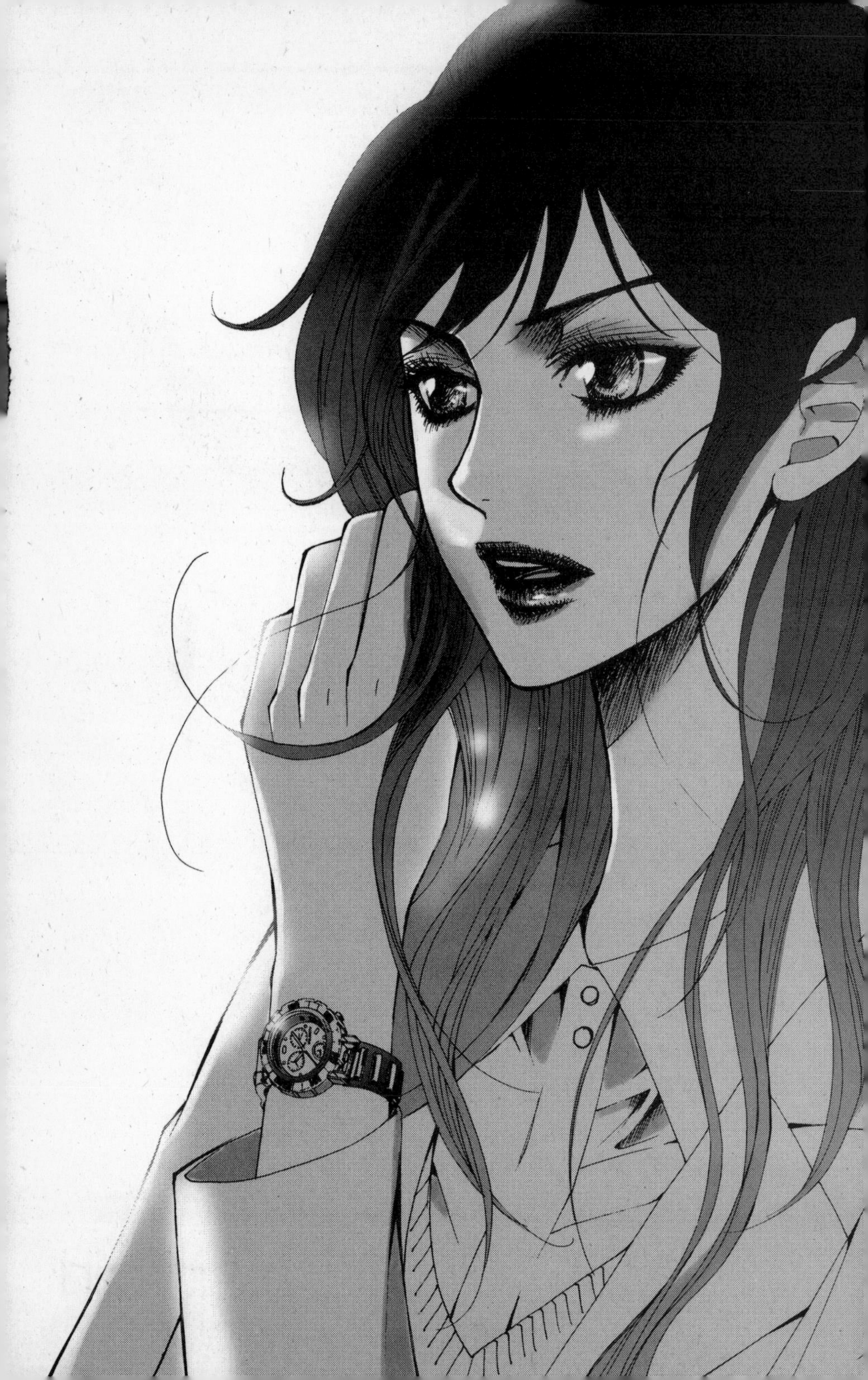

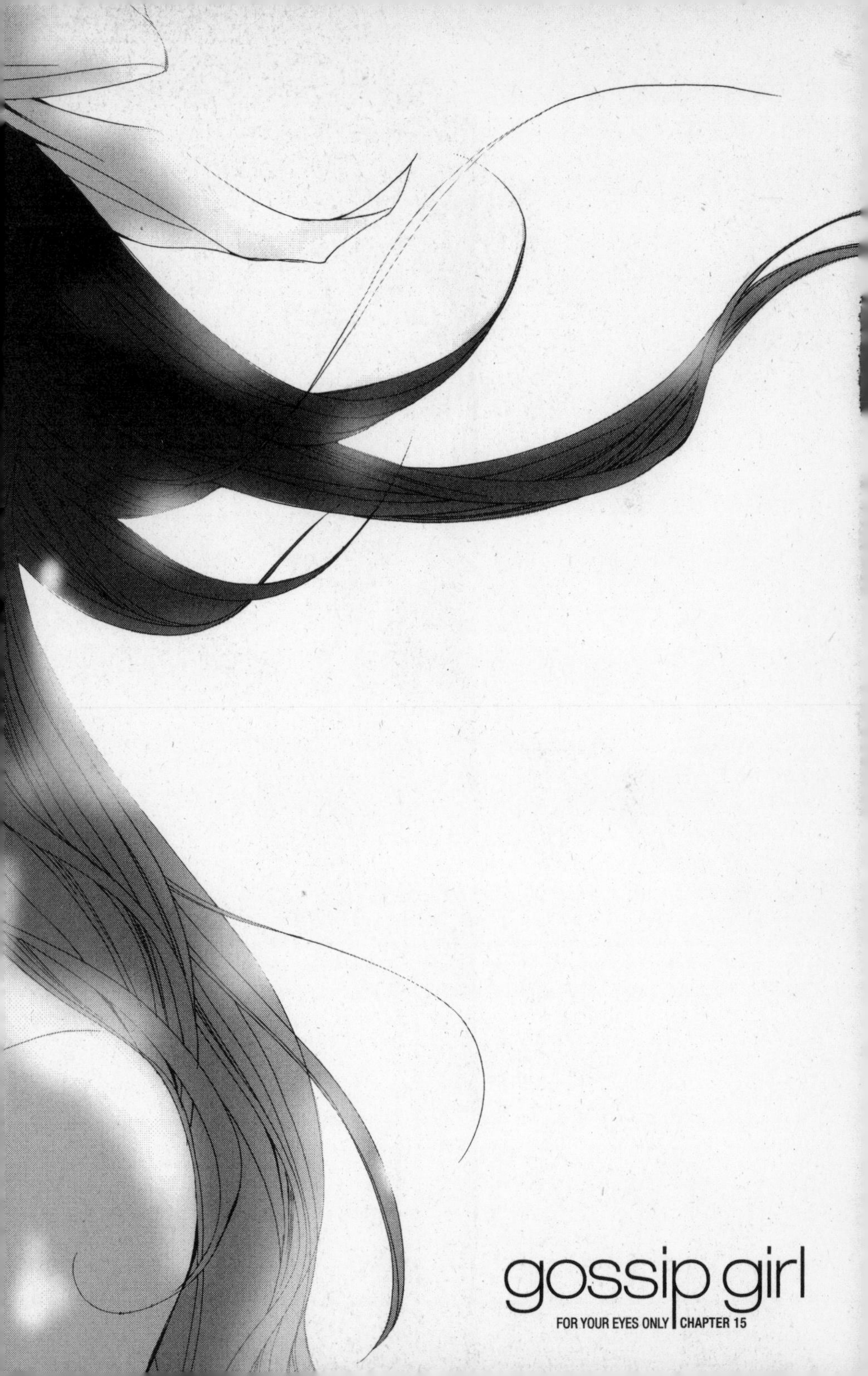
gossip girl
FOR YOUR EYES ONLY | CHAPTER 15

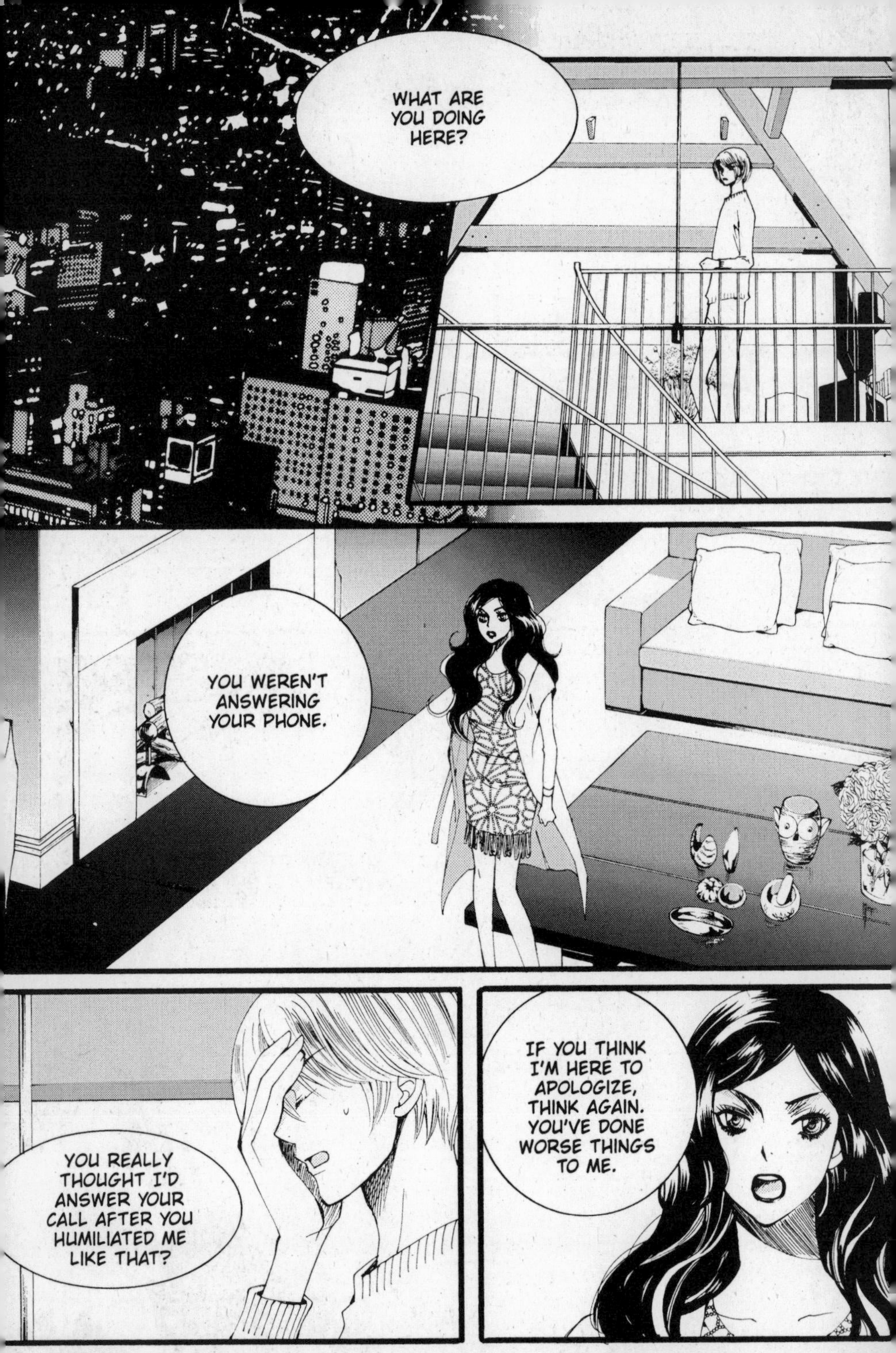
WHAT ARE YOU DOING HERE?
YOU WEREN'T ANSWERING YOUR PHONE.
YOU REALLY THOUGHT I'D ANSWER YOUR CALL AFTER YOU HUMILIATED ME LIKE THAT?
IF YOU THINK I'M HERE TO APOLOGIZE, THINK AGAIN. YOU'VE DONE WORSE THINGS TO ME.

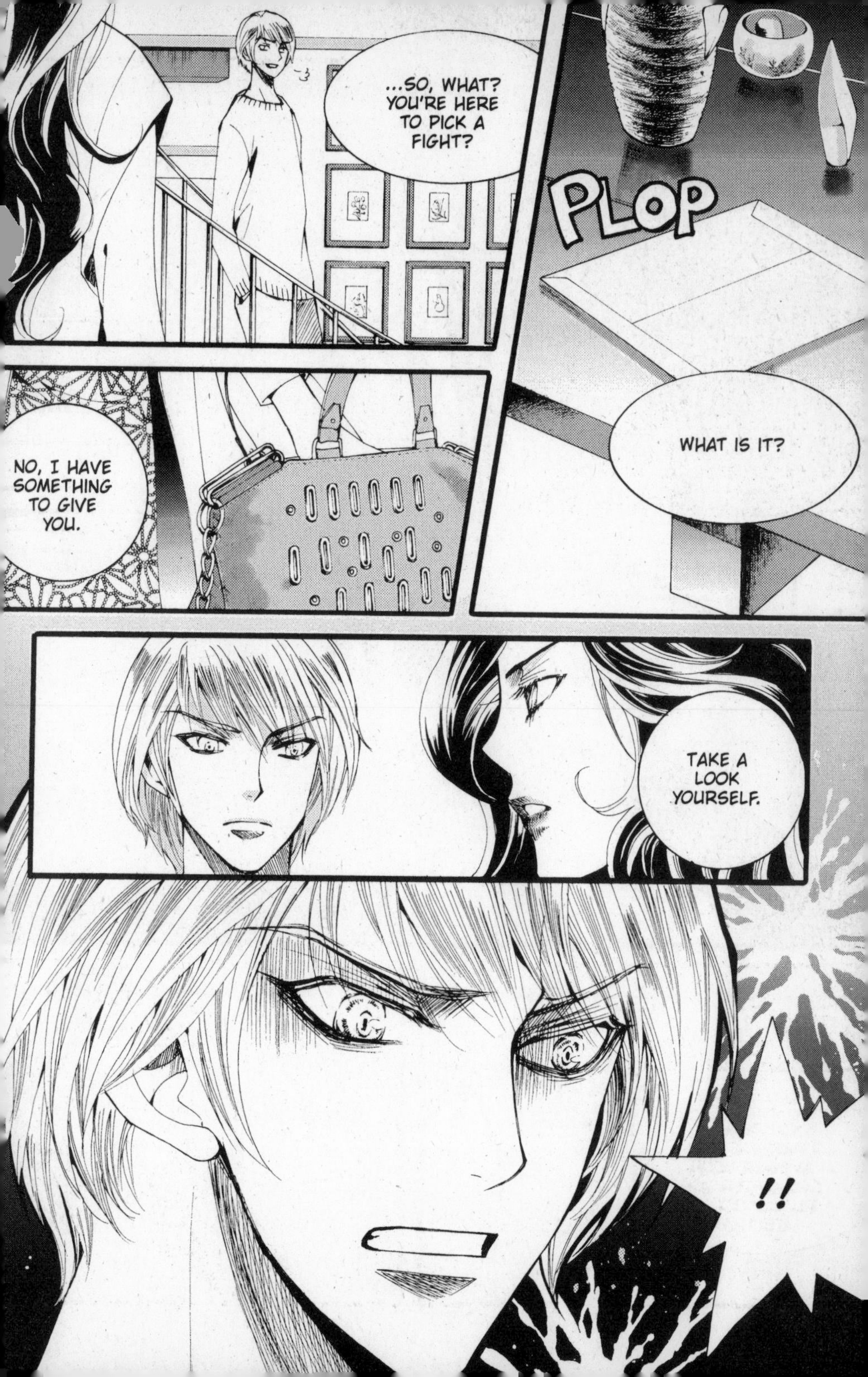
...SO, WHAT? YOU'RE HERE TO PICK A FIGHT?
PLOP
NO, I HAVE SOMETHING TO GIVE YOU.
WHAT IS IT?
TAKE A LOOK YOURSELF.
!!

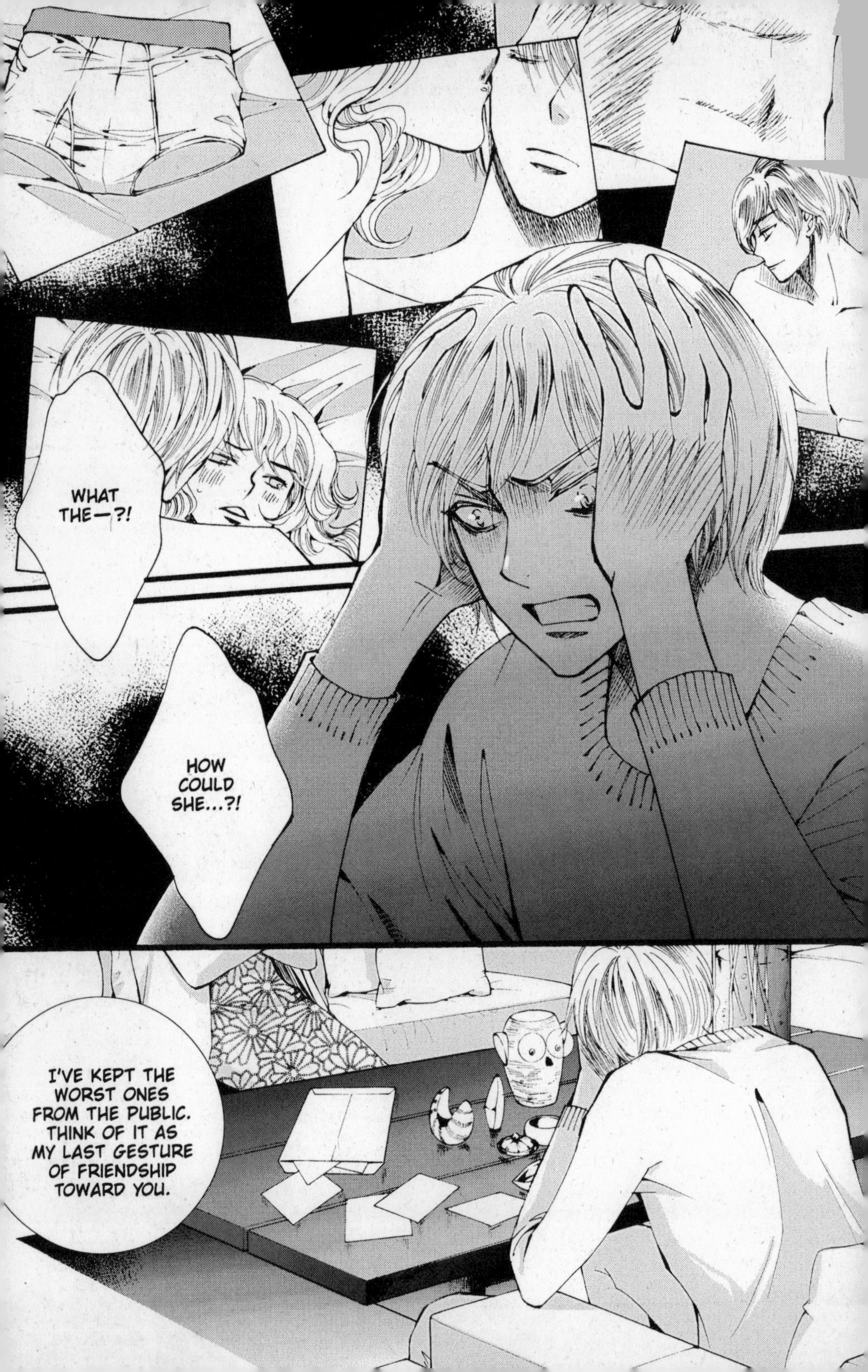
WHAT THE—?!
HOW COULD SHE...?!
I'VE KEPT THE WORST ONES FROM THE PUBLIC. THINK OF IT AS MY LAST GESTURE OF FRIENDSHIP TOWARD YOU.

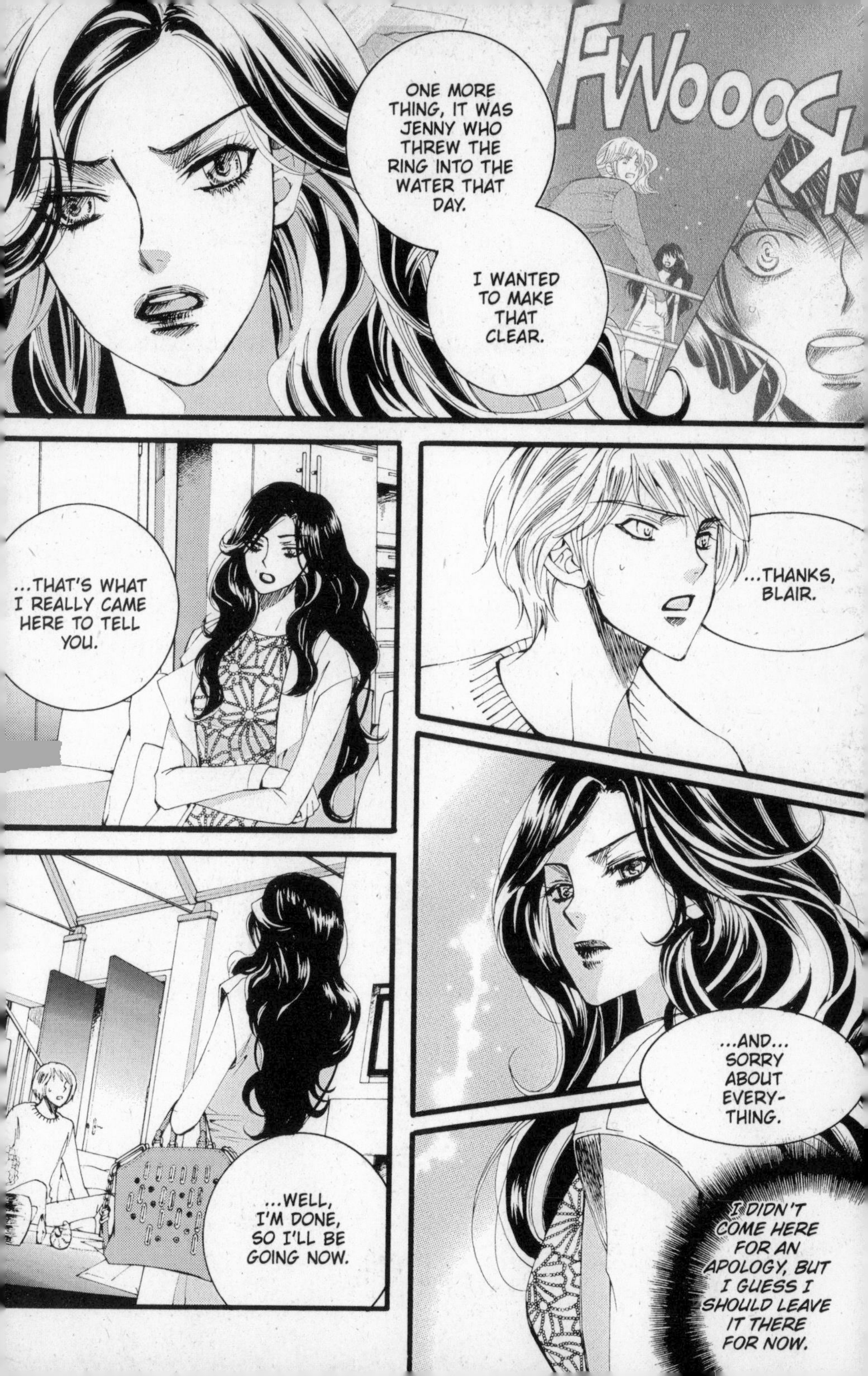
ONE MORE THING, IT WAS JENNY WHO THREW THE RING INTO THE WATER THAT DAY.
I WANTED TO MAKE THAT CLEAR.
FWOOOSH
...THAT'S WHAT I REALLY CAME HERE TO TELL YOU.
...THANKS, BLAIR.
...AND... SORRY ABOUT EVERY-THING.
...WELL, I'M DONE, SO I'LL BE GOING NOW.
I DIDN'T COME HERE FOR AN APOLOGY, BUT I GUESS I SHOULD LEAVE IT THERE FOR NOW.

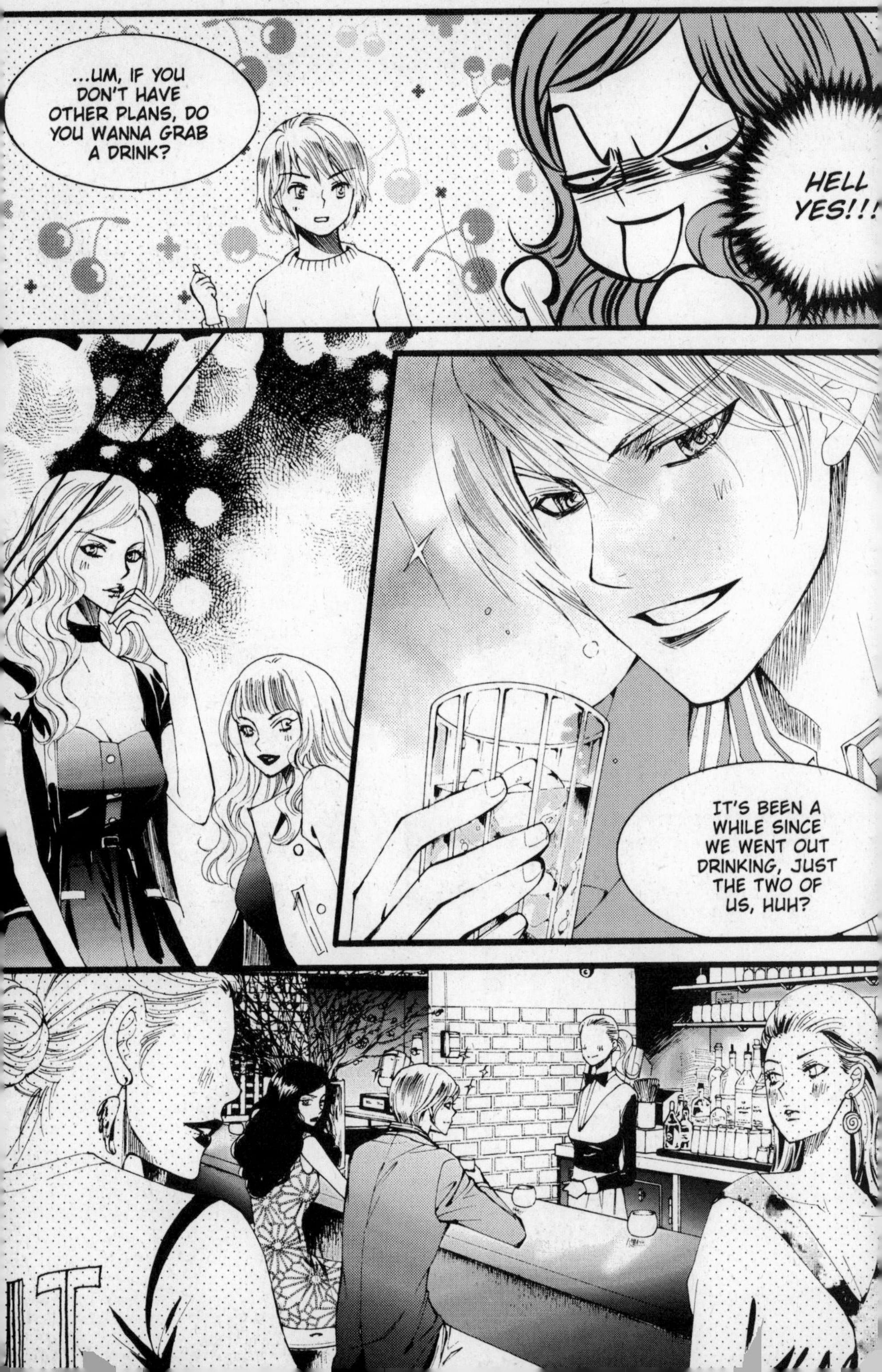
...UM, IF YOU DON'T HAVE OTHER PLANS, DO YOU WANNA GRAB A DRINK?
HELL YES!!!
IT'S BEEN A WHILE SINCE WE WENT OUT DRINKING, JUST THE TWO OF US, HUH?

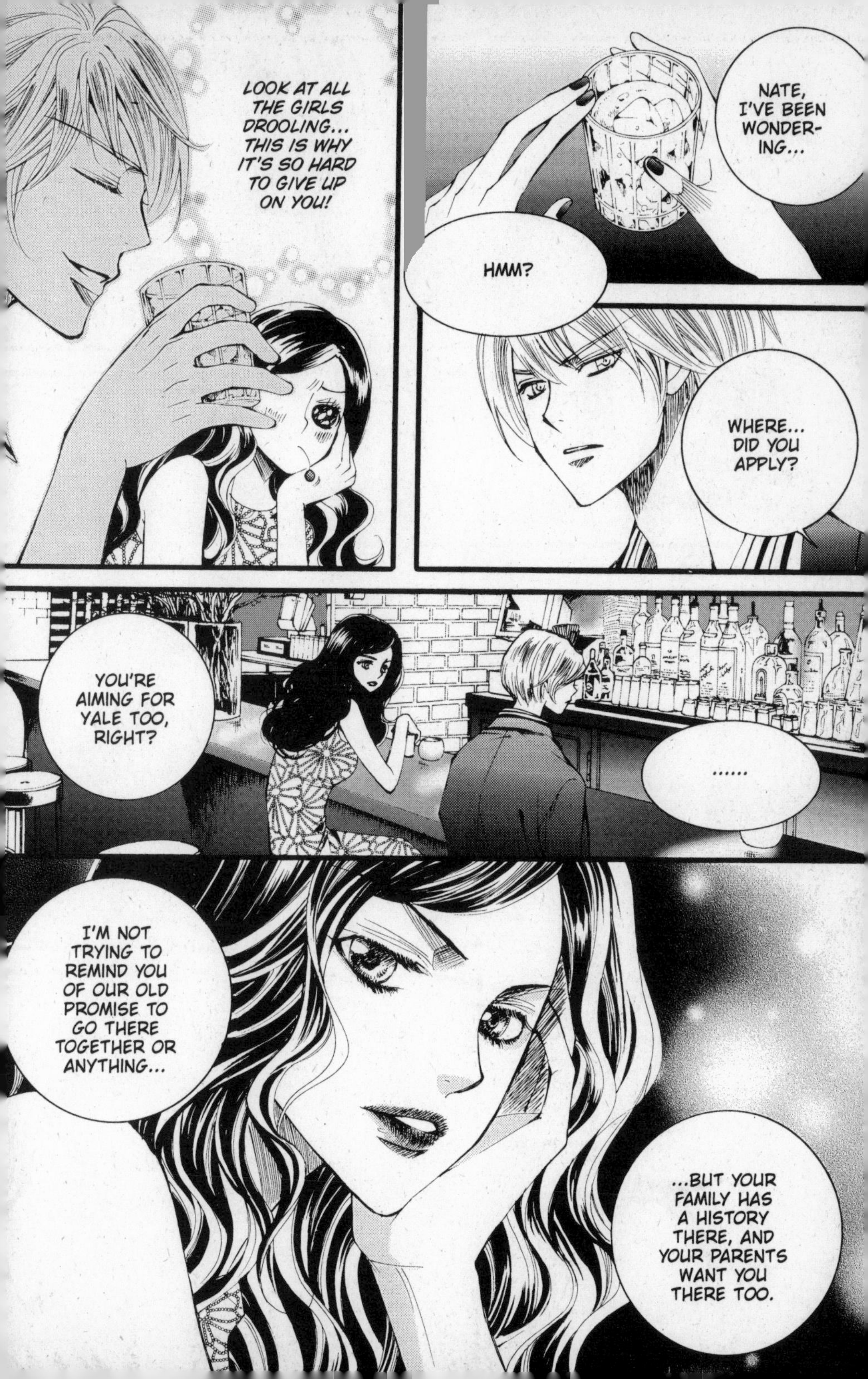
LOOK AT ALL THE GIRLS DROOLING... THIS IS WHY IT'S SO HARD TO GIVE UP ON YOU!
NATE, I'VE BEEN WONDER-ING...
HMM?
WHERE... DID YOU APPLY?
YOU'RE AIMING FOR YALE TOO, RIGHT?
......
I'M NOT TRYING TO REMIND YOU OF OUR OLD PROMISE TO GO THERE TOGETHER OR ANYTHING...
...BUT YOUR FAMILY HAS A HISTORY THERE, AND YOUR PARENTS WANT YOU THERE TOO.

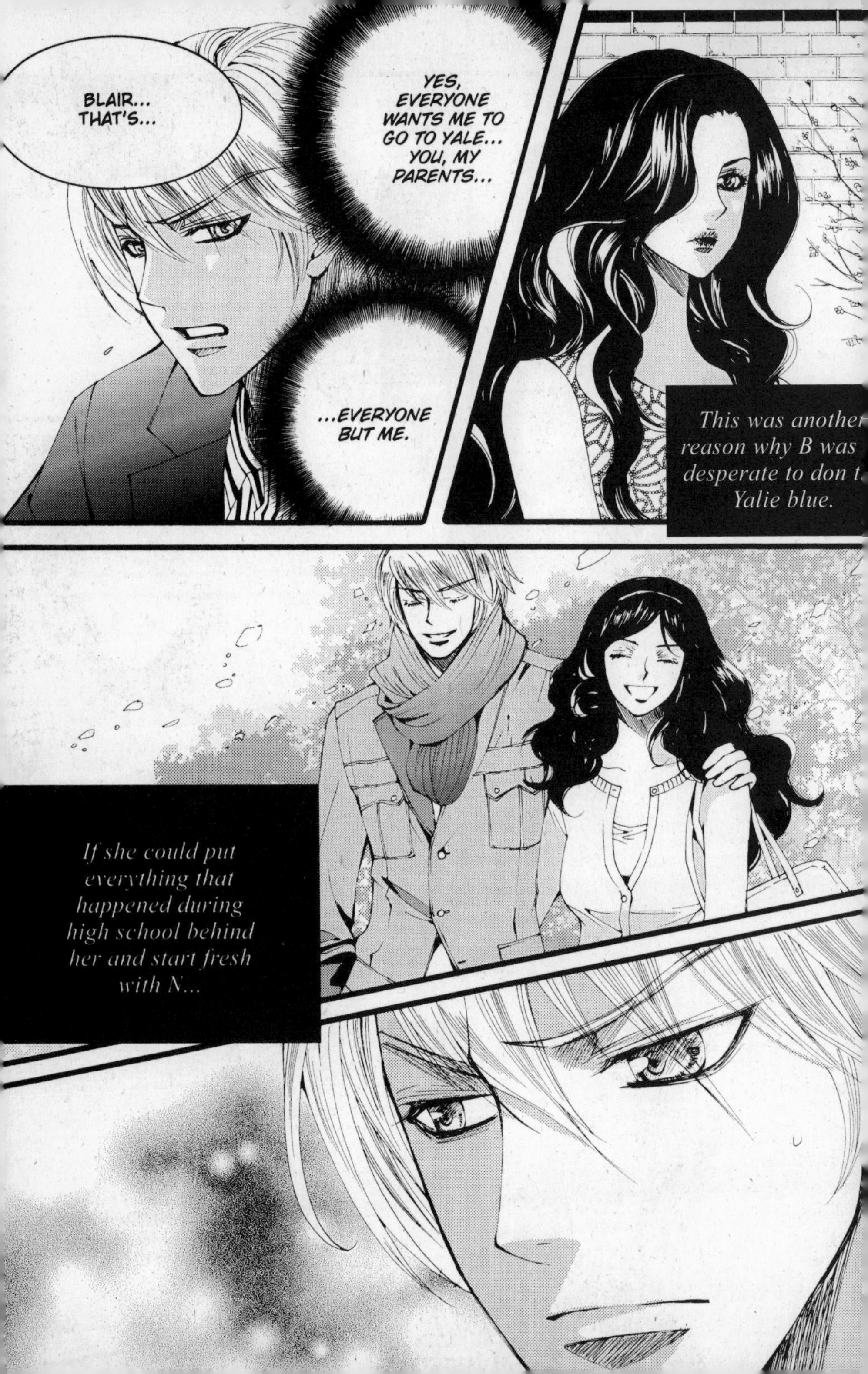
BLAIR... THAT'S...
YES, EVERYONE WANTS ME TO GO TO YALE... YOU, MY PARENTS...
...EVERYONE BUT ME.
This was another reason why B was desperate to don t
Yalie blue.
If she could put everything that happened during high school behind her and start fresh with N...

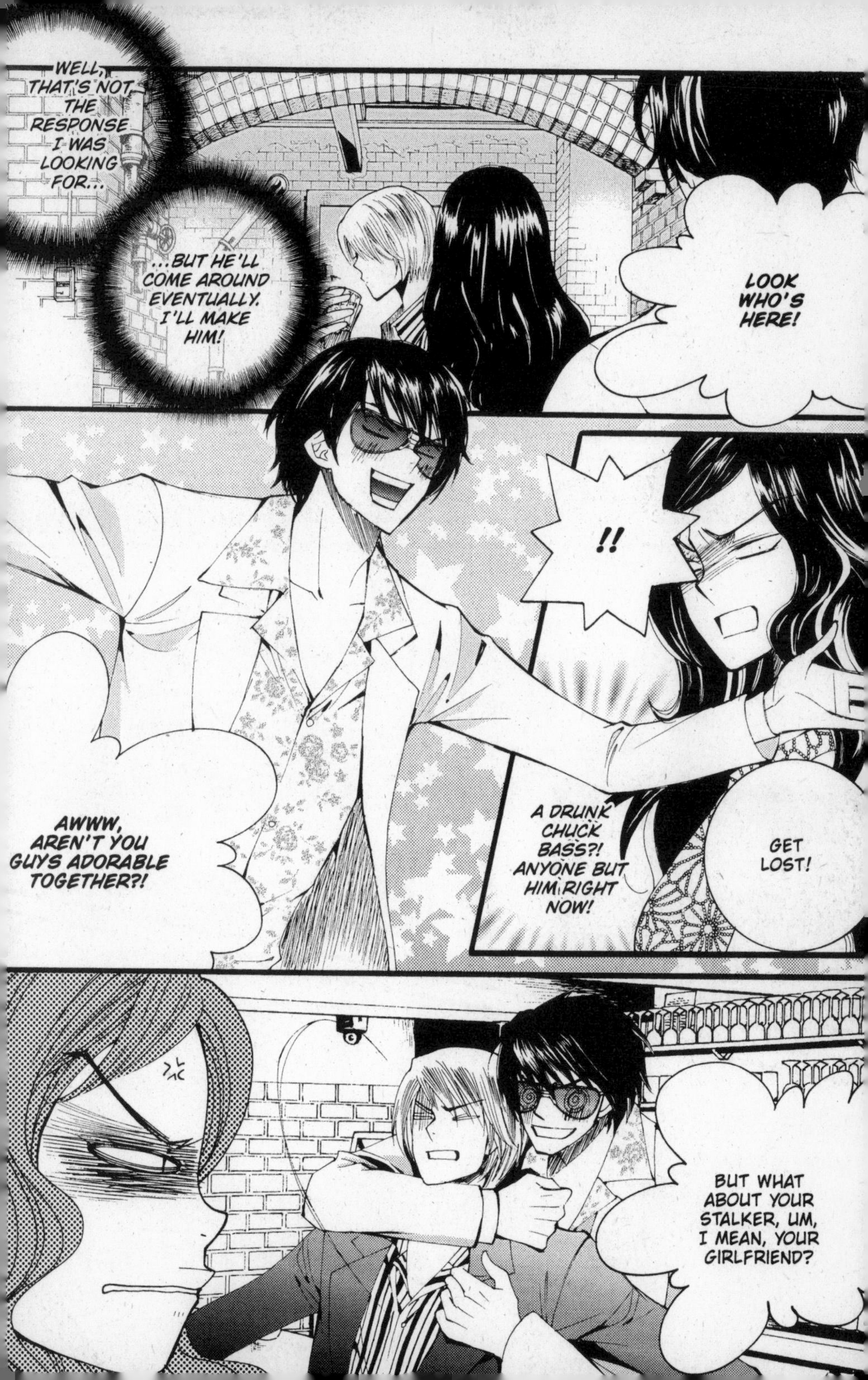
WELL, THAT'S NOT THE RESPONSE I WAS LOOKING FOR...
...BUT HE'LL COME AROUND EVENTUALLY. I'LL MAKE HIM!
LOOK WHO'S HERE!
AWWW, AREN'T YOU GUYS ADORABLE TOGETHER?!
!!
A DRUNK CHUCK BASS?! ANYONE BUT HIM RIGHT NOW!
GET LOST!
BUT WHAT ABOUT YOUR STALKER, UM, I MEAN, YOUR GIRLFRIEND?

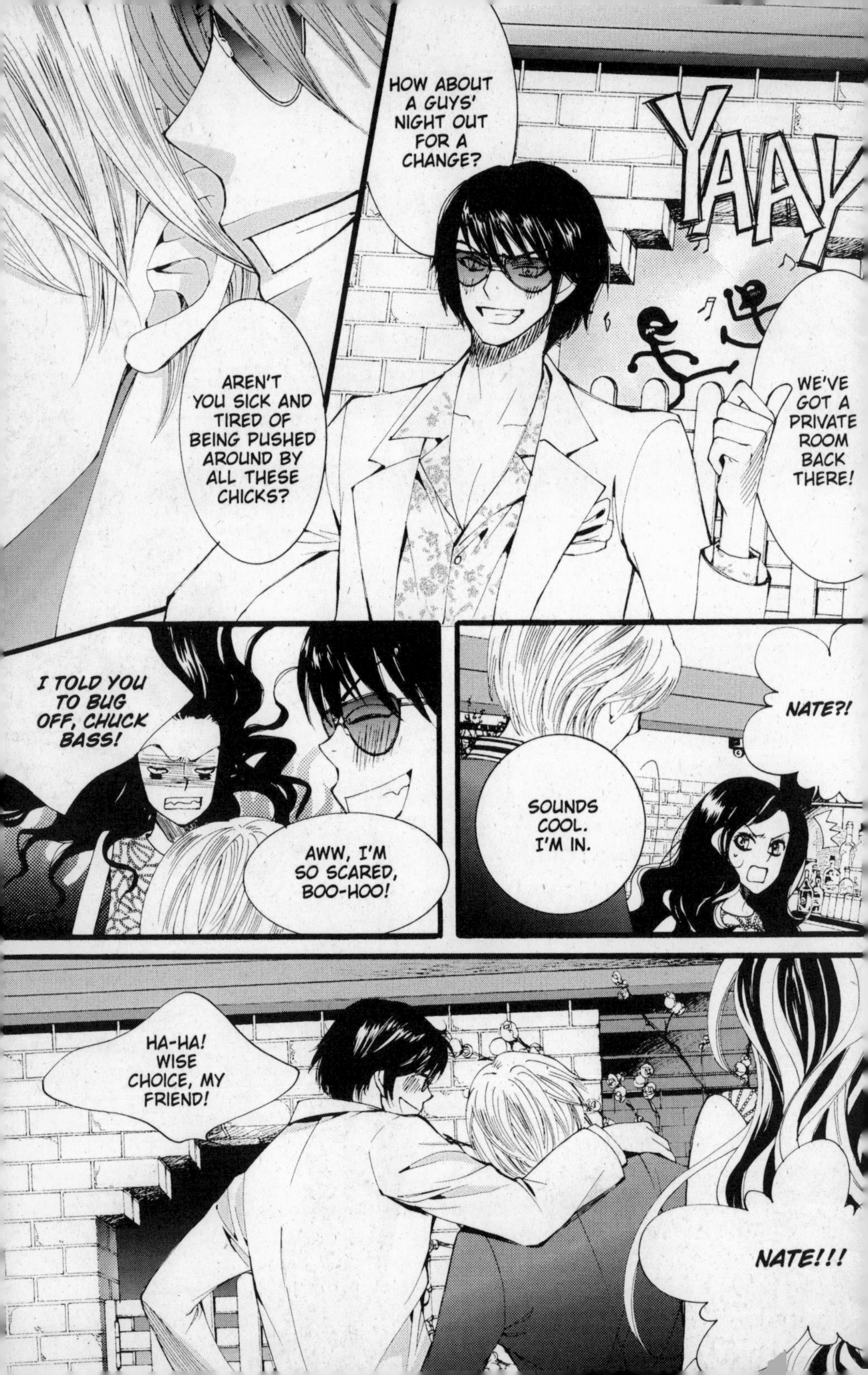
HOW ABOUT A GUYS' NIGHT OUT FOR A CHANGE?
YAAY
AREN'T YOU SICK AND TIRED OF BEING PUSHED AROUND BY ALL THESE CHICKS?
WE'VE GOT A PRIVATE ROOM BACK THERE!
I TOLD YOU TO BUG OFF, CHUCK BASS!
AWW, I'M SO SCARED, BOO-HOO!
NATE?!
SOUNDS COOL. I'M IN.
HA-HA! WISE CHOICE, MY FRIEND!
NATE!!!

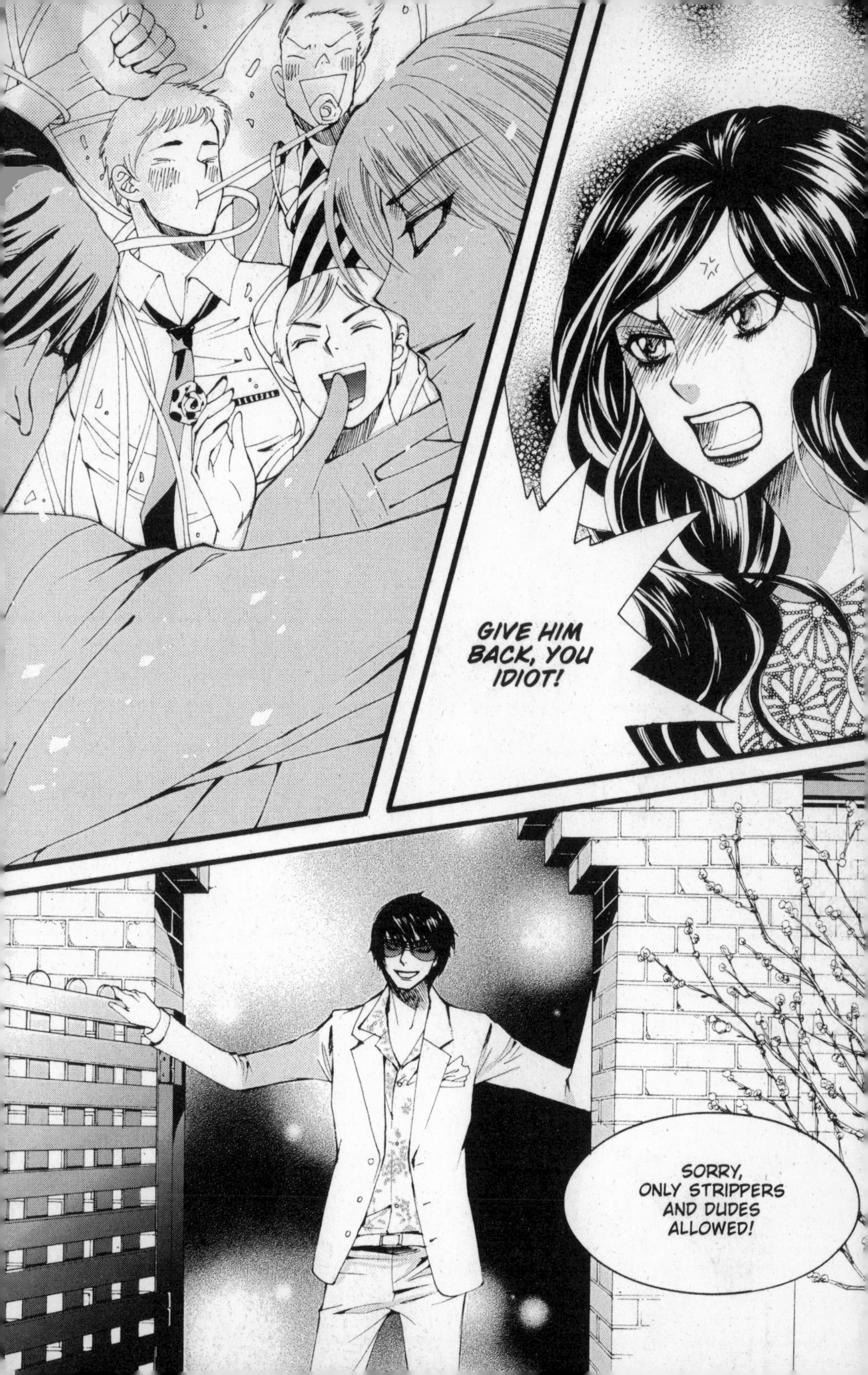
GIVE HIM BACK, YOU IDIOT!
SORRY, ONLY STRIPPERS AND DUDES ALLOWED!

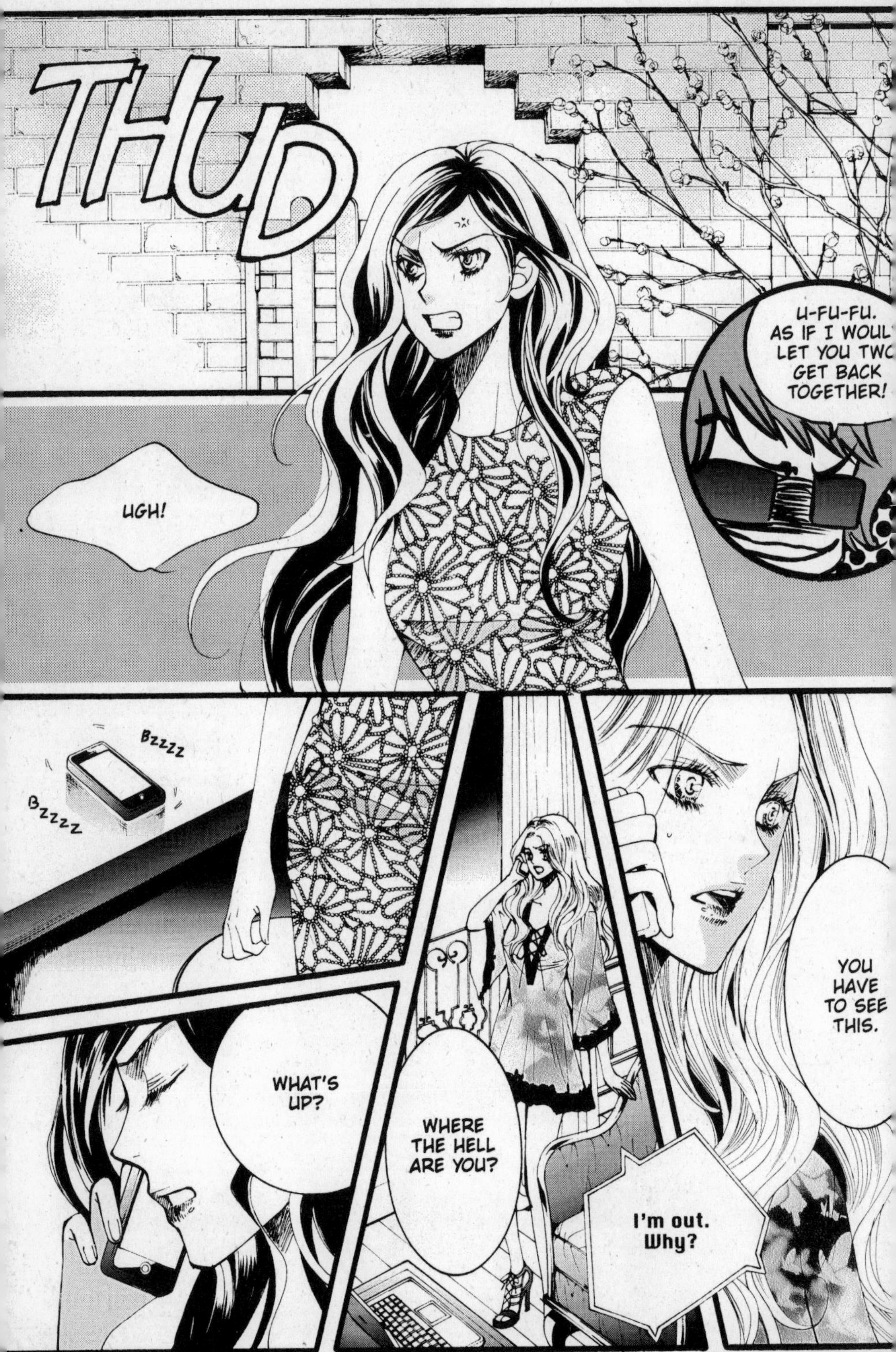
THUD
U-FU-FU. AS IF I WOUL LET YOU TWC GET BACK TOGETHER!
UGH!
Bzzzz
Bzzzz
WHAT'S UP?
WHERE THE HELL ARE YOU?
I'm out. Why?
YOU HAVE TO SEE THIS.

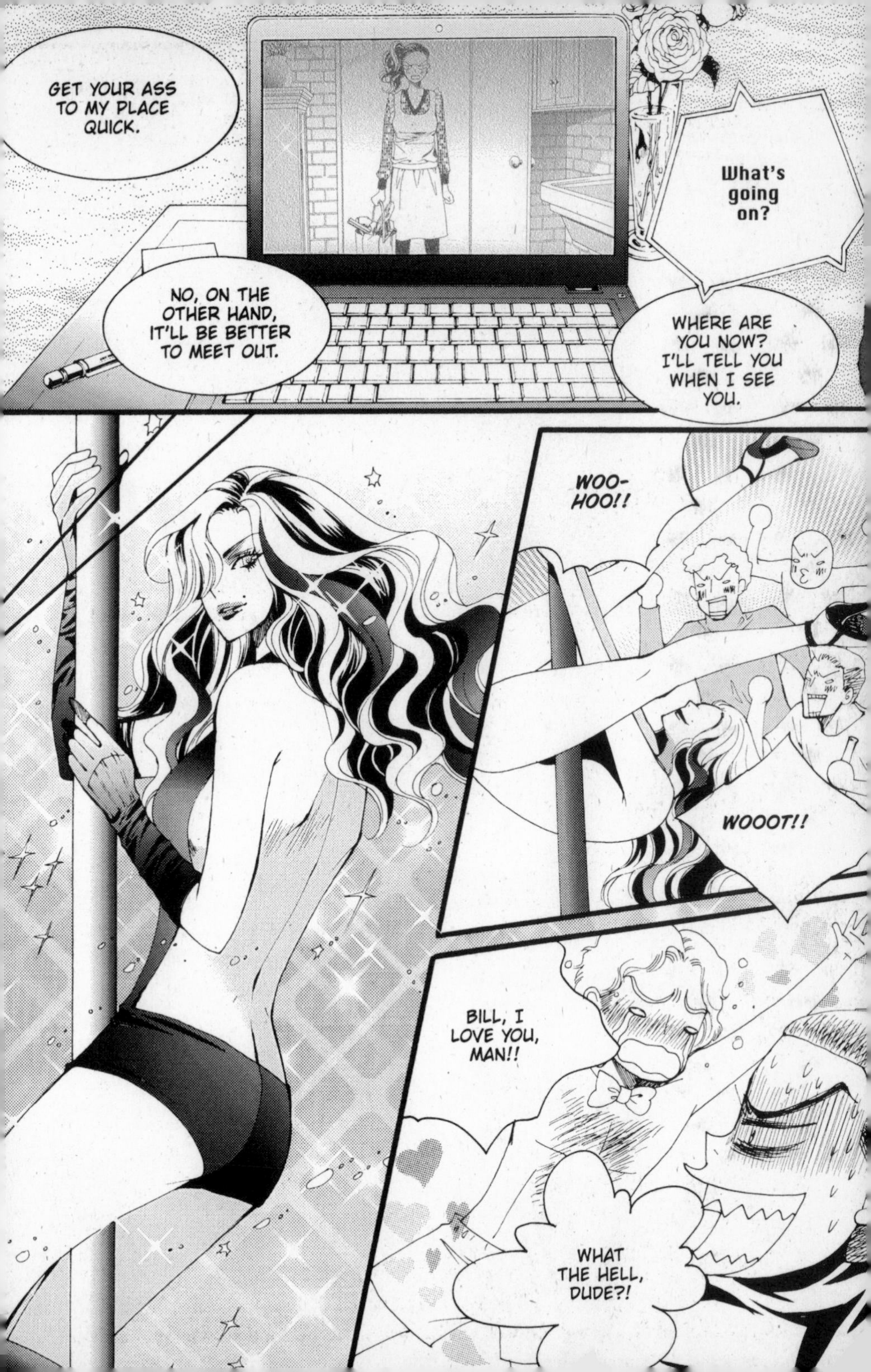

GET YOUR ASS TO MY PLACE QUICK.
What's going on?
NO, ON THE OTHER HAND, IT'LL BE BETTER TO MEET OUT.
WHERE ARE YOU NOW? I'LL TELL YOU WHEN I SEE YOU.
WOO-HOO!!
WOOOT!!
BILL, I LOVE YOU, MAN!!
WHAT THE HELL, DUDE?!

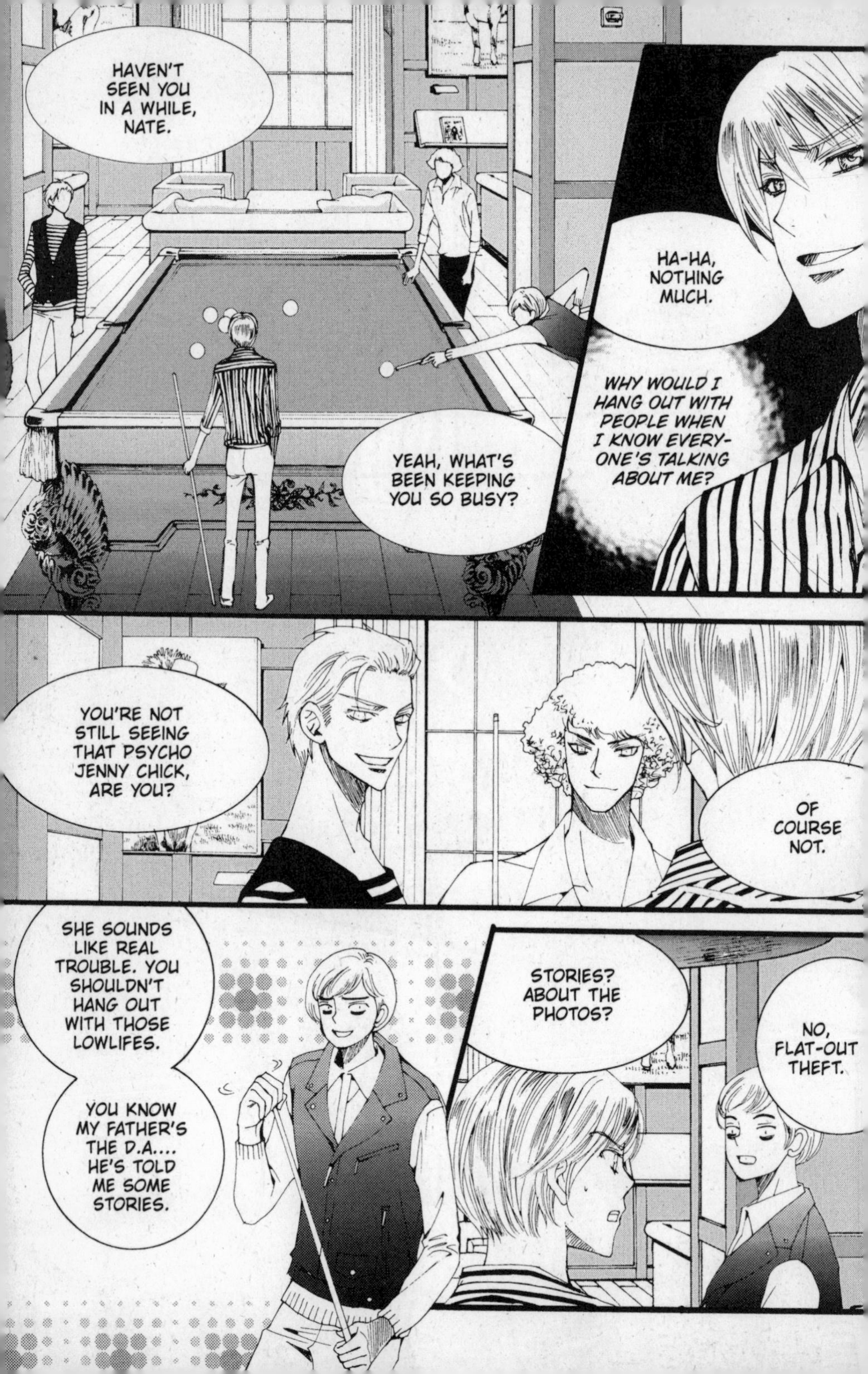
HAVEN'T SEEN YOU IN A WHILE, NATE.
YEAH, WHAT'S BEEN KEEPING YOU SO BUSY?
HA-HA, NOTHING MUCH.
WHY WOULD I HANG OUT WITH PEOPLE WHEN I KNOW EVERY-ONE'S TALKING ABOUT ME?
YOU'RE NOT STILL SEEING THAT PSYCHO JENNY CHICK, ARE YOU?
OF COURSE NOT.
SHE SOUNDS LIKE REAL TROUBLE. YOU SHOULDN'T HANG OUT WITH THOSE LOWLIFES.
YOU KNOW MY FATHER'S THE D.A.... HE'S TOLD ME SOME STORIES.
STORIES? ABOUT THE PHOTOS?
NO, FLAT-OUT THEFT.

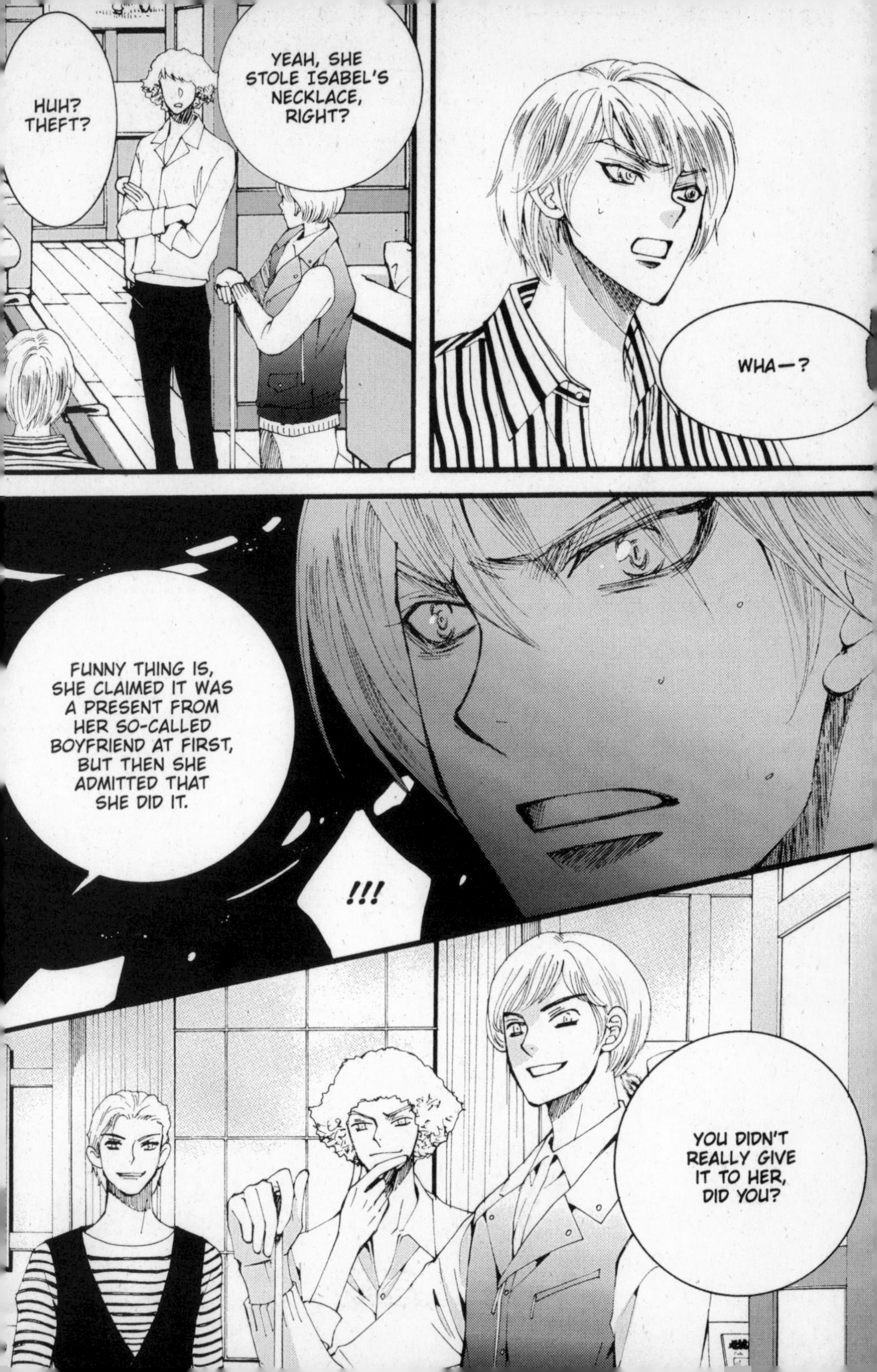
HUH? THEFT?
YEAH, SHE STOLE ISABEL'S NECKLACE, RIGHT?
WHA—?
FUNNY THING IS, SHE CLAIMED IT WAS A PRESENT FROM HER SO-CALLED BOYFRIEND AT FIRST, BUT THEN SHE ADMITTED THAT SHE DID IT.
!!!
YOU DIDN'T REALLY GIVE IT TO HER, DID YOU?

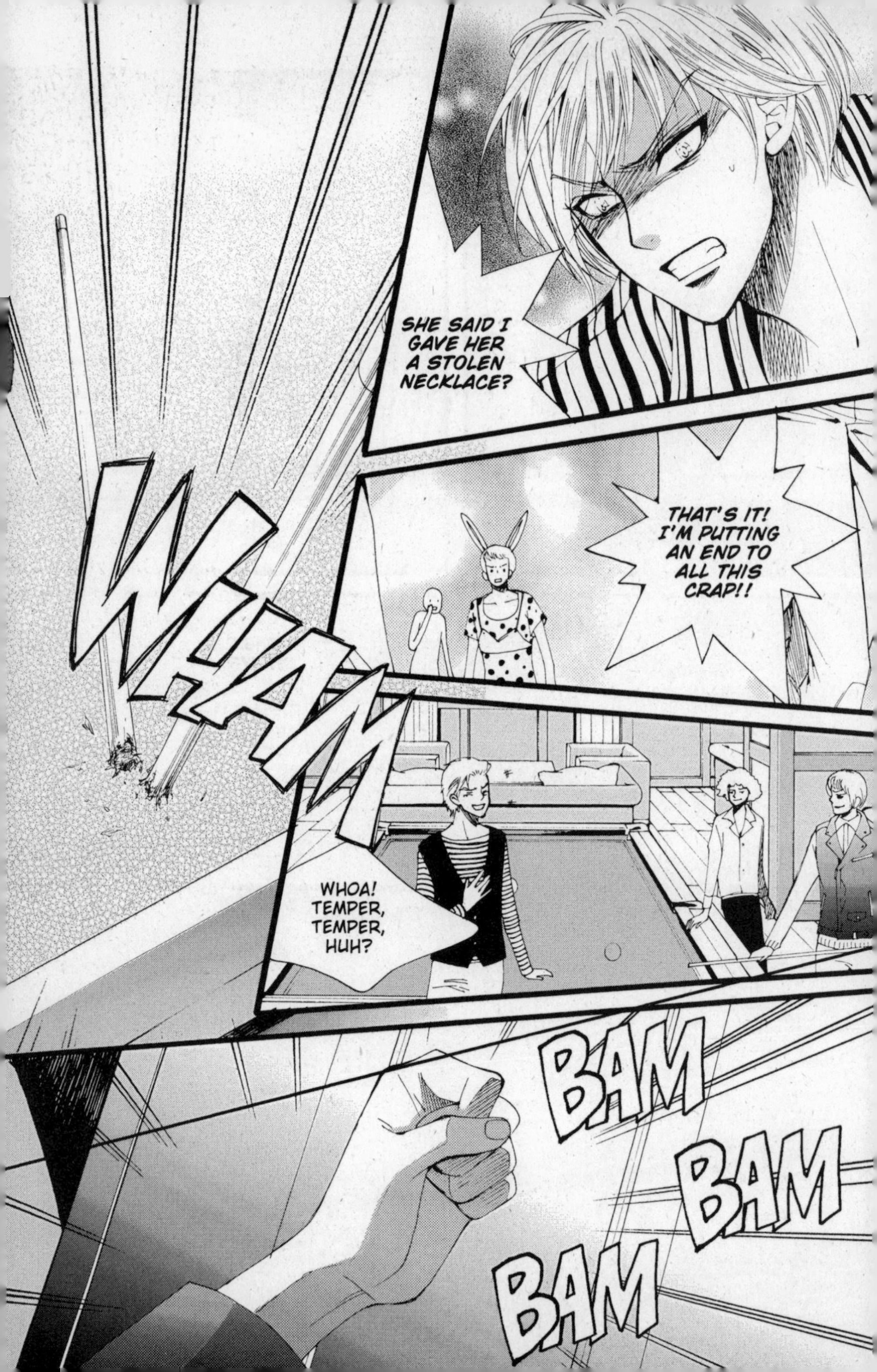
WHAM
SHE SAID I GAVE HER A STOLEN NECKLACE?
THAT'S IT! I'M PUTTING AN END TO ALL THIS CRAP!!
WHOA! TEMPER, TEMPER, HUH?
BAM
BAM
BAM

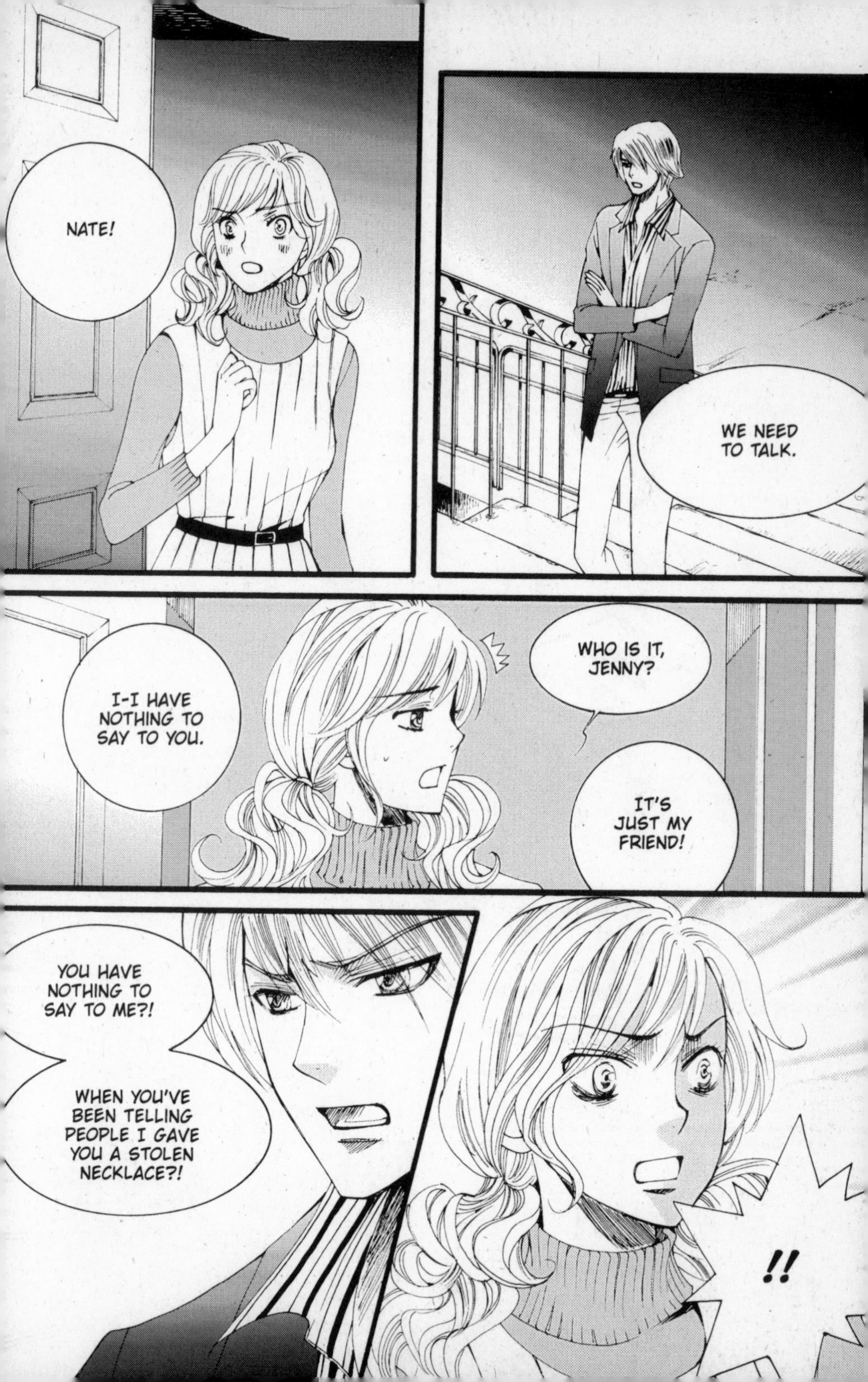
NATE!
WE NEED TO TALK.
I-I HAVE NOTHING TO SAY TO YOU.
WHO IS IT, JENNY?
IT'S JUST MY FRIEND!
YOU HAVE NOTHING TO SAY TO ME?!
WHEN YOU'VE BEEN TELLING PEOPLE I GAVE YOU A STOLEN NECKLACE?!
!!

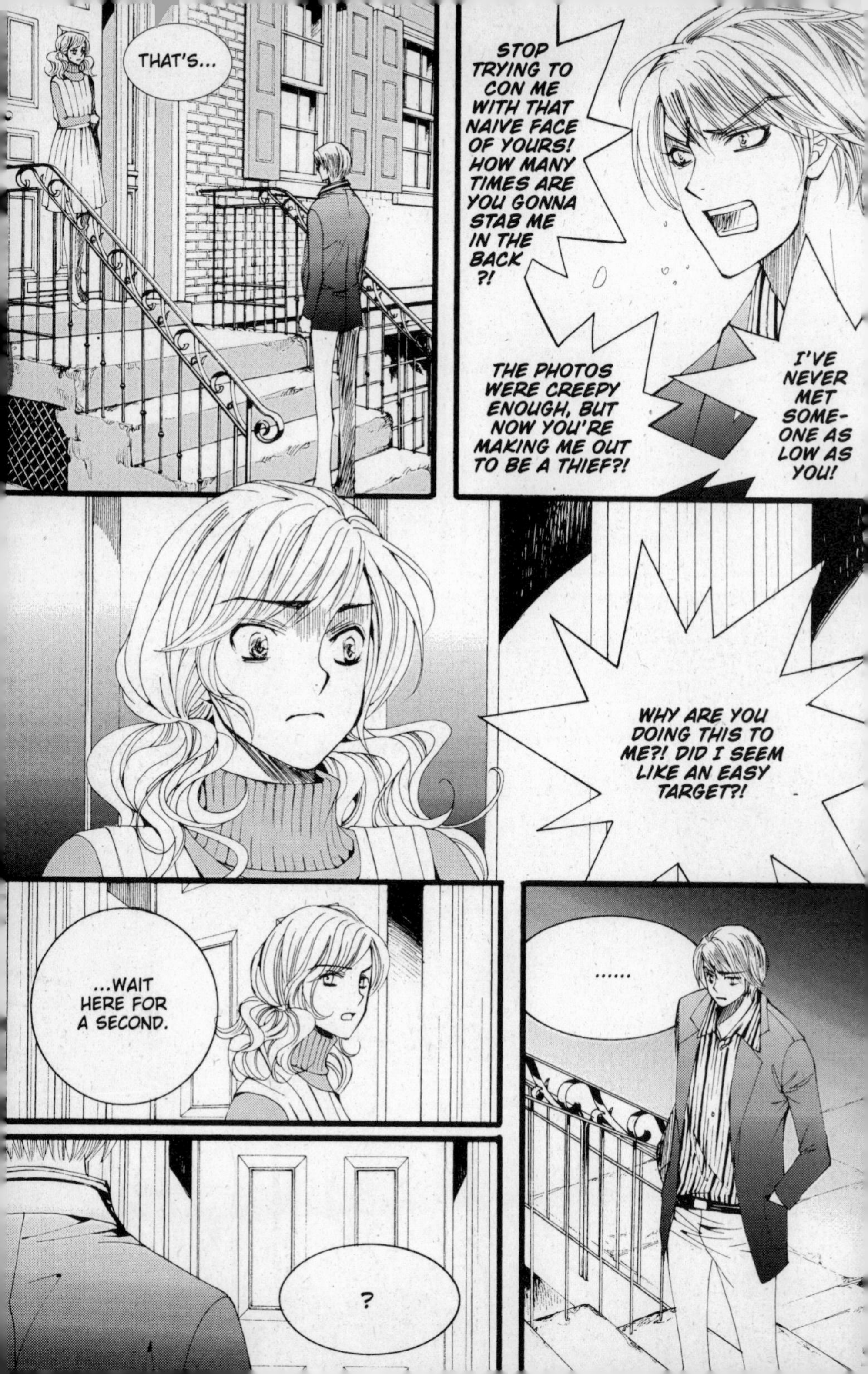
THAT'S...
STOP TRYING TO CON ME WITH THAT NAIVE FACE OF YOURS! HOW MANY TIMES ARE YOU GONNA STAB ME IN THE BACK ?!
THE PHOTOS WERE CREEPY ENOUGH, BUT NOW YOU'RE MAKING ME OUT TO BE A THIEF?!
I'VE NEVER MET SOME-ONE AS LOW AS YOU!
WHY ARE YOU DOING THIS TO ME?! DID I SEEM LIKE AN EASY TARGET?!
...WAIT HERE FOR A SECOND.
......
?

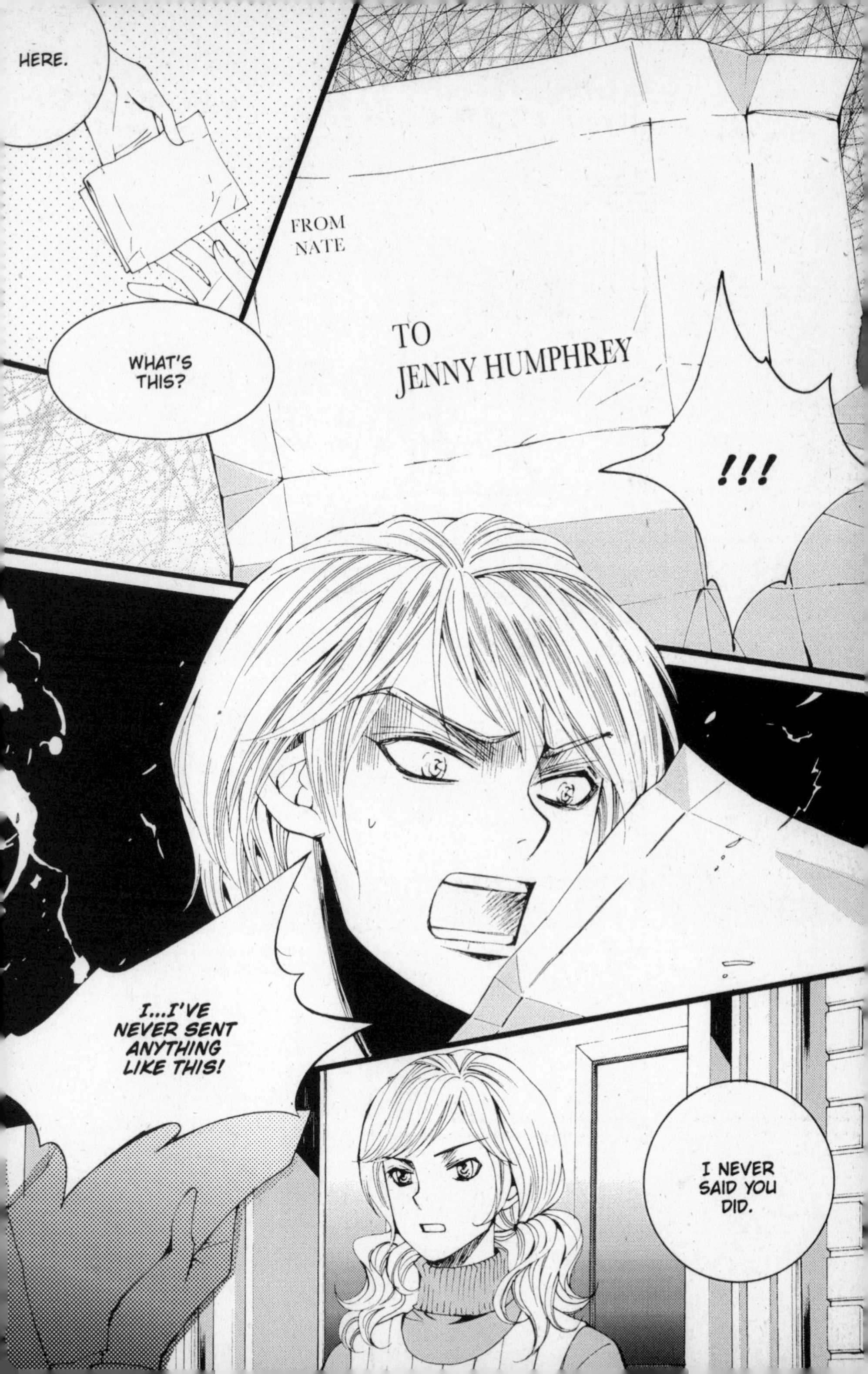
HERE.
WHAT'S THIS?
FROM NATE
TO JENNY HUMPHREY
!!!
I...I'VE NEVER SENT ANYTHING LIKE THIS!
I NEVER SAID YOU DID.

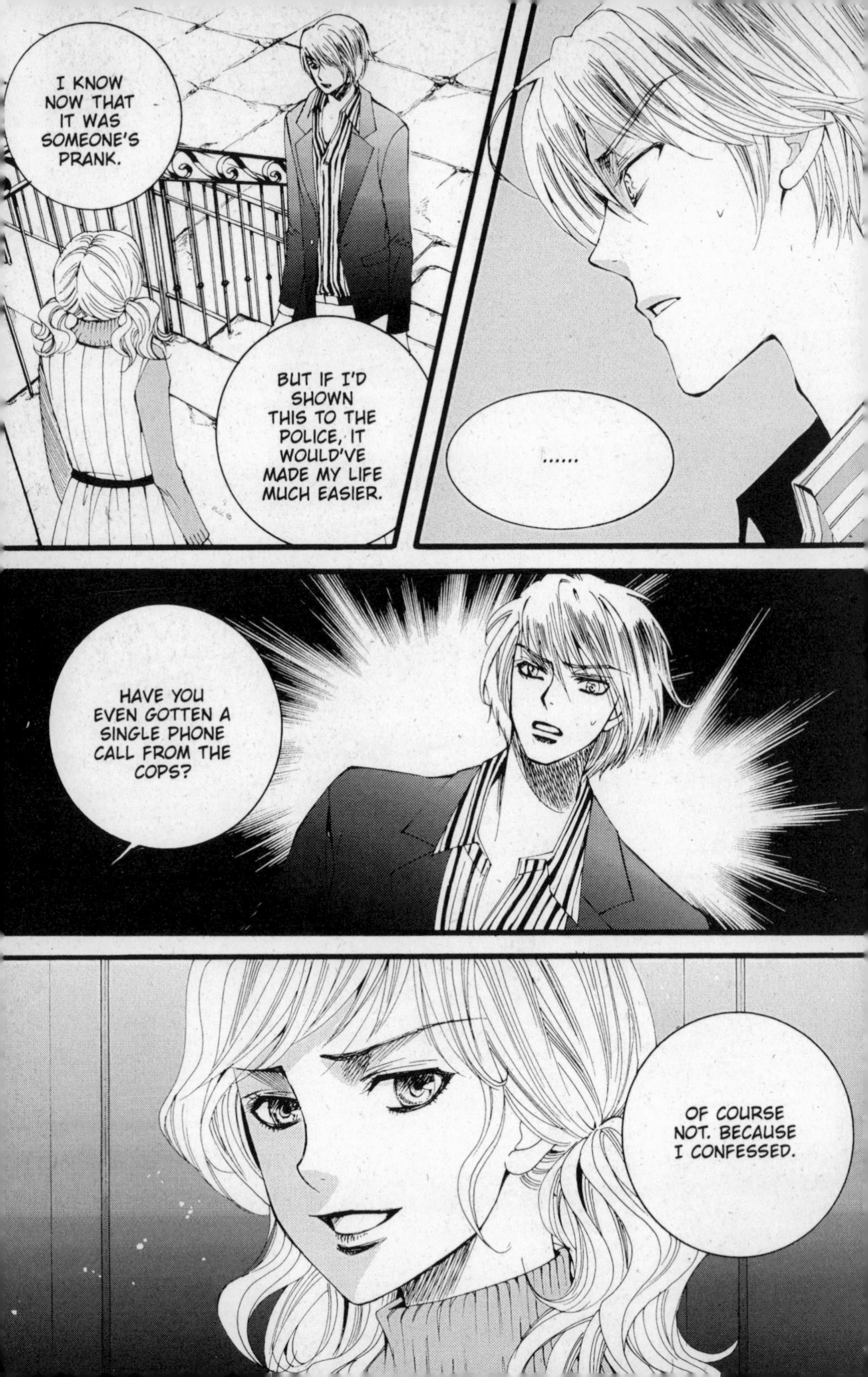
I KNOW NOW THAT IT WAS SOMEONE'S PRANK.
BUT IF I'D SHOWN THIS TO THE POLICE, IT WOULD'VE MADE MY LIFE MUCH EASIER.
......
HAVE YOU EVEN GOTTEN A SINGLE PHONE CALL FROM THE COPS?
OF COURSE NOT. BECAUSE I CONFESSED.

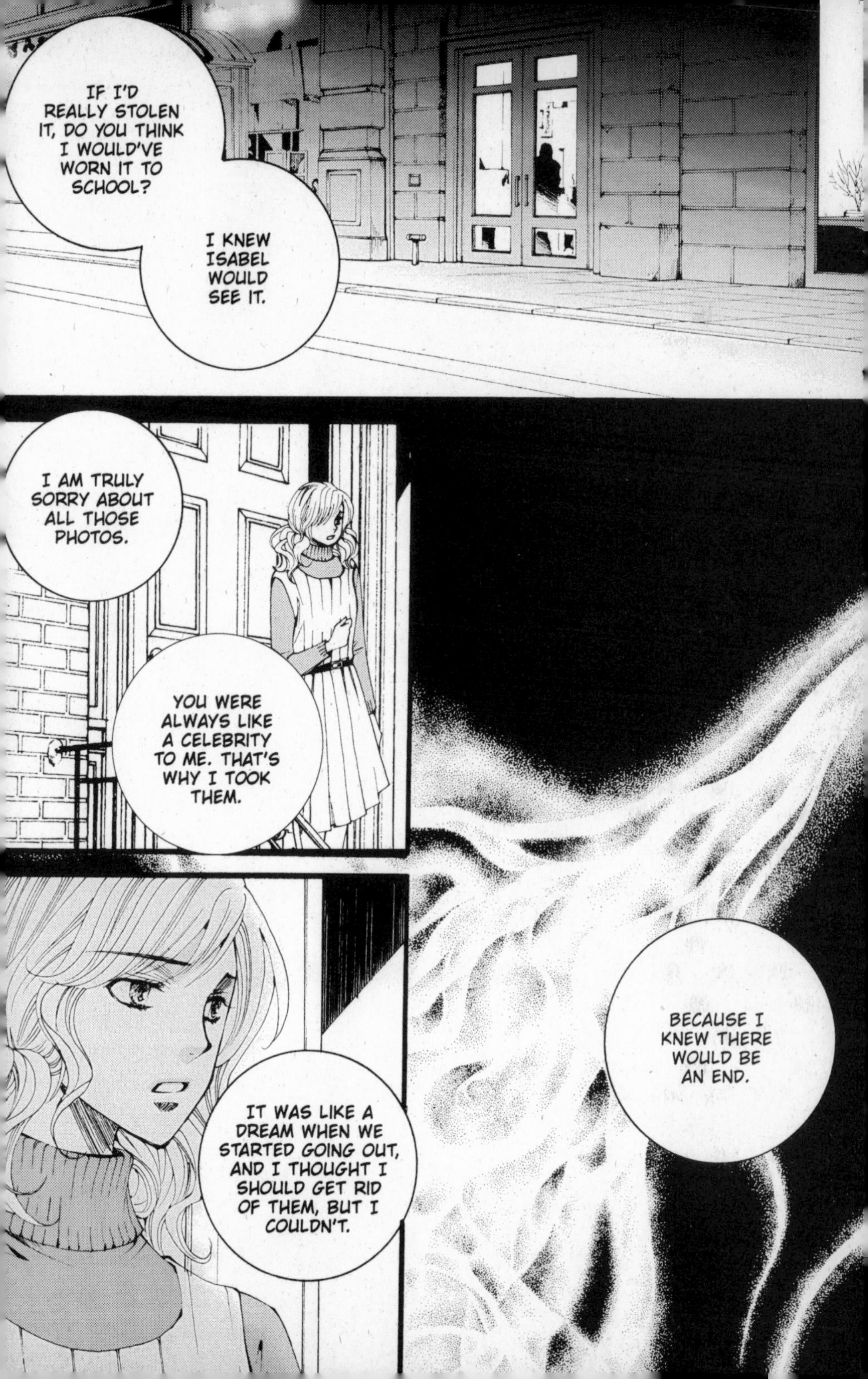
IF I'D REALLY STOLEN IT, DO YOU THINK I WOULD'VE WORN IT TO SCHOOL?
I KNEW ISABEL WOULD SEE IT.
I AM TRULY SORRY ABOUT ALL THOSE PHOTOS.
YOU WERE ALWAYS LIKE A CELEBRITY TO ME. THAT'S WHY I TOOK THEM.
IT WAS LIKE A DREAM WHEN WE STARTED GOING OUT, AND I THOUGHT I SHOULD GET RID OF THEM, BUT I COULDN'T.
BECAUSE I KNEW THERE WOULD BE AN END.

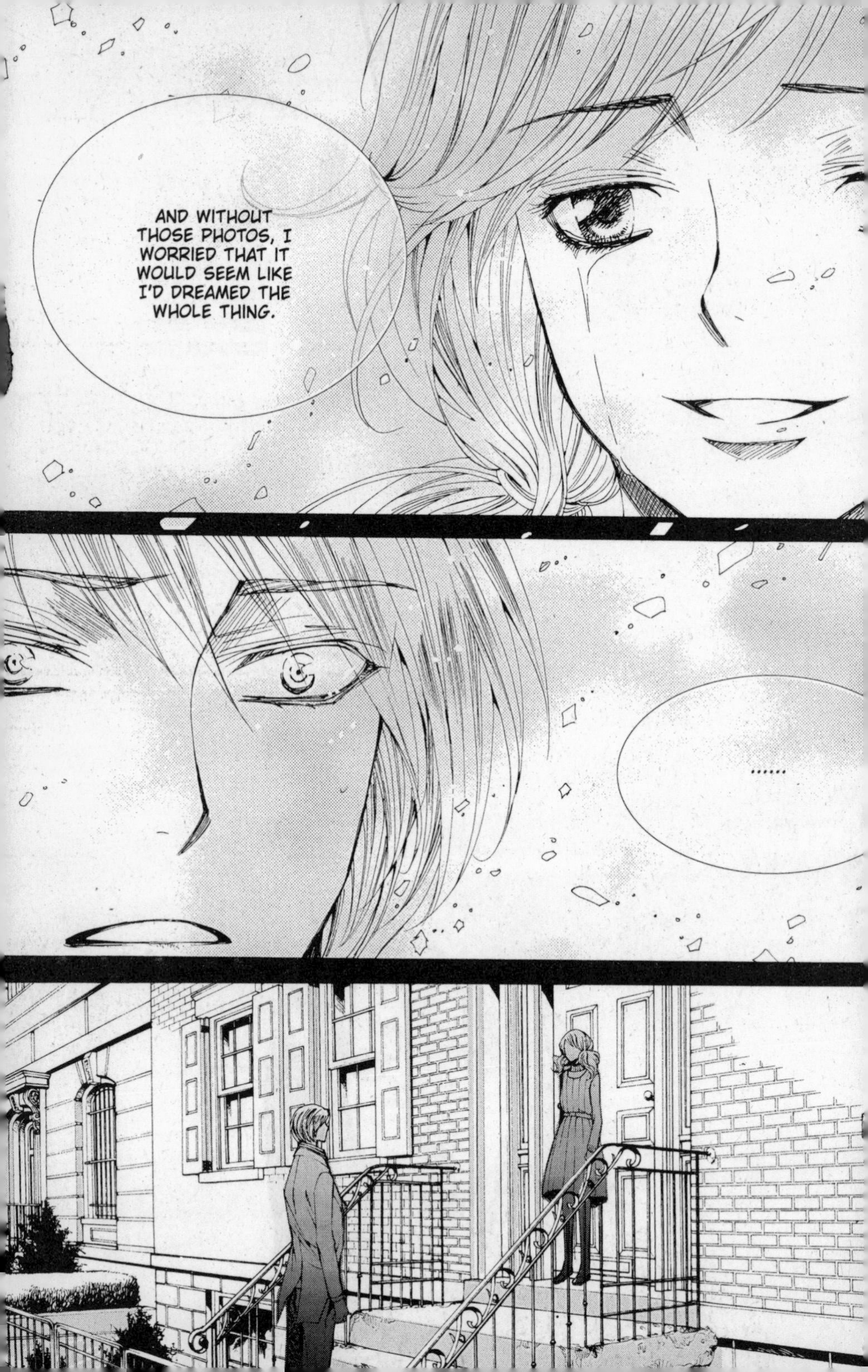
AND WITHOUT THOSE PHOTOS, I WORRIED THAT IT WOULD SEEM LIKE I'D DREAMED THE WHOLE THING.
......

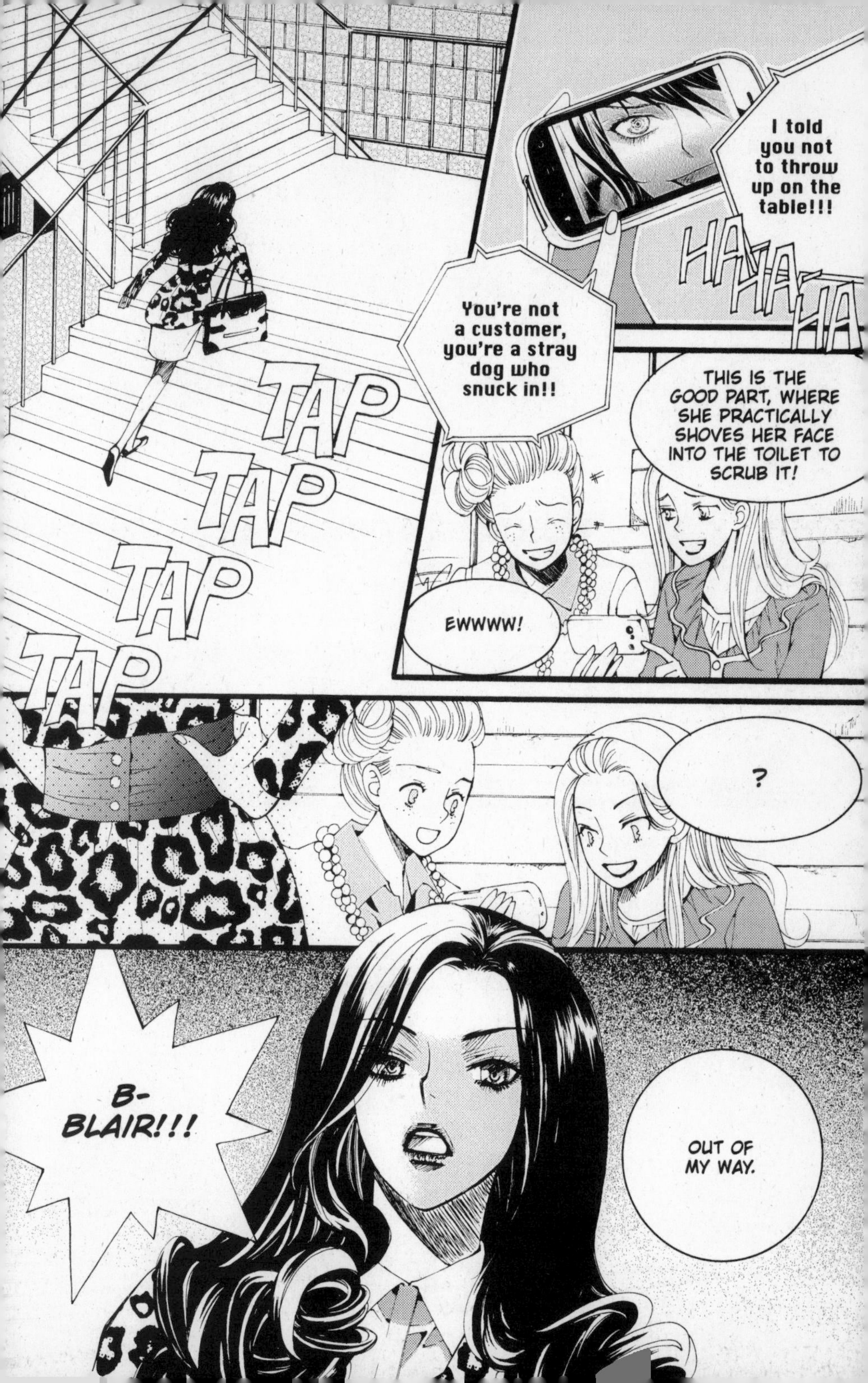
TAP
TAP
TAP
TAP
I told you not to throw up on the table!!!
You're not a customer, you're a stray dog who snuck in!!
HA-HA-HA
THIS IS THE GOOD PART, WHERE SHE PRACTICALLY SHOVES HER FACE INTO THE TOILET TO SCRUB IT!
EWWWW!
?
B-BLAIR!!!
OUT OF MY WAY.

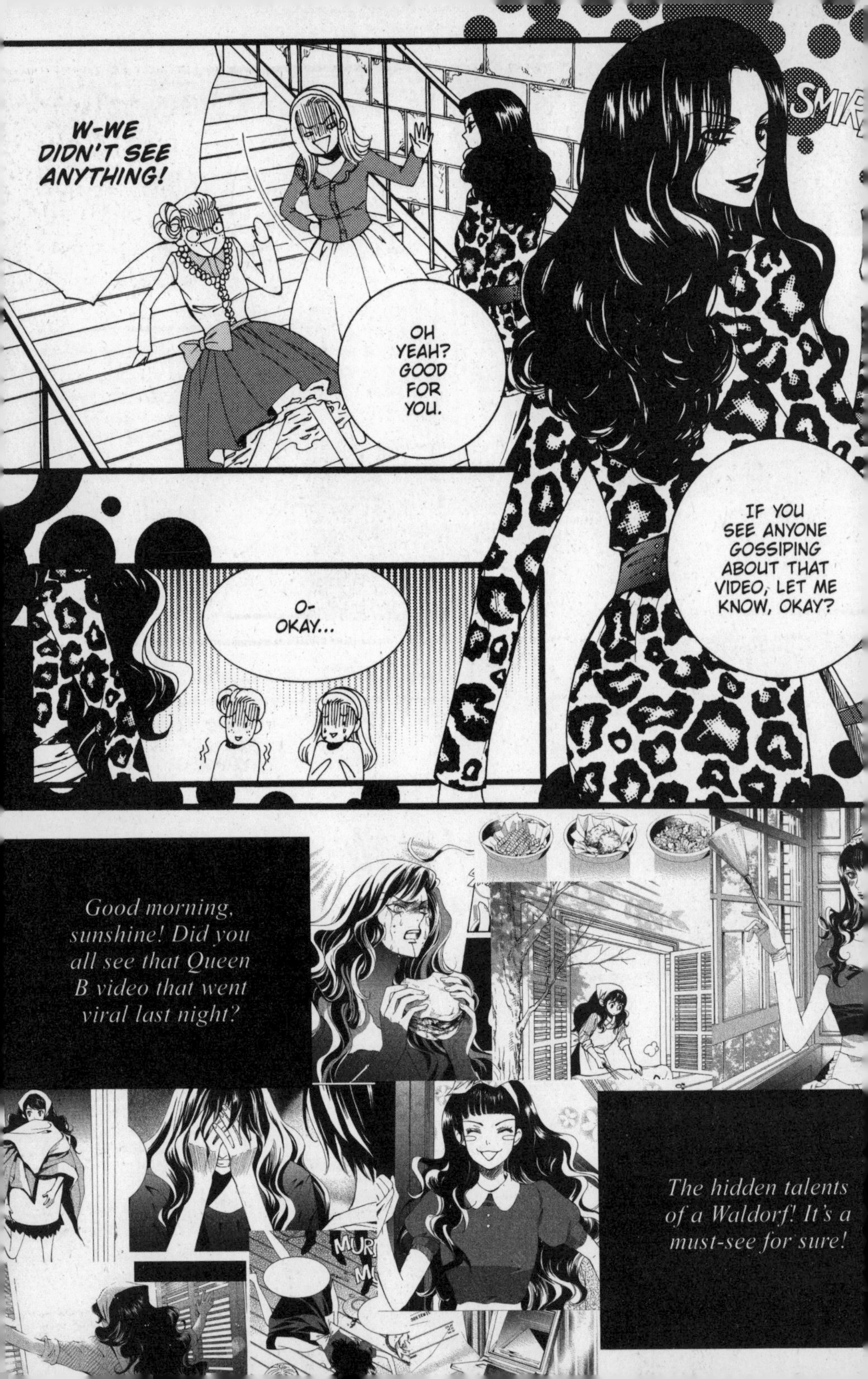
W-WE DIDN'T SEE ANYTHING!
OH YEAH? GOOD FOR YOU.
SMIR
O-OKAY...
IF YOU SEE ANYONE GOSSIPING ABOUT THAT VIDEO, LET ME KNOW, OKAY?
Good morning, sunshine! Did you all see that Queen B video that went viral last night?
The hidden talents of a Waldorf! It's a must-see for sure!

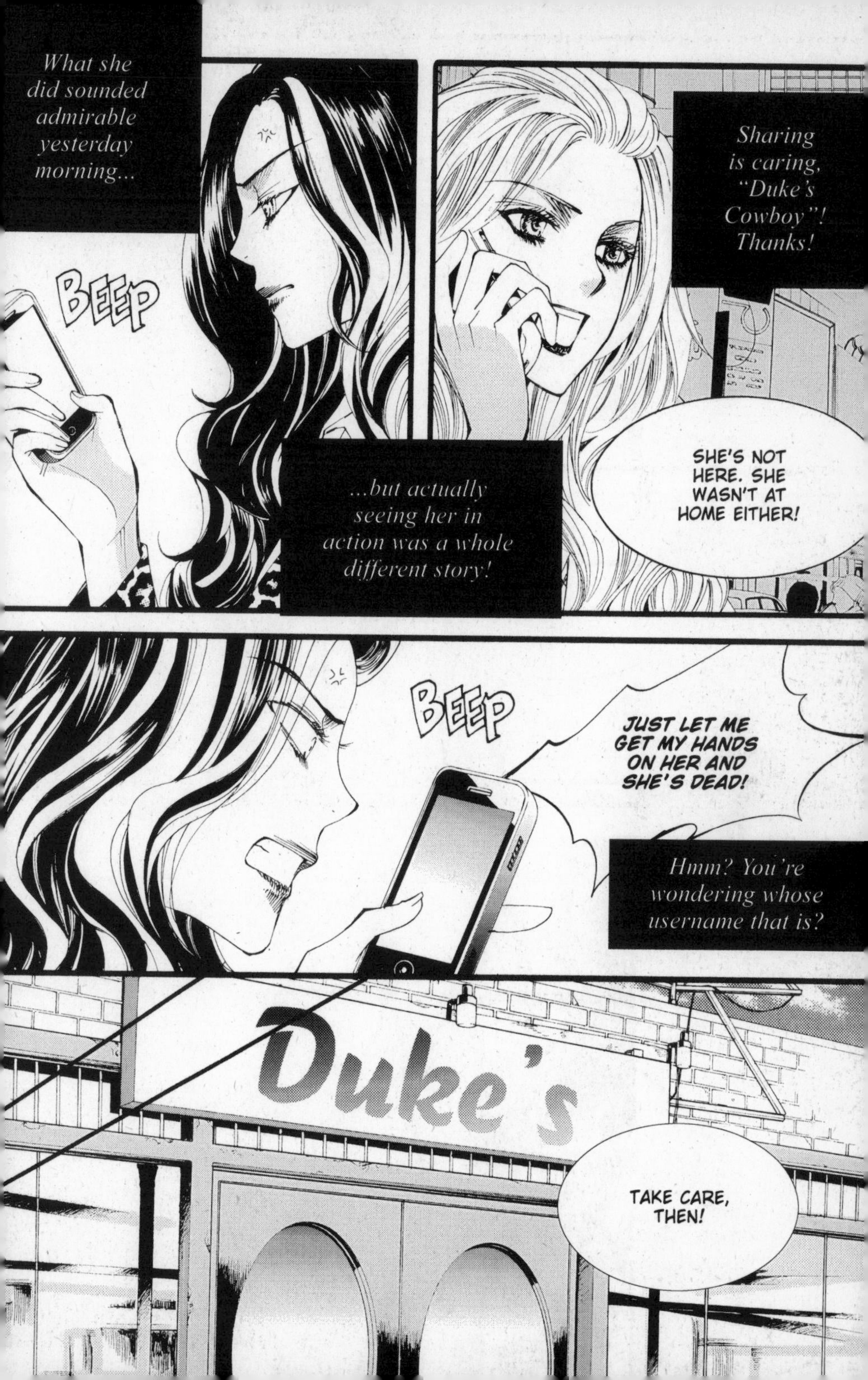
What she did sounded admirable yesterday morning...
BEEP
...but actually seeing her in action was a whole different story!
Sharing is caring, "Duke's Cowboy"! Thanks!
SHE'S NOT HERE. SHE WASN'T AT HOME EITHER!
BEEP
JUST LET ME GET MY HANDS ON HER AND SHE'S DEAD!
Hmm? You're wondering whose username that is?
Duke's
TAKE CARE, THEN!

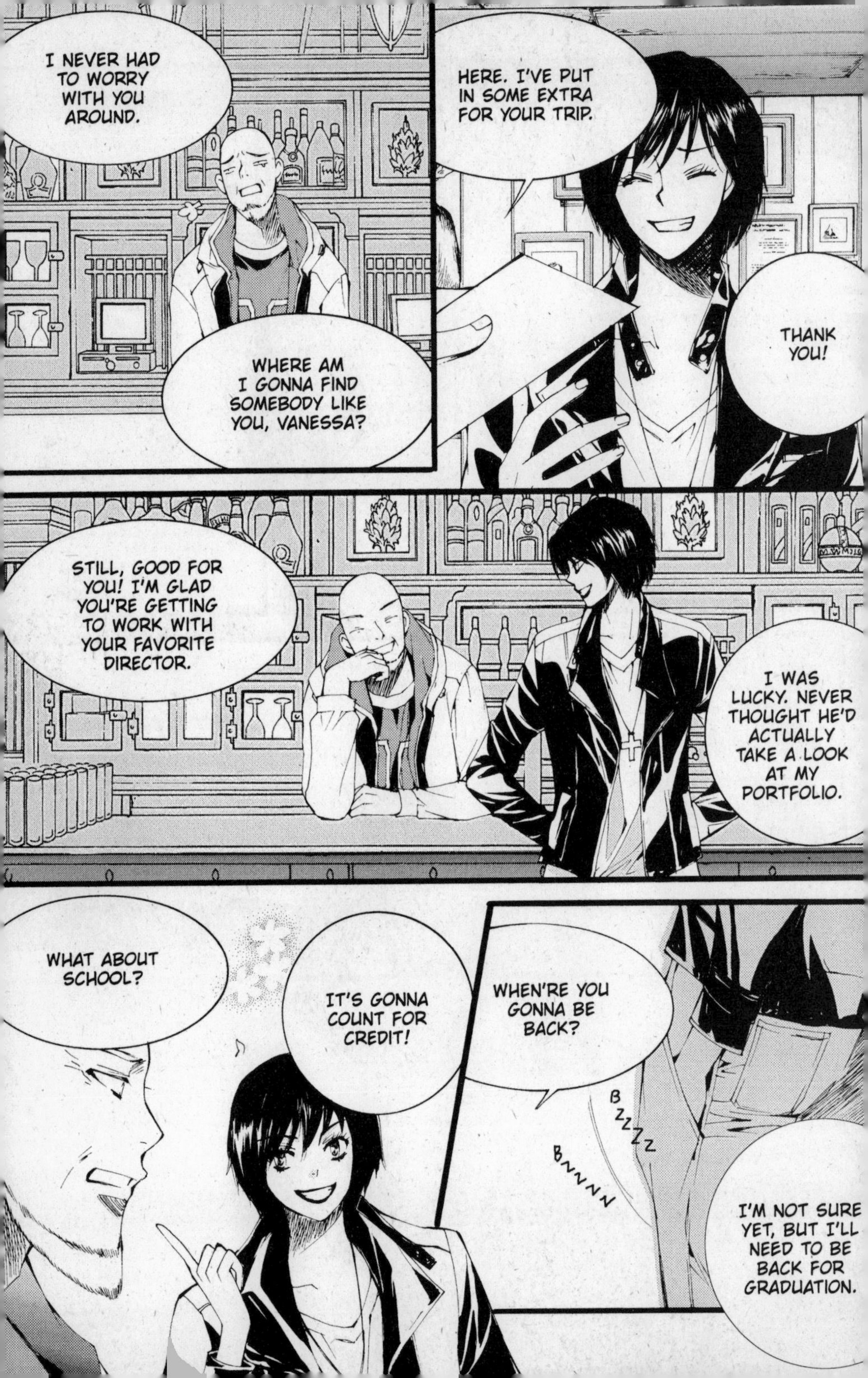
I NEVER HAD TO WORRY WITH YOU AROUND.
WHERE AM I GONNA FIND SOMEBODY LIKE YOU, VANESSA?
HERE. I'VE PUT IN SOME EXTRA FOR YOUR TRIP.
THANK YOU!
STILL, GOOD FOR YOU! I'M GLAD YOU'RE GETTING TO WORK WITH YOUR FAVORITE DIRECTOR.
I WAS LUCKY. NEVER THOUGHT HE'D ACTUALLY TAKE A LOOK AT MY PORTFOLIO.
WHAT ABOUT SCHOOL?
IT'S GONNA COUNT FOR CREDIT!
WHEN'RE YOU GONNA BE BACK?
BZZZZ
BNNNN
I'M NOT SURE YET, BUT I'LL NEED TO BE BACK FOR GRADUATION.

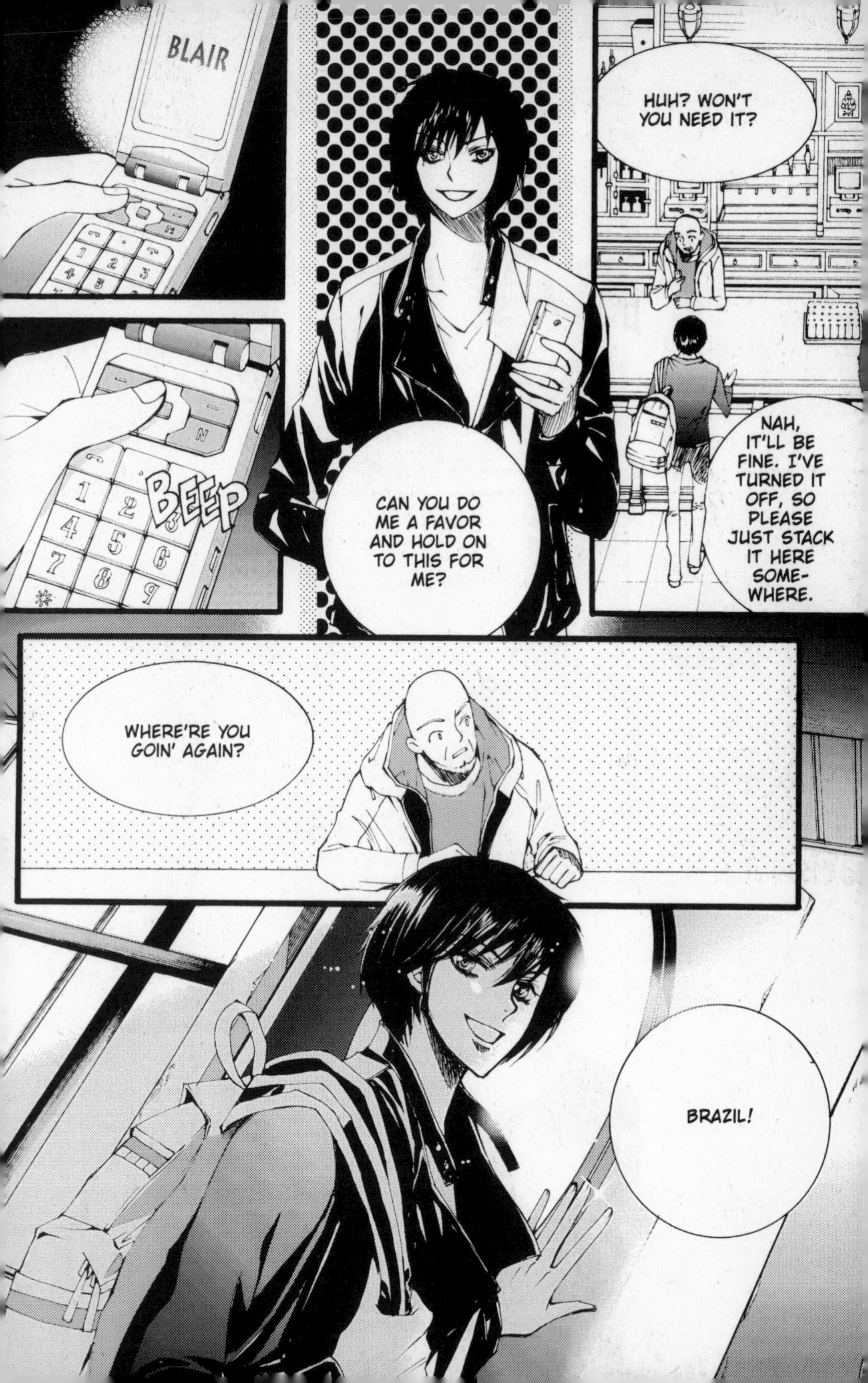
BLAIR
BEEP
CAN YOU DO ME A FAVOR AND HOLD ON TO THIS FOR ME?
HUH? WON'T YOU NEED IT?
NAH, IT'LL BE FINE. I'VE TURNED IT OFF, SO PLEASE JUST STACK IT HERE SOME-WHERE.
WHERE'RE YOU GOIN' AGAIN?
BRAZIL!

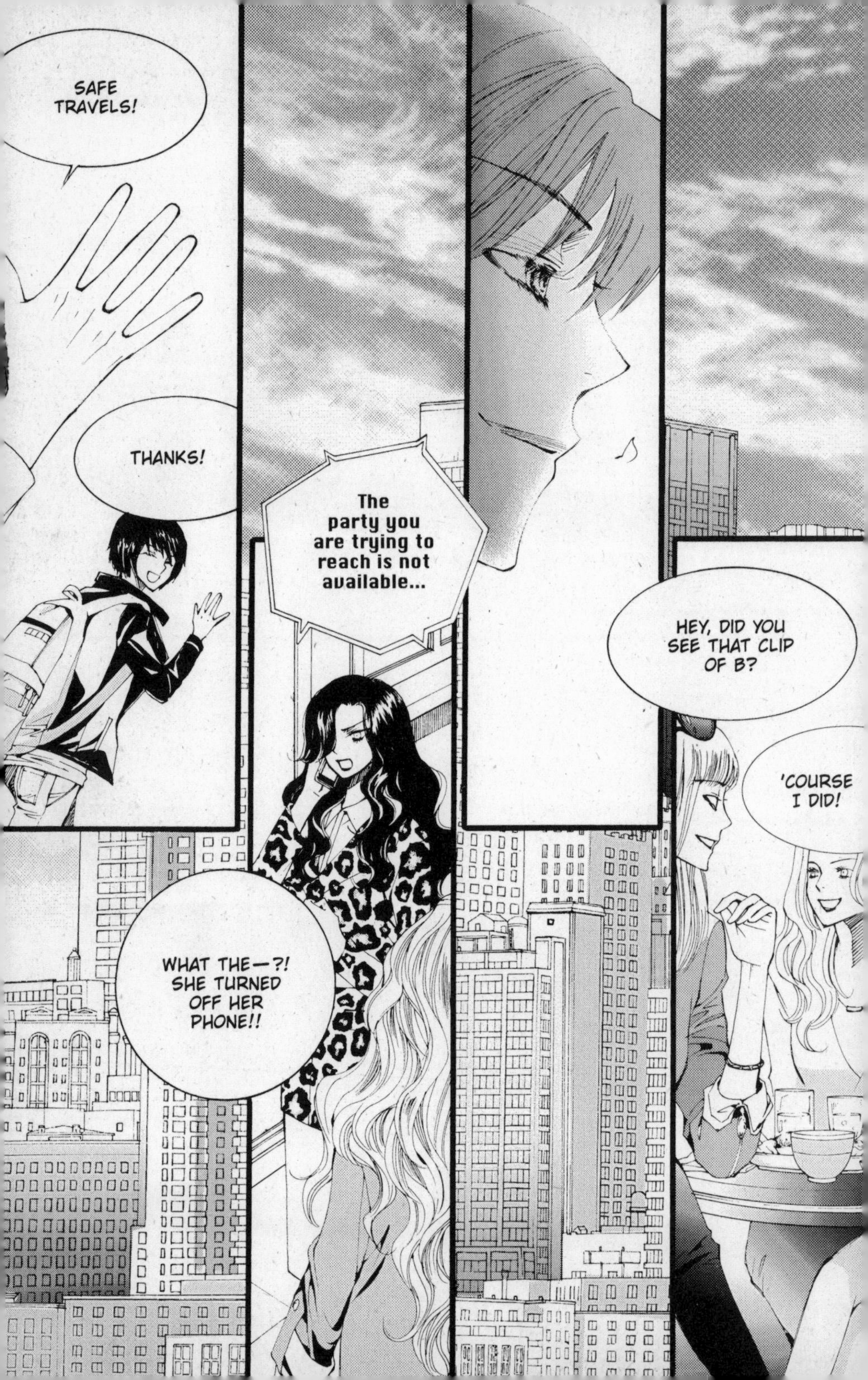
SAFE TRAVELS!
THANKS!
The party you are trying to reach is not available...
WHAT THE—?! SHE TURNED OFF HER PHONE!!
HEY, DID YOU SEE THAT CLIP OF B?
'COURSE I DID!

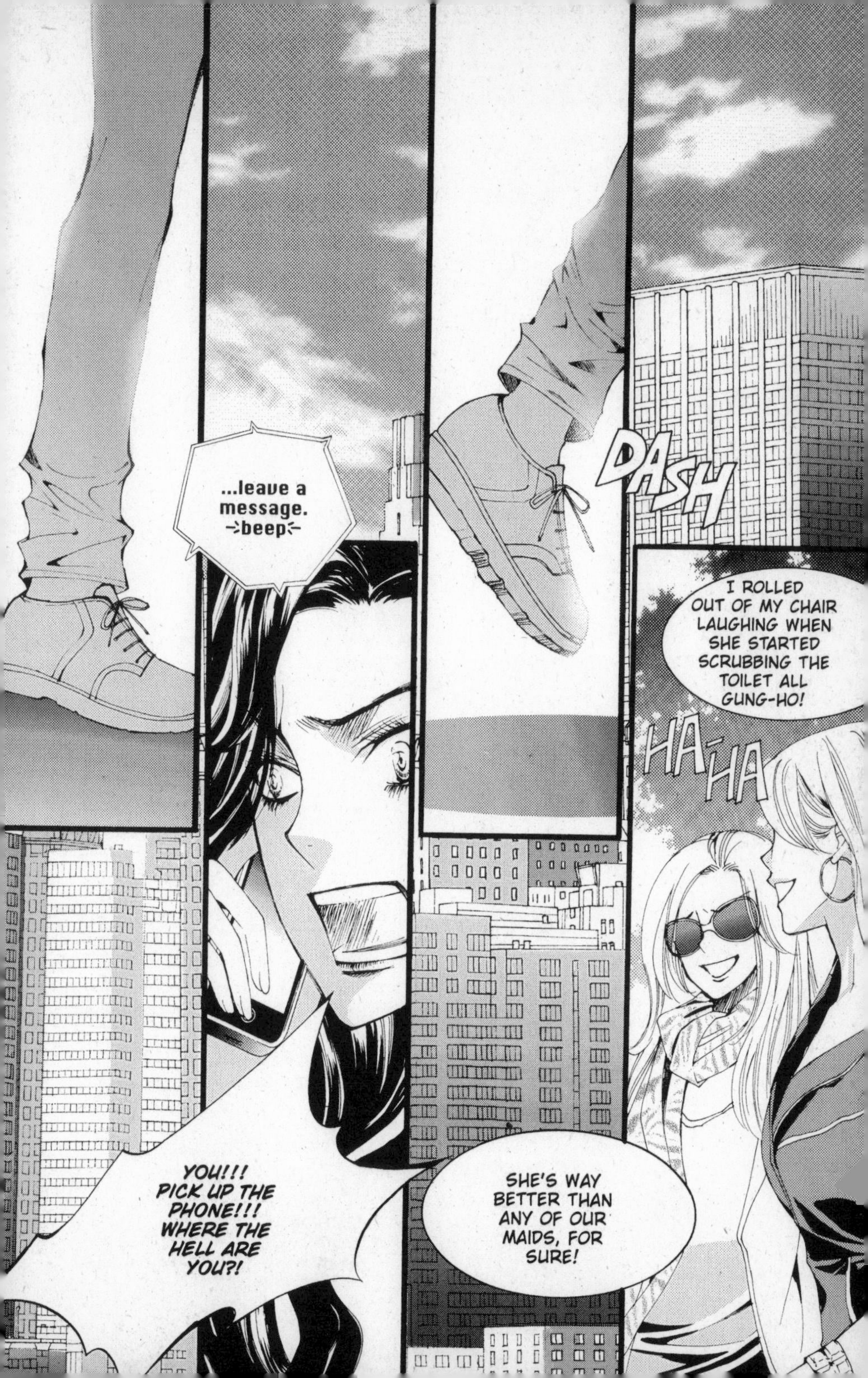

...leave a message. -beep-
DASH
I ROLLED OUT OF MY CHAIR LAUGHING WHEN SHE STARTED SCRUBBING THE TOILET ALL GUNG-HO!
HA-HA
YOU!!! PICK UP THE PHONE!!! WHERE THE HELL ARE YOU?!
SHE'S WAY BETTER THAN ANY OF OUR MAIDS, FOR SURE!

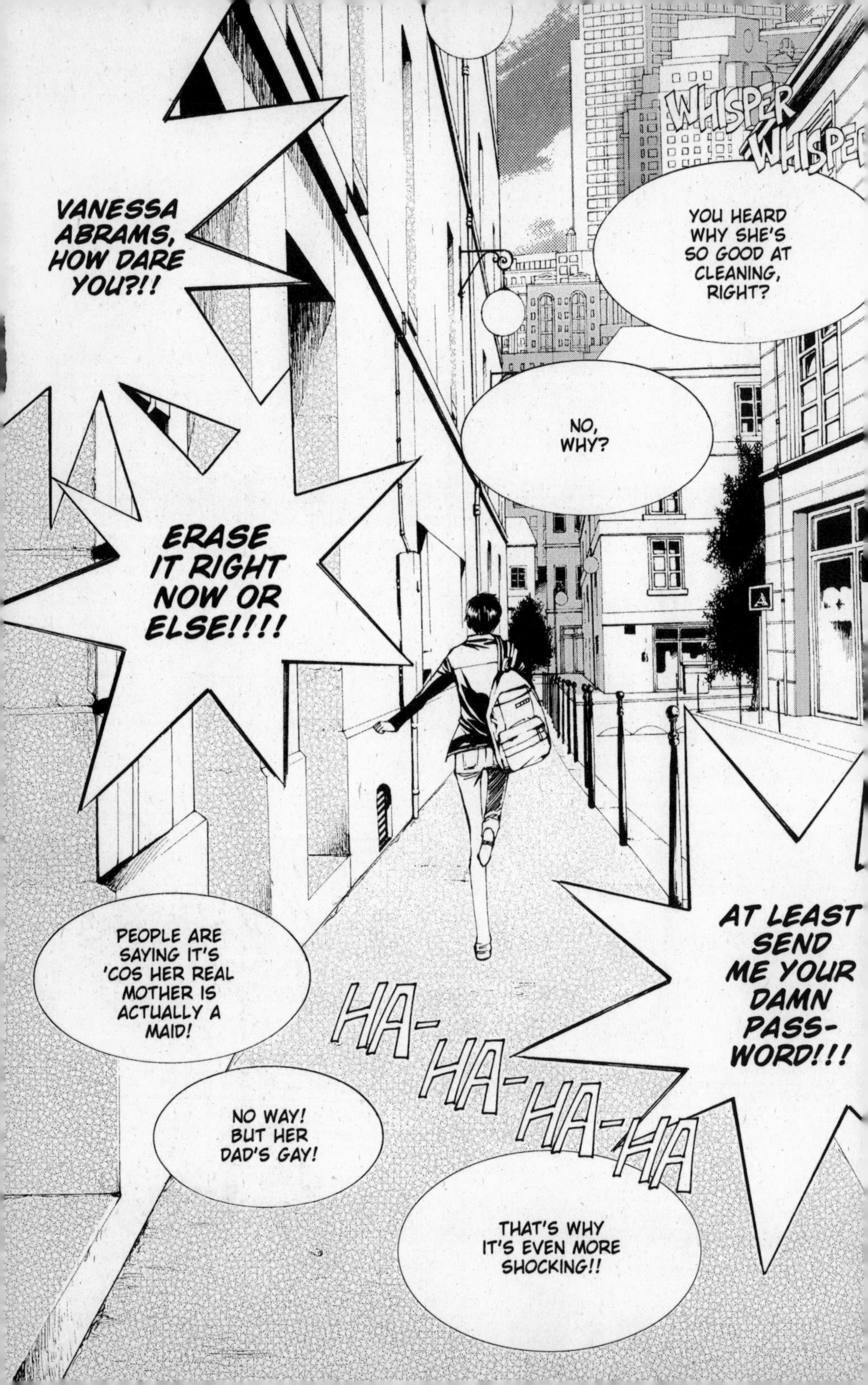
VANESSA ABRAMS, HOW DARE YOU?!!
ERASE IT RIGHT NOW OR ELSE!!!!
WHISPER
YOU HEARD WHY SHE'S SO GOOD AT CLEANING, RIGHT?
NO, WHY?
AT LEAST SEND ME YOUR DAMN PASS-WORD!!!
PEOPLE ARE SAYING IT'S 'COS HER REAL MOTHER IS ACTUALLY A MAID!
HA-HA-HA-HA
NO WAY! BUT HER DAD'S GAY!
THAT'S WHY IT'S EVEN MORE SHOCKING!!

gossip girl

FOR YOUR EYES ONLY

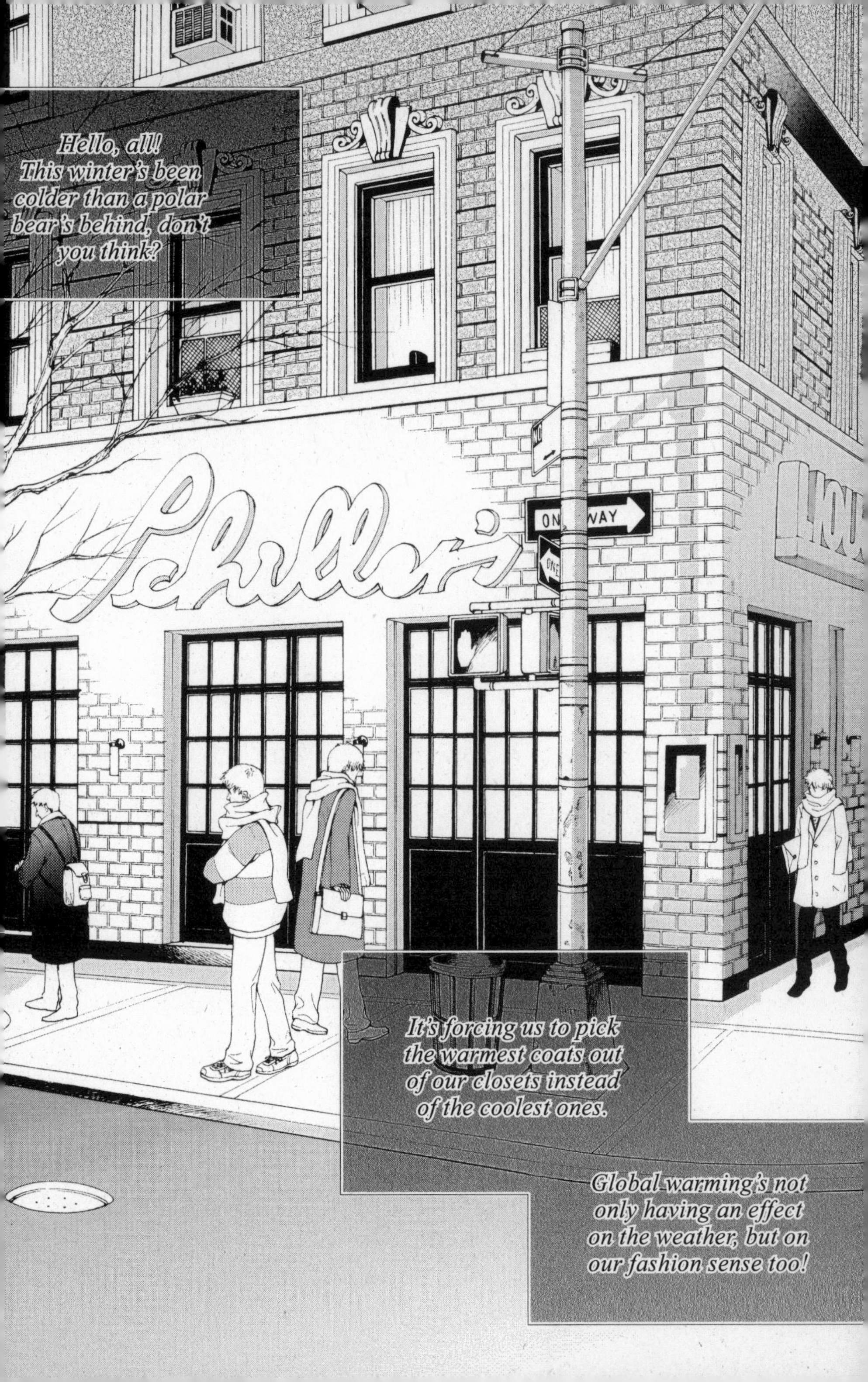
Hello, all! This winter's been colder than a polar bear's behind, don't you think?
Schiller's
ONE WAY
ONE
It's forcing us to pick the warmest coats out of our closets instead of the coolest ones.
Global warming's not only having an effect on the weather, but on our fashion sense too!

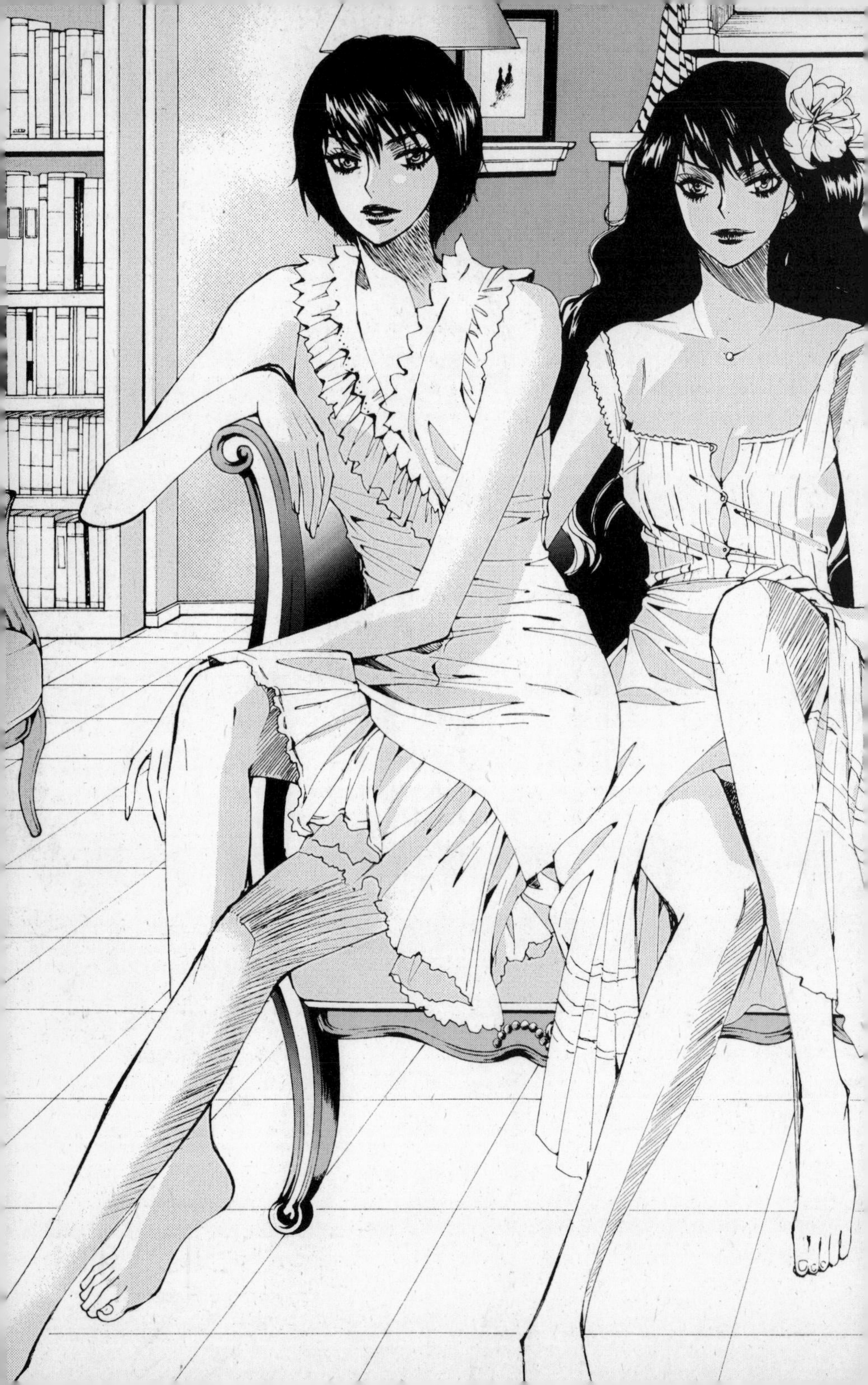

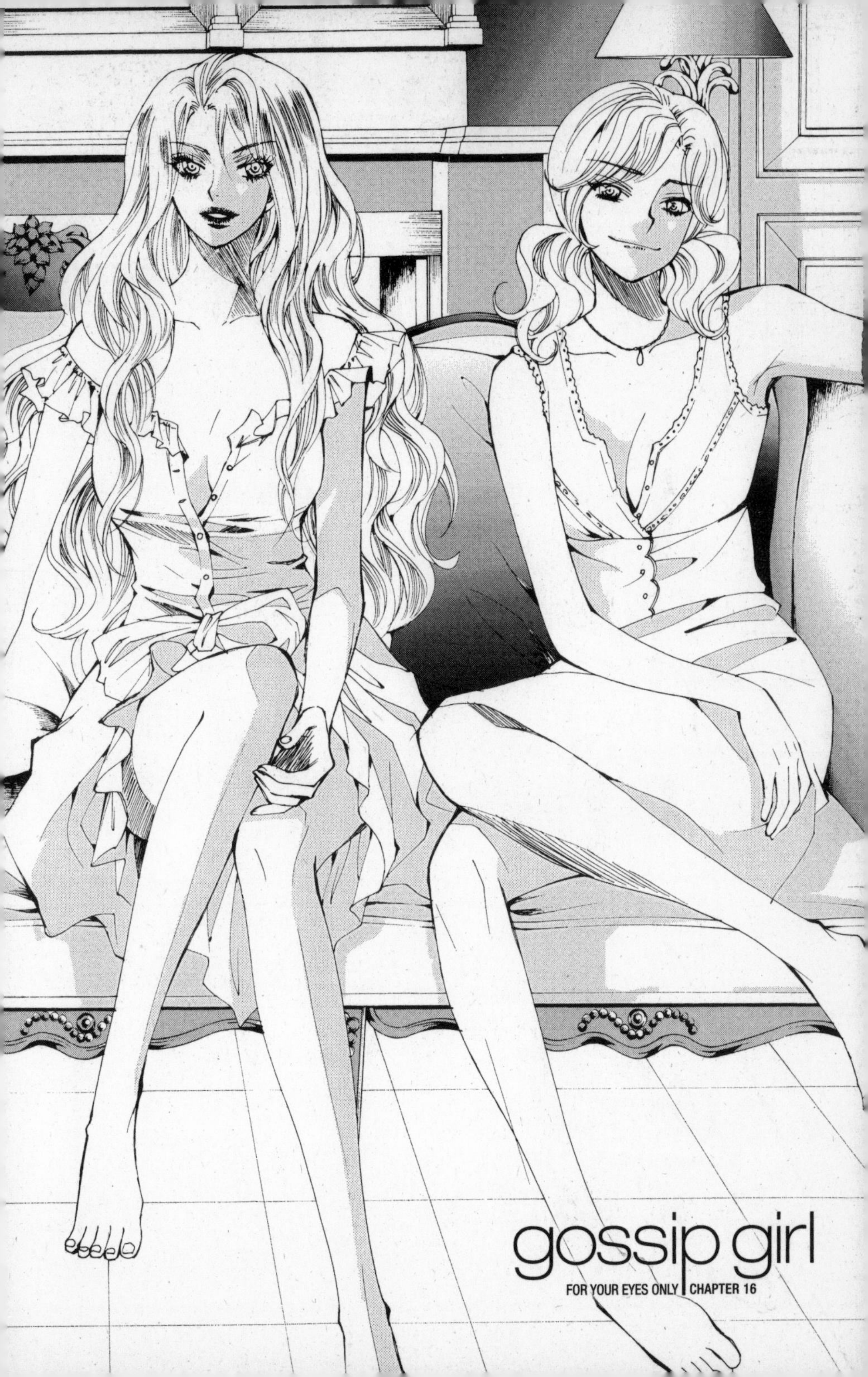
gossip girl
FOR YOUR EYES ONLY | CHAPTER 16

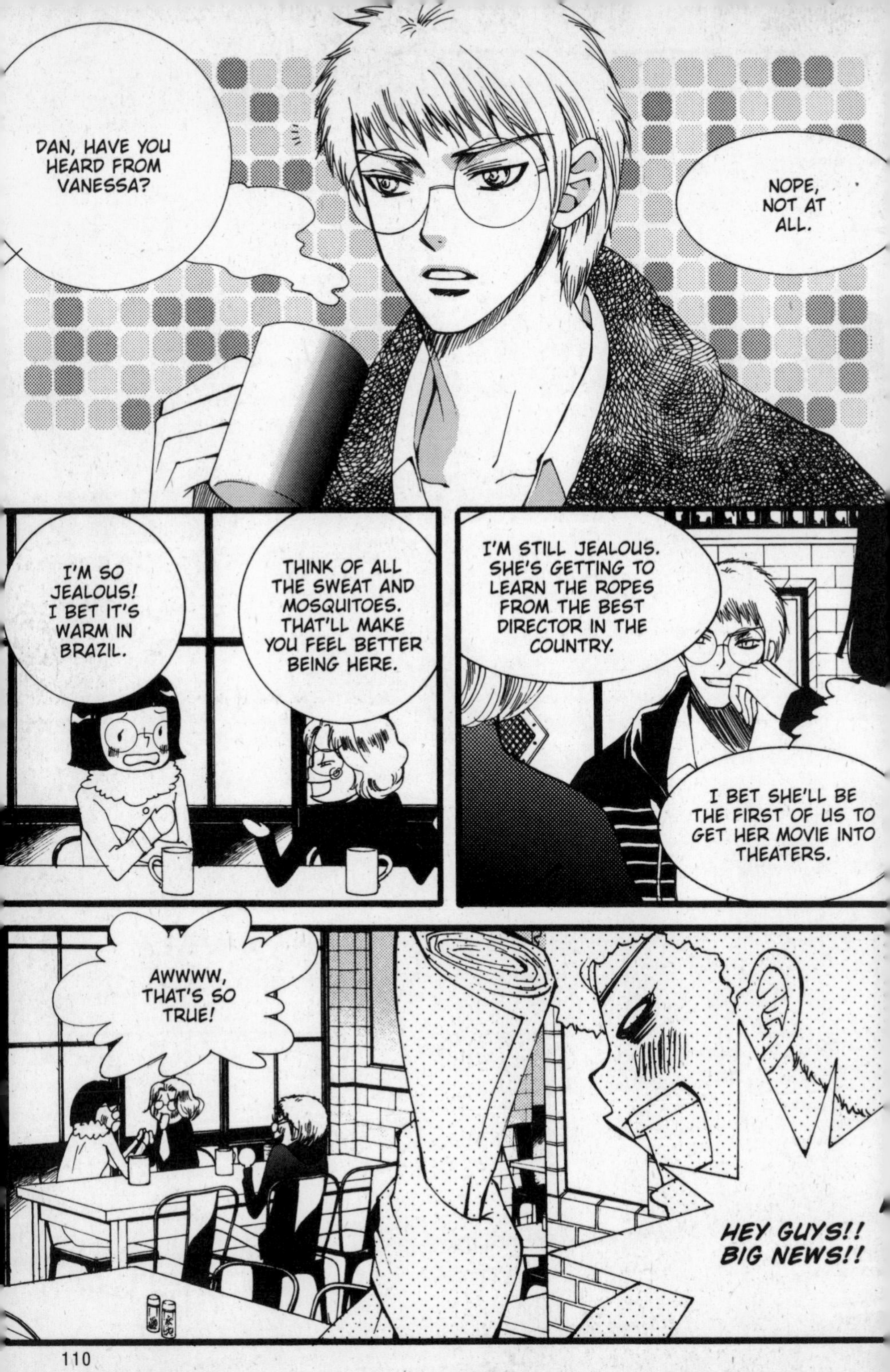
DAN, HAVE YOU HEARD FROM VANESSA?
NOPE, NOT AT ALL.
I'M SO JEALOUS! I BET IT'S WARM IN BRAZIL.
THINK OF ALL THE SWEAT AND MOSQUITOES. THAT'LL MAKE YOU FEEL BETTER BEING HERE.
I'M STILL JEALOUS. SHE'S GETTING TO LEARN THE ROPES FROM THE BEST DIRECTOR IN THE COUNTRY.
I BET SHE'LL BE THE FIRST OF US TO GET HER MOVIE INTO THEATERS.
AWWWW, THAT'S SO TRUE!
HEY GUYS!! BIG NEWS!!

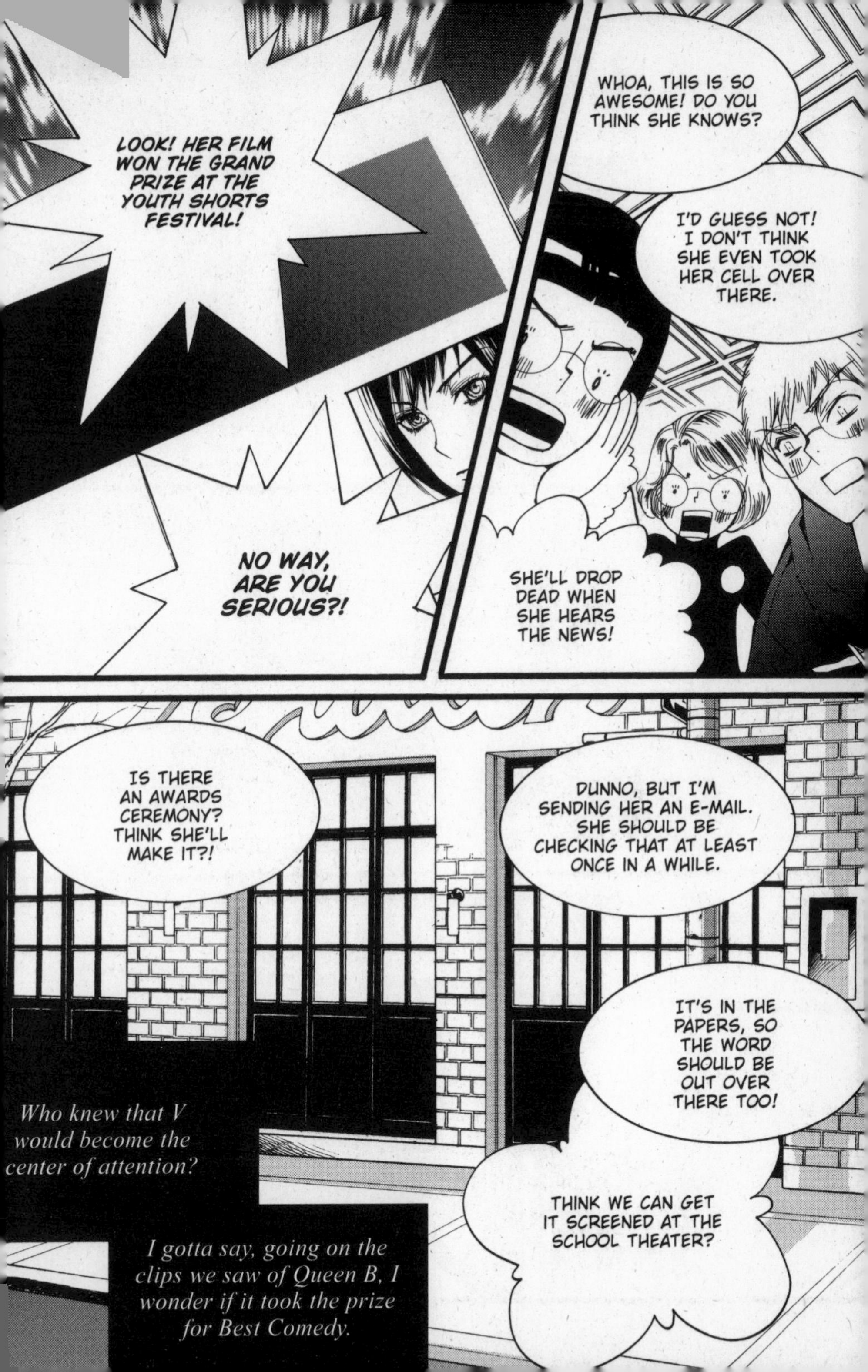
LOOK! HER FILM WON THE GRAND PRIZE AT THE YOUTH SHORTS FESTIVAL!
NO WAY, ARE YOU SERIOUS?!
WHOA, THIS IS SO AWESOME! DO YOU THINK SHE KNOWS?
I'D GUESS NOT! I DON'T THINK SHE EVEN TOOK HER CELL OVER THERE.
SHE'LL DROP DEAD WHEN SHE HEARS THE NEWS!
IS THERE AN AWARDS CEREMONY? THINK SHE'LL MAKE IT?!
DUNNO, BUT I'M SENDING HER AN E-MAIL. SHE SHOULD BE CHECKING THAT AT LEAST ONCE IN A WHILE.
IT'S IN THE PAPERS, SO THE WORD SHOULD BE OUT OVER THERE TOO!
Who knew that V would become the center of attention?
THINK WE CAN GET IT SCREENED AT THE SCHOOL THEATER?
I gotta say, going on the clips we saw of Queen B, I wonder if it took the prize for Best Comedy.

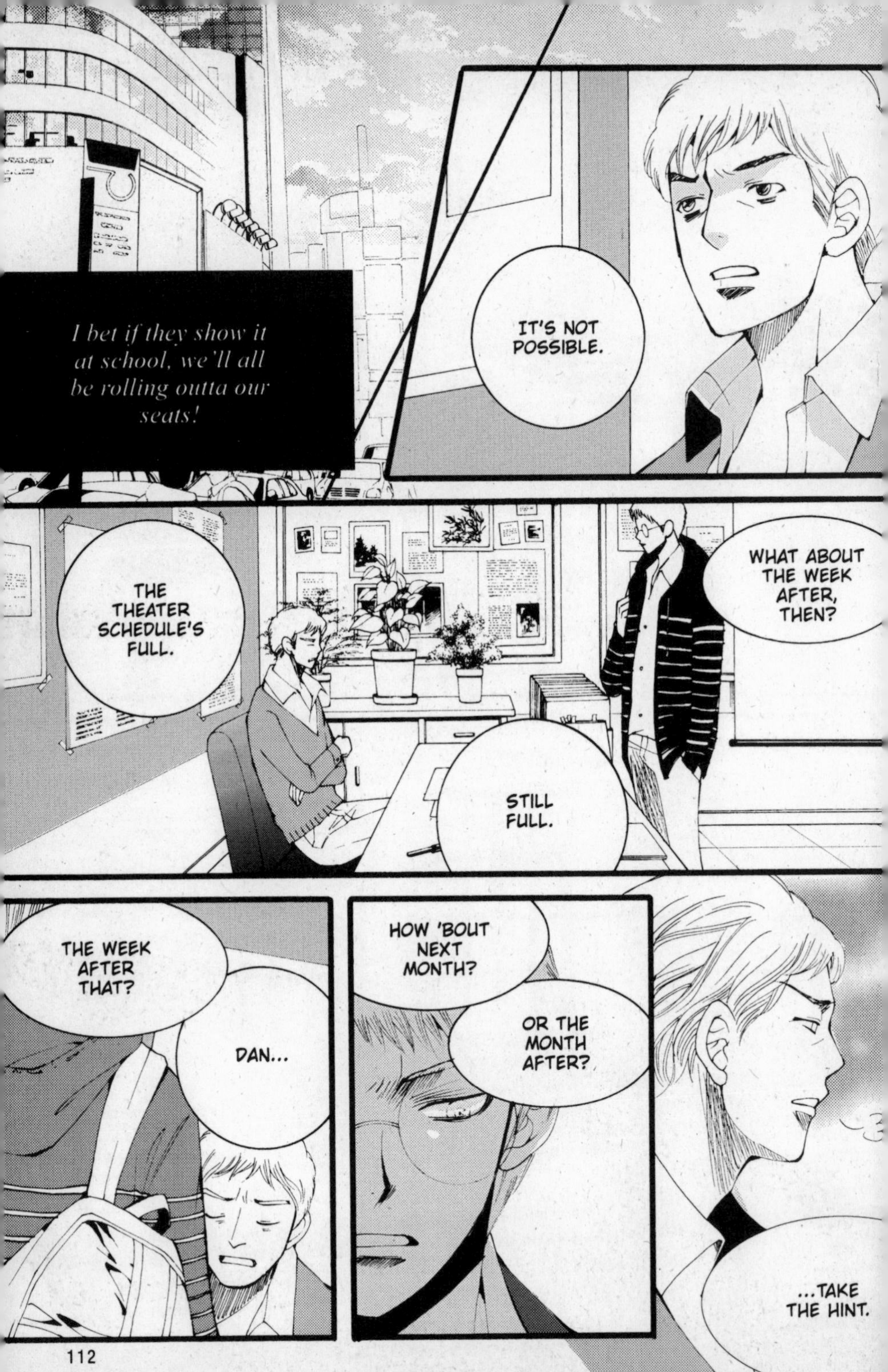
I bet if they show it at school, we'll all be rolling outta our seats!
IT'S NOT POSSIBLE.
THE THEATER SCHEDULE'S FULL.
WHAT ABOUT THE WEEK AFTER, THEN?
STILL FULL.
THE WEEK AFTER THAT?
DAN...
HOW 'BOUT NEXT MONTH?
OR THE MONTH AFTER?
...TAKE THE HINT.

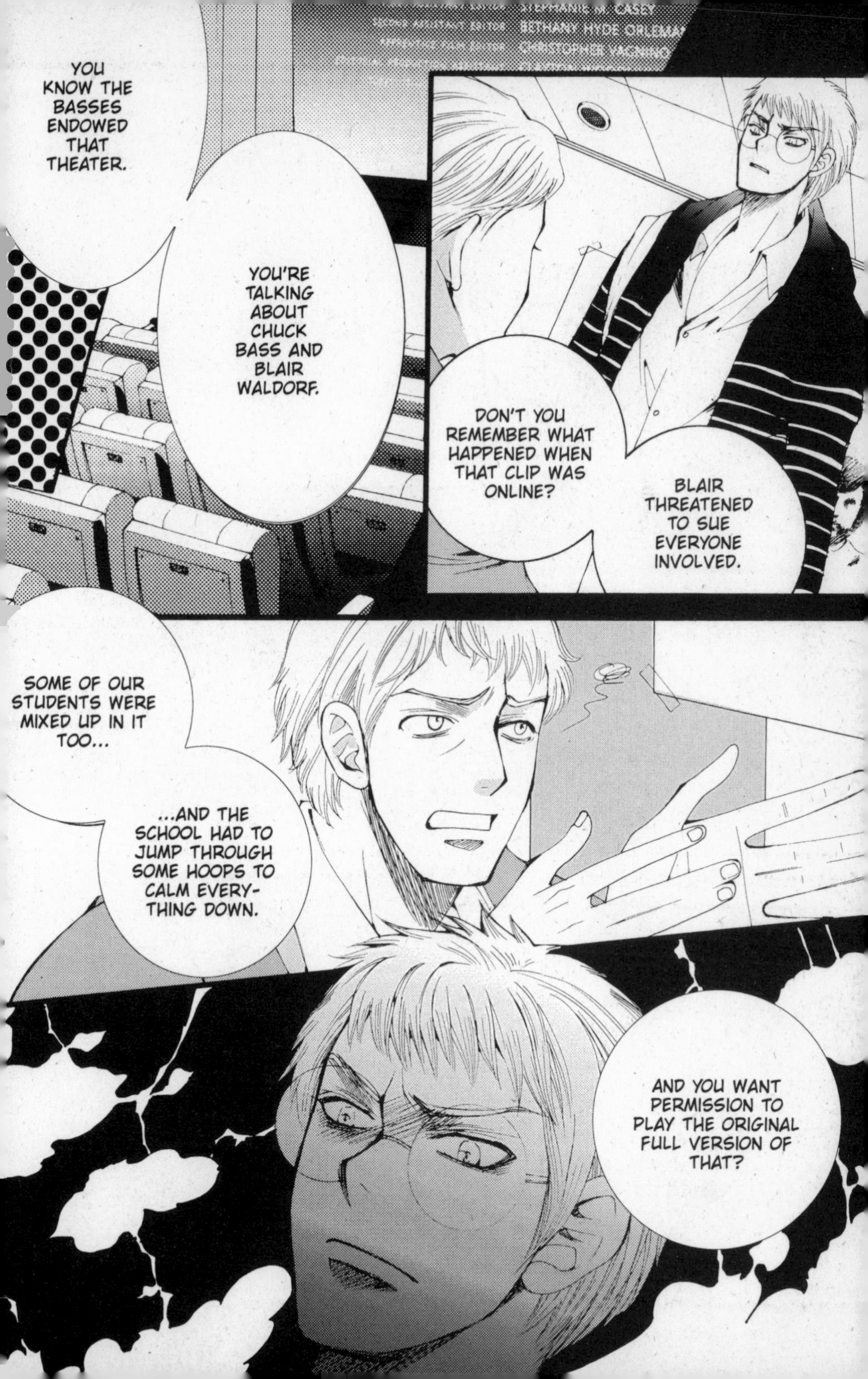
YOU KNOW THE BASSES ENDOWED THAT THEATER.
YOU'RE TALKING ABOUT CHUCK BASS AND BLAIR WALDORF.
DON'T YOU REMEMBER WHAT HAPPENED WHEN THAT CLIP WAS ONLINE?
BLAIR THREATENED TO SUE EVERYONE INVOLVED.
SOME OF OUR STUDENTS WERE MIXED UP IN IT TOO...
...AND THE SCHOOL HAD TO JUMP THROUGH SOME HOOPS TO CALM EVERY-THING DOWN.
AND YOU WANT PERMISSION TO PLAY THE ORIGINAL FULL VERSION OF THAT?

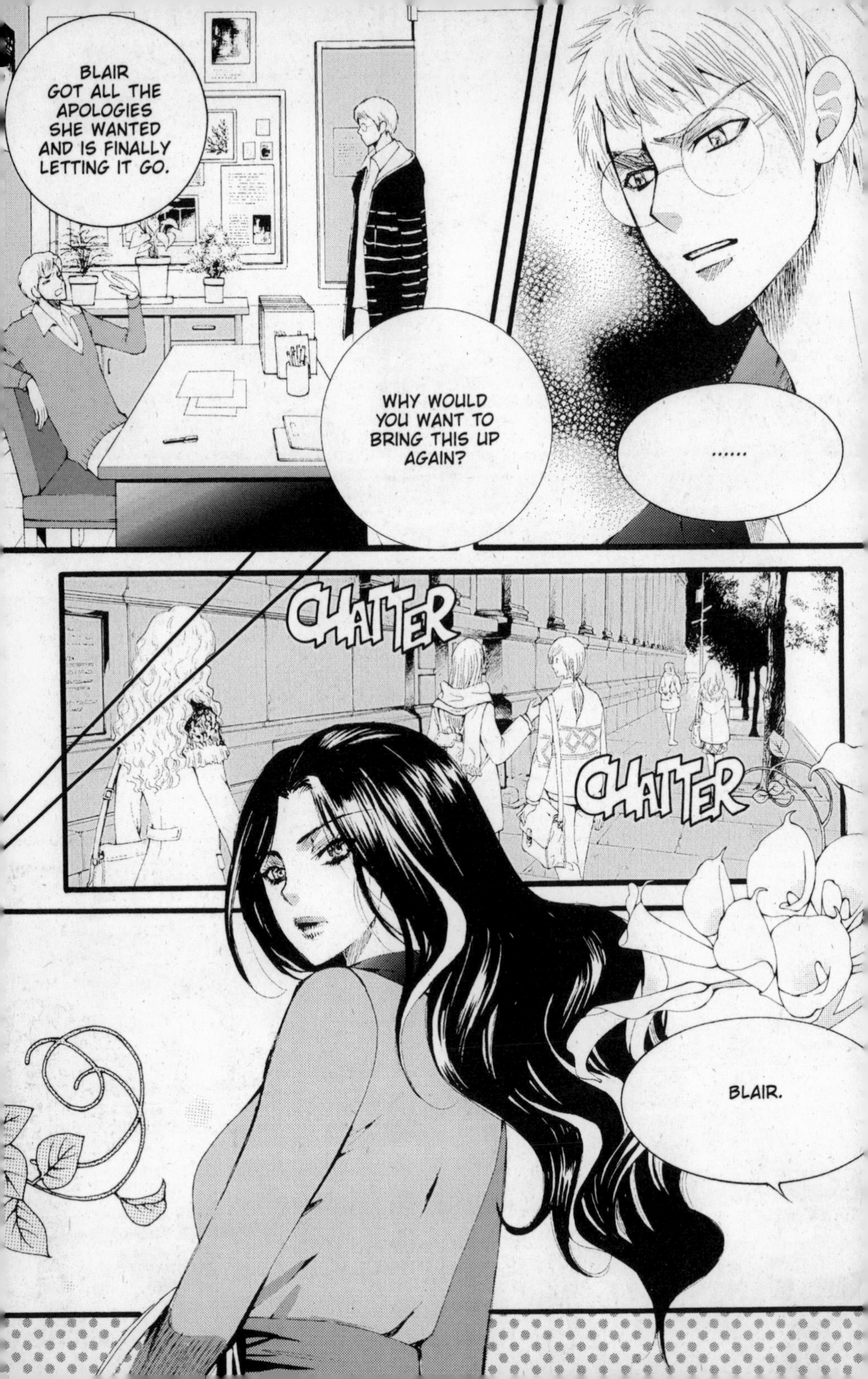
BLAIR GOT ALL THE APOLOGIES SHE WANTED AND IS FINALLY LETTING IT GO.
WHY WOULD YOU WANT TO BRING THIS UP AGAIN?
......
CHATTER
CHATTER
BLAIR.

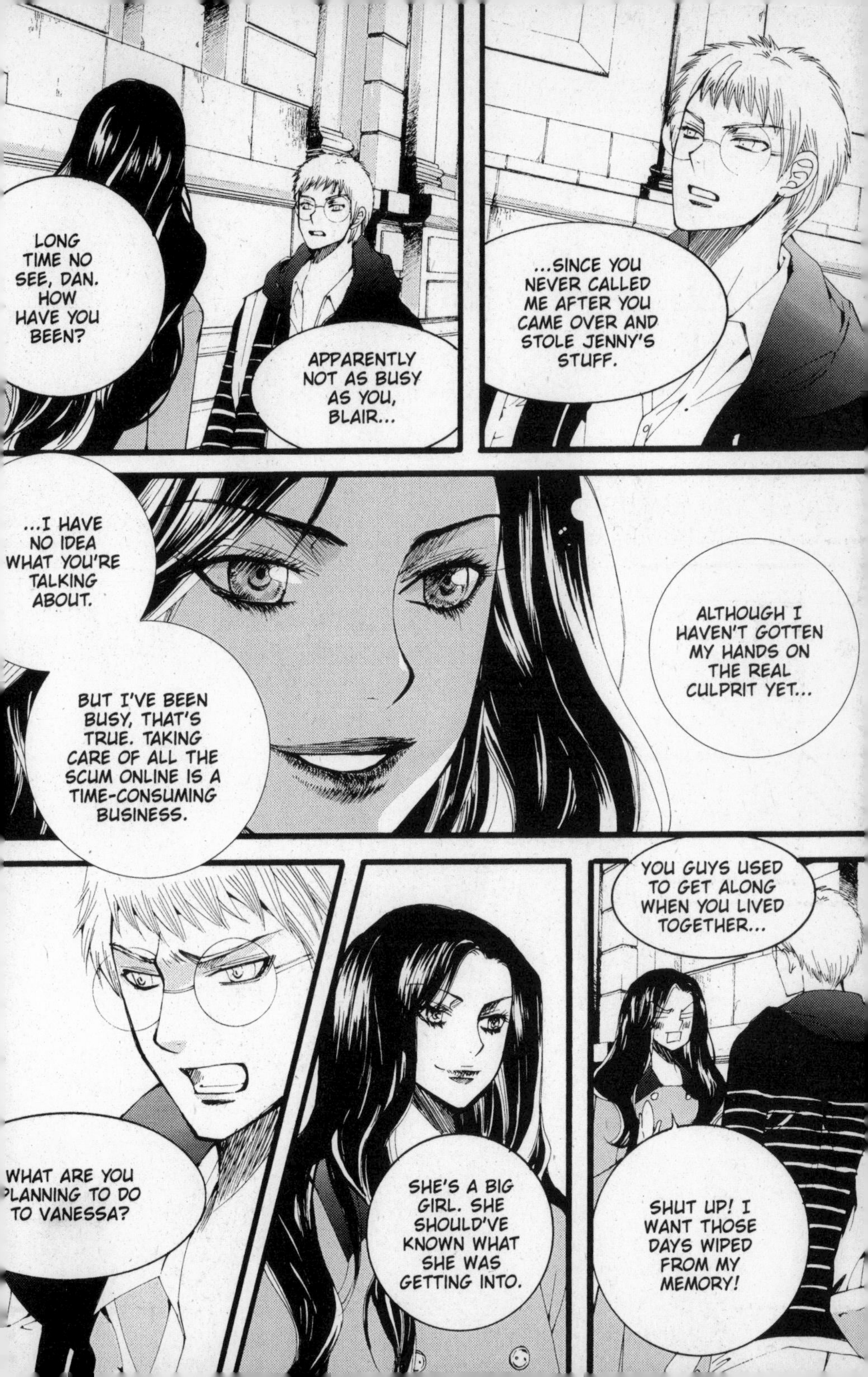
LONG TIME NO SEE, DAN. HOW HAVE YOU BEEN?
APPARENTLY NOT AS BUSY AS YOU, BLAIR...
...SINCE YOU NEVER CALLED ME AFTER YOU CAME OVER AND STOLE JENNY'S STUFF.
...I HAVE NO IDEA WHAT YOU'RE TALKING ABOUT.
BUT I'VE BEEN BUSY, THAT'S TRUE. TAKING CARE OF ALL THE SCUM ONLINE IS A TIME-CONSUMING BUSINESS.
ALTHOUGH I HAVEN'T GOTTEN MY HANDS ON THE REAL CULPRIT YET...
WHAT ARE YOU PLANNING TO DO TO VANESSA?
SHE'S A BIG GIRL. SHE SHOULD'VE KNOWN WHAT SHE WAS GETTING INTO.
YOU GUYS USED TO GET ALONG WHEN YOU LIVED TOGETHER...
SHUT UP! I WANT THOSE DAYS WIPED FROM MY MEMORY!

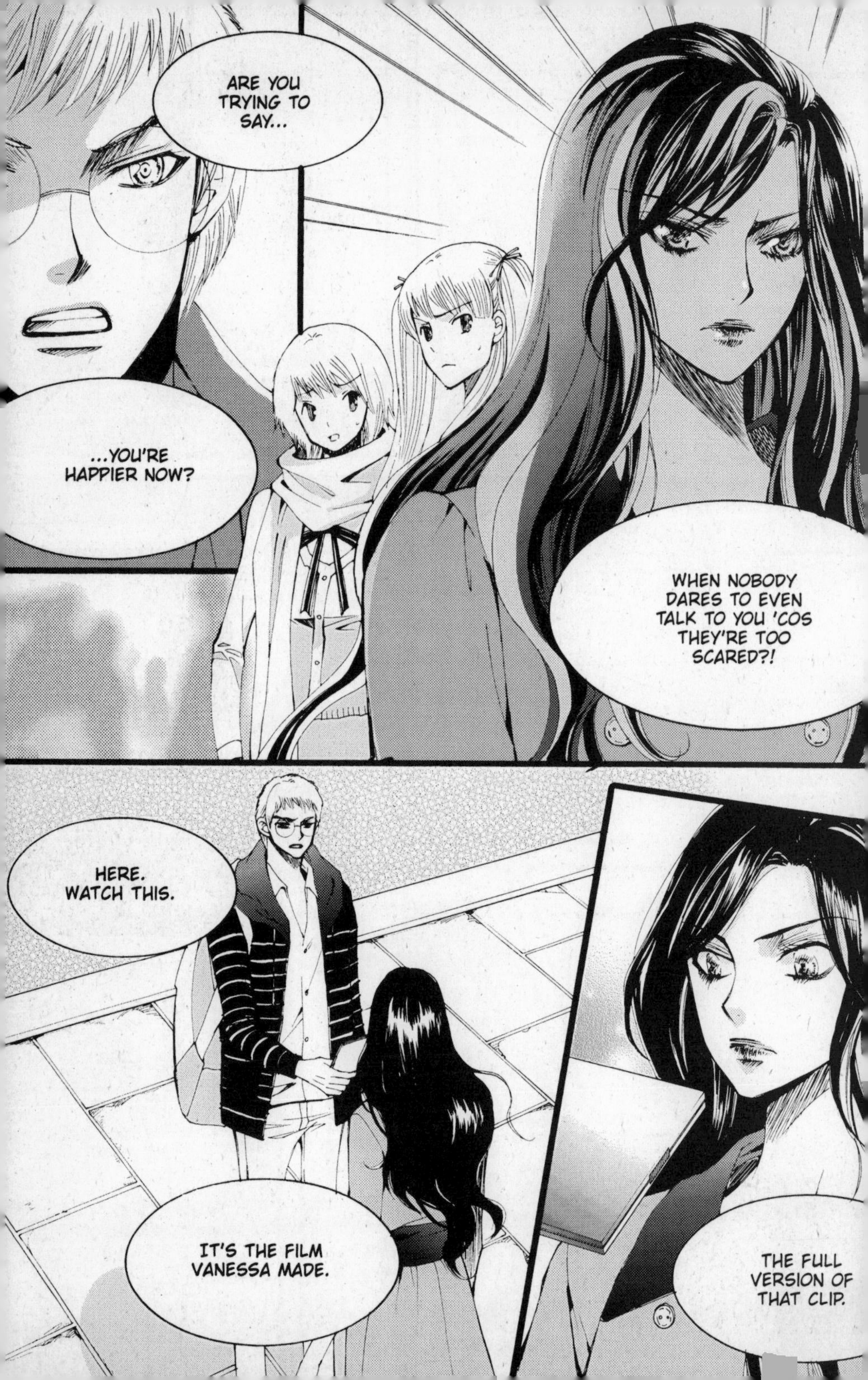
ARE YOU TRYING TO SAY...
...YOU'RE HAPPIER NOW?
WHEN NOBODY DARES TO EVEN TALK TO YOU 'COS THEY'RE TOO SCARED?!
HERE. WATCH THIS.
IT'S THE FILM VANESSA MADE.
THE FULL VERSION OF THAT CLIP.

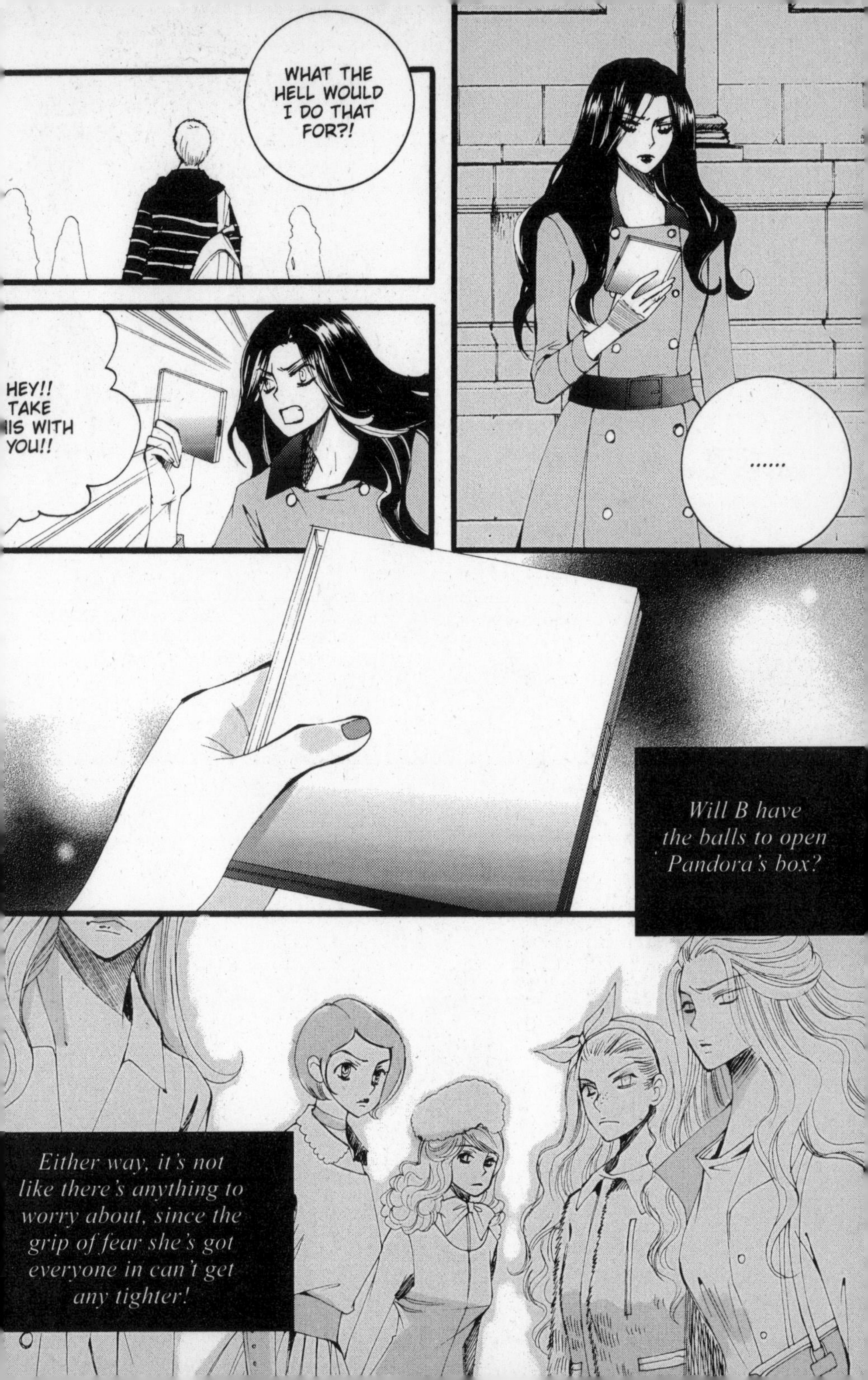

WHAT THE HELL WOULD I DO THAT FOR?!
HEY!! TAKE IIS WITH YOU!!
......
Will B have the balls to open Pandora's box?
Either way, it's not like there's anything to worry about, since the grip of fear she's got everyone in can't get any tighter!

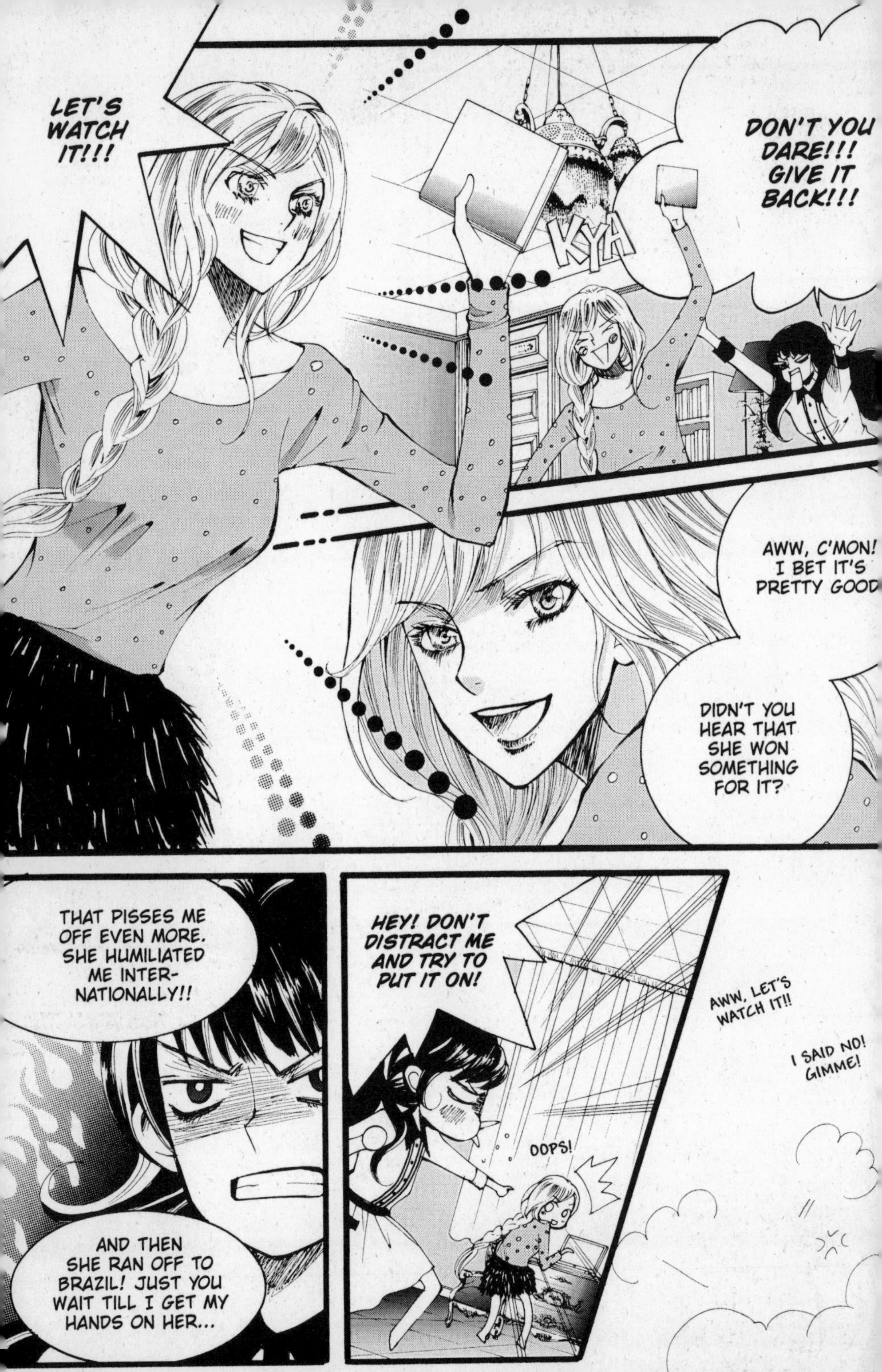
LET'S WATCH IT!!!
KYA
DON'T YOU DARE!!! GIVE IT BACK!!!
AWW, C'MON! I BET IT'S PRETTY GOOD
DIDN'T YOU HEAR THAT SHE WON SOMETHING FOR IT?
THAT PISSES ME OFF EVEN MORE. SHE HUMILIATED ME INTER-NATIONALLY!!
AND THEN SHE RAN OFF TO BRAZIL! JUST YOU WAIT TILL I GET MY HANDS ON HER...
HEY! DON'T DISTRACT ME AND TRY TO PUT IT ON!
OOPS!
AWW, LET'S WATCH IT!!
I SAID NO! GIMME!

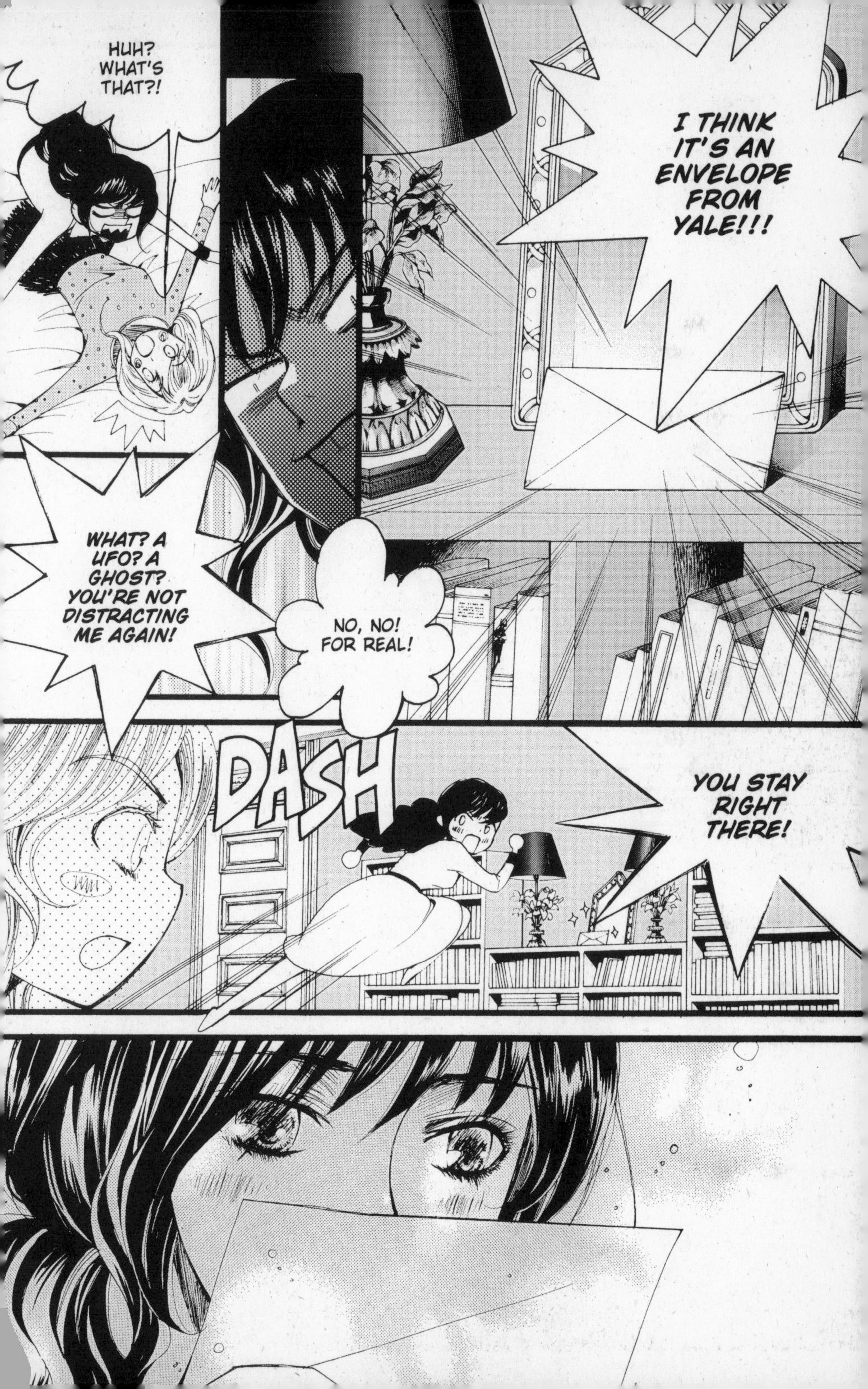
HUH? WHAT'S THAT?!
I THINK IT'S AN ENVELOPE FROM YALE!!!
WHAT? A UFO? A GHOST? YOU'RE NOT DISTRACTING ME AGAIN!
NO, NO! FOR REAL!
DASH
YOU STAY RIGHT THERE!

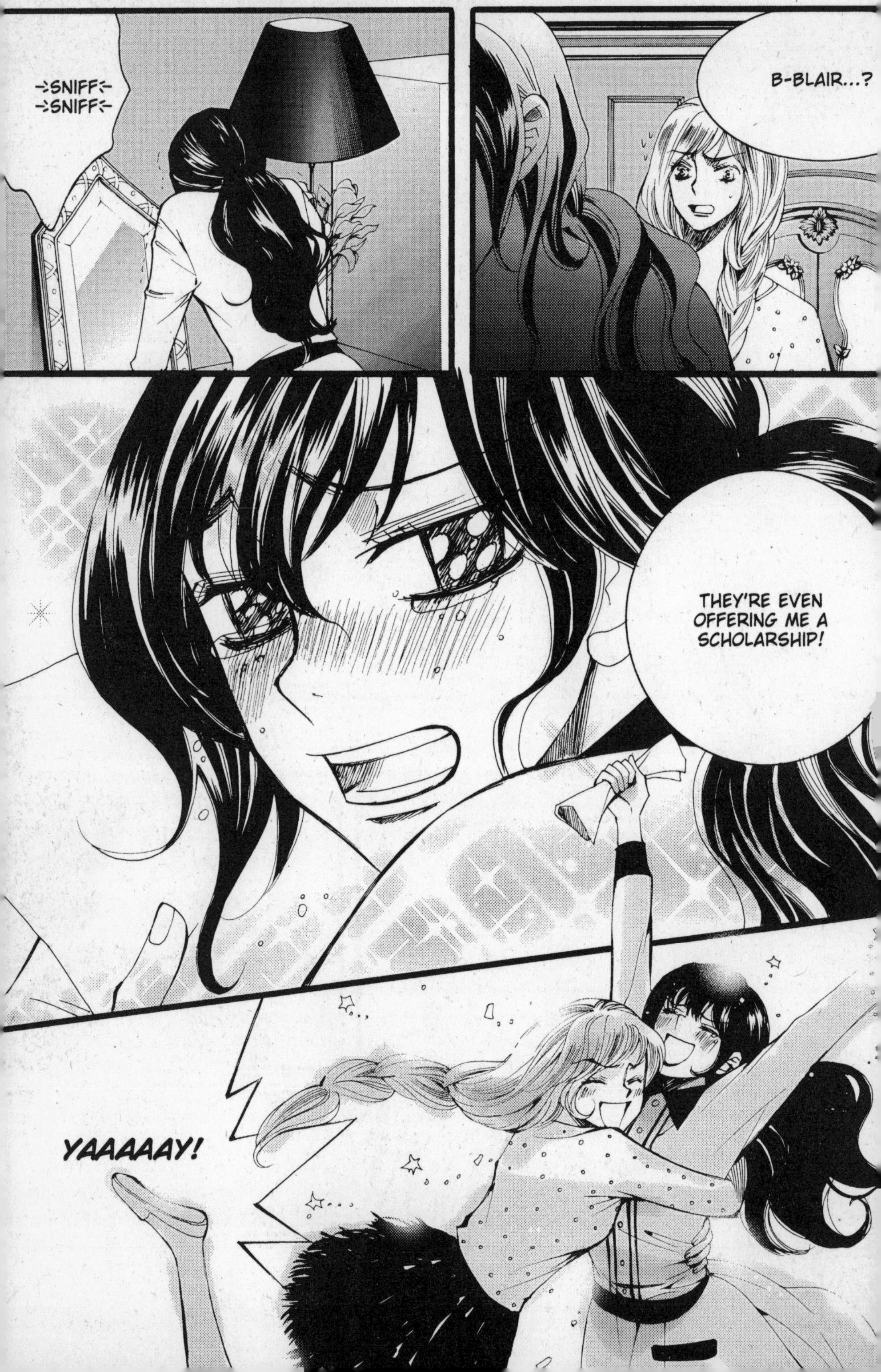
B-BLAIR...?
-SNIFF-
-SNIFF-
THEY'RE EVEN OFFERING ME A SCHOLARSHIP!
YAAAAAY!

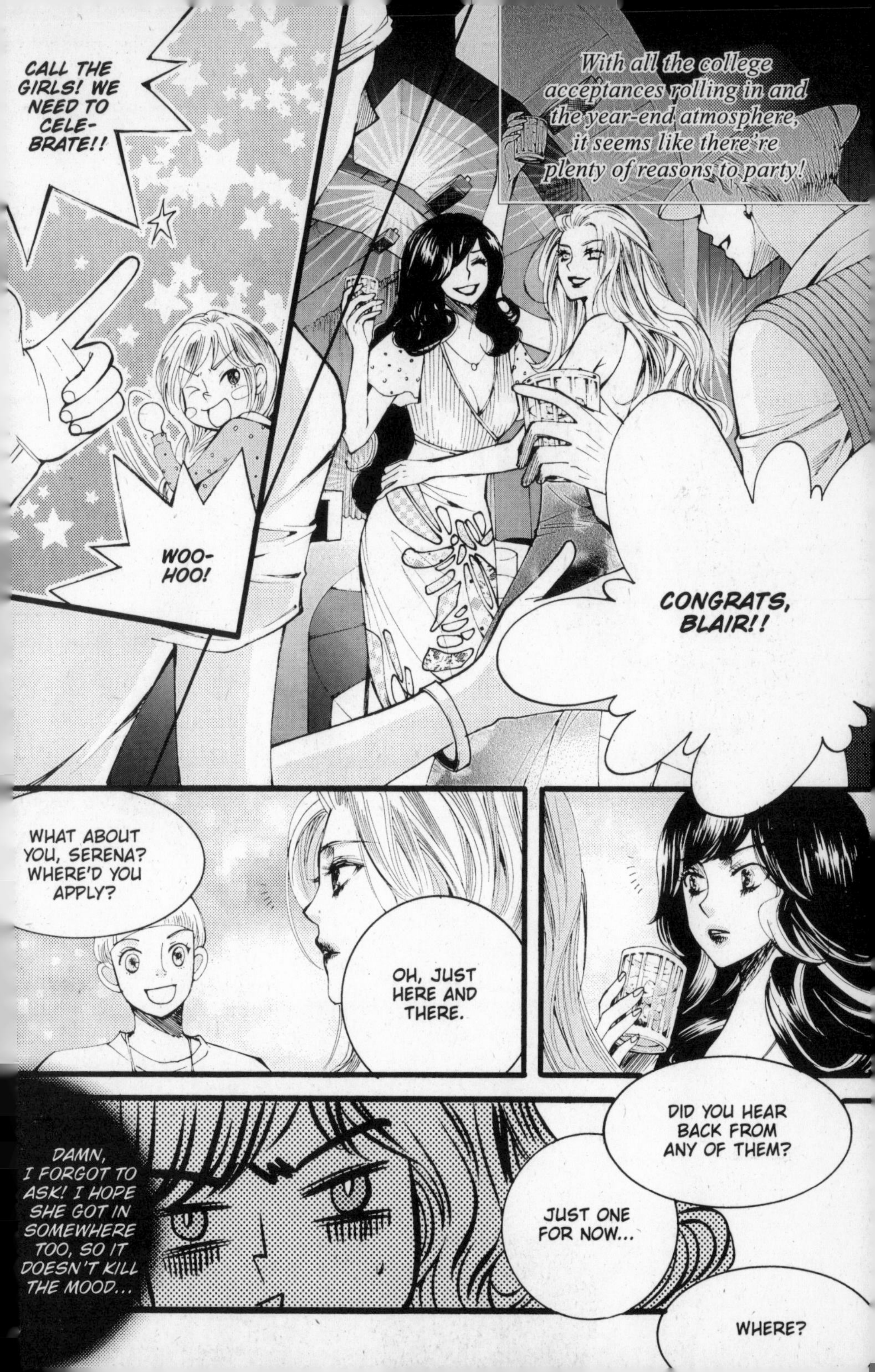

With all the college acceptances rolling in and the year-end atmosphere, it seems like there're plenty of reasons to party!
CALL THE GIRLS! WE NEED TO CELE-BRATE!!
WOO-HOO!
CONGRATS, BLAIR!!
WHAT ABOUT YOU, SERENA? WHERE'D YOU APPLY?
OH, JUST HERE AND THERE.
DID YOU HEAR BACK FROM ANY OF THEM?
JUST ONE FOR NOW...
WHERE?
DAMN, I FORGOT TO ASK! I HOPE SHE GOT IN SOMEWHERE TOO, SO IT DOESN'T KILL THE MOOD...

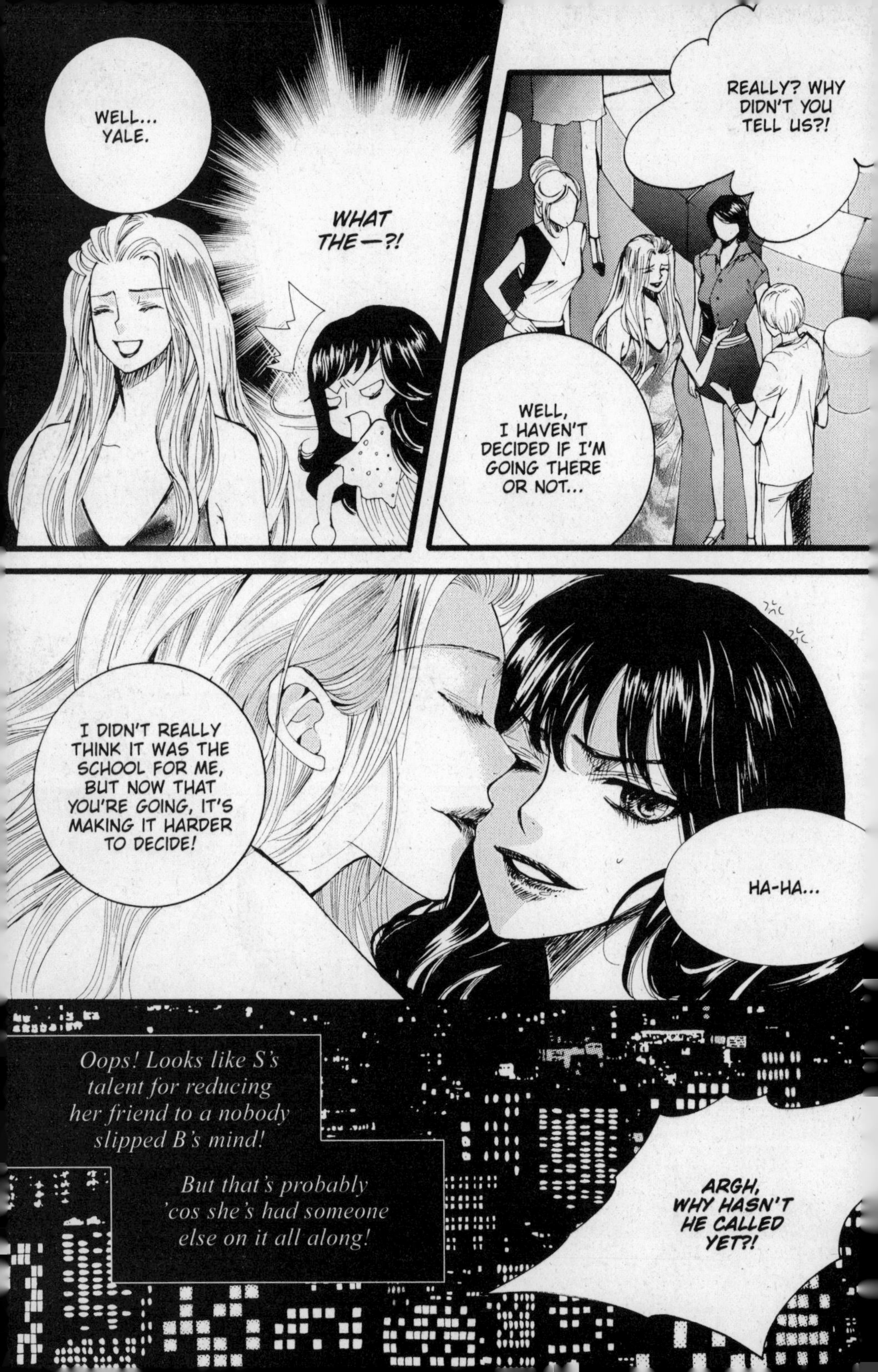
WELL... YALE.
WHAT THE—?!
REALLY? WHY DIDN'T YOU TELL US?!
WELL, I HAVEN'T DECIDED IF I'M GOING THERE OR NOT...
I DIDN'T REALLY THINK IT WAS THE SCHOOL FOR ME, BUT NOW THAT YOU'RE GOING, IT'S MAKING IT HARDER TO DECIDE!
HA-HA...
Oops! Looks like S's talent for reducing her friend to a nobody slipped B's mind!
But that's probably 'cos she's had someone else on it all along!
ARGH, WHY HASN'T HE CALLED YET?!

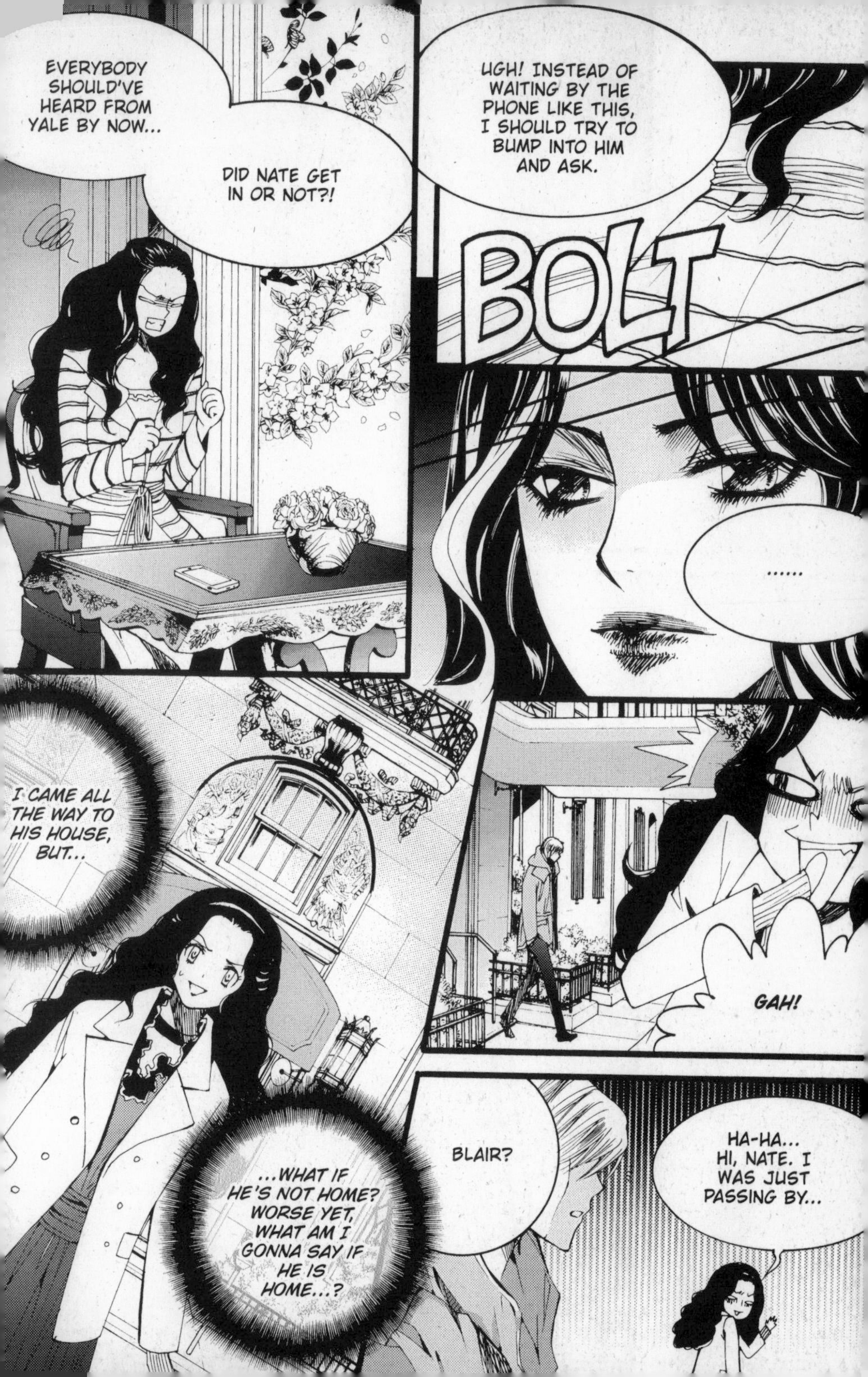
EVERYBODY SHOULD'VE HEARD FROM YALE BY NOW...
DID NATE GET IN OR NOT?!
UGH! INSTEAD OF WAITING BY THE PHONE LIKE THIS, I SHOULD TRY TO BUMP INTO HIM AND ASK.
BOLT
......
I CAME ALL THE WAY TO HIS HOUSE, BUT...
...WHAT IF HE'S NOT HOME? WORSE YET, WHAT AM I GONNA SAY IF HE IS HOME...?
GAH!
BLAIR?
HA-HA... HI, NATE. I WAS JUST PASSING BY...

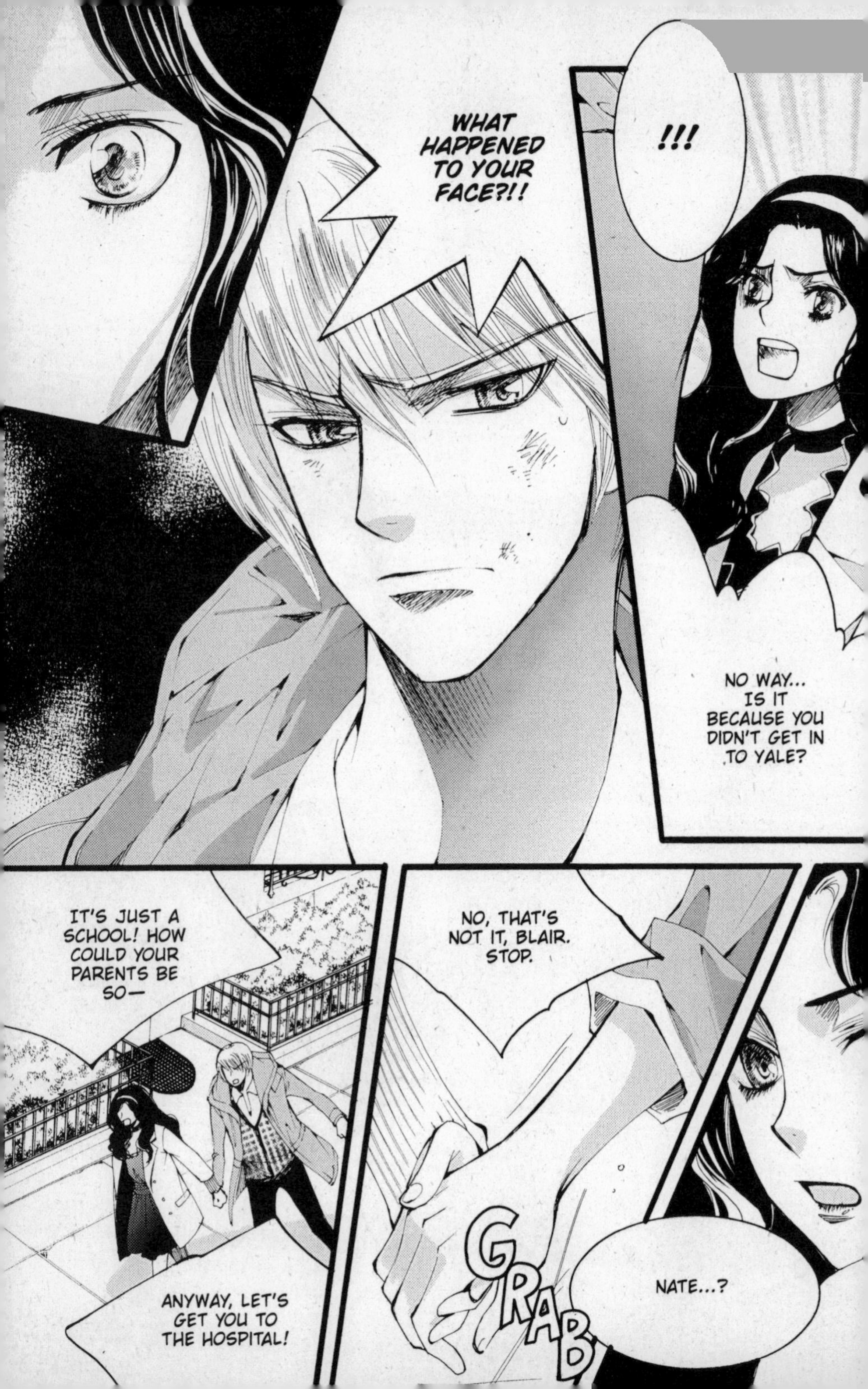
WHAT HAPPENED TO YOUR FACE?!!
!!!
NO WAY... IS IT BECAUSE YOU DIDN'T GET IN TO YALE?
IT'S JUST A SCHOOL! HOW COULD YOUR PARENTS BE SO—
ANYWAY, LET'S GET YOU TO THE HOSPITAL!
NO, THAT'S NOT IT, BLAIR. STOP.
GRAB
NATE...?

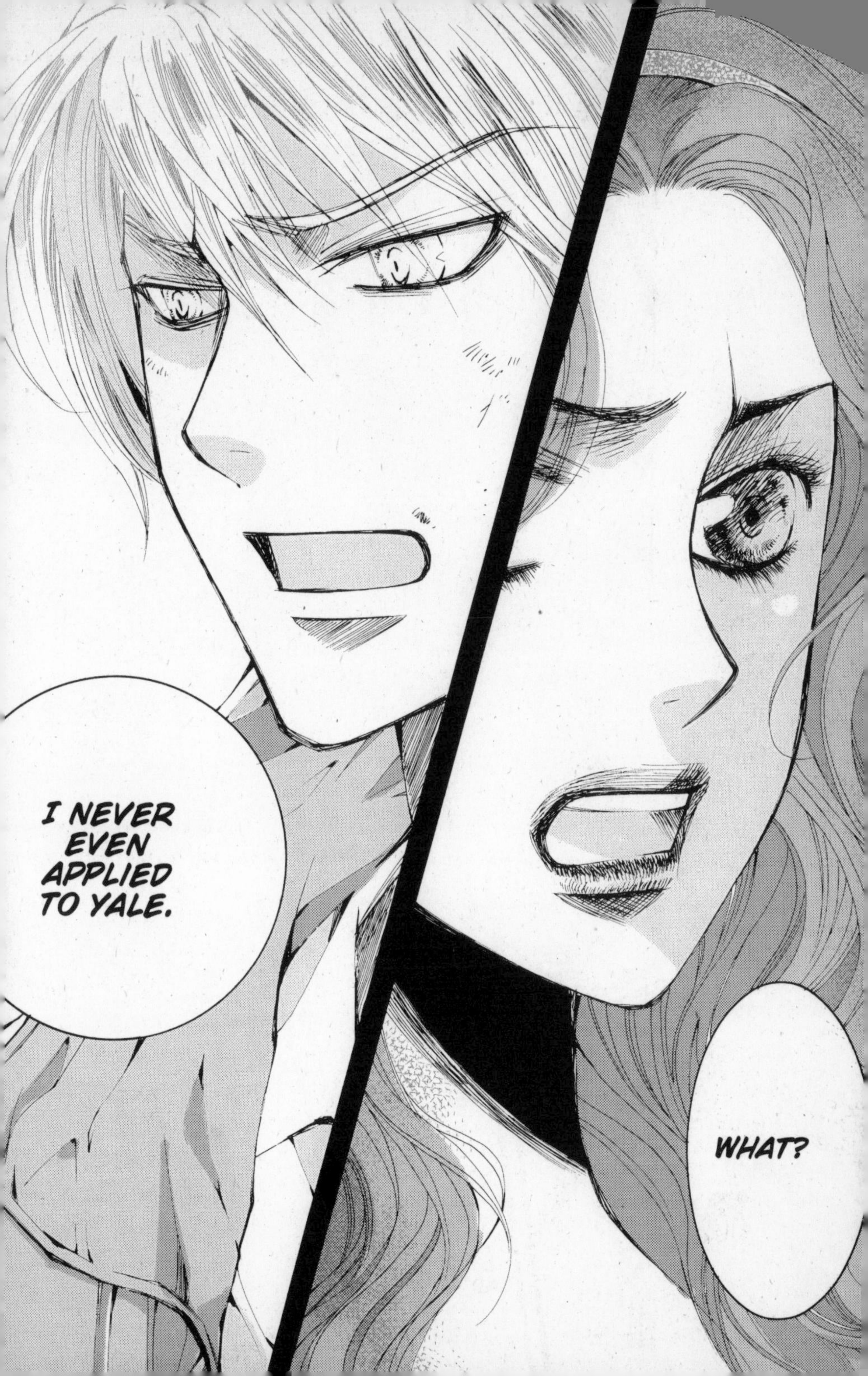
I NEVER EVEN APPLIED TO YALE.
WHAT?

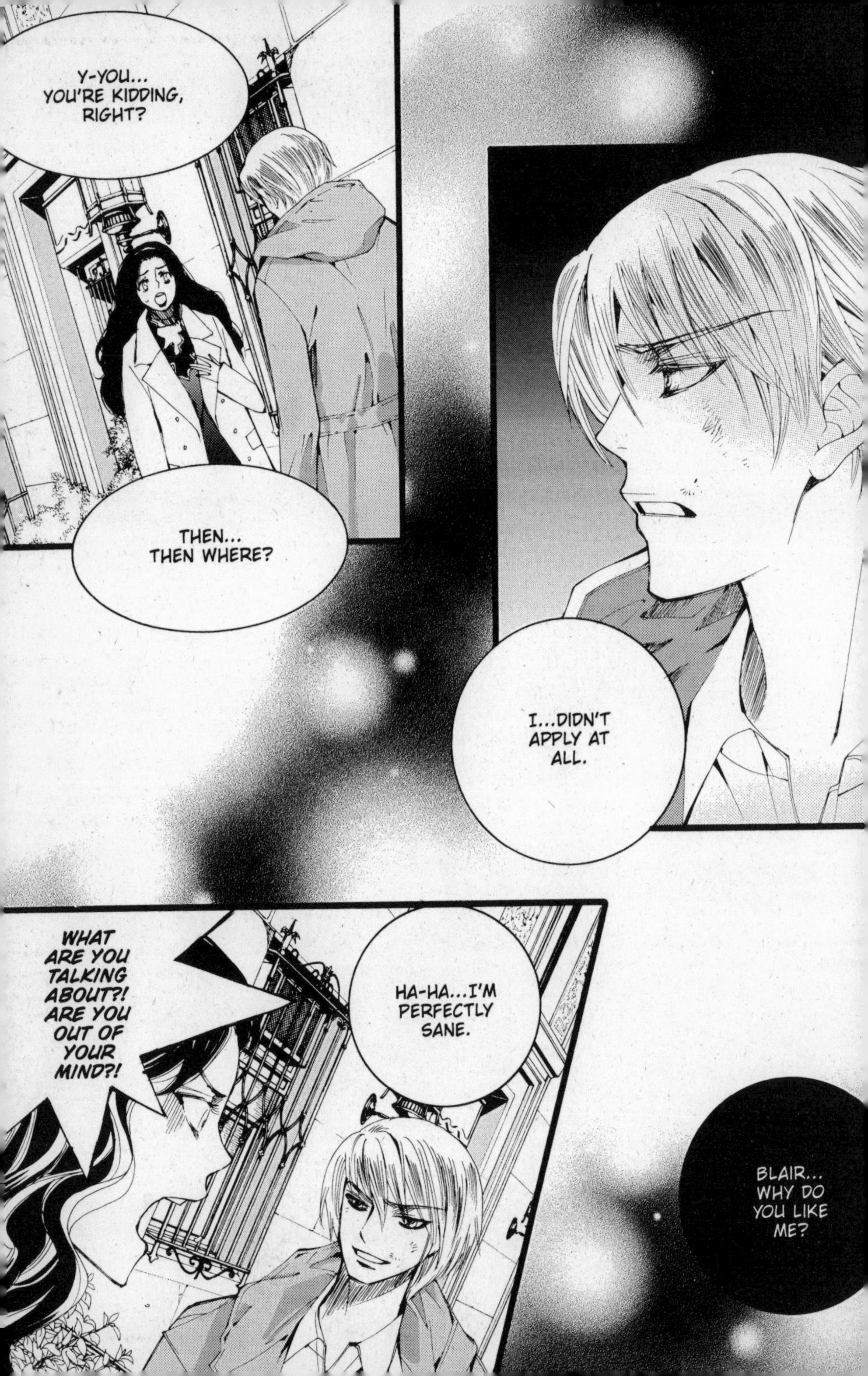
Y-YOU... YOU'RE KIDDING, RIGHT?
THEN... THEN WHERE?
I...DIDN'T APPLY AT ALL.
WHAT ARE YOU TALKING ABOUT?! ARE YOU OUT OF YOUR MIND?!
HA-HA...I'M PERFECTLY SANE.
BLAIR... WHY DO YOU LIKE ME?

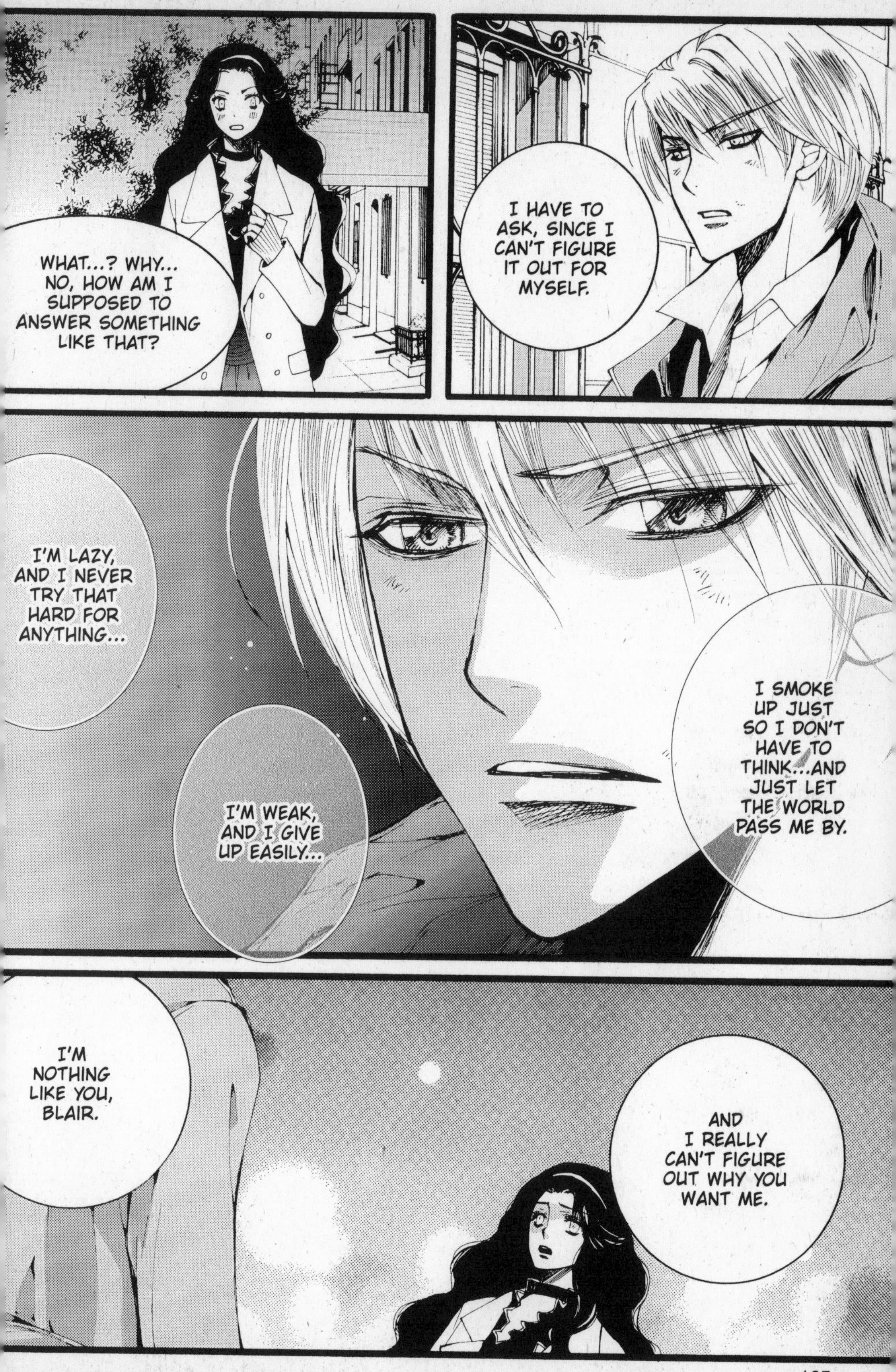
WHAT...? WHY... NO, HOW AM I SUPPOSED TO ANSWER SOMETHING LIKE THAT?
I HAVE TO ASK, SINCE I CAN'T FIGURE IT OUT FOR MYSELF.
I'M LAZY, AND I NEVER TRY THAT HARD FOR ANYTHING...
I'M WEAK, AND I GIVE UP EASILY...
I SMOKE UP JUST SO I DON'T HAVE TO THINK...AND JUST LET THE WORLD PASS ME BY.
I'M NOTHING LIKE YOU, BLAIR.
AND I REALLY CAN'T FIGURE OUT WHY YOU WANT ME.

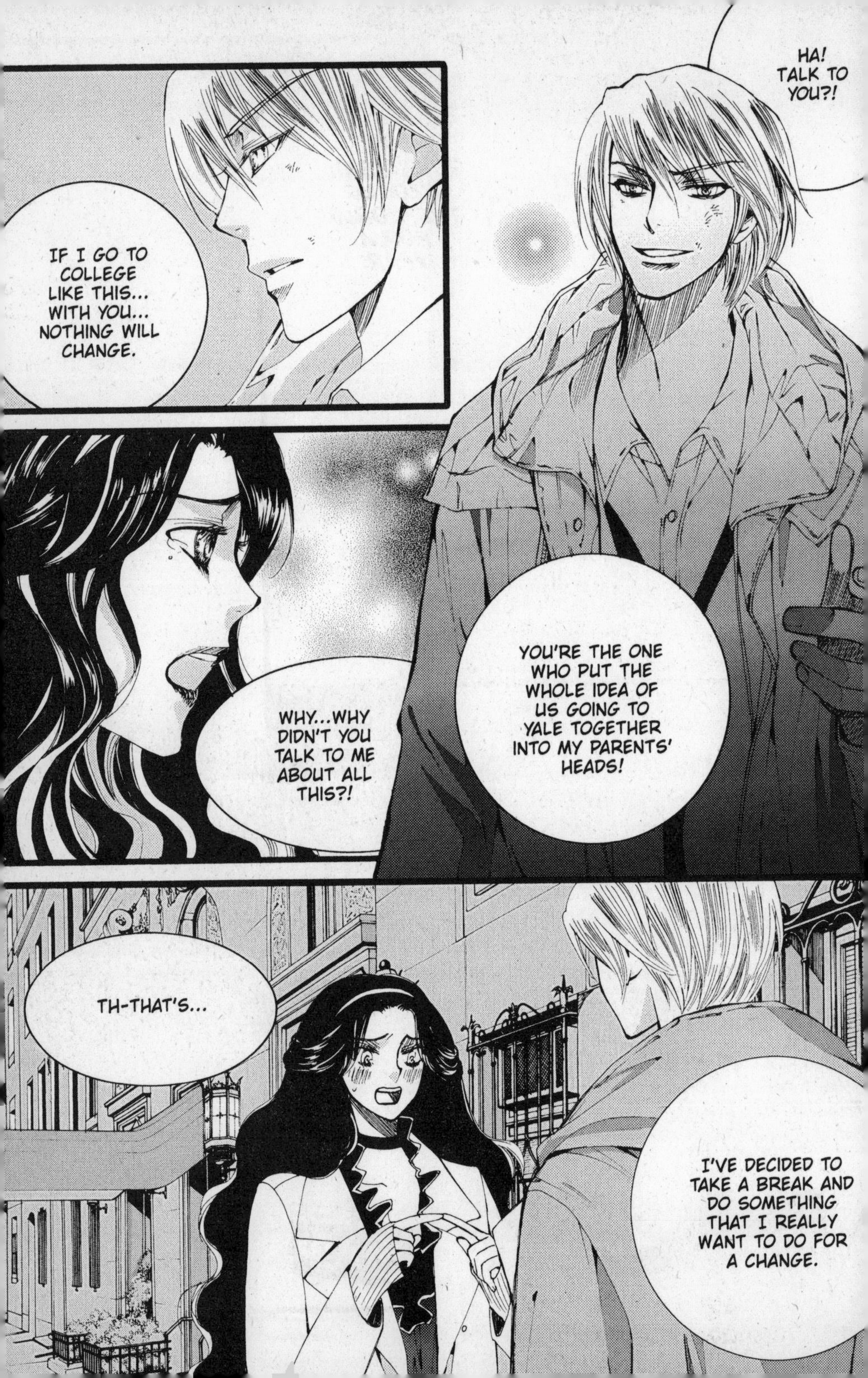
IF I GO TO COLLEGE LIKE THIS... WITH YOU... NOTHING WILL CHANGE.
WHY...WHY DIDN'T YOU TALK TO ME ABOUT ALL THIS?!
HA! TALK TO YOU?!
YOU'RE THE ONE WHO PUT THE WHOLE IDEA OF US GOING TO YALE TOGETHER INTO MY PARENTS' HEADS!
TH-THAT'S...
I'VE DECIDED TO TAKE A BREAK AND DO SOMETHING THAT I REALLY WANT TO DO FOR A CHANGE.

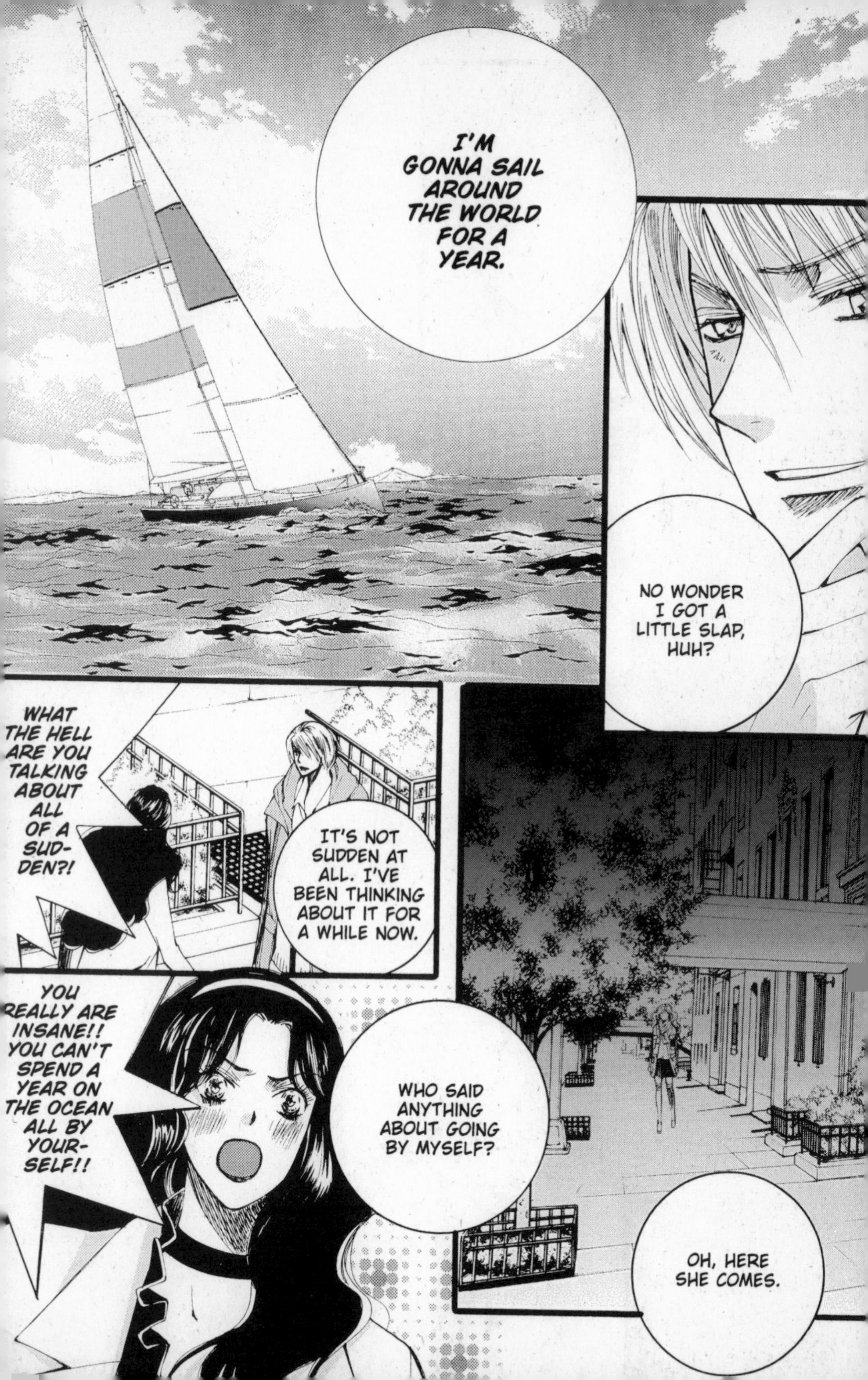
I'M GONNA SAIL AROUND THE WORLD FOR A YEAR.
NO WONDER I GOT A LITTLE SLAP, HUH?
WHAT THE HELL ARE YOU TALKING ABOUT ALL OF A SUD-DEN?!
IT'S NOT SUDDEN AT ALL. I'VE BEEN THINKING ABOUT IT FOR A WHILE NOW.
YOU REALLY ARE INSANE!! YOU CAN'T SPEND A YEAR ON THE OCEAN ALL BY YOUR-SELF!!
WHO SAID ANYTHING ABOUT GOING BY MYSELF?
OH, HERE SHE COMES.

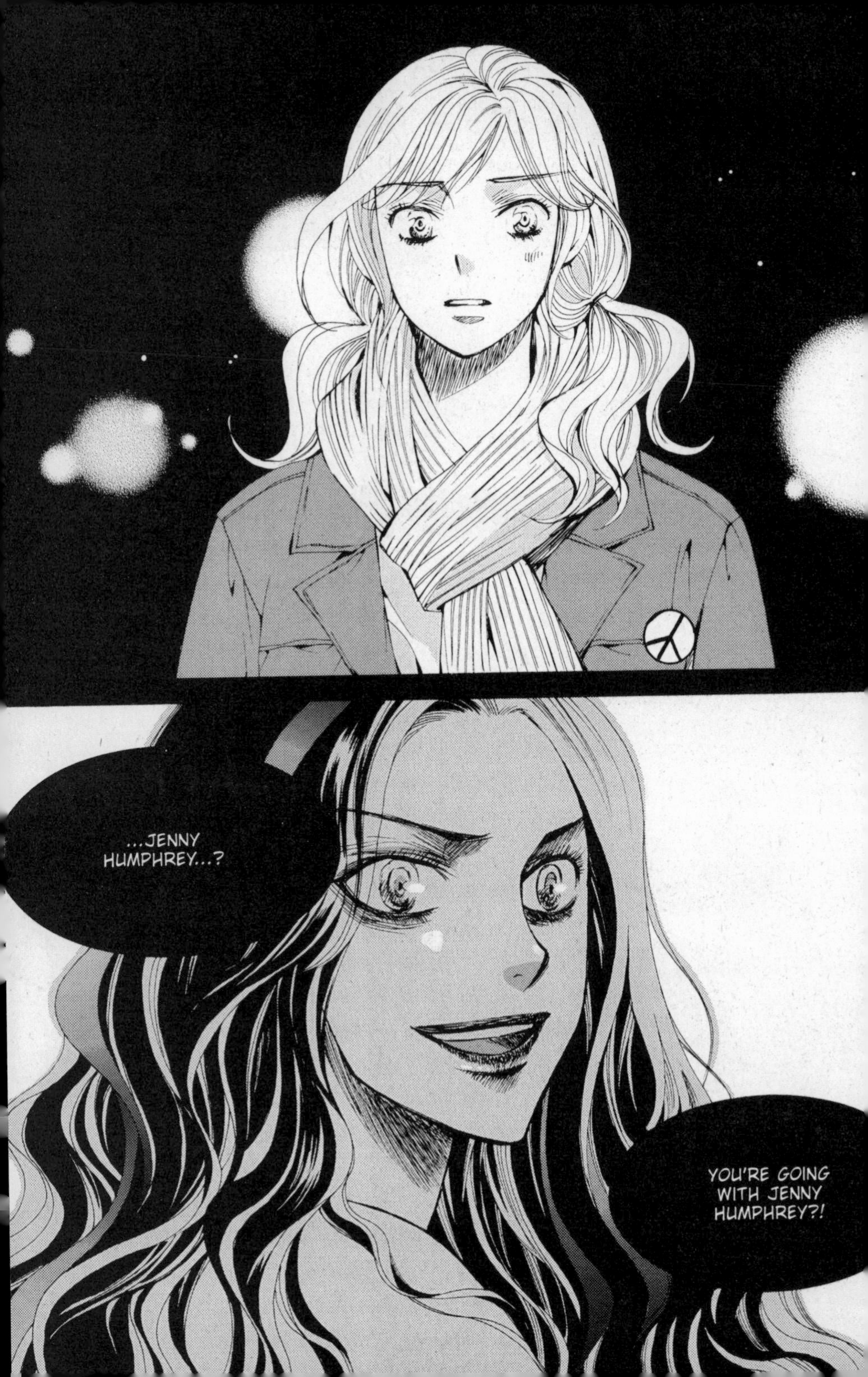
...JENNY HUMPHREY...?
YOU'RE GOING WITH JENNY HUMPHREY?!

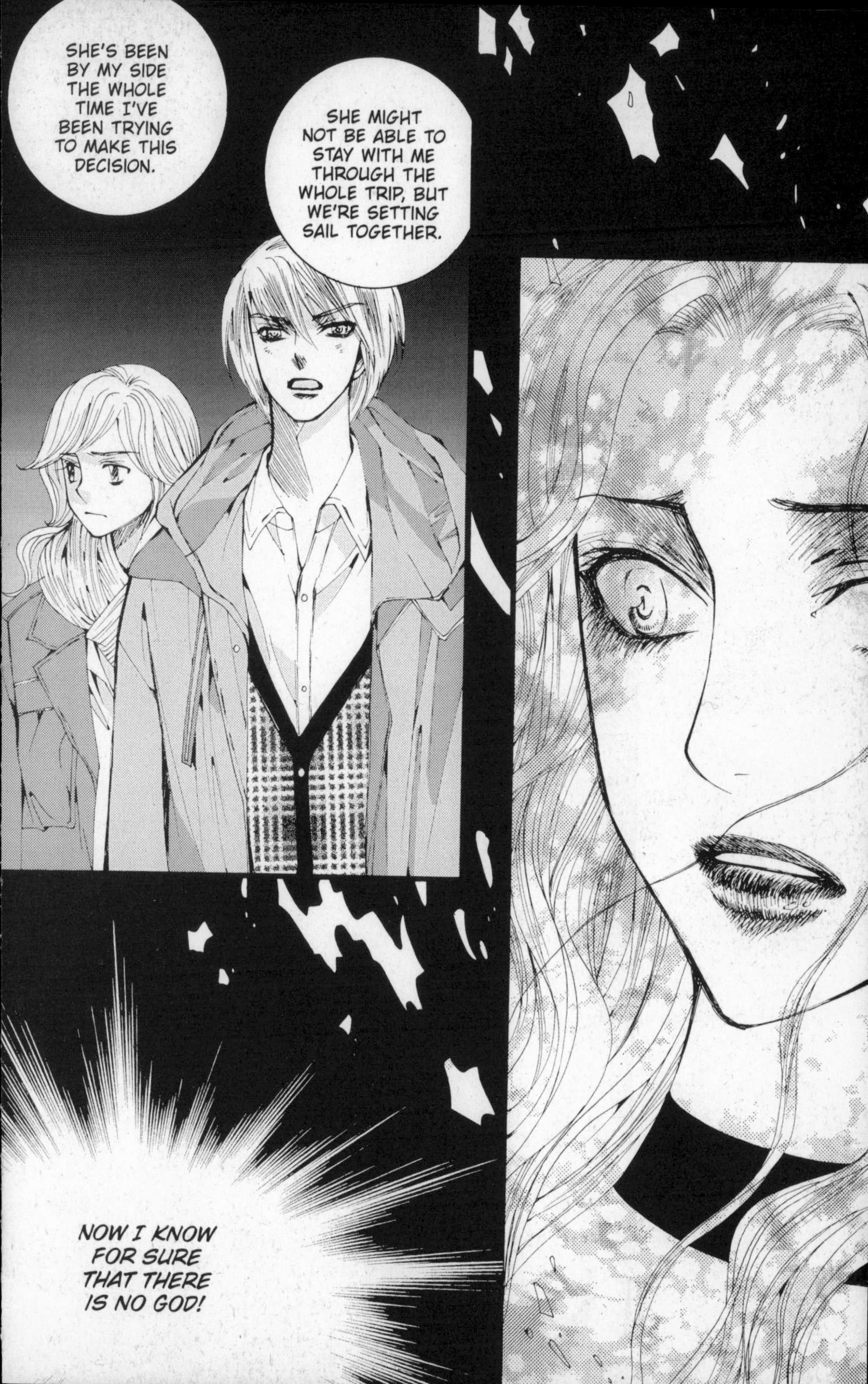
SHE'S BEEN BY MY SIDE THE WHOLE TIME I'VE BEEN TRYING TO MAKE THIS DECISION.
SHE MIGHT NOT BE ABLE TO STAY WITH ME THROUGH THE WHOLE TRIP, BUT WE'RE SETTING SAIL TOGETHER.
NOW I KNOW FOR SURE THAT THERE IS NO GOD!

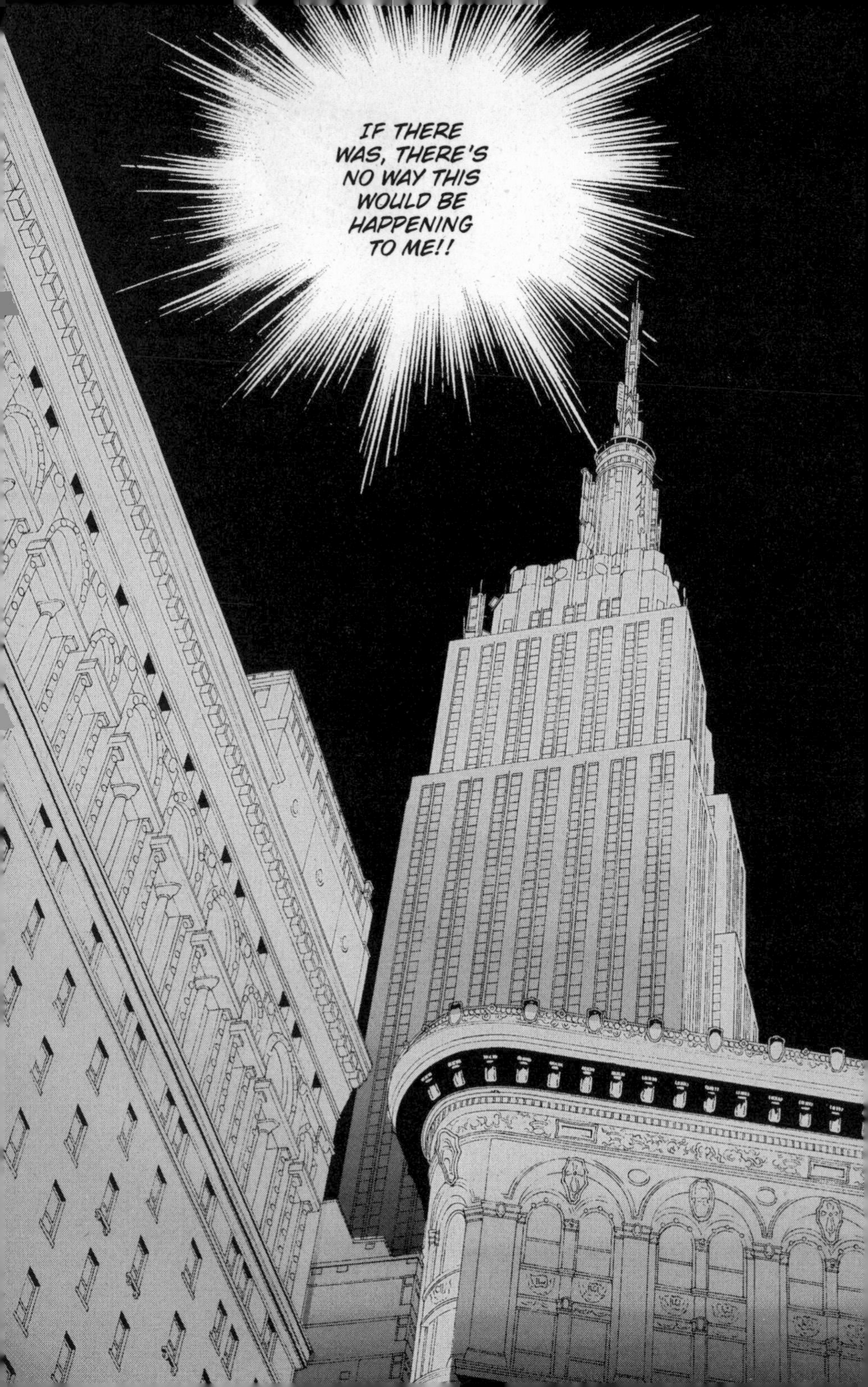
IF THERE WAS, THERE'S NO WAY THIS WOULD BE HAPPENING TO ME!!

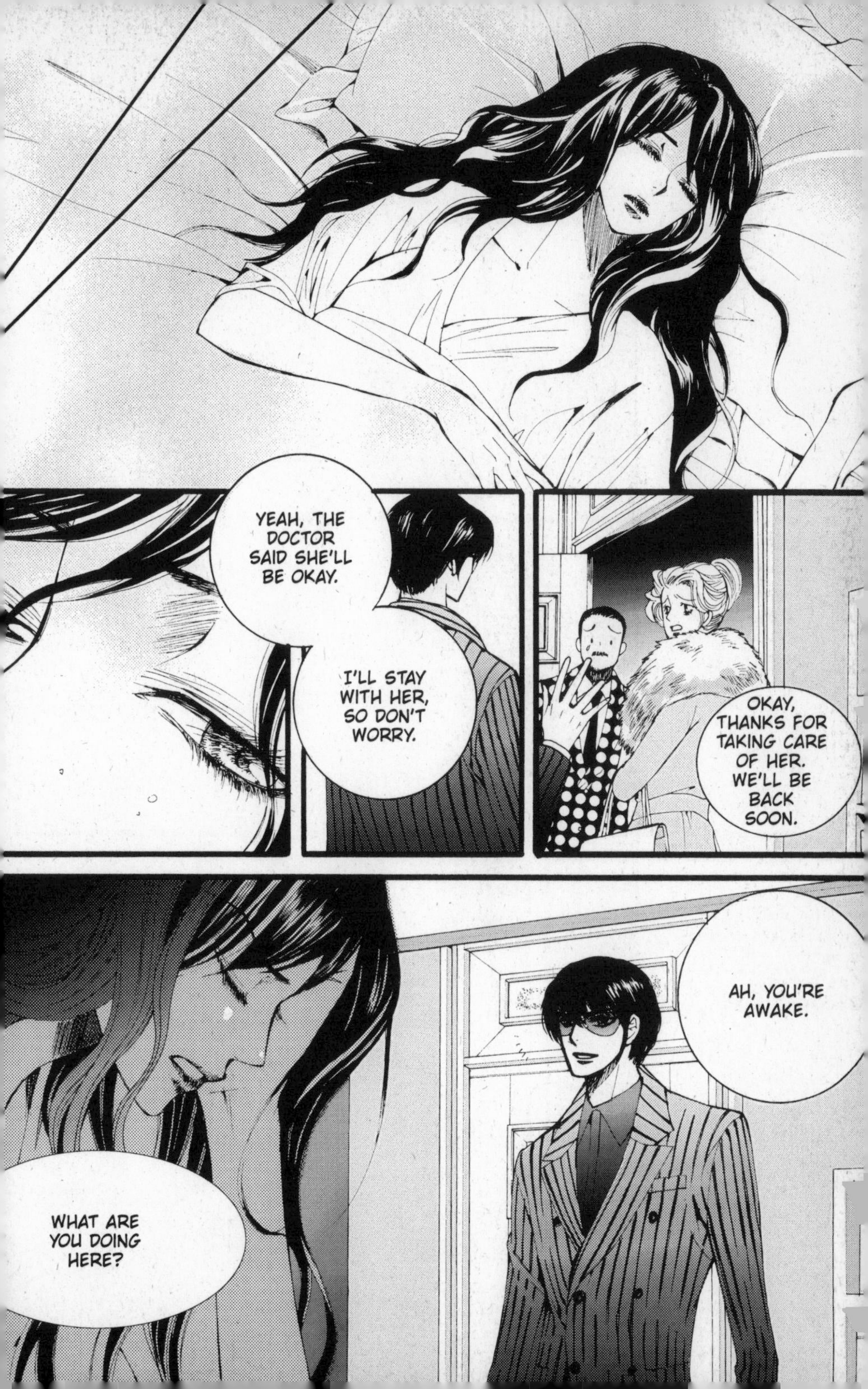
YEAH, THE DOCTOR SAID SHE'LL BE OKAY.
I'LL STAY WITH HER, SO DON'T WORRY.
OKAY, THANKS FOR TAKING CARE OF HER. WE'LL BE BACK SOON.
WHAT ARE YOU DOING HERE?
AH, YOU'RE AWAKE.

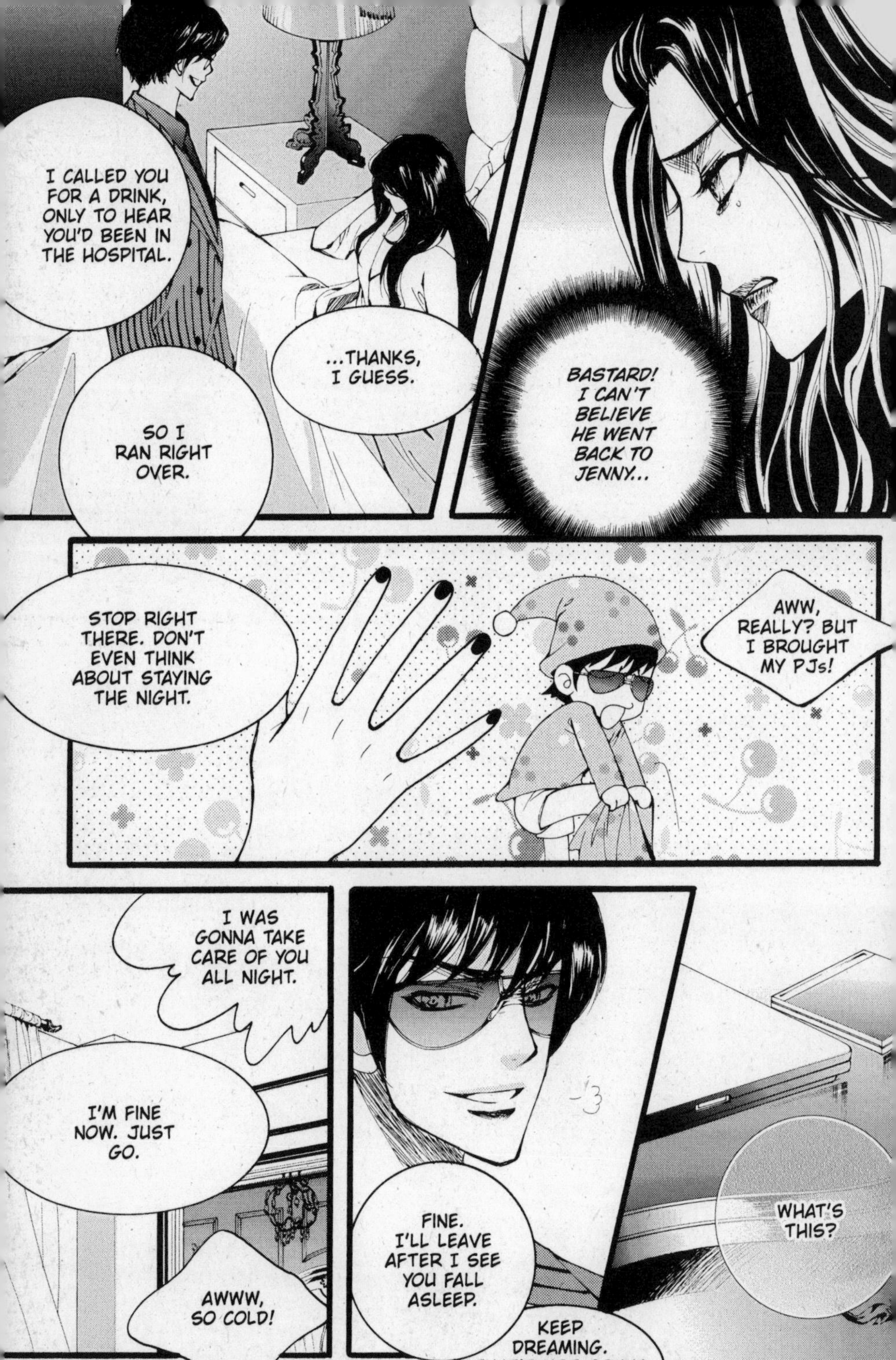
I CALLED YOU FOR A DRINK, ONLY TO HEAR YOU'D BEEN IN THE HOSPITAL.
SO I RAN RIGHT OVER.
...THANKS, I GUESS.
BASTARD! I CAN'T BELIEVE HE WENT BACK TO JENNY...
STOP RIGHT THERE. DON'T EVEN THINK ABOUT STAYING THE NIGHT.
AWW, REALLY? BUT I BROUGHT MY PJs!
I WAS GONNA TAKE CARE OF YOU ALL NIGHT.
I'M FINE NOW. JUST GO.
AWWW, SO COLD!
FINE. I'LL LEAVE AFTER I SEE YOU FALL ASLEEP.
KEEP DREAMING. THAT'S NOT GONNA HAPPEN.
WHAT'S THIS?

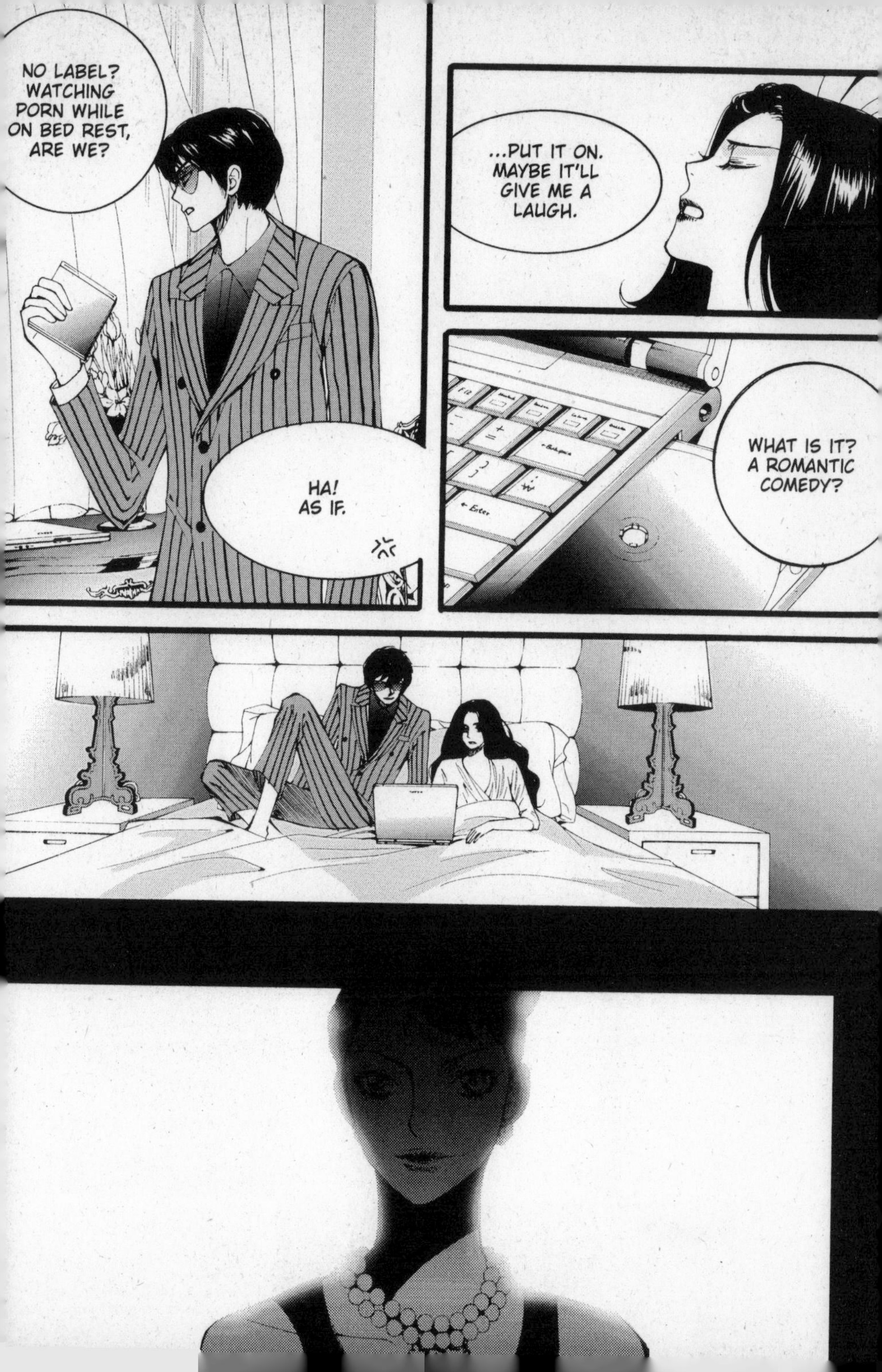
NO LABEL? WATCHING PORN WHILE ON BED REST, ARE WE?
HA! AS IF.
...PUT IT ON. MAYBE IT'LL GIVE ME A LAUGH.
WHAT IS IT? A ROMANTIC COMEDY?

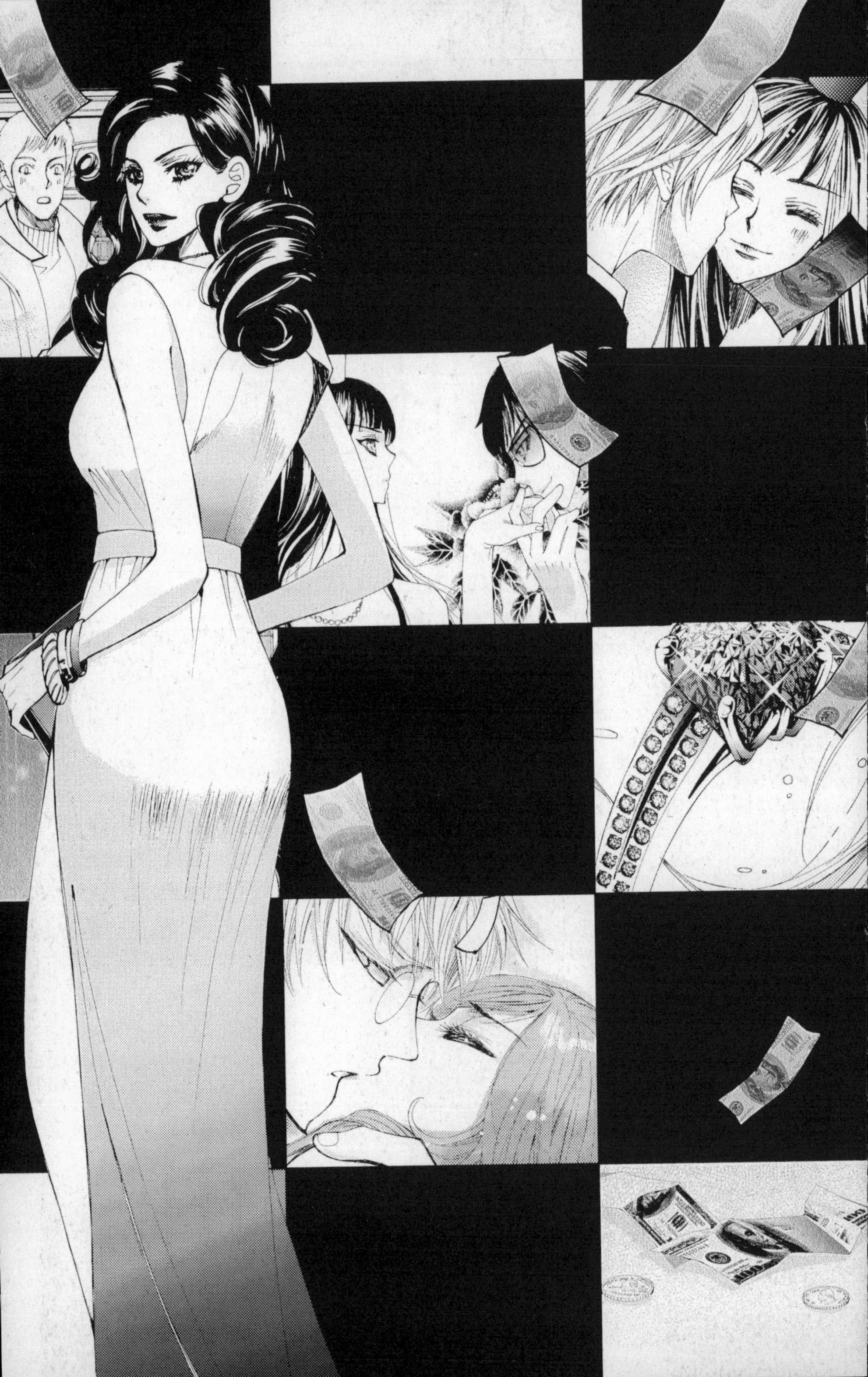

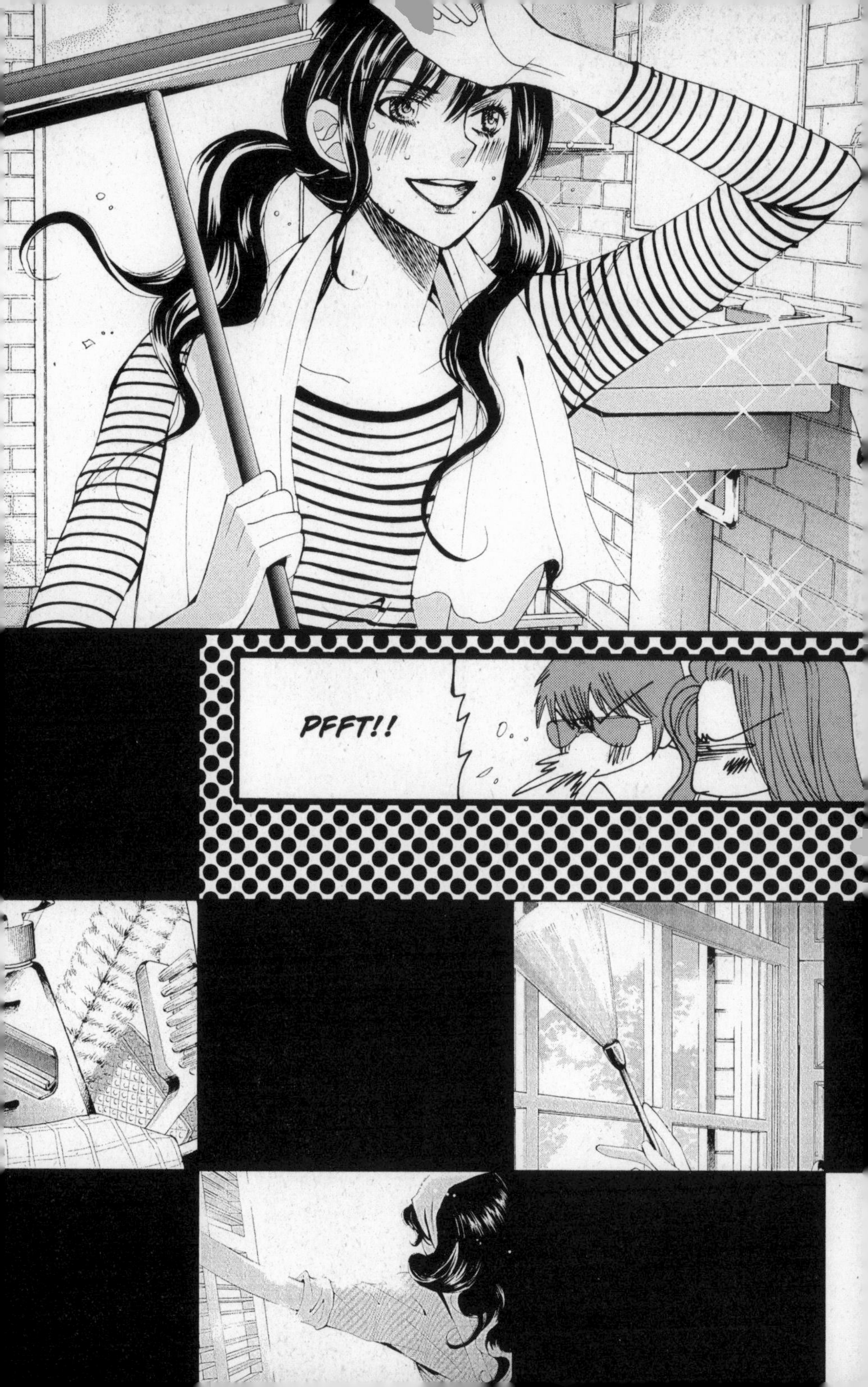
PFFT!!

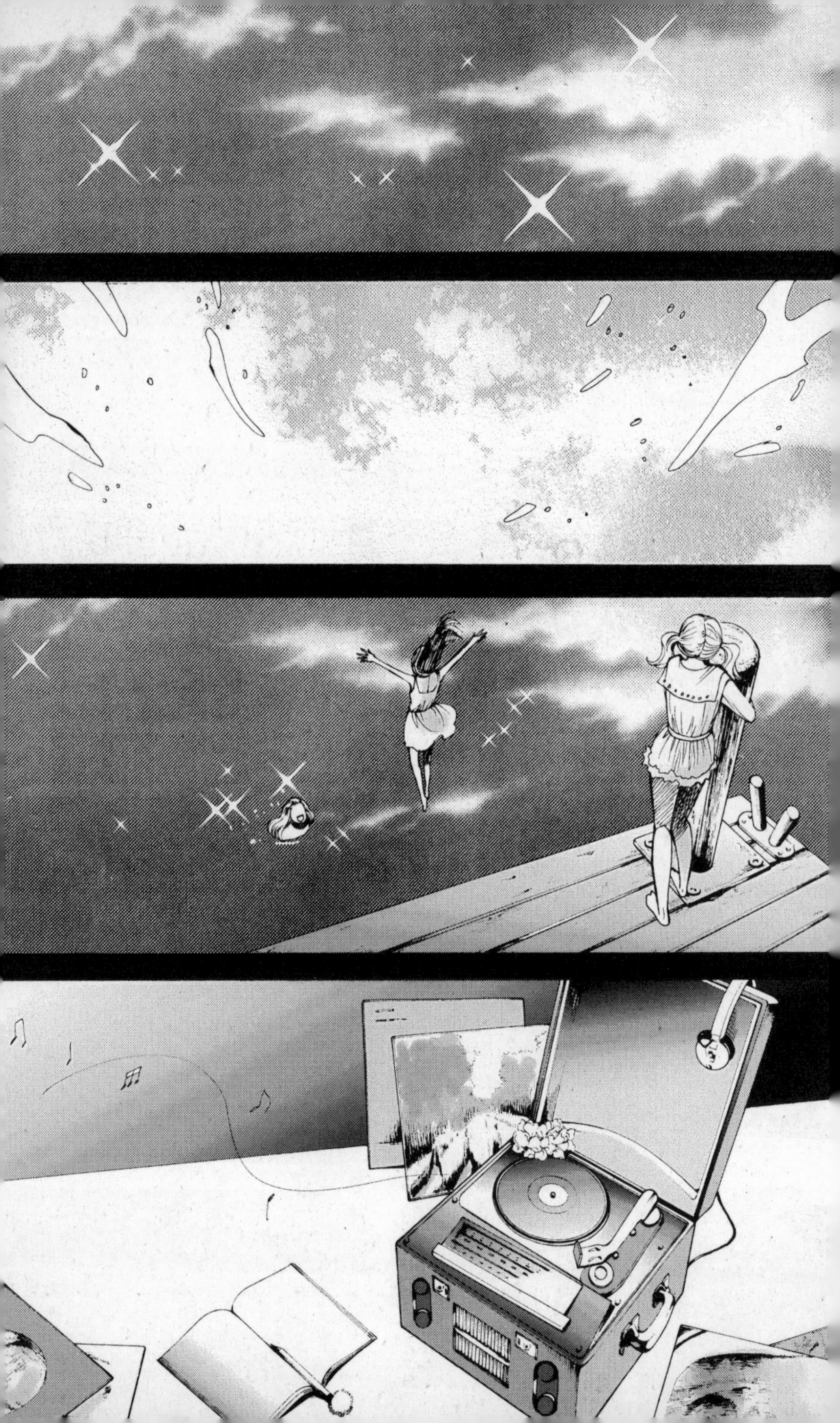

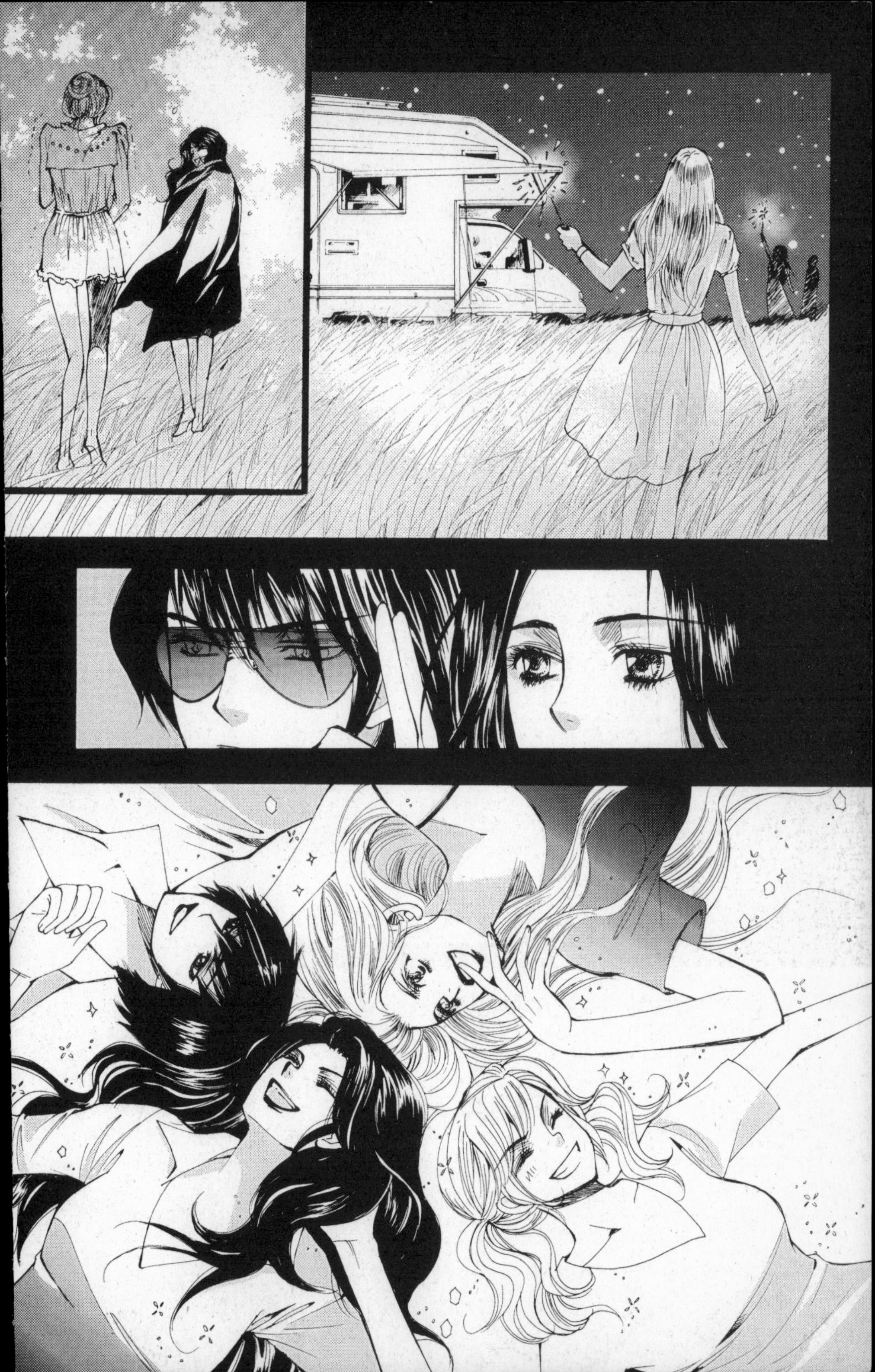

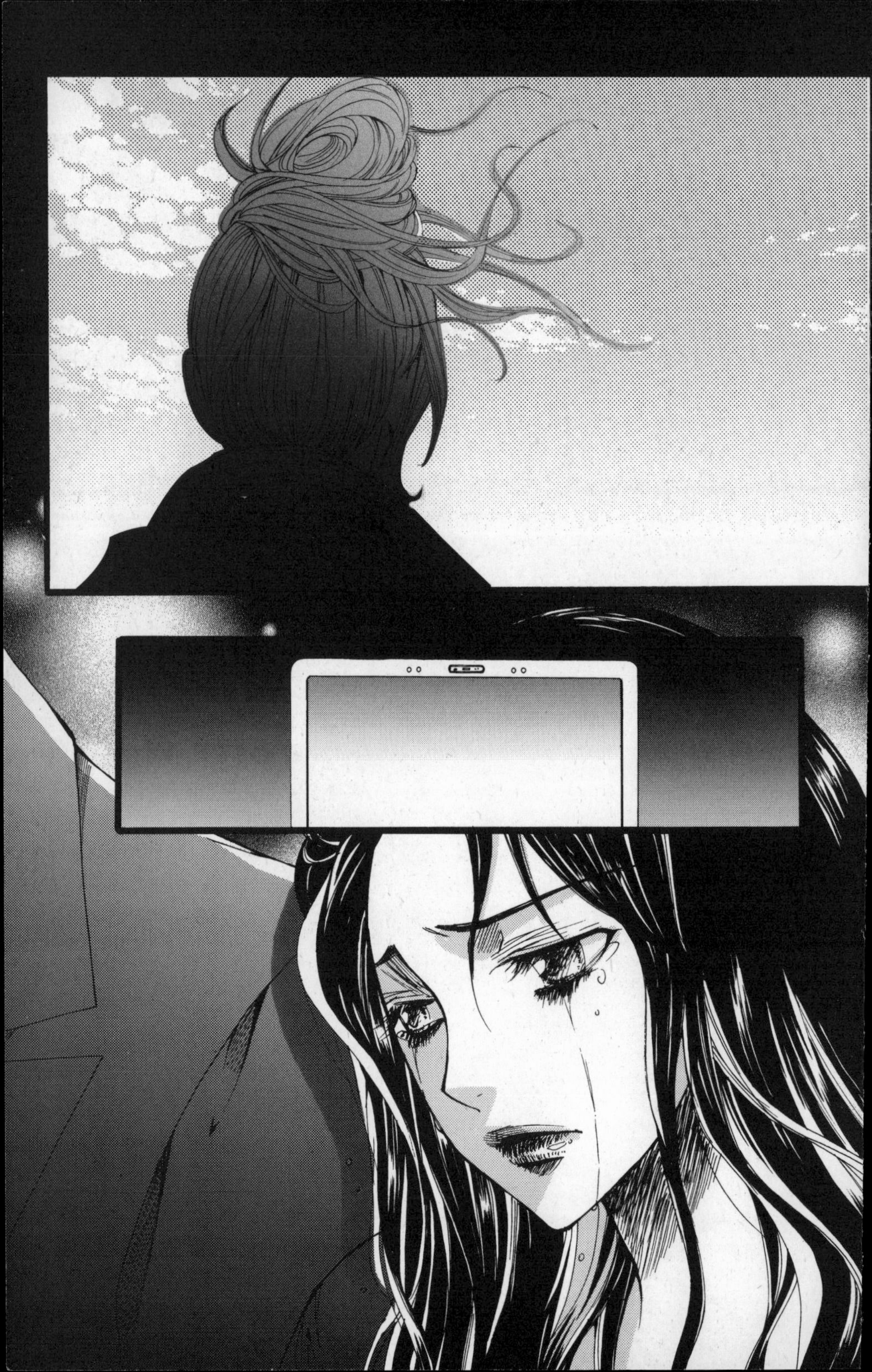

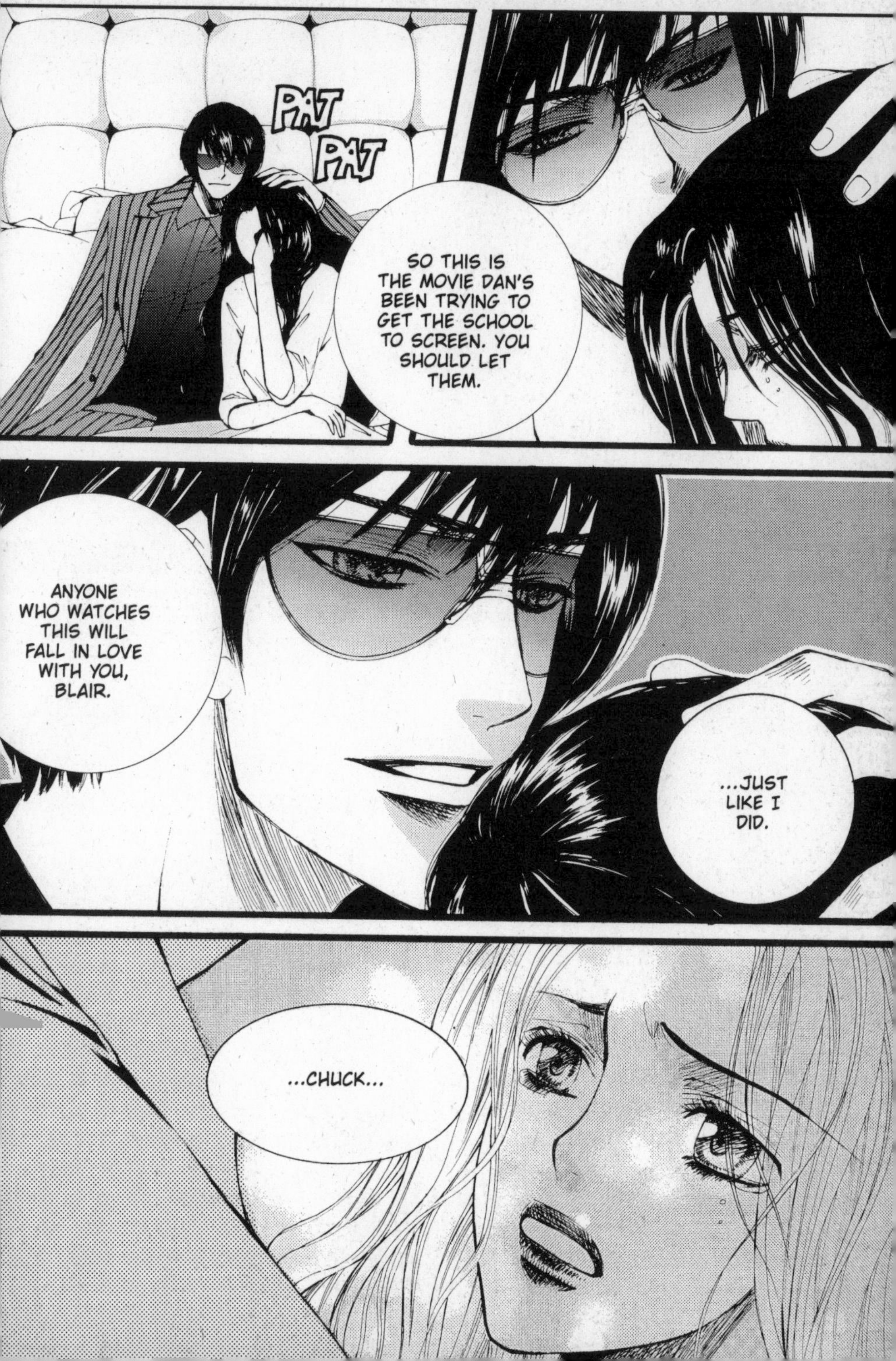
PAT PAT
SO THIS IS THE MOVIE DAN'S BEEN TRYING TO GET THE SCHOOL TO SCREEN. YOU SHOULD LET THEM.
ANYONE WHO WATCHES THIS WILL FALL IN LOVE WITH YOU, BLAIR.
...JUST LIKE I DID.
...CHUCK...

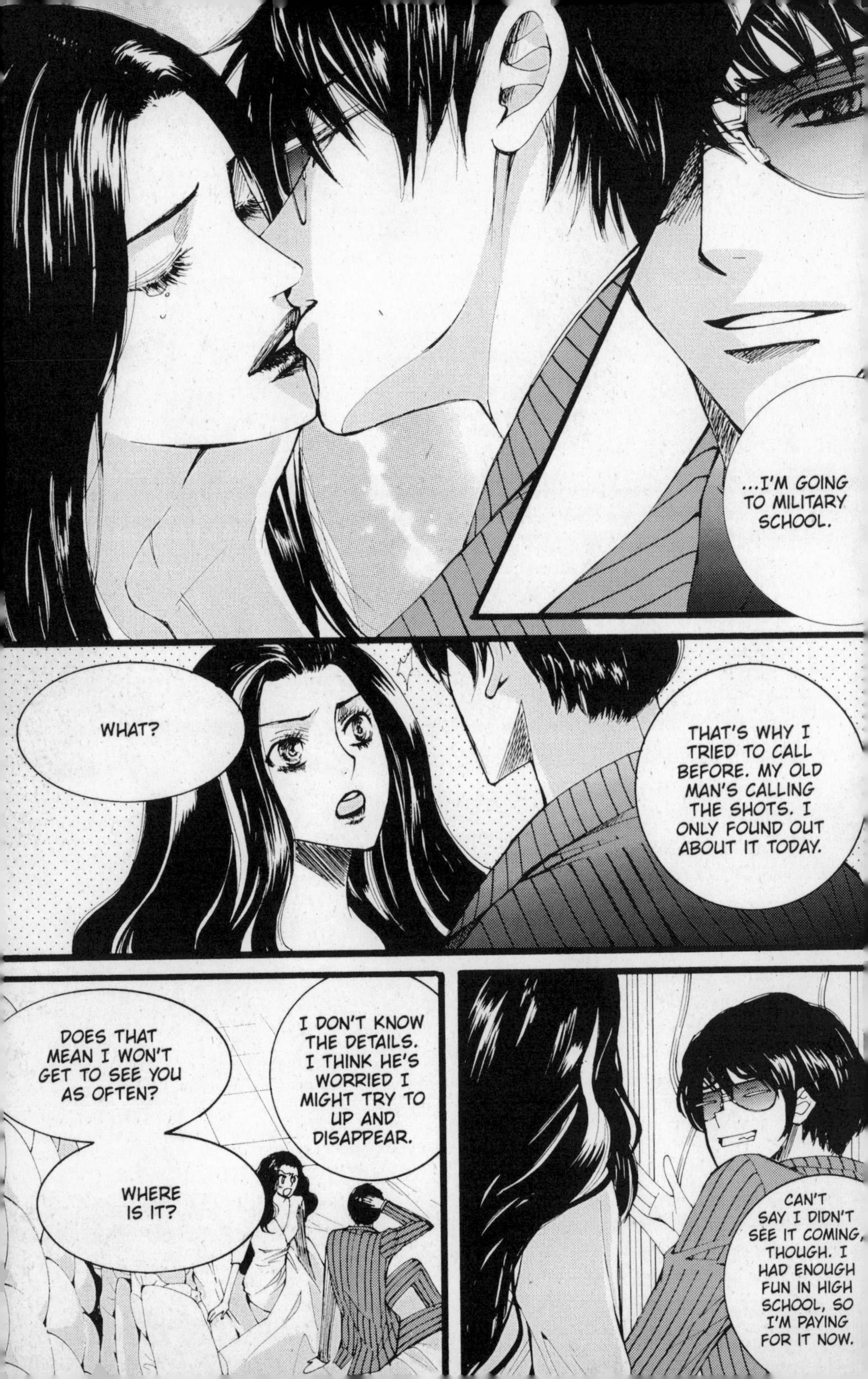
...I'M GOING TO MILITARY SCHOOL.
WHAT?
THAT'S WHY I TRIED TO CALL BEFORE. MY OLD MAN'S CALLING THE SHOTS. I ONLY FOUND OUT ABOUT IT TODAY.
DOES THAT MEAN I WON'T GET TO SEE YOU AS OFTEN?
WHERE IS IT?
I DON'T KNOW THE DETAILS. I THINK HE'S WORRIED I MIGHT TRY TO UP AND DISAPPEAR.
CAN'T SAY I DIDN'T SEE IT COMING, THOUGH. I HAD ENOUGH FUN IN HIGH SCHOOL, SO I'M PAYING FOR IT NOW.

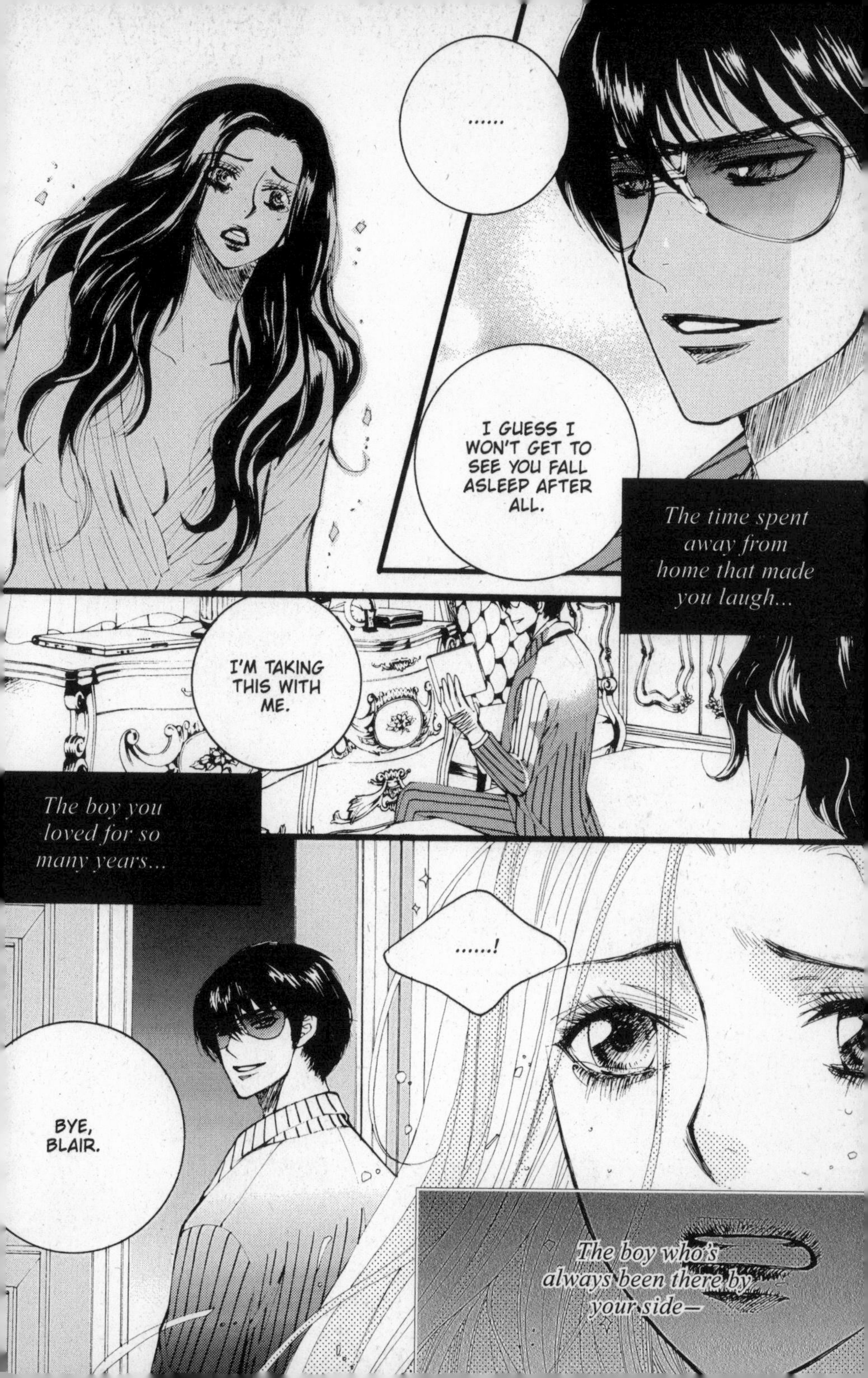
......
I GUESS I WON'T GET TO SEE YOU FALL ASLEEP AFTER ALL.
The time spent away from home that made you laugh...
I'M TAKING THIS WITH ME.
The boy you loved for so many years...
BYE, BLAIR.
......!
The boy who's always been there by your side—

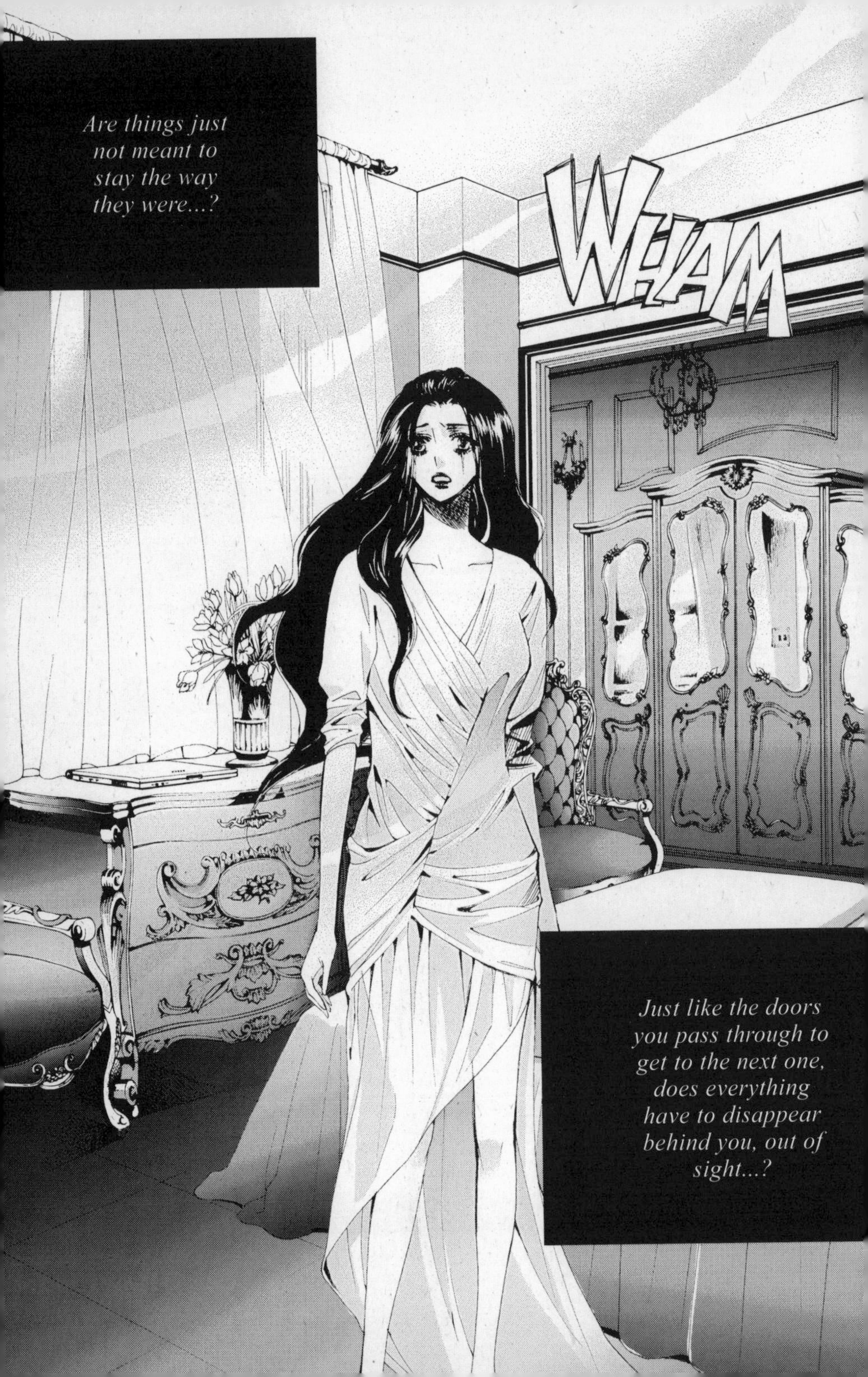

Are things just not meant to stay the way they were...?
WHAM
Just like the doors you pass through to get to the next one, does everything have to disappear behind you, out of sight...?

gossip girl

FOR YOUR EYES ONLY

gossip girl

FOR YOUR EYES ONLY | CHAPTER 17

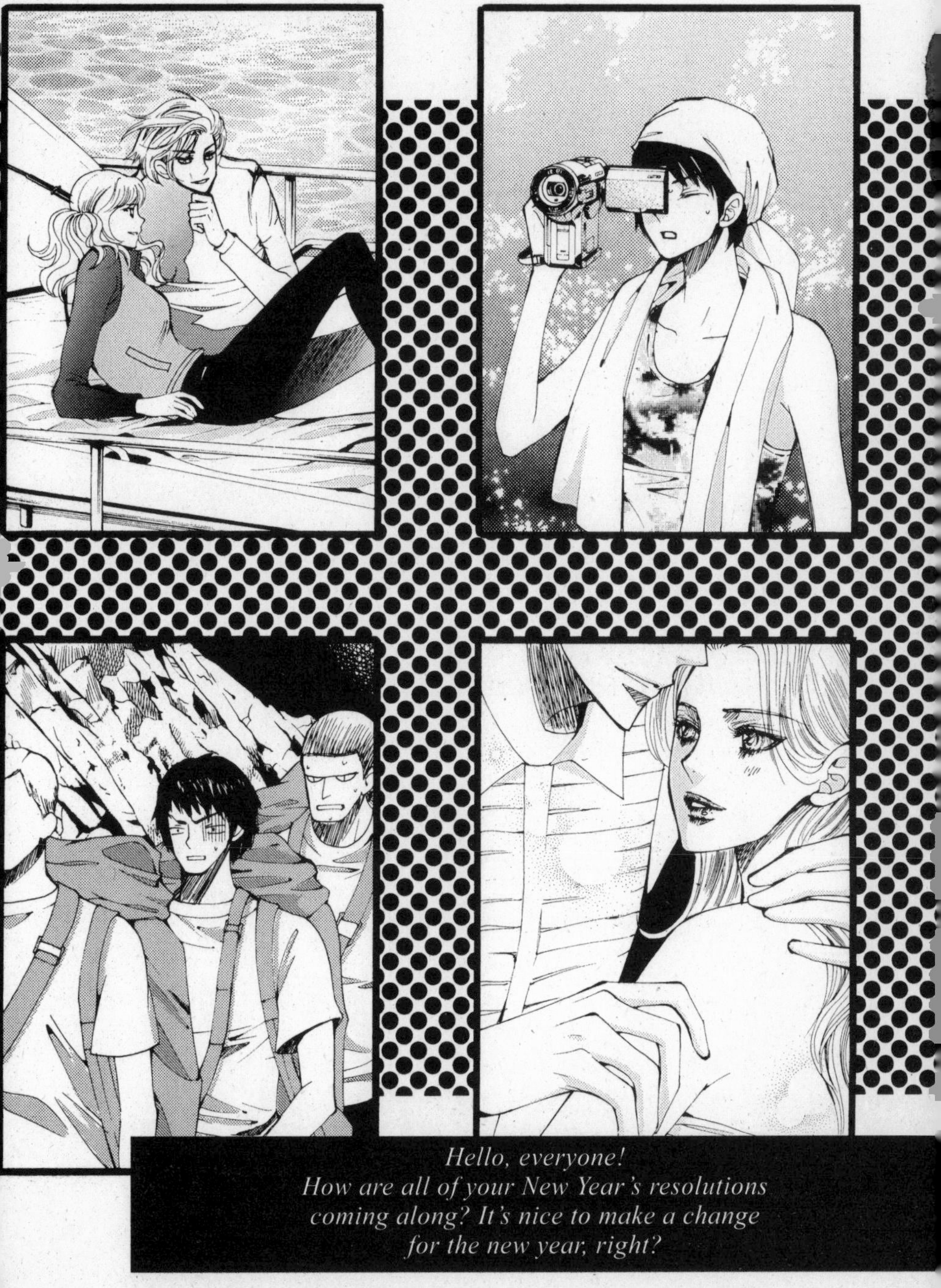
Hello, everyone!
How are all of your New Year's resolutions coming along? It's nice to make a change for the new year, right?

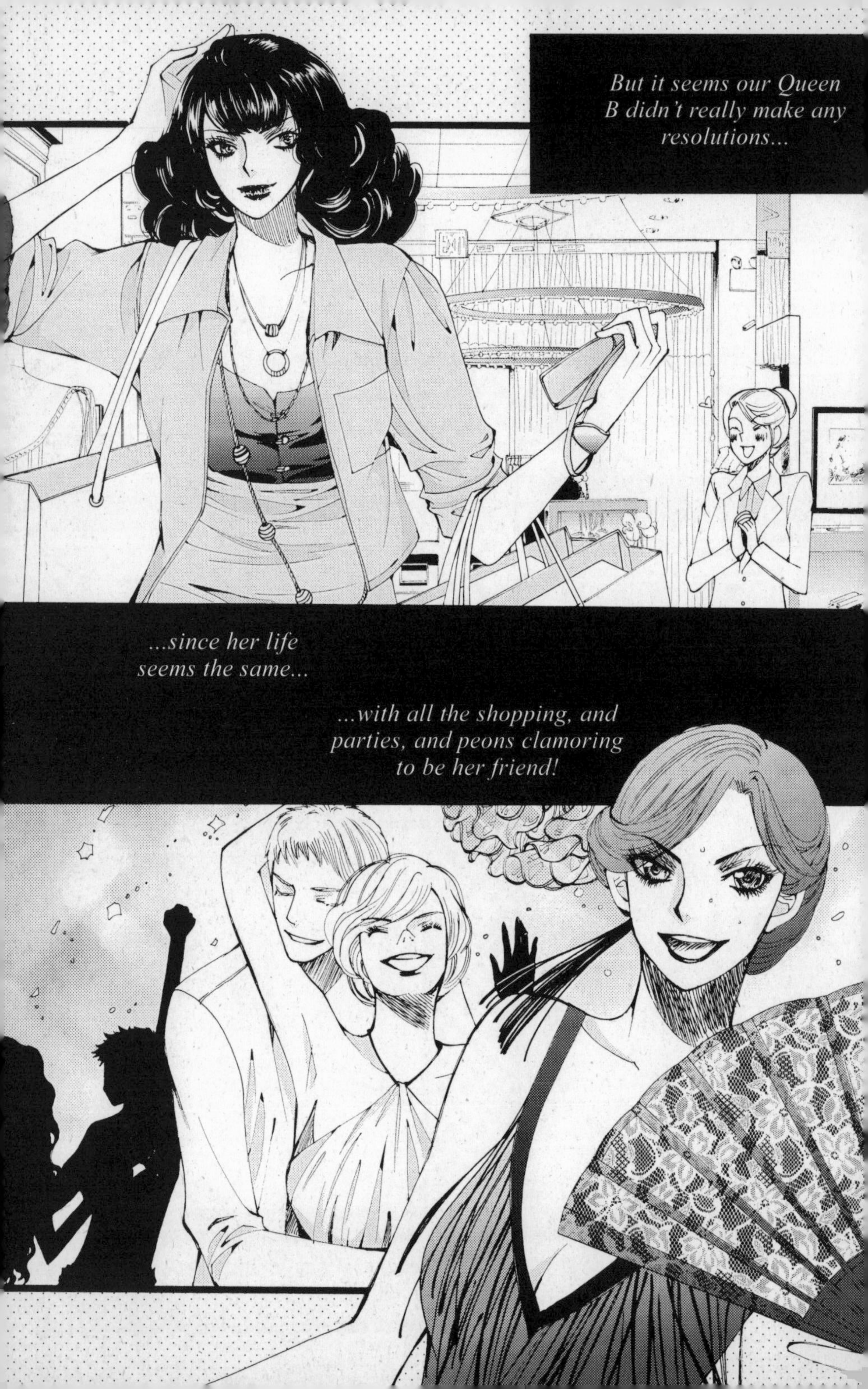
But it seems our Queen B didn't really make any resolutions...
...since her life seems the same...
...with all the shopping, and parties, and peons clamoring to be her friend!

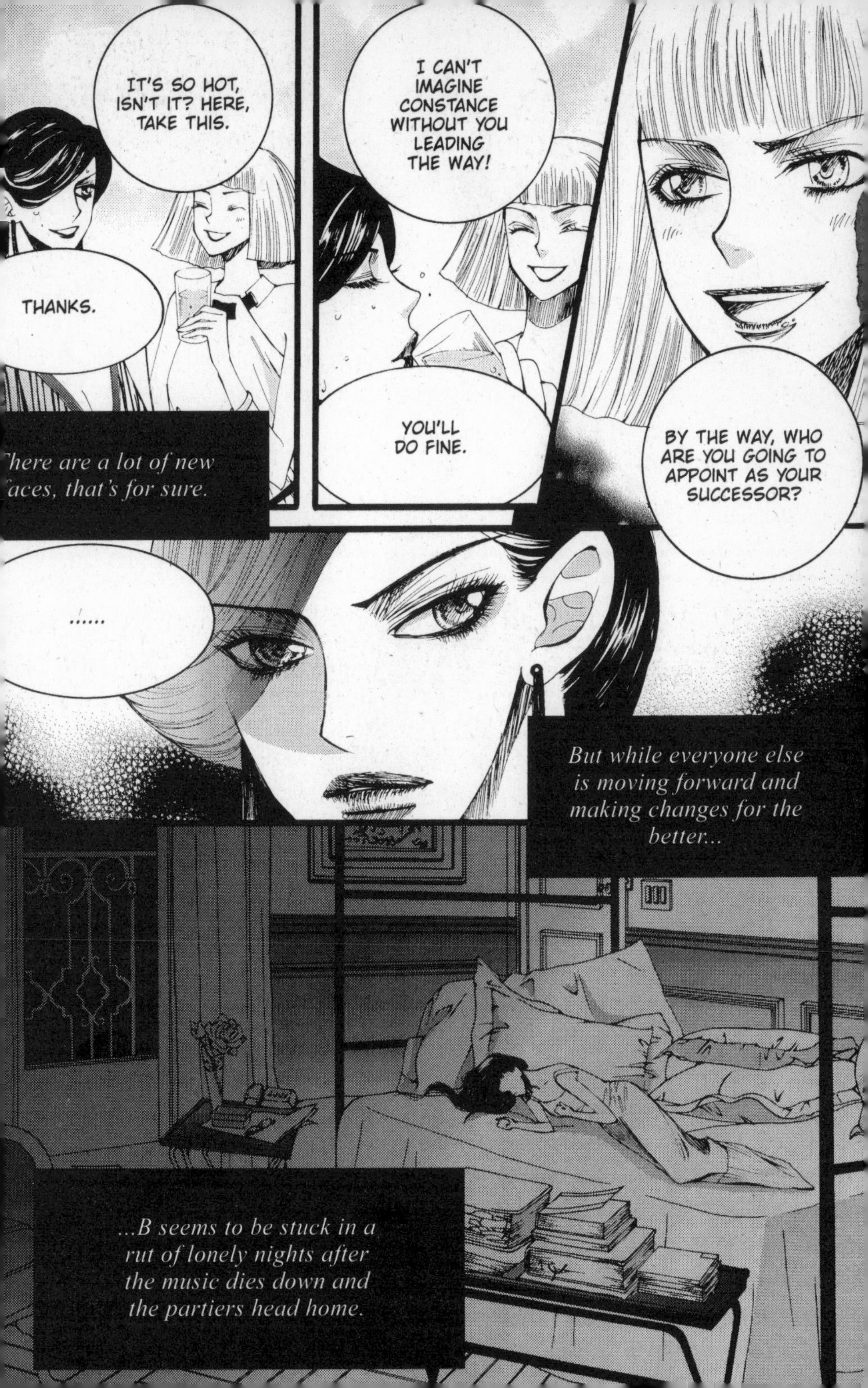
IT'S SO HOT, ISN'T IT? HERE, TAKE THIS.
THANKS.
There are a lot of new faces, that's for sure.
I CAN'T IMAGINE CONSTANCE WITHOUT YOU LEADING THE WAY!
YOU'LL DO FINE.
BY THE WAY, WHO ARE YOU GOING TO APPOINT AS YOUR SUCCESSOR?
......
But while everyone else is moving forward and making changes for the better...
...B seems to be stuck in a rut of lonely nights after the music dies down and the partiers head home.

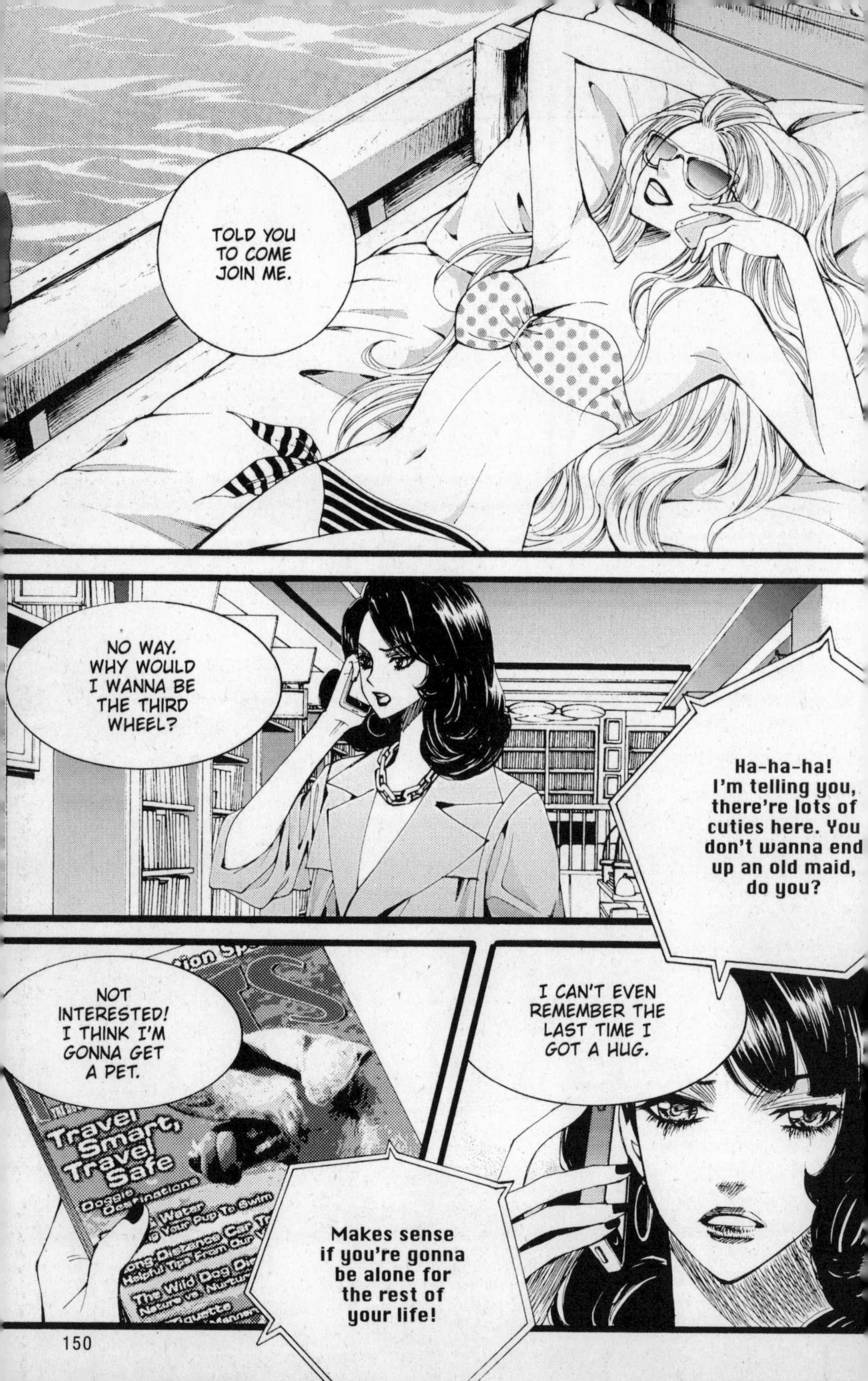
TOLD YOU TO COME JOIN ME.
NO WAY. WHY WOULD I WANNA BE THE THIRD WHEEL?
Ha-ha-ha! I'm telling you, there're lots of cuties here. You don't wanna end up an old maid, do you?
NOT INTERESTED! I THINK I'M GONNA GET A PET.
Travel Smart, Travel Safe
Doggie Destinations
I CAN'T EVEN REMEMBER THE LAST TIME I GOT A HUG.
Makes sense if you're gonna be alone for the rest of your life!

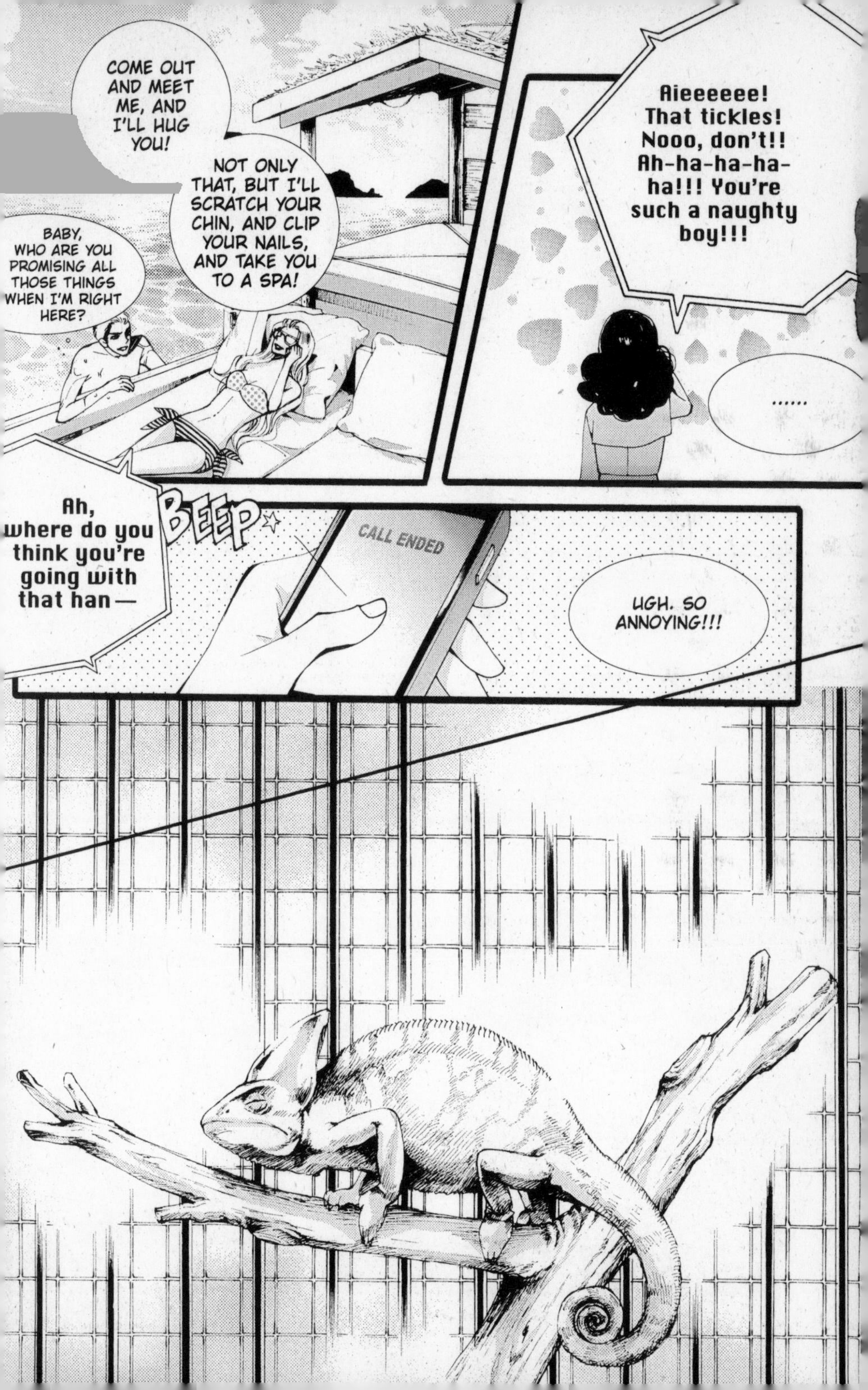
COME OUT AND MEET ME, AND I'LL HUG YOU!
NOT ONLY THAT, BUT I'LL SCRATCH YOUR CHIN, AND CLIP YOUR NAILS, AND TAKE YOU TO A SPA!
BABY, WHO ARE YOU PROMISING ALL THOSE THINGS WHEN I'M RIGHT HERE?
Aieeeeee! That tickles! Nooo, don't!! Ah-ha-ha-ha-ha!!! You're such a naughty boy!!!
......
Ah, where do you think you're going with that han—
BEEP
CALL ENDED
UGH. SO ANNOYING!!!

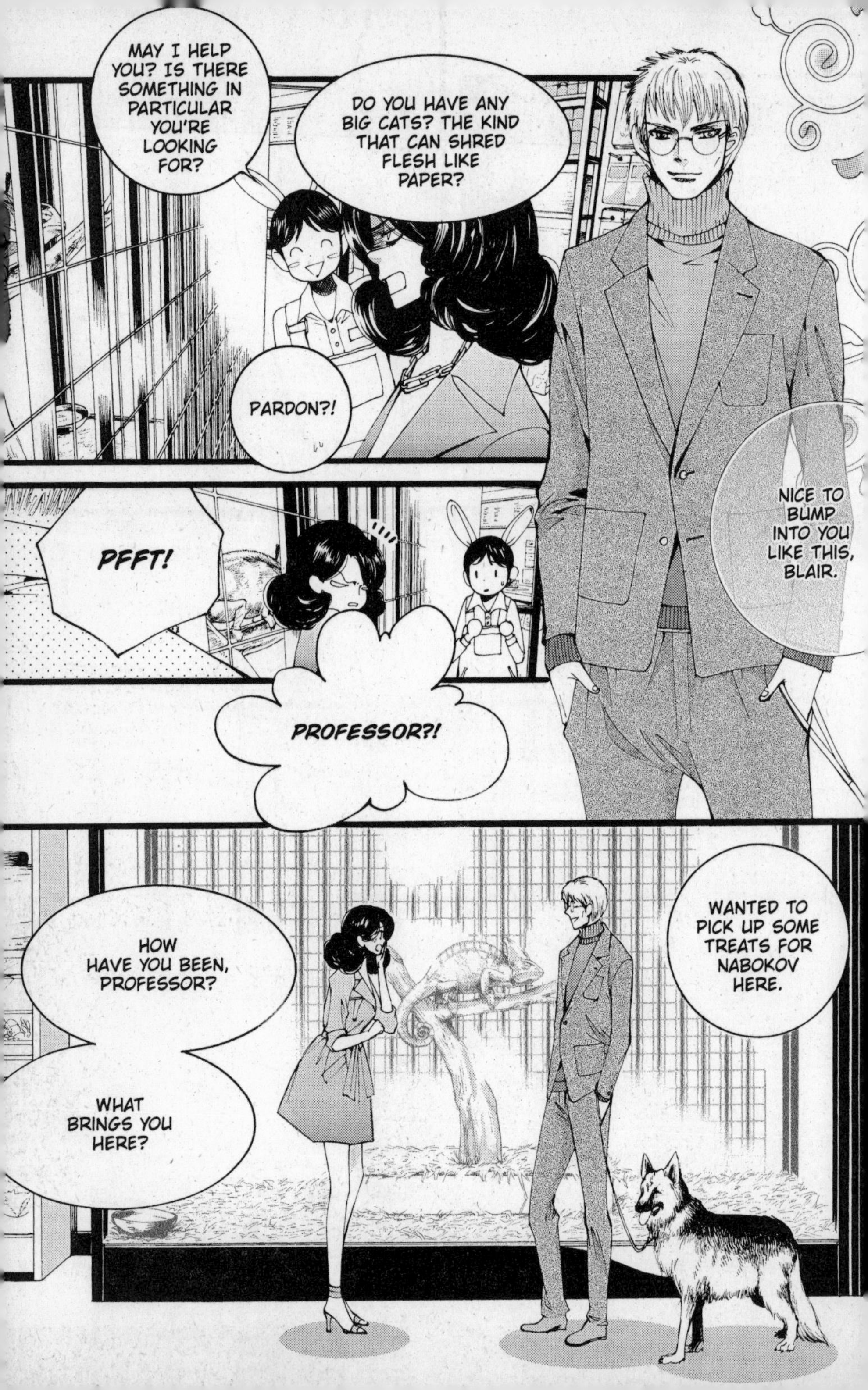
MAY I HELP YOU? IS THERE SOMETHING IN PARTICULAR YOU'RE LOOKING FOR?
DO YOU HAVE ANY BIG CATS? THE KIND THAT CAN SHRED FLESH LIKE PAPER?
PARDON?!
PFFT!
PROFESSOR?!
NICE TO BUMP INTO YOU LIKE THIS, BLAIR.
HOW HAVE YOU BEEN, PROFESSOR?
WHAT BRINGS YOU HERE?
WANTED TO PICK UP SOME TREATS FOR NABOKOV HERE.

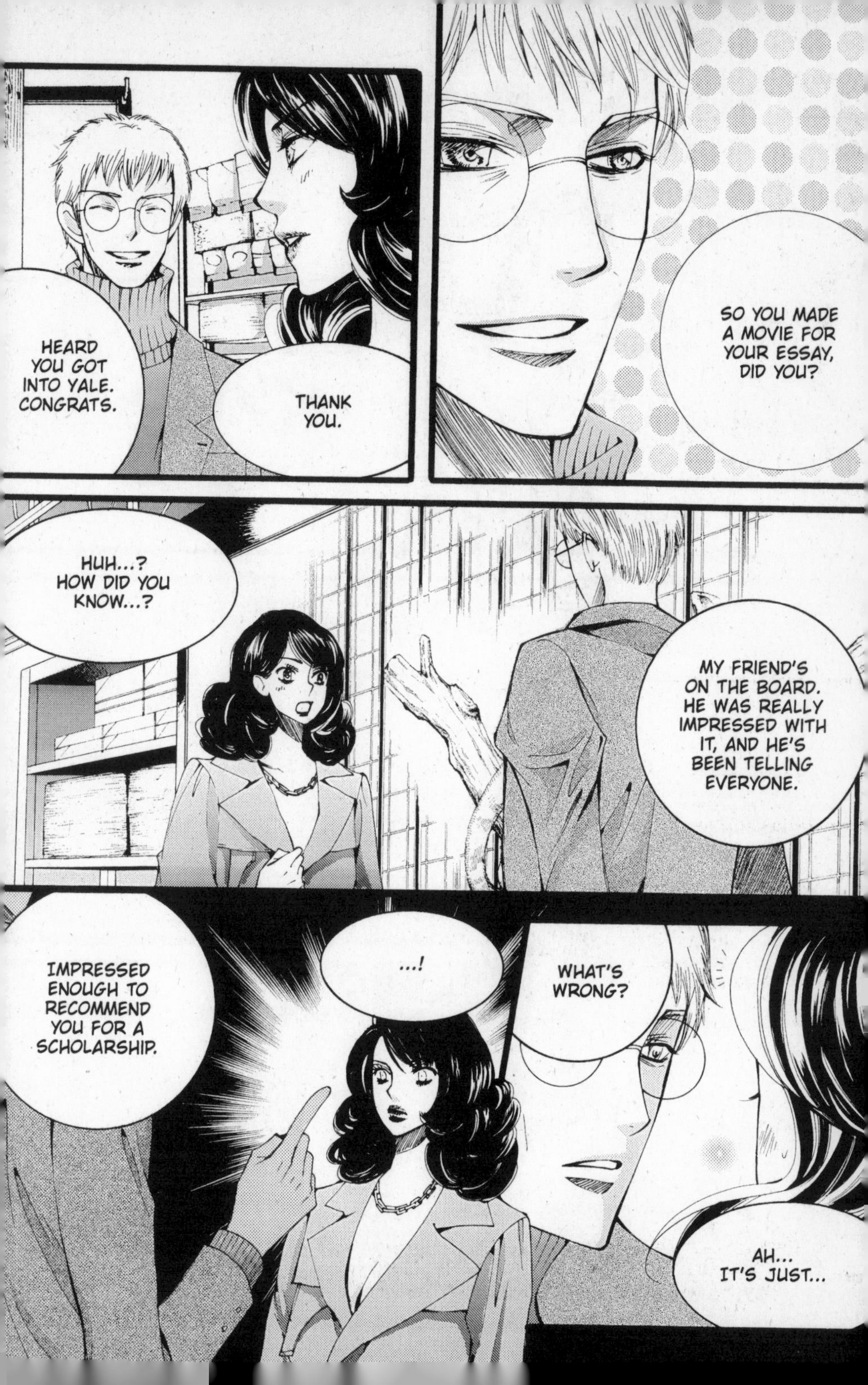

HEARD YOU GOT INTO YALE. CONGRATS.
THANK YOU.
SO YOU MADE A MOVIE FOR YOUR ESSAY, DID YOU?
HUH...? HOW DID YOU KNOW...?
MY FRIEND'S ON THE BOARD. HE WAS REALLY IMPRESSED WITH IT, AND HE'S BEEN TELLING EVERYONE.
IMPRESSED ENOUGH TO RECOMMEND YOU FOR A SCHOLARSHIP.
...!
WHAT'S WRONG?
AH... IT'S JUST...

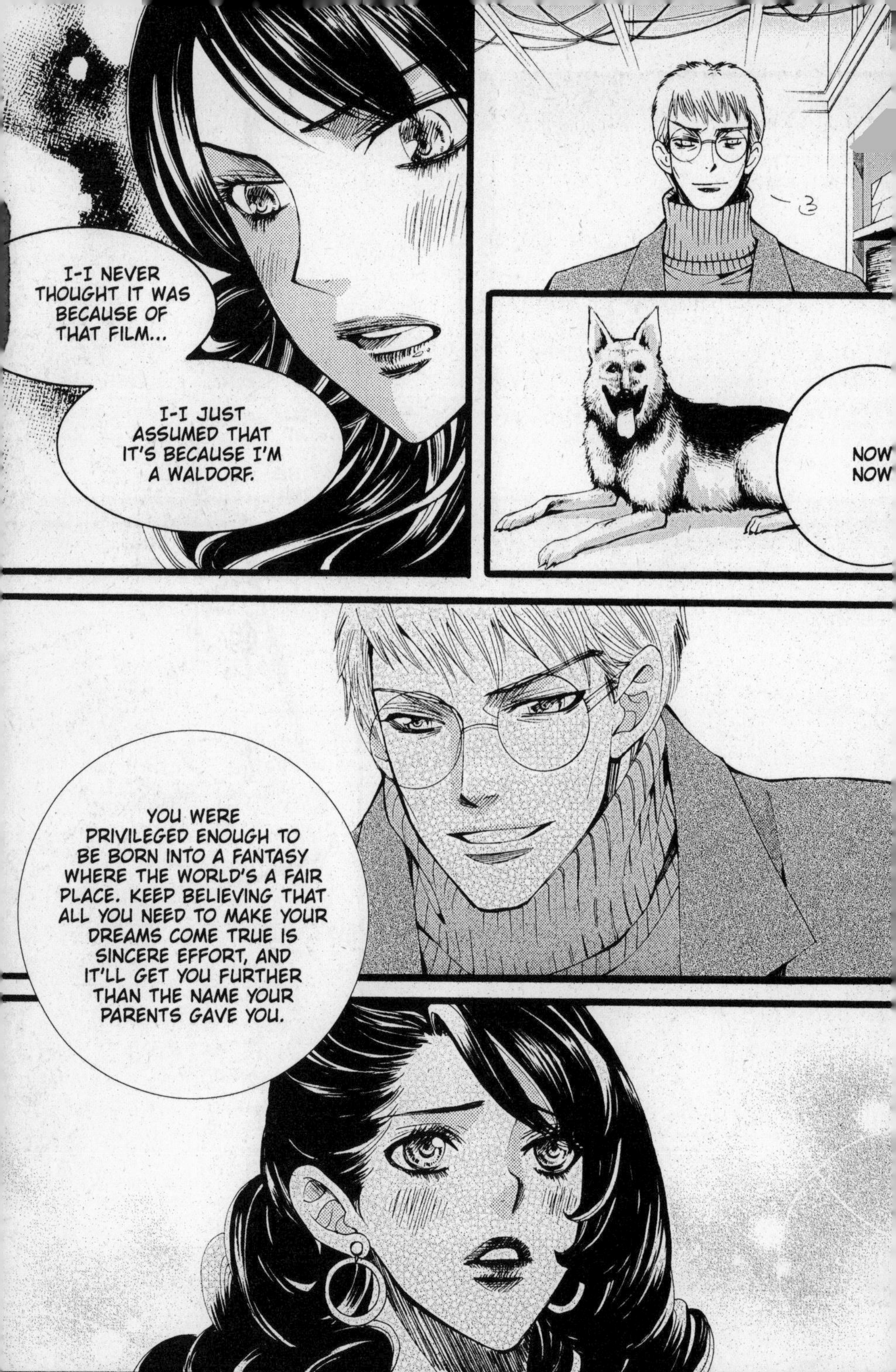
I-I NEVER THOUGHT IT WAS BECAUSE OF THAT FILM...
I-I JUST ASSUMED THAT IT'S BECAUSE I'M A WALDORF.
NOW NOW
YOU WERE PRIVILEGED ENOUGH TO BE BORN INTO A FANTASY WHERE THE WORLD'S A FAIR PLACE. KEEP BELIEVING THAT ALL YOU NEED TO MAKE YOUR DREAMS COME TRUE IS SINCERE EFFORT, AND IT'LL GET YOU FURTHER THAN THE NAME YOUR PARENTS GAVE YOU.

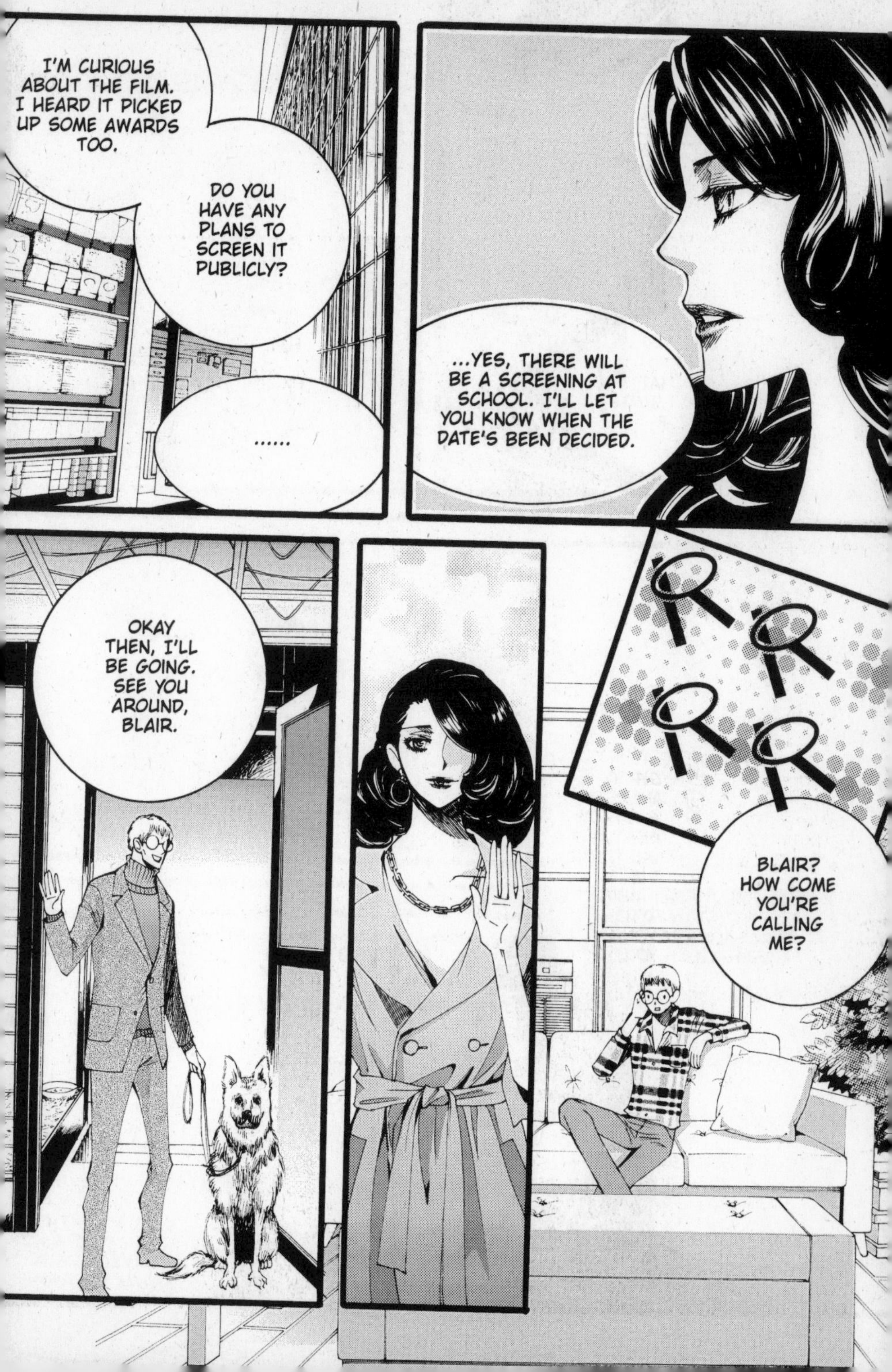
I'M CURIOUS ABOUT THE FILM. I HEARD IT PICKED UP SOME AWARDS TOO.
DO YOU HAVE ANY PLANS TO SCREEN IT PUBLICLY?
......
...YES, THERE WILL BE A SCREENING AT SCHOOL. I'LL LET YOU KNOW WHEN THE DATE'S BEEN DECIDED.
OKAY THEN, I'LL BE GOING. SEE YOU AROUND, BLAIR.
BLAIR? HOW COME YOU'RE CALLING ME?

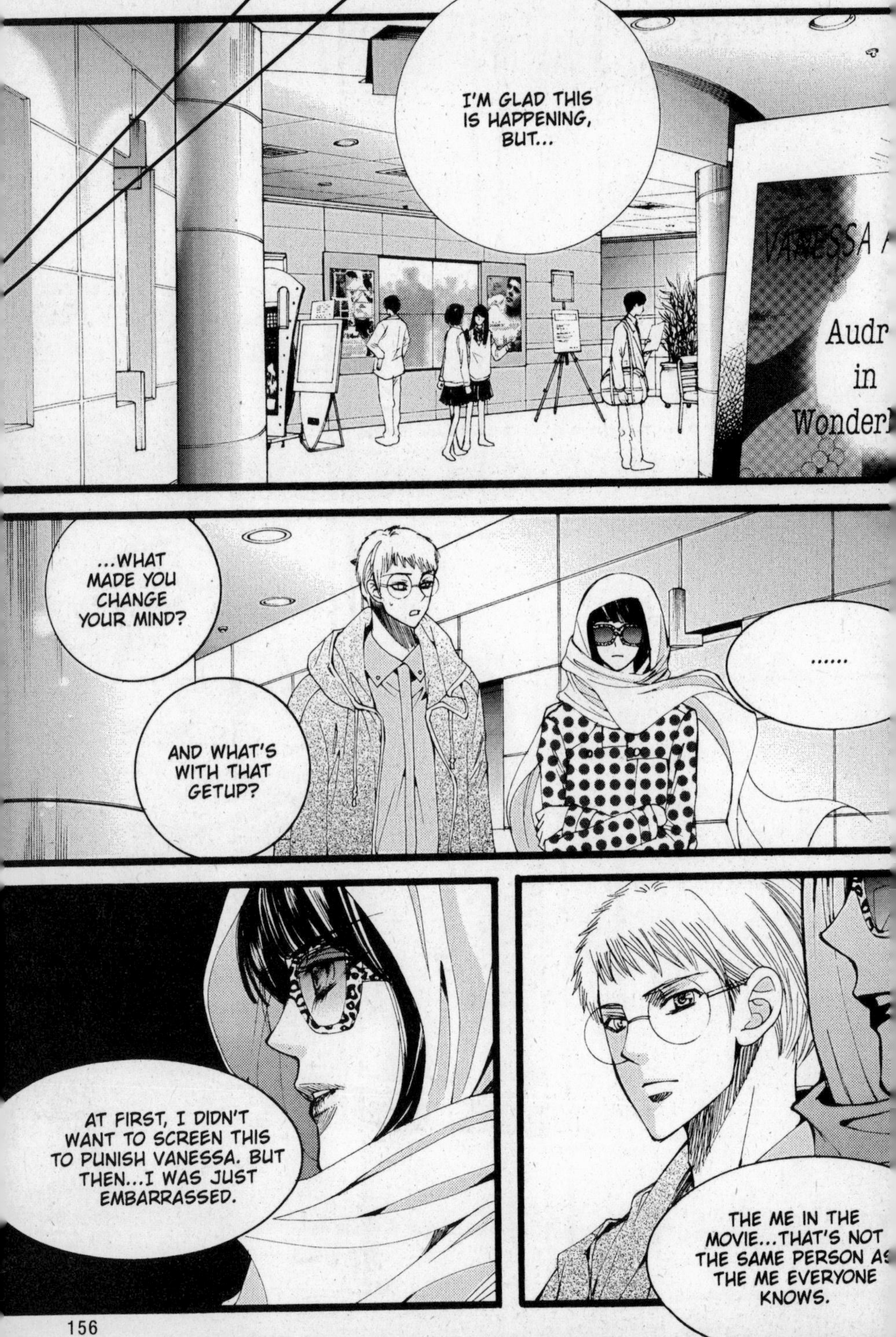
I'M GLAD THIS IS HAPPENING, BUT...
...WHAT MADE YOU CHANGE YOUR MIND?
AND WHAT'S WITH THAT GETUP?
......
AT FIRST, I DIDN'T WANT TO SCREEN THIS TO PUNISH VANESSA. BUT THEN...I WAS JUST EMBARRASSED.
THE ME IN THE MOVIE...THAT'S NOT THE SAME PERSON AS THE ME EVERYONE KNOWS.

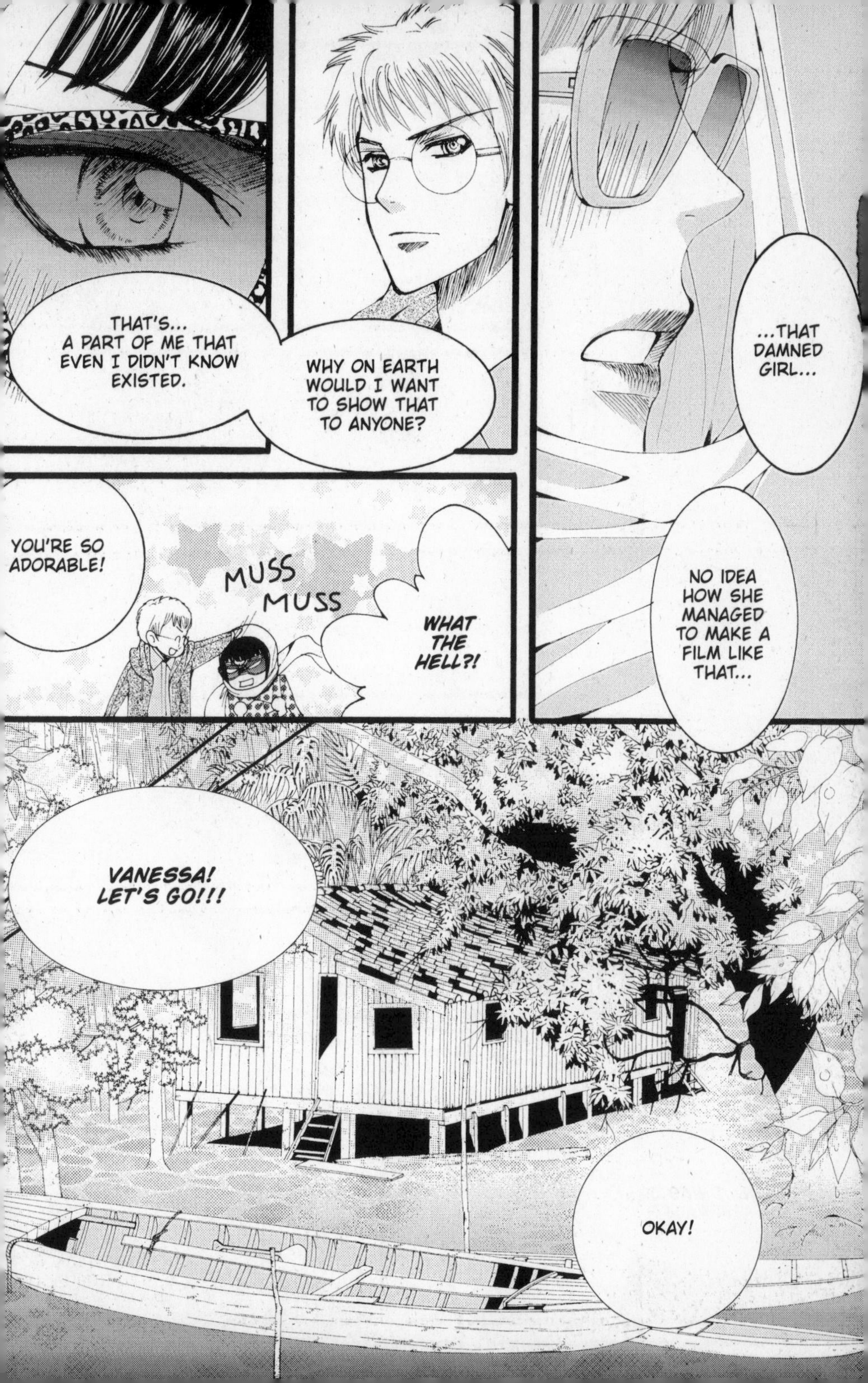
THAT'S... A PART OF ME THAT EVEN I DIDN'T KNOW EXISTED.
WHY ON EARTH WOULD I WANT TO SHOW THAT TO ANYONE?
YOU'RE SO ADORABLE!
MUSS MUSS
WHAT THE HELL?!
...THAT DAMNED GIRL...
NO IDEA HOW SHE MANAGED TO MAKE A FILM LIKE THAT...
VANESSA! LET'S GO!!!
OKAY!

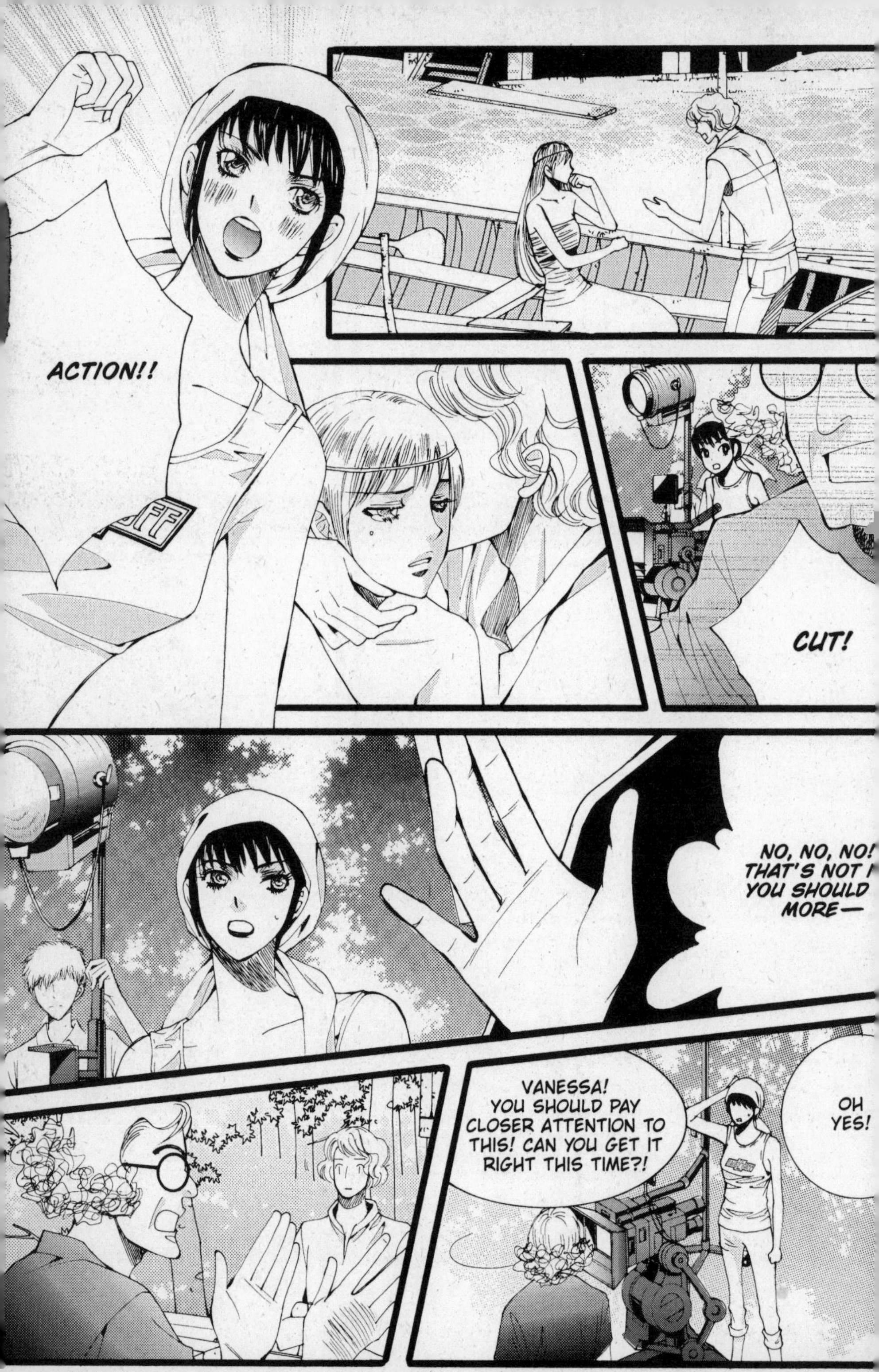
ACTION!!
CUT!
NO, NO, NO! THAT'S NOT I YOU SHOULD MORE—
VANESSA! YOU SHOULD PAY CLOSER ATTENTION TO THIS! CAN YOU GET IT RIGHT THIS TIME?!
OH YES!

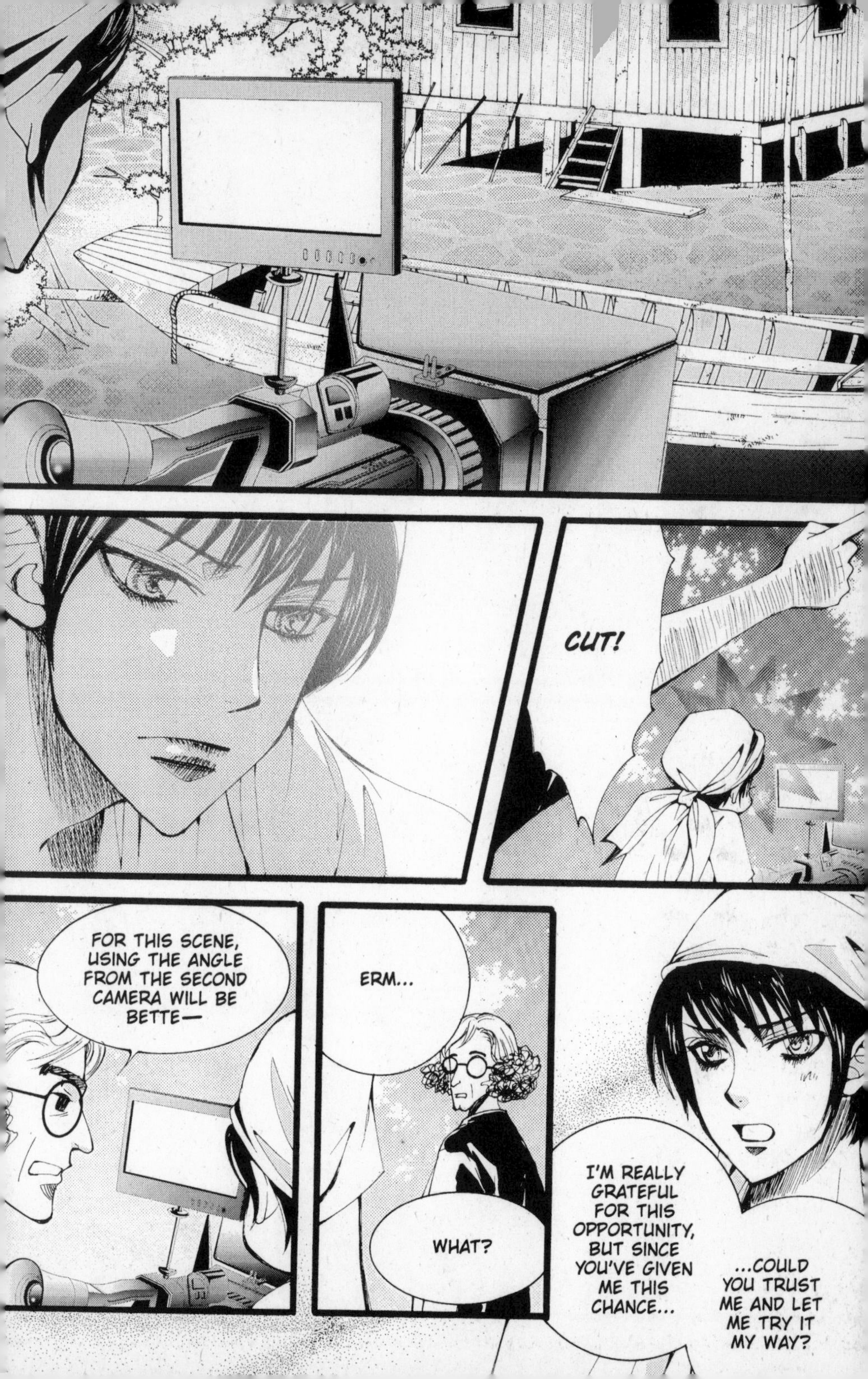
CUT!
FOR THIS SCENE, USING THE ANGLE FROM THE SECOND CAMERA WILL BE BETTE—
ERM...
WHAT?
I'M REALLY GRATEFUL FOR THIS OPPORTUNITY, BUT SINCE YOU'VE GIVEN ME THIS CHANCE...
...COULD YOU TRUST ME AND LET ME TRY IT MY WAY?

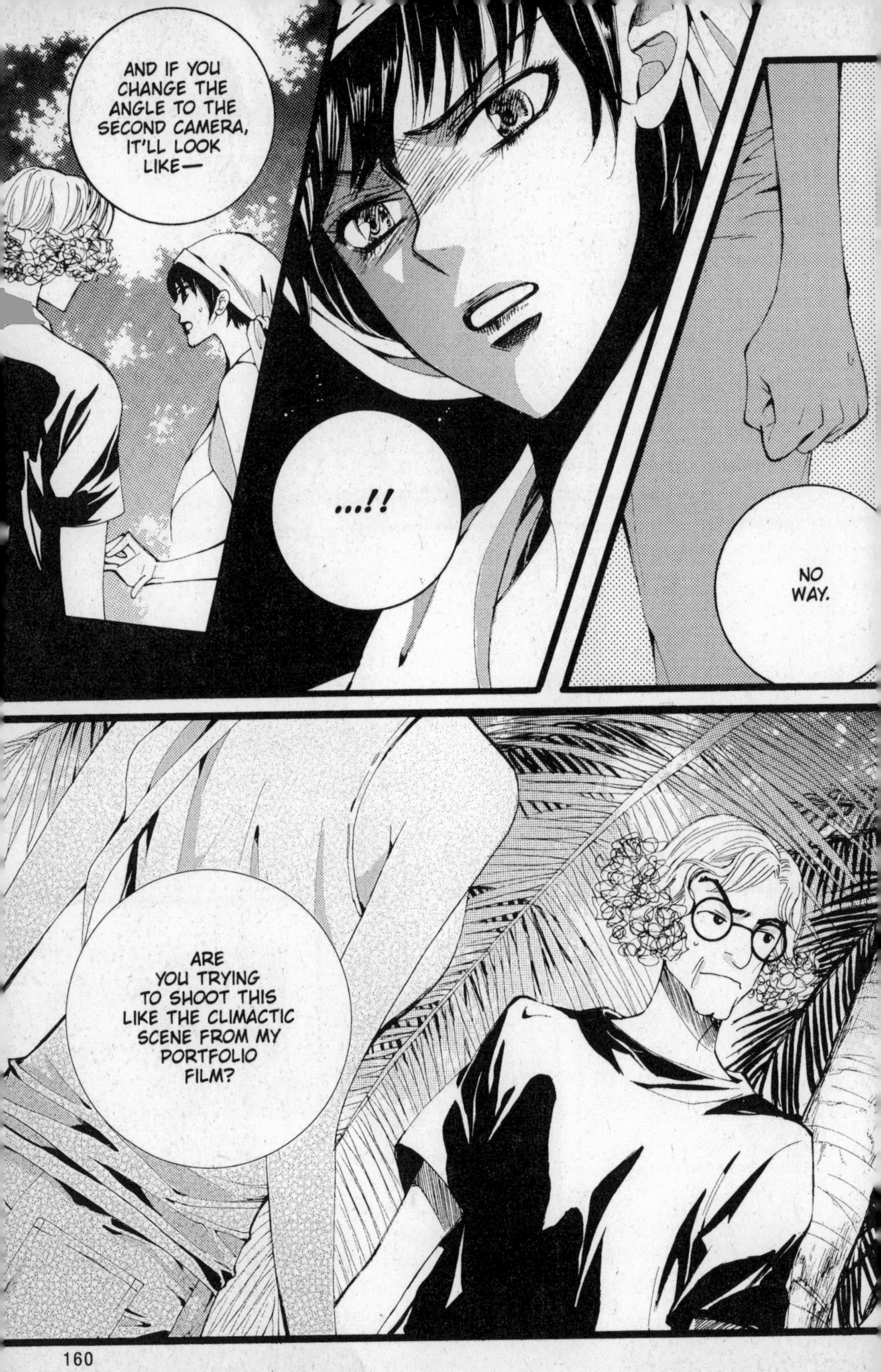
AND IF YOU CHANGE THE ANGLE TO THE SECOND CAMERA, IT'LL LOOK LIKE—
...!!
NO WAY.
ARE YOU TRYING TO SHOOT THIS LIKE THE CLIMACTIC SCENE FROM MY PORTFOLIO FILM?

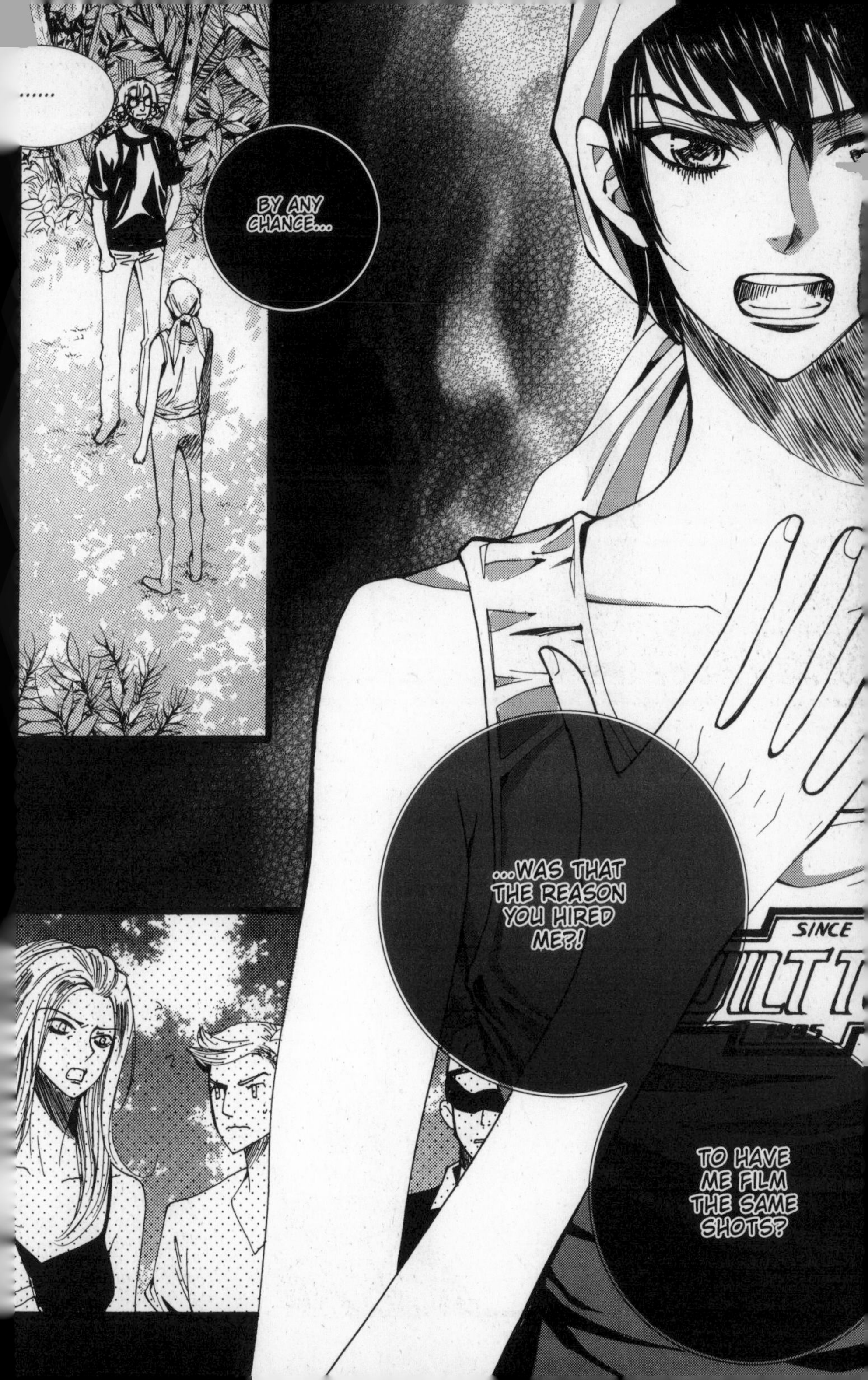
......
BY ANY CHANCE...
...WAS THAT THE REASON YOU HIRED ME?!
TO HAVE ME FILM THE SAME SHOTS?
SINCE

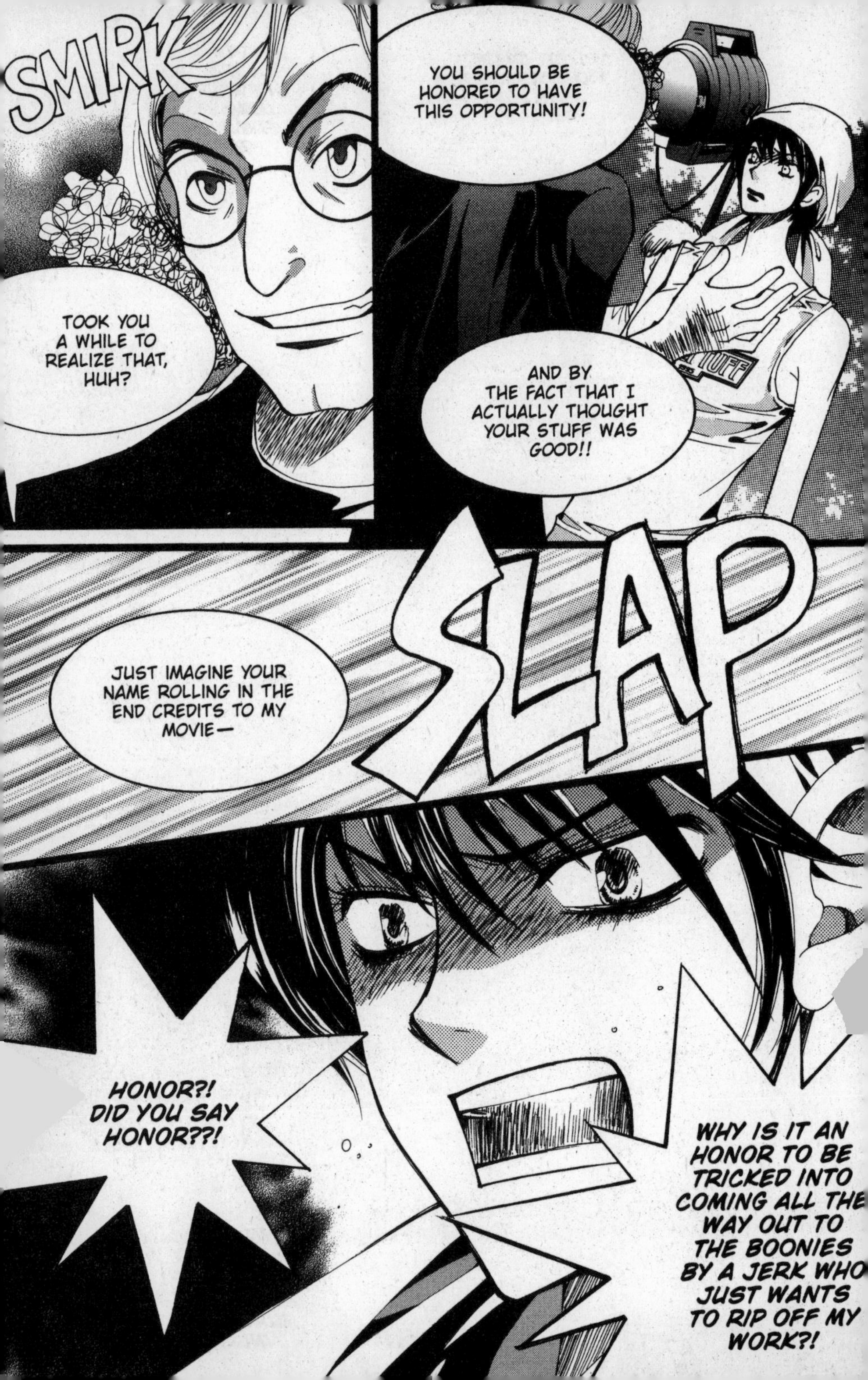
SMIRK
TOOK YOU A WHILE TO REALIZE THAT, HUH?
YOU SHOULD BE HONORED TO HAVE THIS OPPORTUNITY!
AND BY THE FACT THAT I ACTUALLY THOUGHT YOUR STUFF WAS GOOD!!
JUST IMAGINE YOUR NAME ROLLING IN THE END CREDITS TO MY MOVIE—
SLAP
HONOR?! DID YOU SAY HONOR??!
WHY IS IT AN HONOR TO BE TRICKED INTO COMING ALL THE WAY OUT TO THE BOONIES BY A JERK WHO JUST WANTS TO RIP OFF MY WORK?!

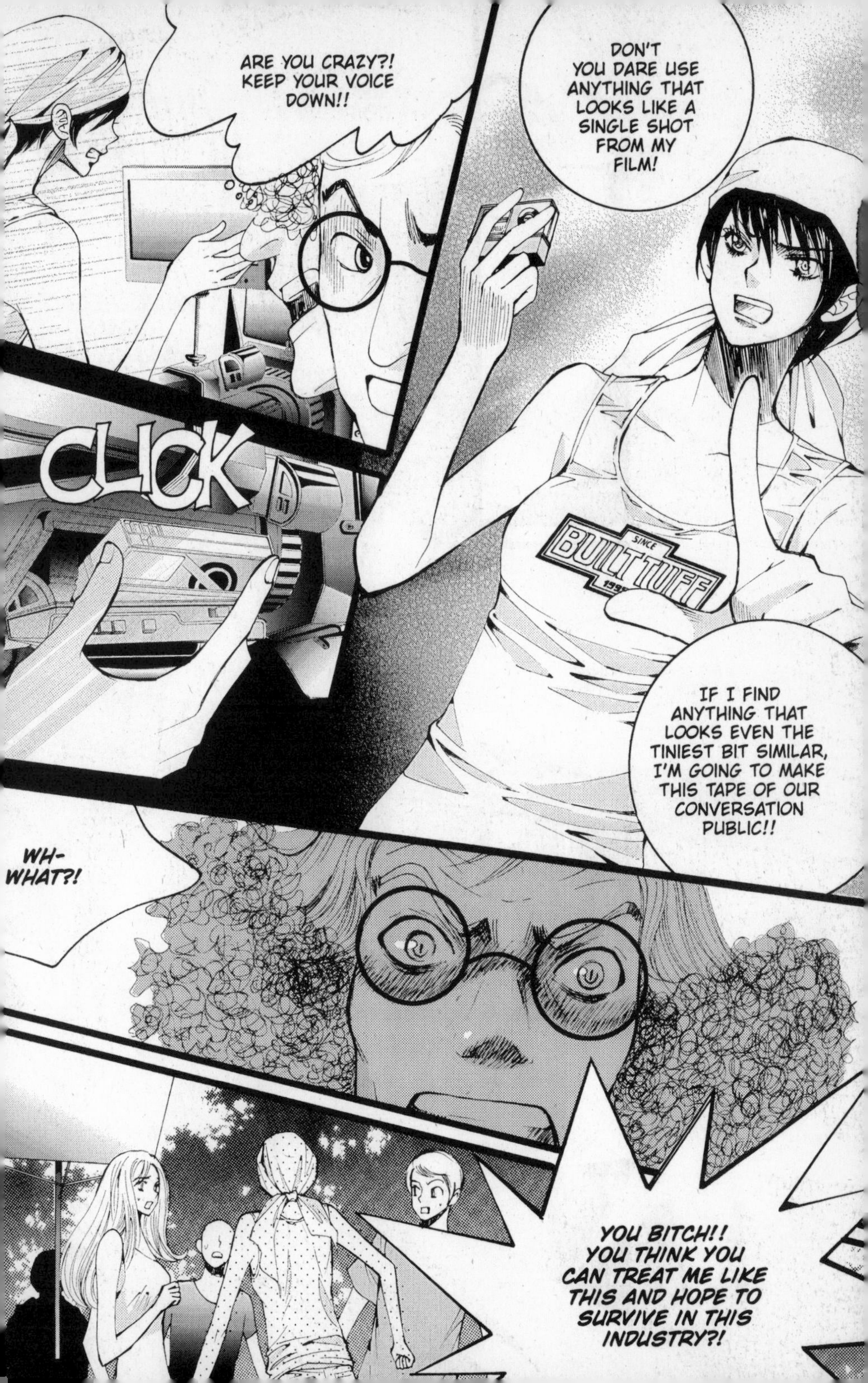
ARE YOU CRAZY?! KEEP YOUR VOICE DOWN!!
DON'T YOU DARE USE ANYTHING THAT LOOKS LIKE A SINGLE SHOT FROM MY FILM!
CLICK
SINCE BUILTTUFF
IF I FIND ANYTHING THAT LOOKS EVEN THE TINIEST BIT SIMILAR, I'M GOING TO MAKE THIS TAPE OF OUR CONVERSATION PUBLIC!!
WH- WHAT?!
YOU BITCH!! YOU THINK YOU CAN TREAT ME LIKE THIS AND HOPE TO SURVIVE IN THIS INDUSTRY?!

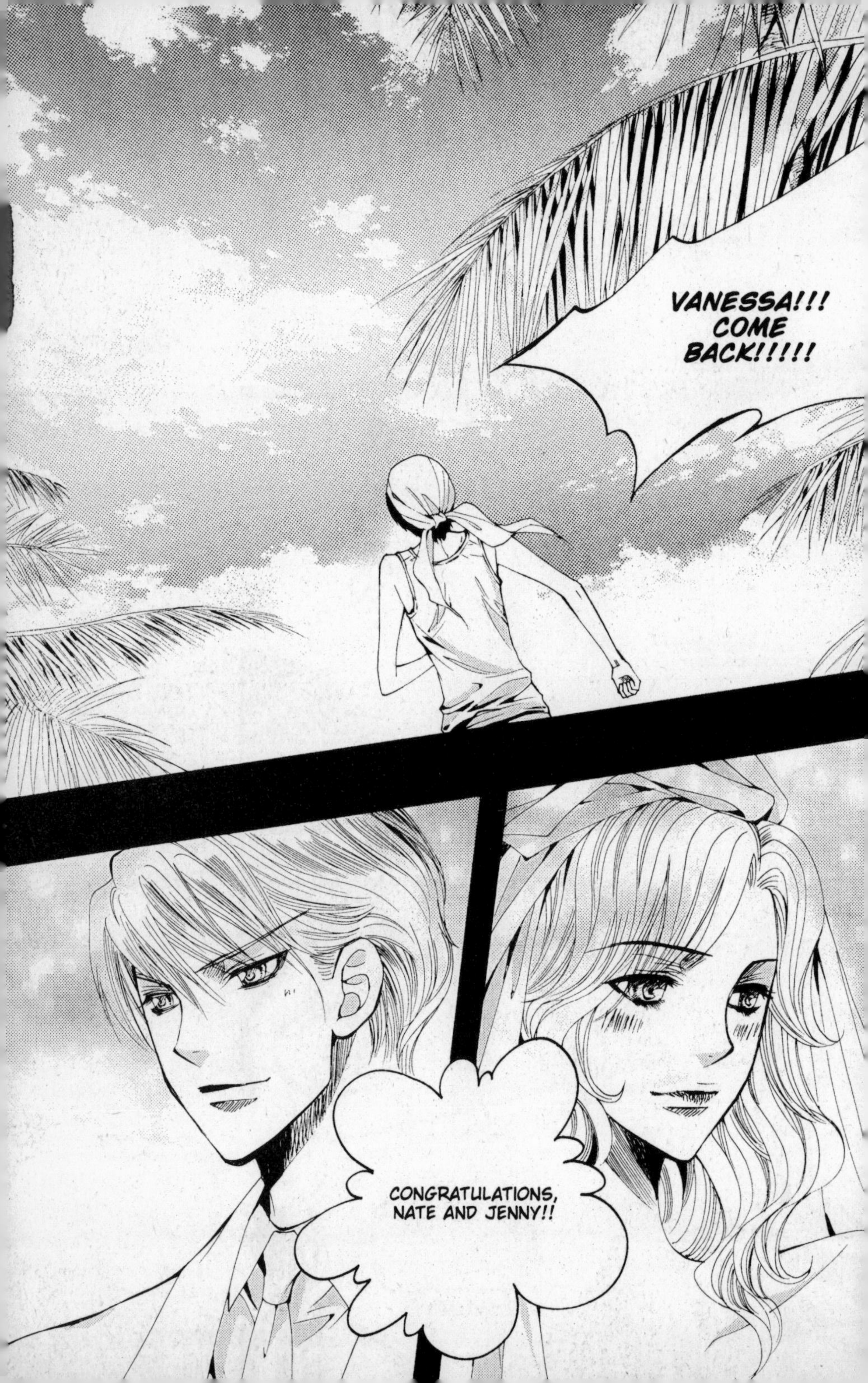
VANESSA!!! COME BACK!!!!!
CONGRATULATIONS, NATE AND JENNY!!

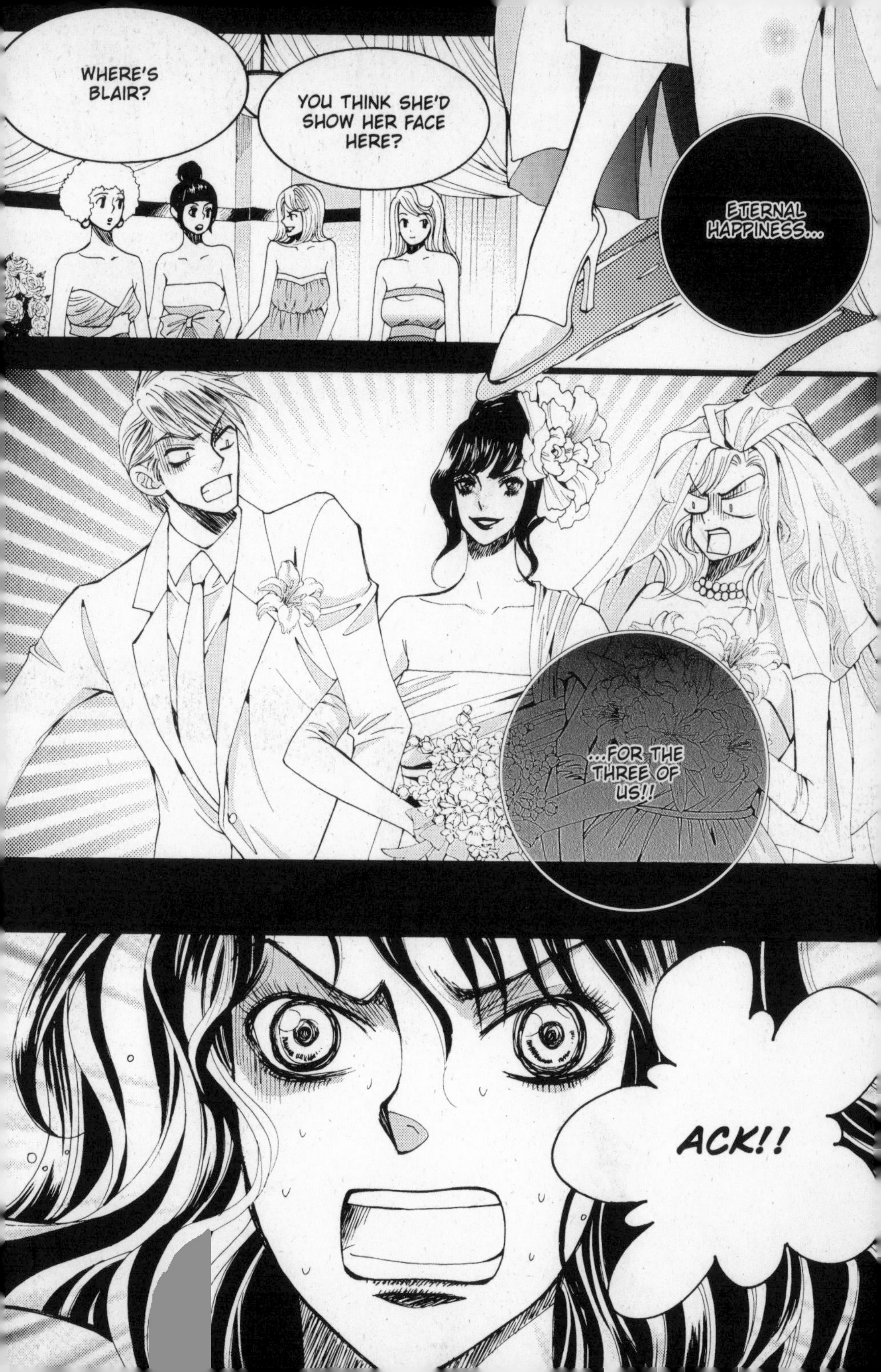
WHERE'S BLAIR?
YOU THINK SHE'D SHOW HER FACE HERE?
ETERNAL HAPPINESS...
...FOR THE THREE OF US!!
ACK!!

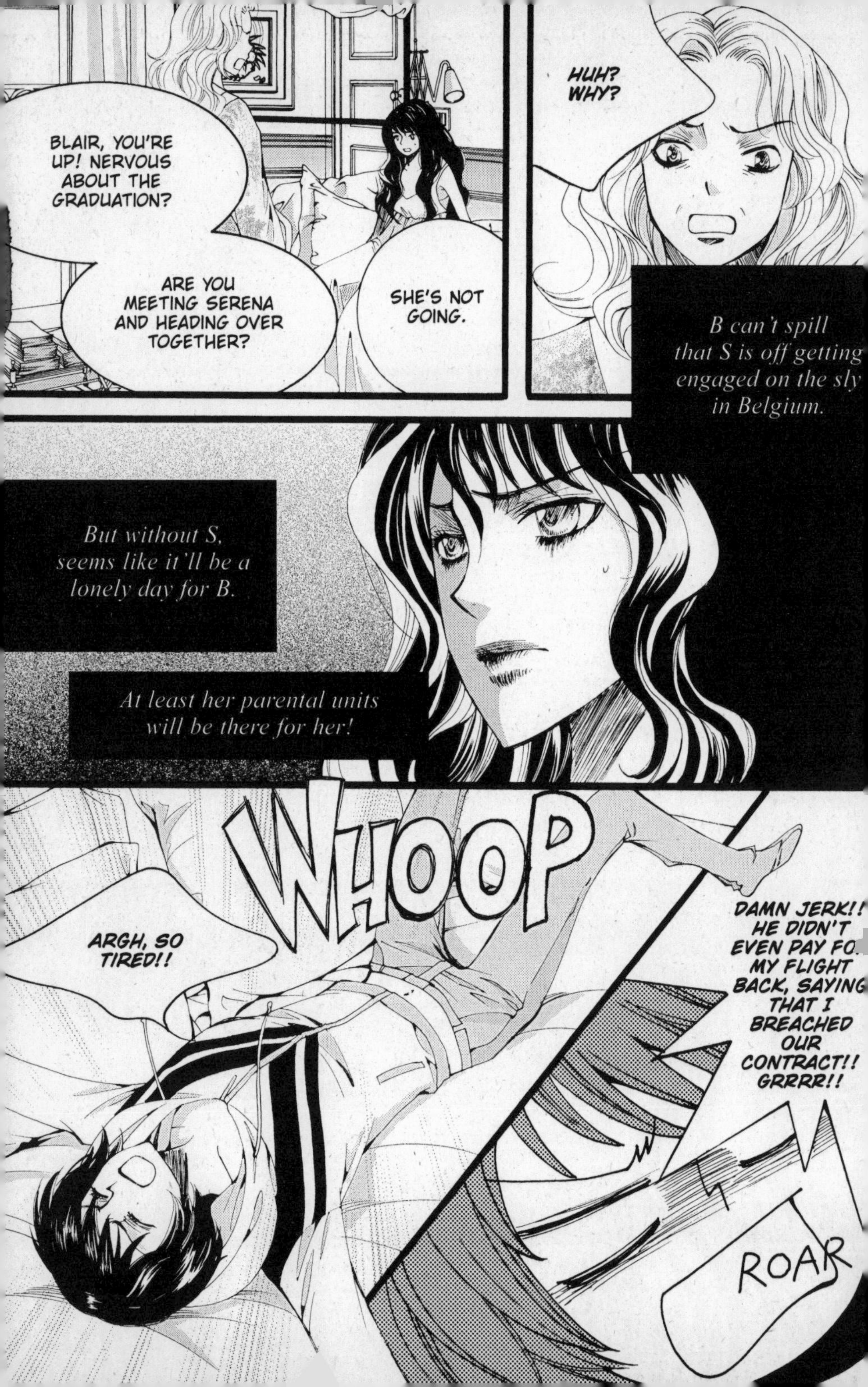
BLAIR, YOU'RE UP! NERVOUS ABOUT THE GRADUATION?
ARE YOU MEETING SERENA AND HEADING OVER TOGETHER?
SHE'S NOT GOING.
HUH? WHY?
B can't spill that S is off getting engaged on the sly in Belgium.
But without S, seems like it'll be a lonely day for B.
At least her parental units will be there for her!
WHOOP
ARGH, SO TIRED!!
DAMN JERK!! HE DIDN'T EVEN PAY FO MY FLIGHT BACK, SAYING THAT I BREACHED OUR CONTRACT!! GRRRR!!
ROAR

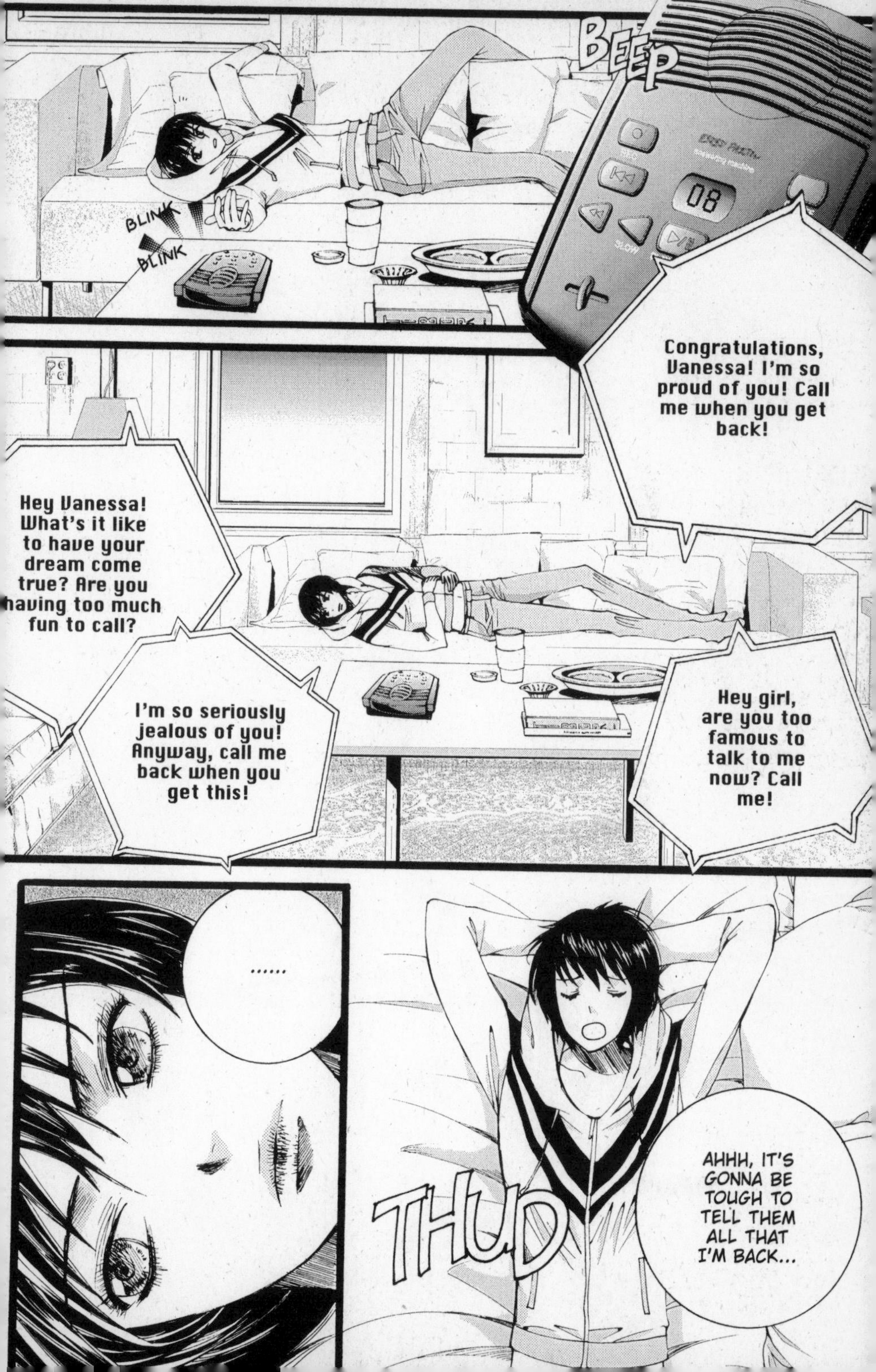
BLINK
BLINK
BEEP
Congratulations, Vanessa! I'm so proud of you! Call me when you get back!
Hey Vanessa! What's it like to have your dream come true? Are you having too much fun to call?
I'm so seriously jealous of you! Anyway, call me back when you get this!
Hey girl, are you too famous to talk to me now? Call me!
......
THUD
AHHH, IT'S GONNA BE TOUGH TO TELL THEM ALL THAT I'M BACK...

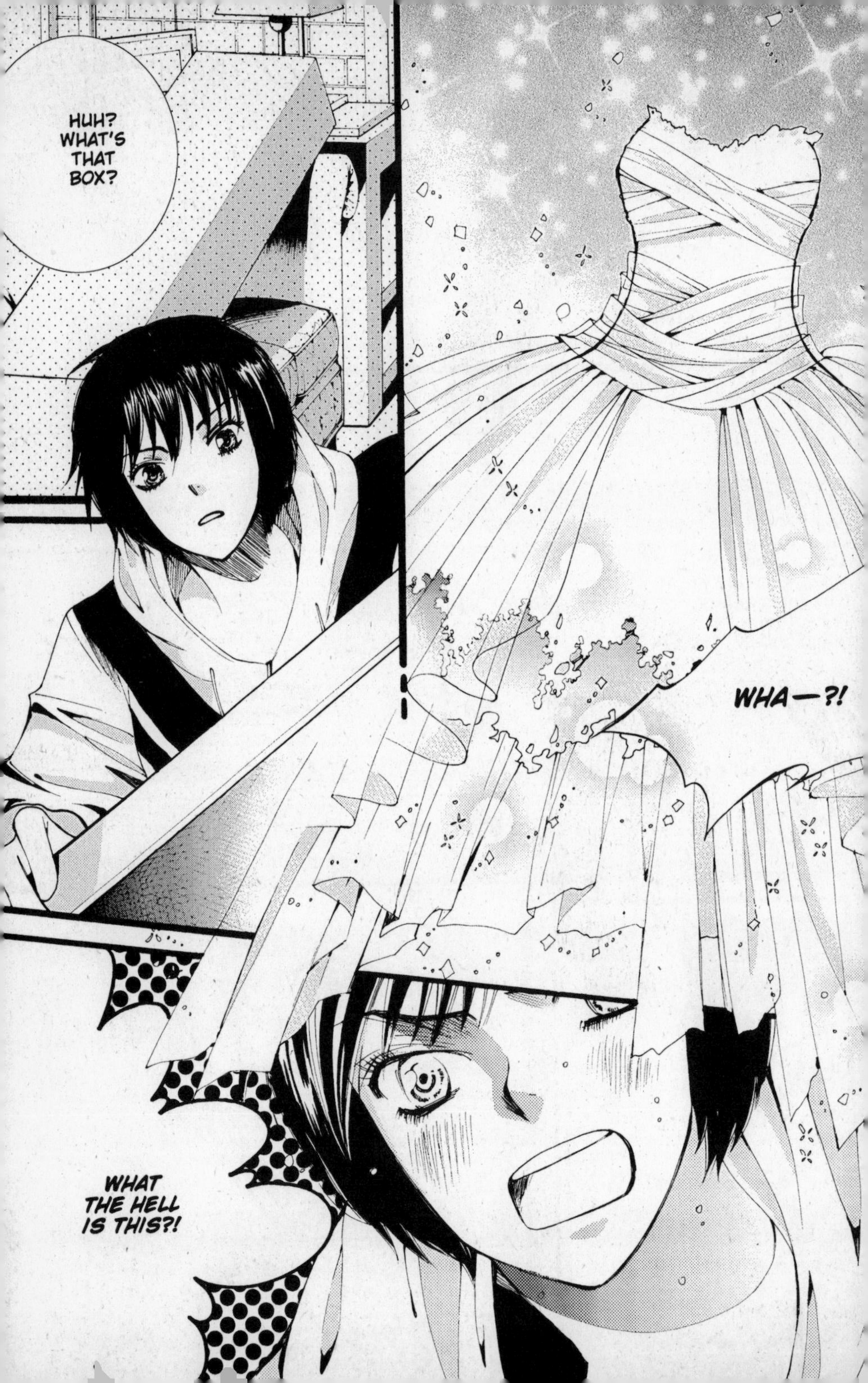
HUH? WHAT'S THAT BOX?
WHA—?!
WHAT THE HELL IS THIS?!

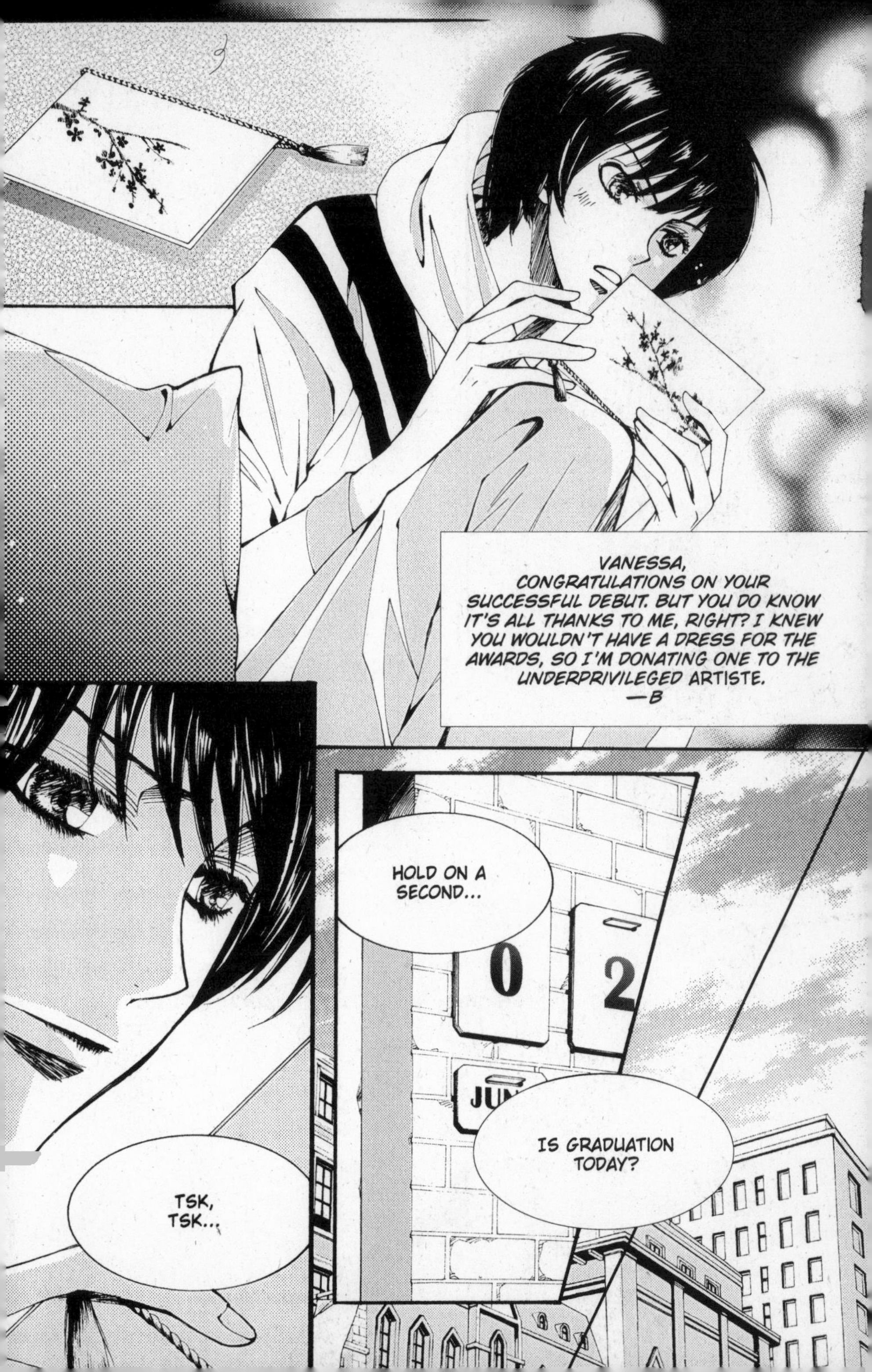
VANESSA,
CONGRATULATIONS ON YOUR SUCCESSFUL DEBUT. BUT YOU DO KNOW IT'S ALL THANKS TO ME, RIGHT? I KNEW YOU WOULDN'T HAVE A DRESS FOR THE AWARDS, SO I'M DONATING ONE TO THE UNDERPRIVILEGED ARTISTE.
—B
TSK, TSK...
HOLD ON A SECOND...
02
IS GRADUATION TODAY?

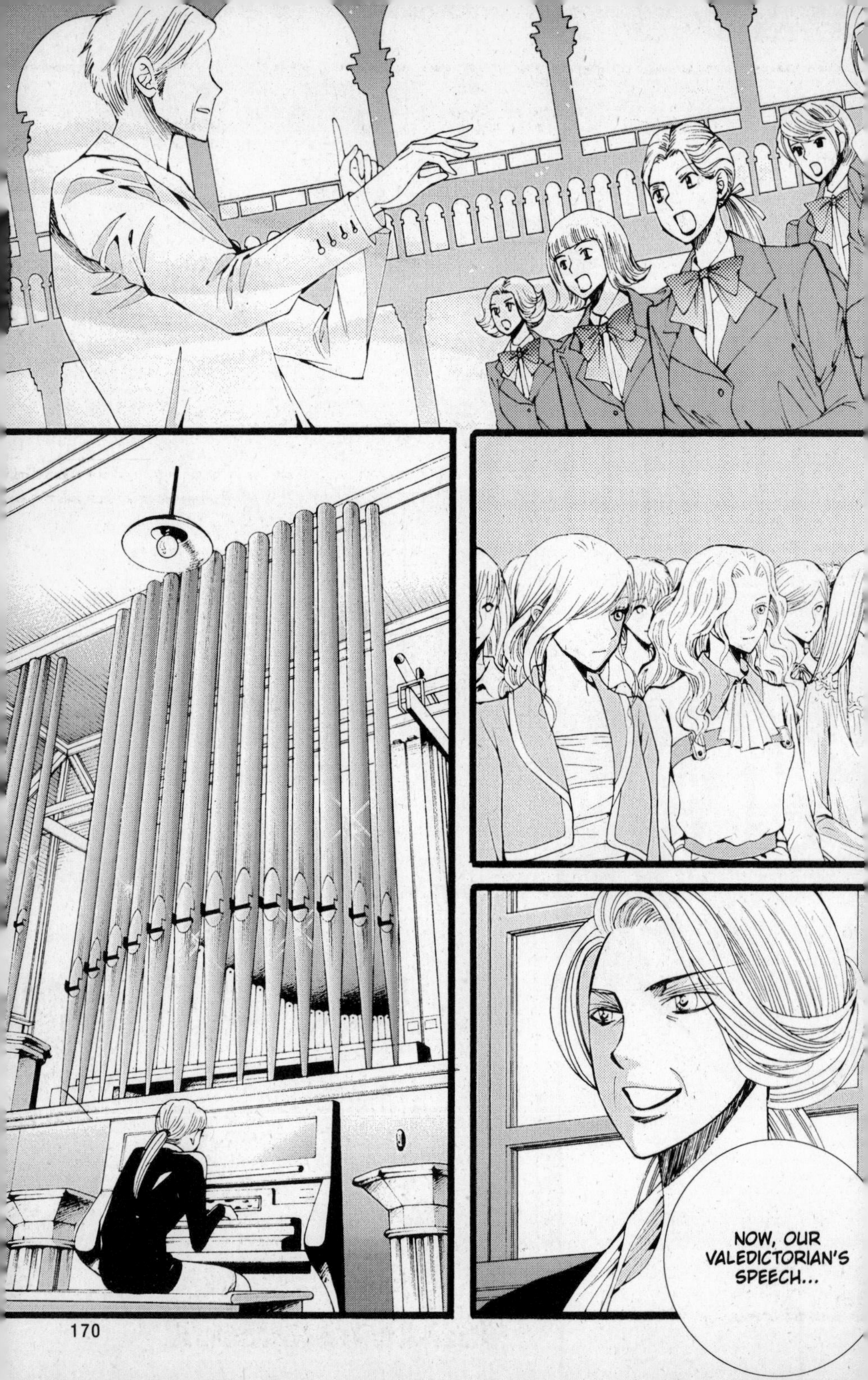
NOW, OUR VALEDICTORIAN'S SPEECH...

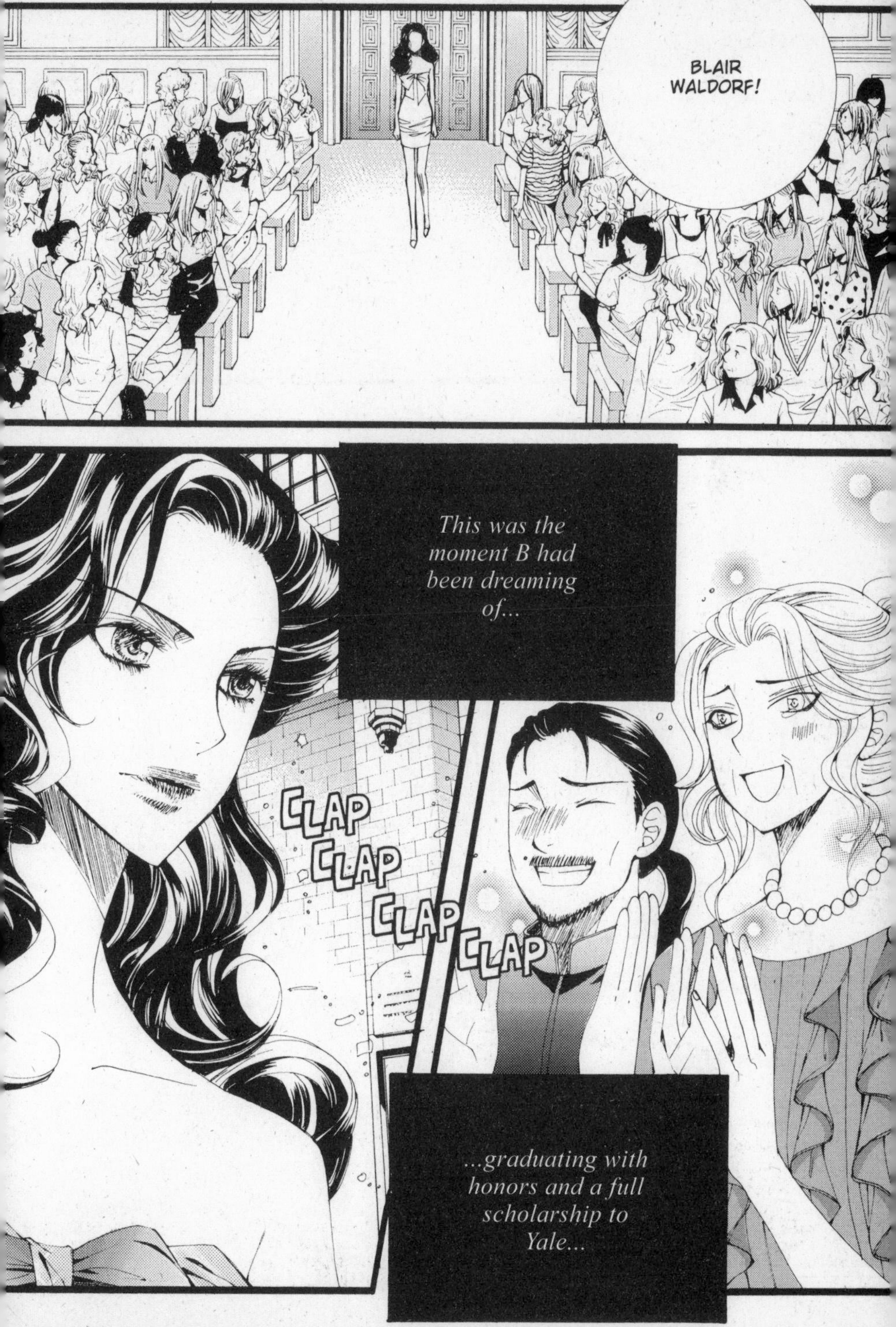
BLAIR WALDORF!
This was the moment B had been dreaming of...
CLAP CLAP CLAP CLAP
...graduating with honors and a full scholarship to Yale...

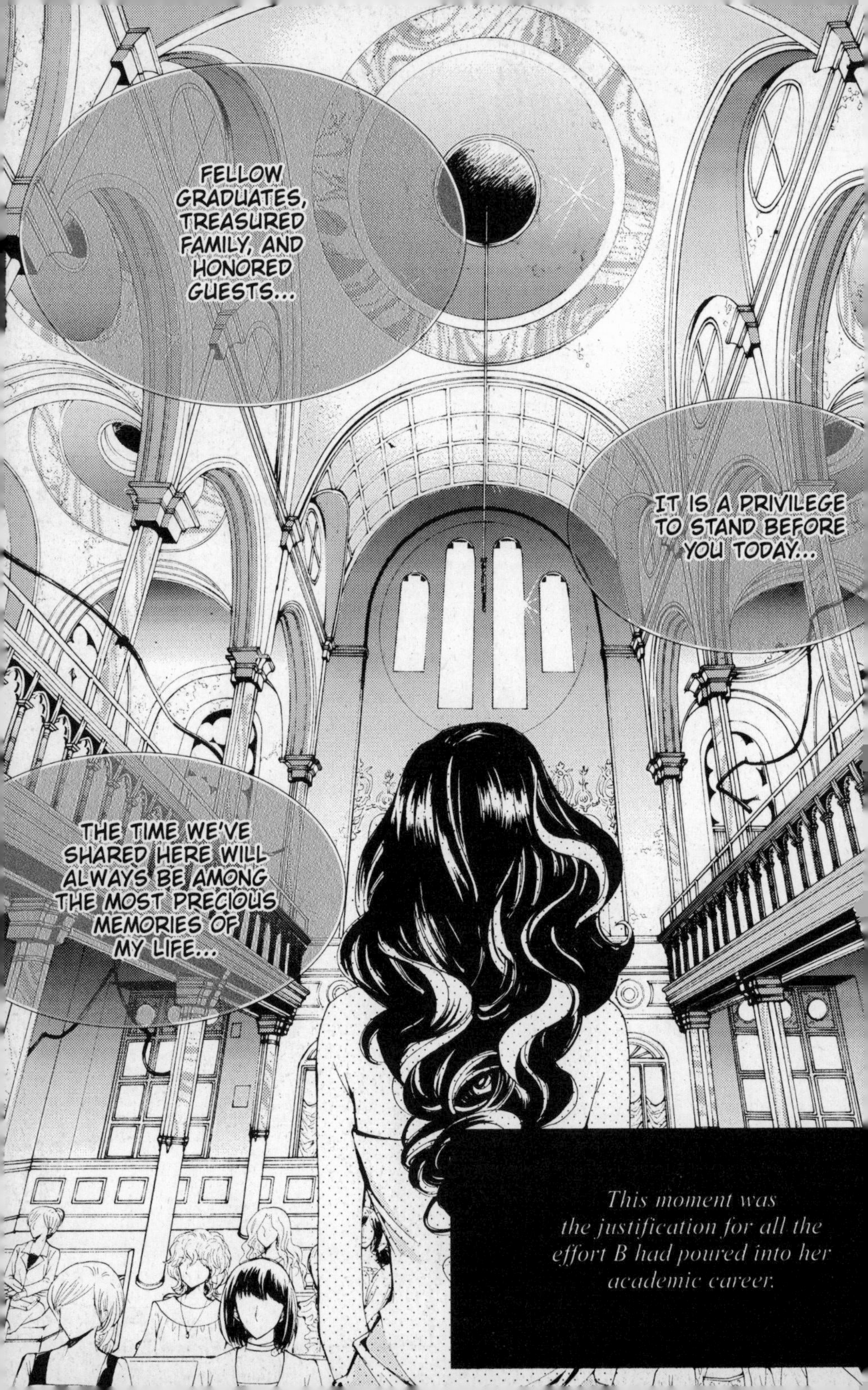
FELLOW GRADUATES, TREASURED FAMILY, AND HONORED GUESTS...
IT IS A PRIVILEGE TO STAND BEFORE YOU TODAY...
THE TIME WE'VE SHARED HERE WILL ALWAYS BE AMONG THE MOST PRECIOUS MEMORIES OF MY LIFE...
This moment was the justification for all the effort B had poured into her academic career.

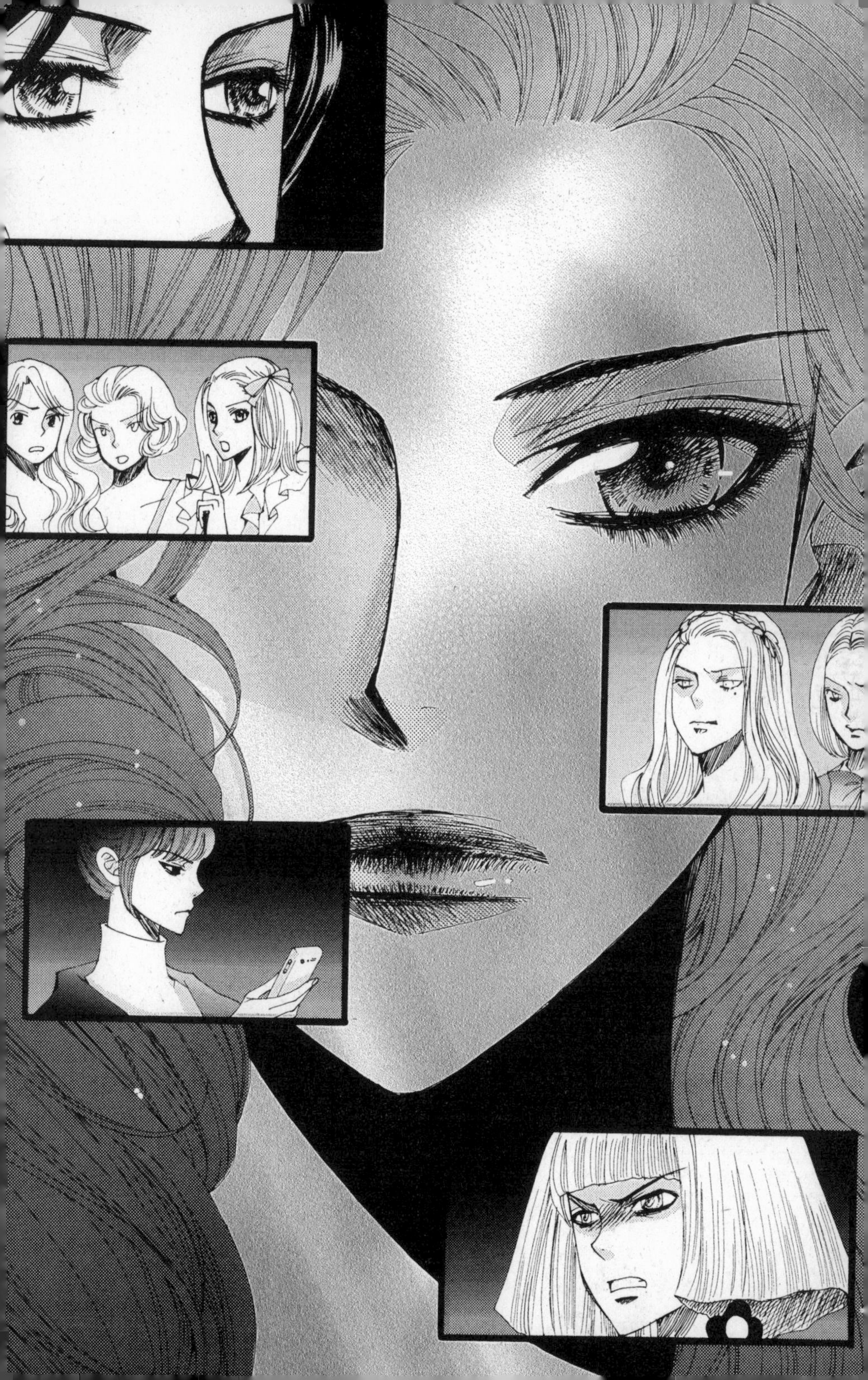

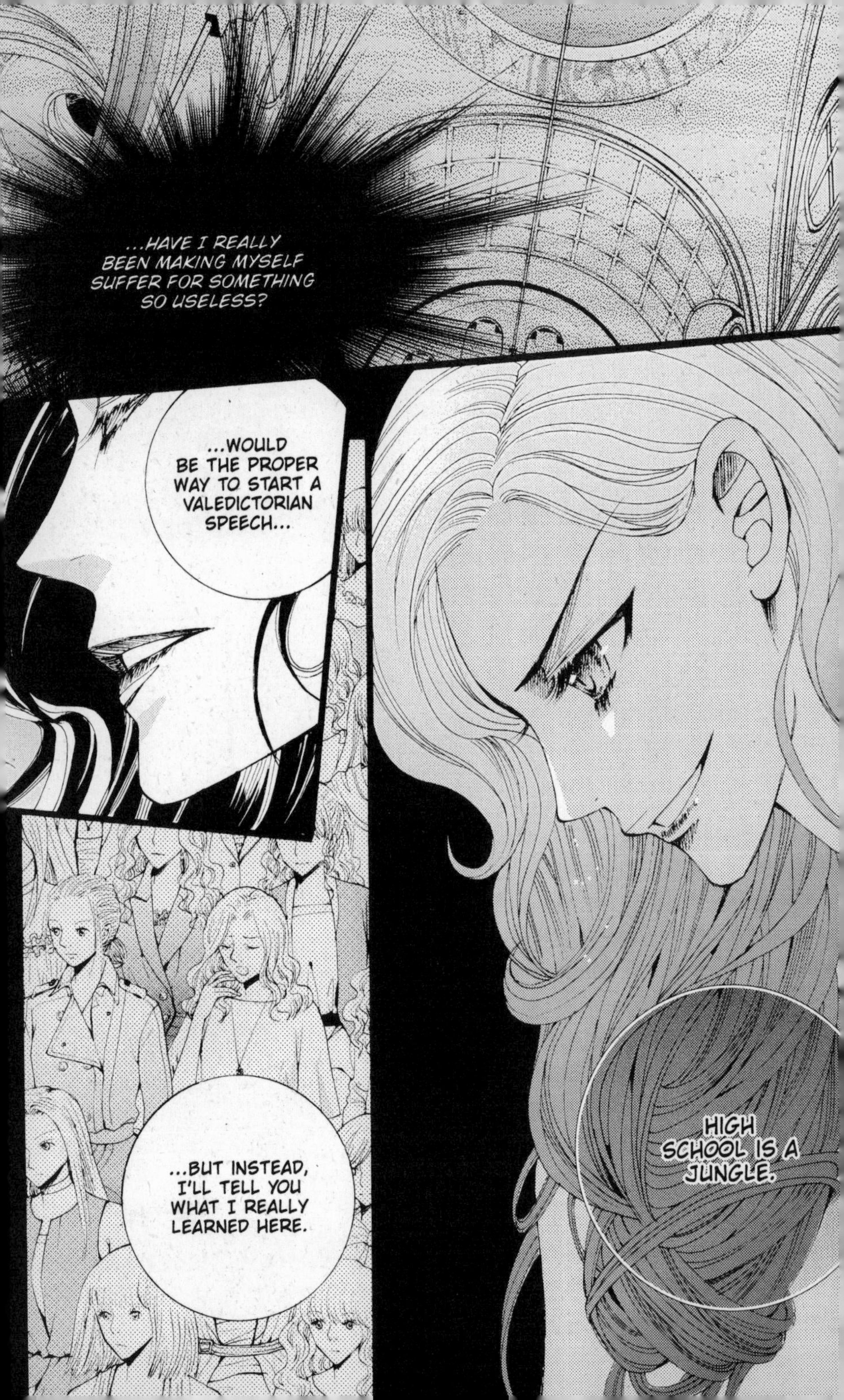
...HAVE I REALLY BEEN MAKING MYSELF SUFFER FOR SOMETHING SO USELESS?
...WOULD BE THE PROPER WAY TO START A VALEDICTORIAN SPEECH...
...BUT INSTEAD, I'LL TELL YOU WHAT I REALLY LEARNED HERE.
HIGH SCHOOL IS A JUNGLE.

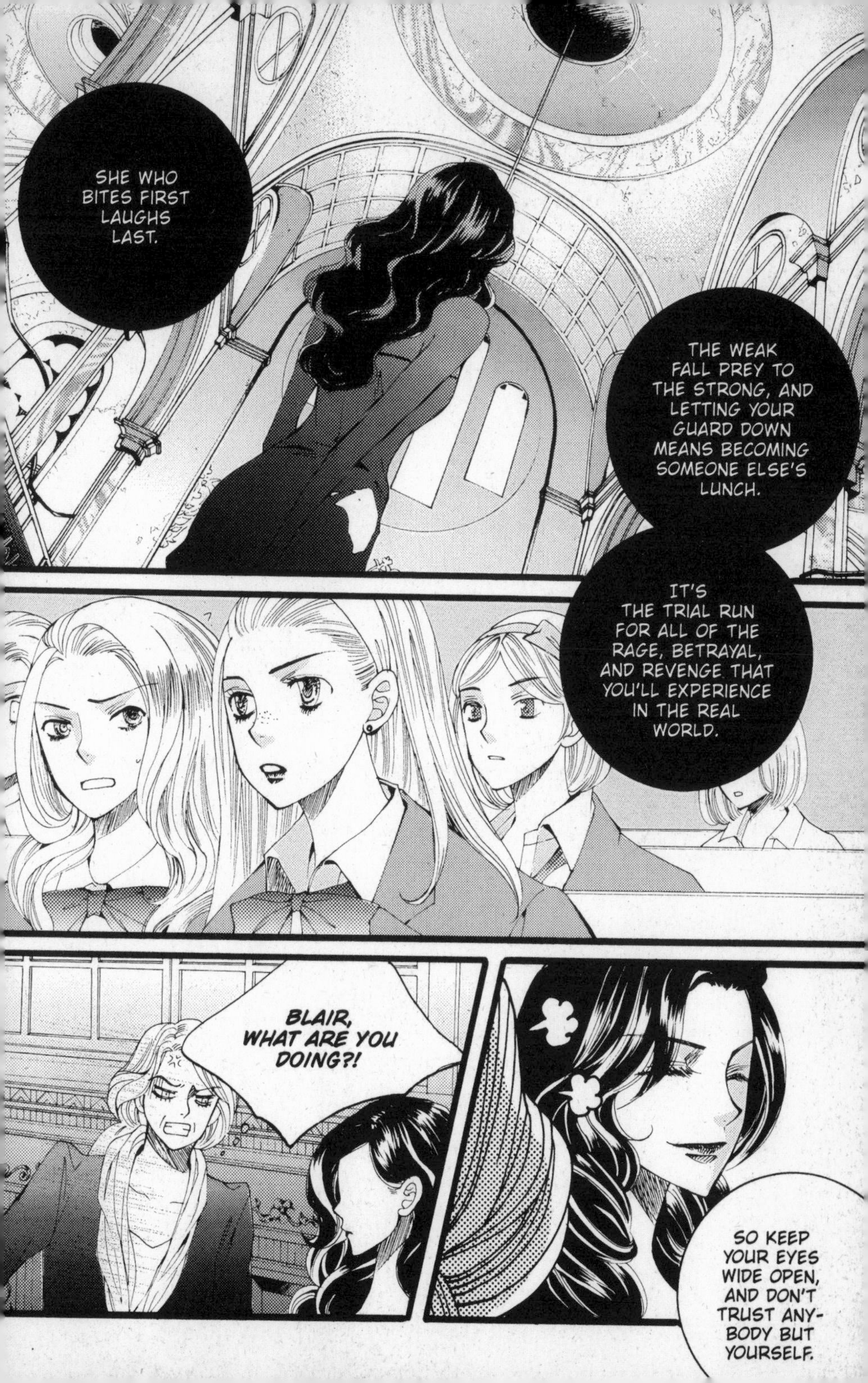
SHE WHO BITES FIRST LAUGHS LAST.
THE WEAK FALL PREY TO THE STRONG, AND LETTING YOUR GUARD DOWN MEANS BECOMING SOMEONE ELSE'S LUNCH.
IT'S THE TRIAL RUN FOR ALL OF THE RAGE, BETRAYAL, AND REVENGE THAT YOU'LL EXPERIENCE IN THE REAL WORLD.
BLAIR, WHAT ARE YOU DOING?!
SO KEEP YOUR EYES WIDE OPEN, AND DON'T TRUST ANY-BODY BUT YOURSELF.

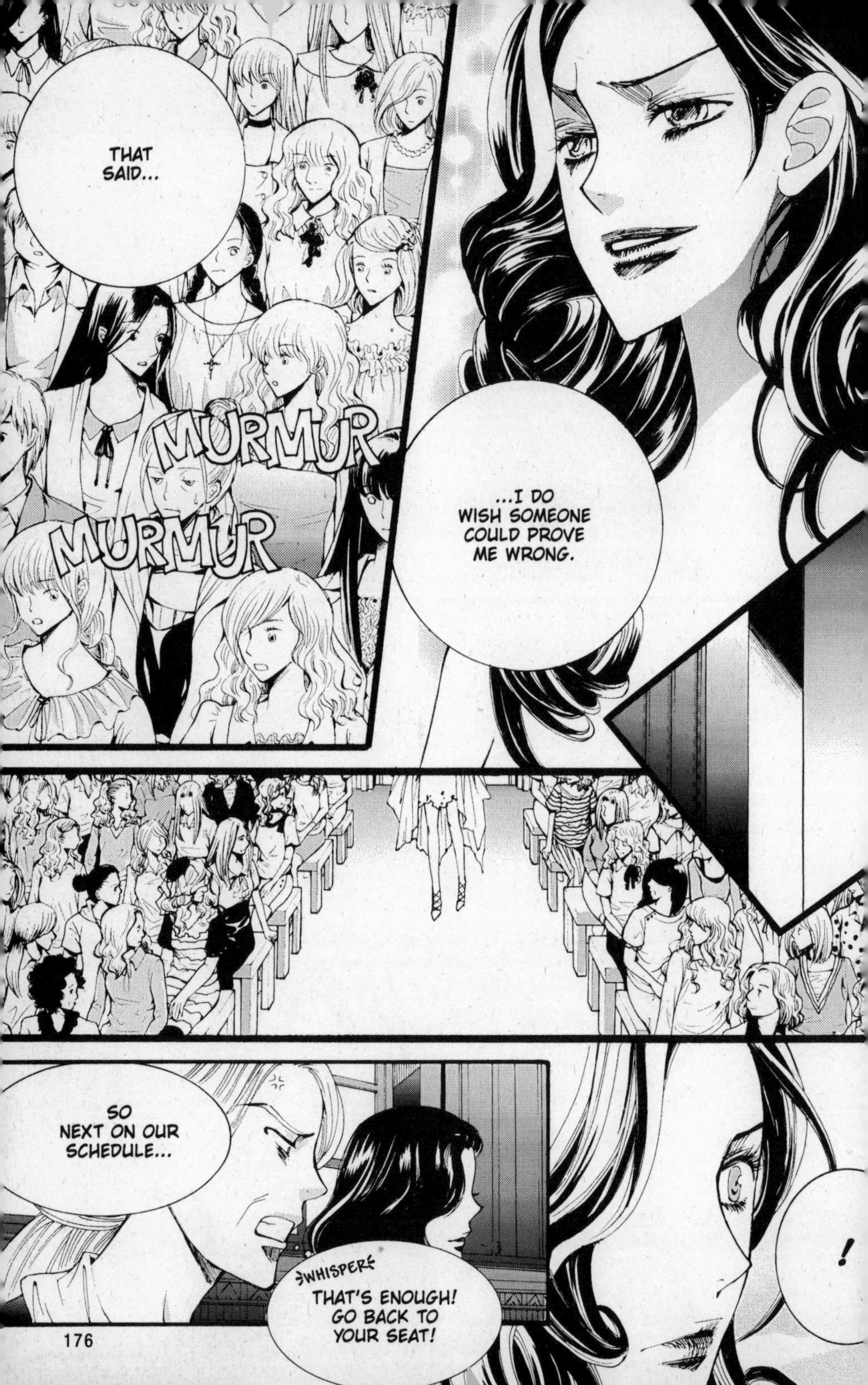
THAT SAID...
MURMUR
MURMUR
...I DO WISH SOMEONE COULD PROVE ME WRONG.
SO NEXT ON OUR SCHEDULE...
WHISPER
THAT'S ENOUGH! GO BACK TO YOUR SEAT!
!

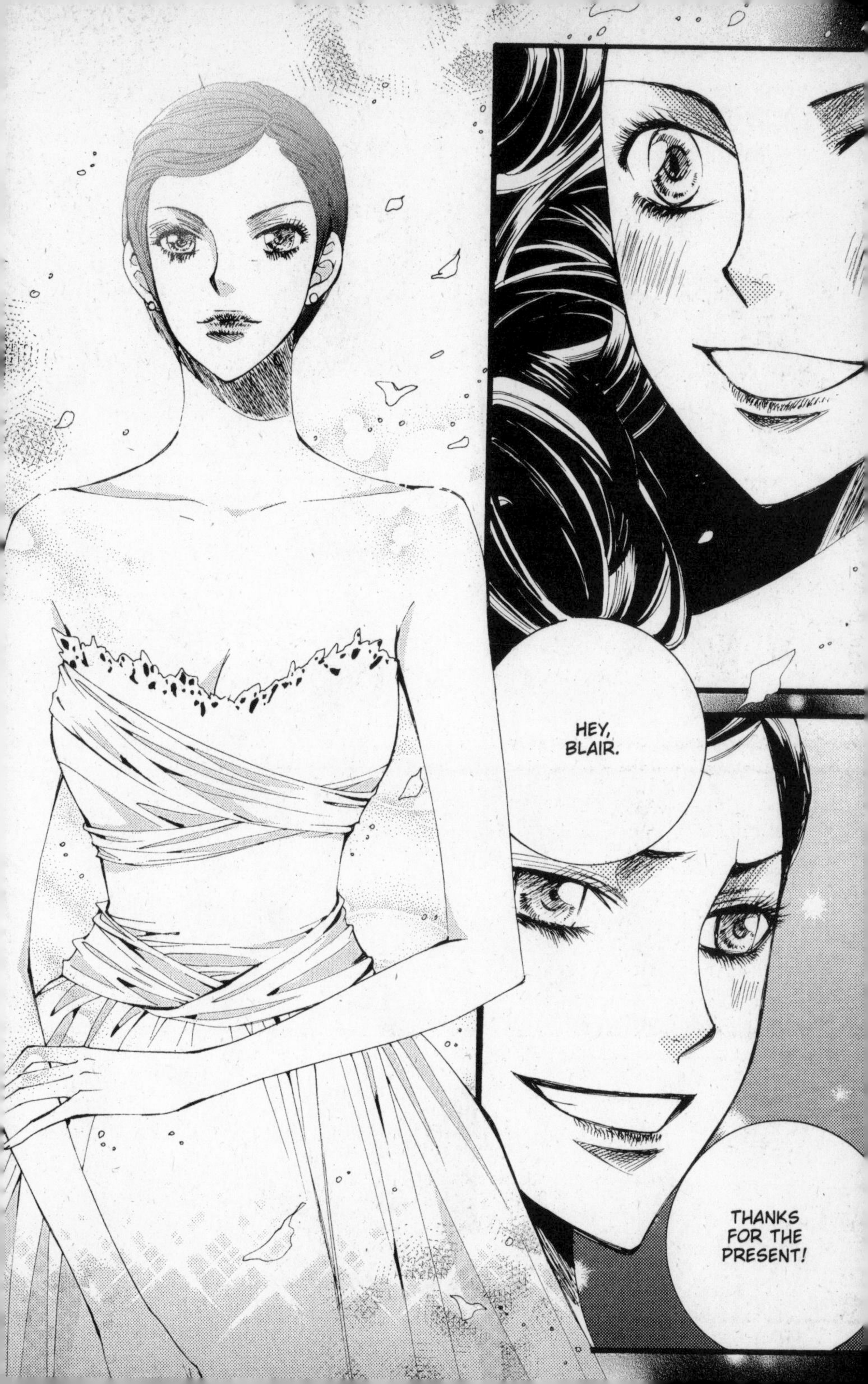
HEY, BLAIR.
THANKS FOR THE PRESENT!

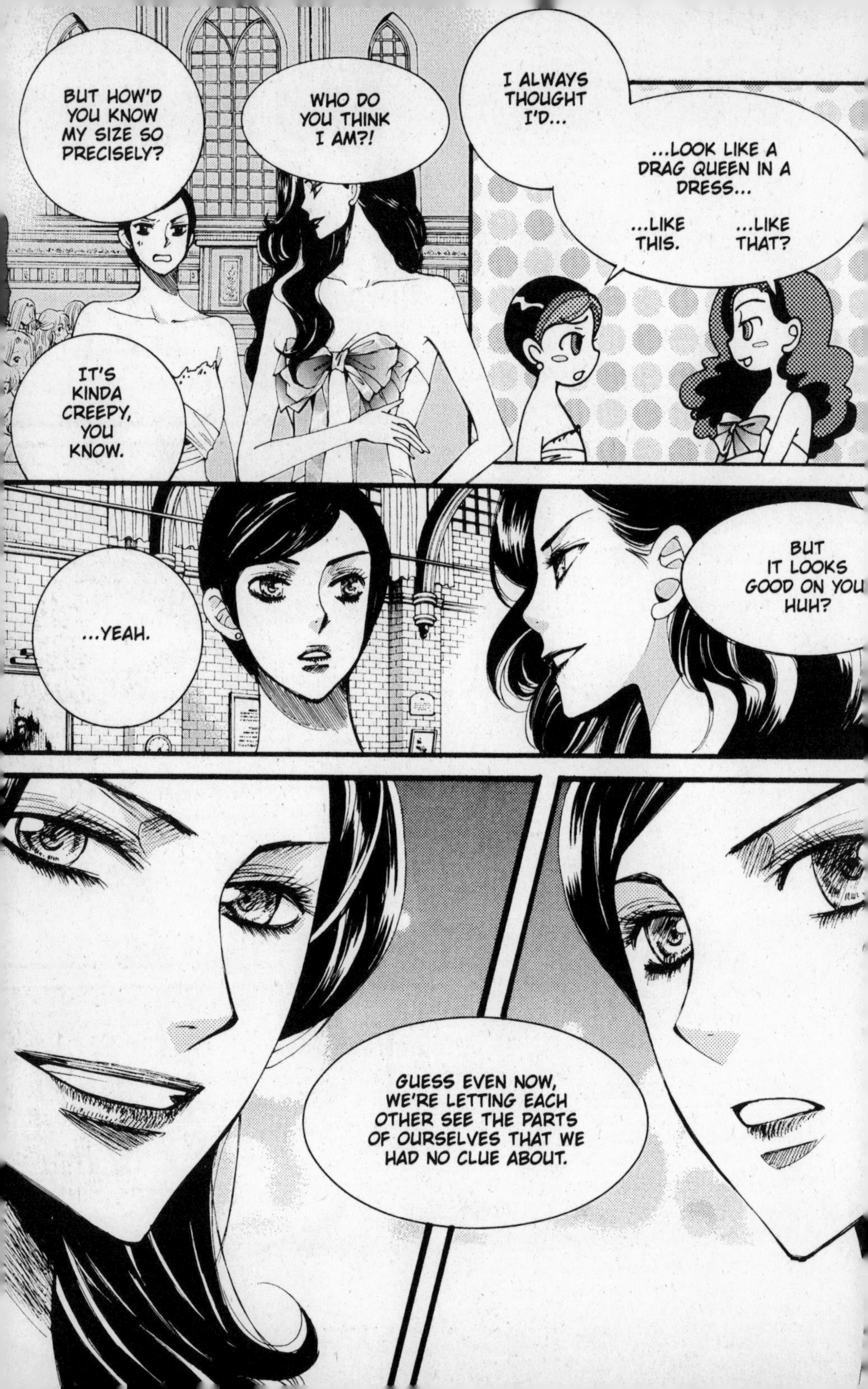
BUT HOW'D YOU KNOW MY SIZE SO PRECISELY?
IT'S KINDA CREEPY, YOU KNOW.
WHO DO YOU THINK I AM?!
I ALWAYS THOUGHT I'D...
...LOOK LIKE A DRAG QUEEN IN A DRESS...
...LIKE THIS.
...LIKE THAT?
...YEAH.
BUT IT LOOKS GOOD ON YOU HUH?
GUESS EVEN NOW, WE'RE LETTING EACH OTHER SEE THE PARTS OF OURSELVES THAT WE HAD NO CLUE ABOUT.

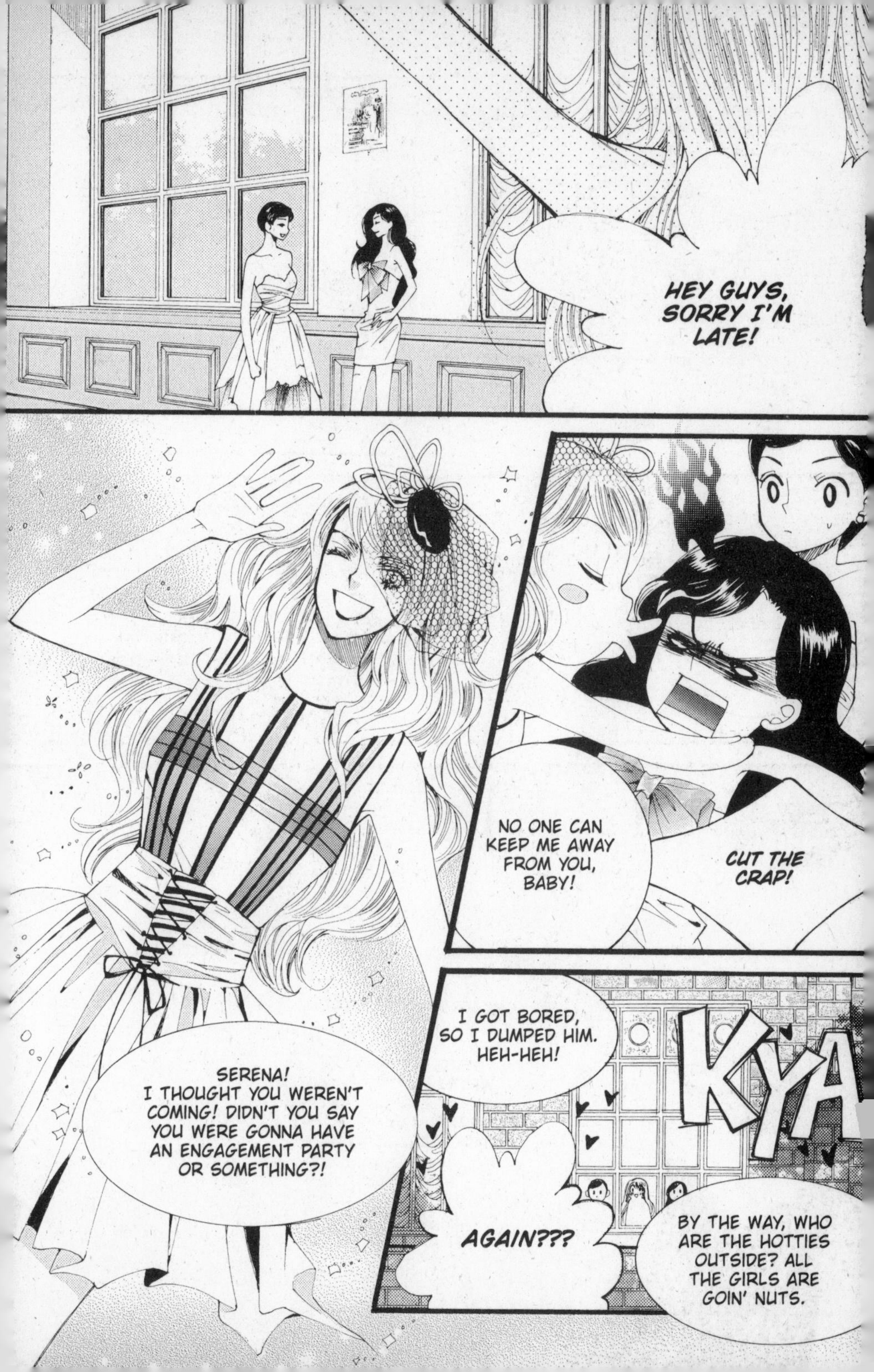
HEY GUYS, SORRY I'M LATE!
SERENA! I THOUGHT YOU WEREN'T COMING! DIDN'T YOU SAY YOU WERE GONNA HAVE AN ENGAGEMENT PARTY OR SOMETHING?!
NO ONE CAN KEEP ME AWAY FROM YOU, BABY!
CUT THE CRAP!
I GOT BORED, SO I DUMPED HIM. HEH-HEH!
KYA
AGAIN???
BY THE WAY, WHO ARE THE HOTTIES OUTSIDE? ALL THE GIRLS ARE GOIN' NUTS.

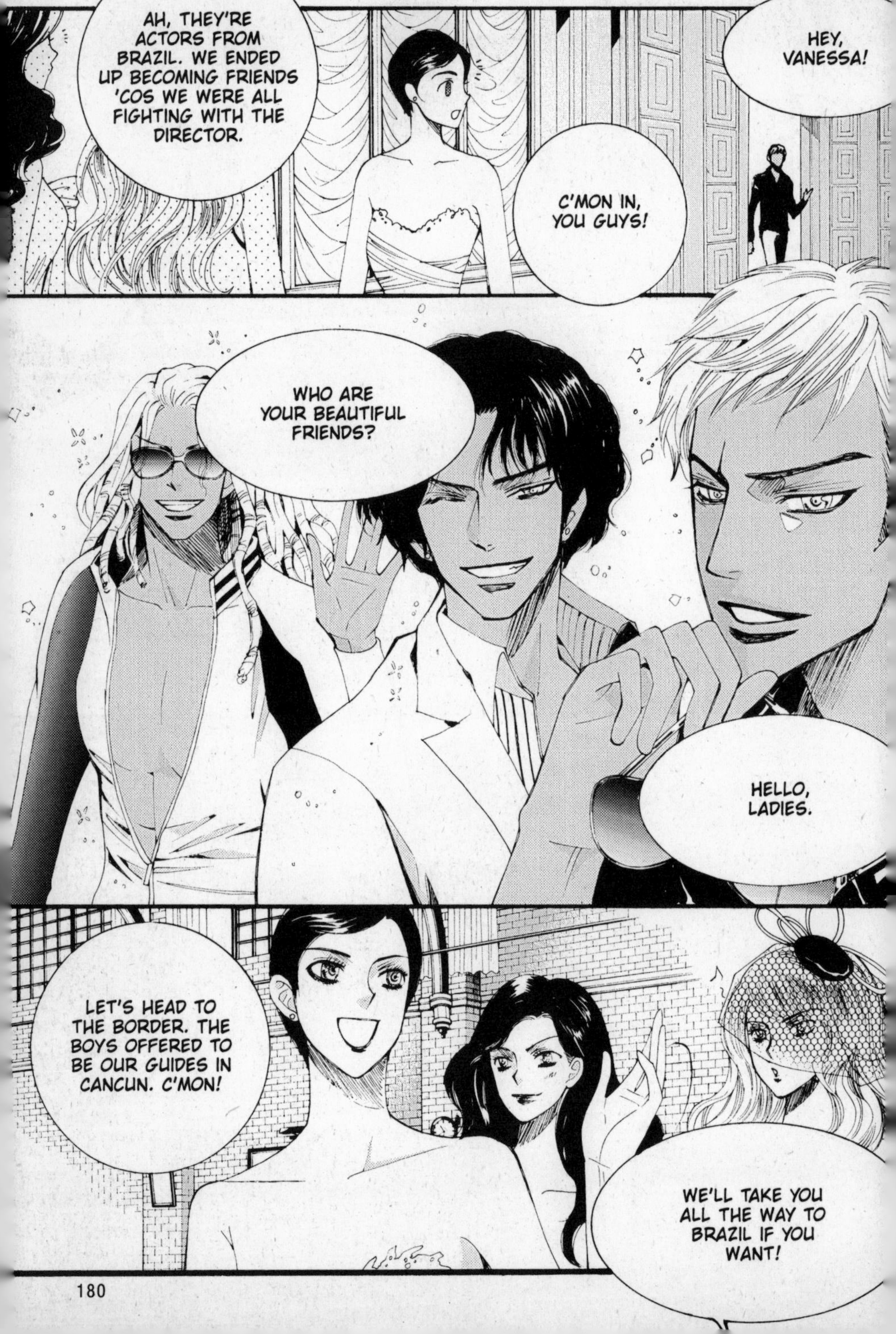
AH, THEY'RE ACTORS FROM BRAZIL. WE ENDED UP BECOMING FRIENDS 'COS WE WERE ALL FIGHTING WITH THE DIRECTOR.
HEY, VANESSA!
C'MON IN, YOU GUYS!
WHO ARE YOUR BEAUTIFUL FRIENDS?
HELLO, LADIES.
LET'S HEAD TO THE BORDER. THE BOYS OFFERED TO BE OUR GUIDES IN CANCUN. C'MON!
WE'LL TAKE YOU ALL THE WAY TO BRAZIL IF YOU WANT!

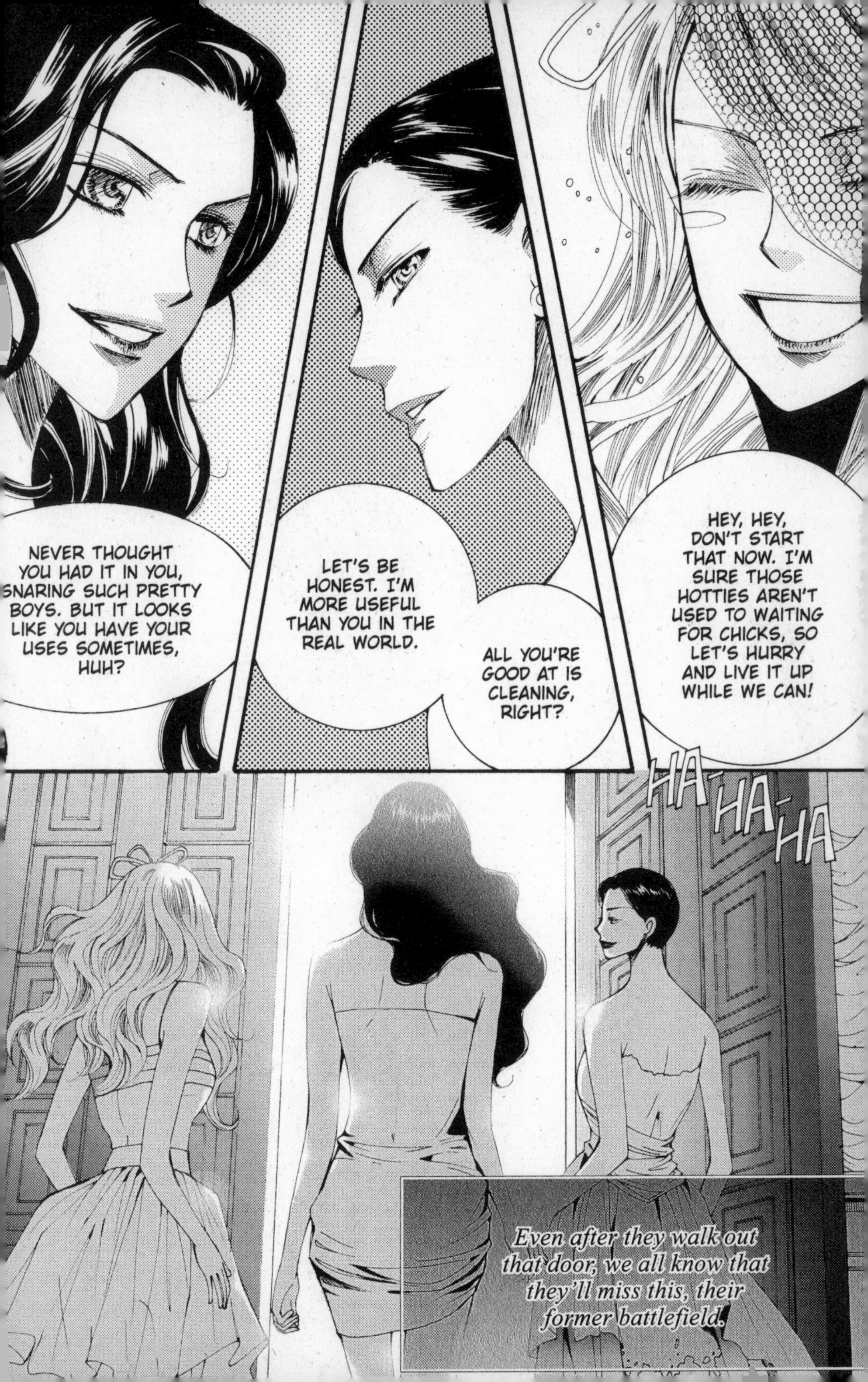
NEVER THOUGHT YOU HAD IT IN YOU, SNARING SUCH PRETTY BOYS. BUT IT LOOKS LIKE YOU HAVE YOUR USES SOMETIMES, HUH?
LET'S BE HONEST. I'M MORE USEFUL THAN YOU IN THE REAL WORLD.
ALL YOU'RE GOOD AT IS CLEANING, RIGHT?
HEY, HEY, DON'T START THAT NOW. I'M SURE THOSE HOTTIES AREN'T USED TO WAITING FOR CHICKS, SO LET'S HURRY AND LIVE IT UP WHILE WE CAN!
HA-HA-HA
Even after they walk out that door, we all know that they'll miss this, their former battlefield.

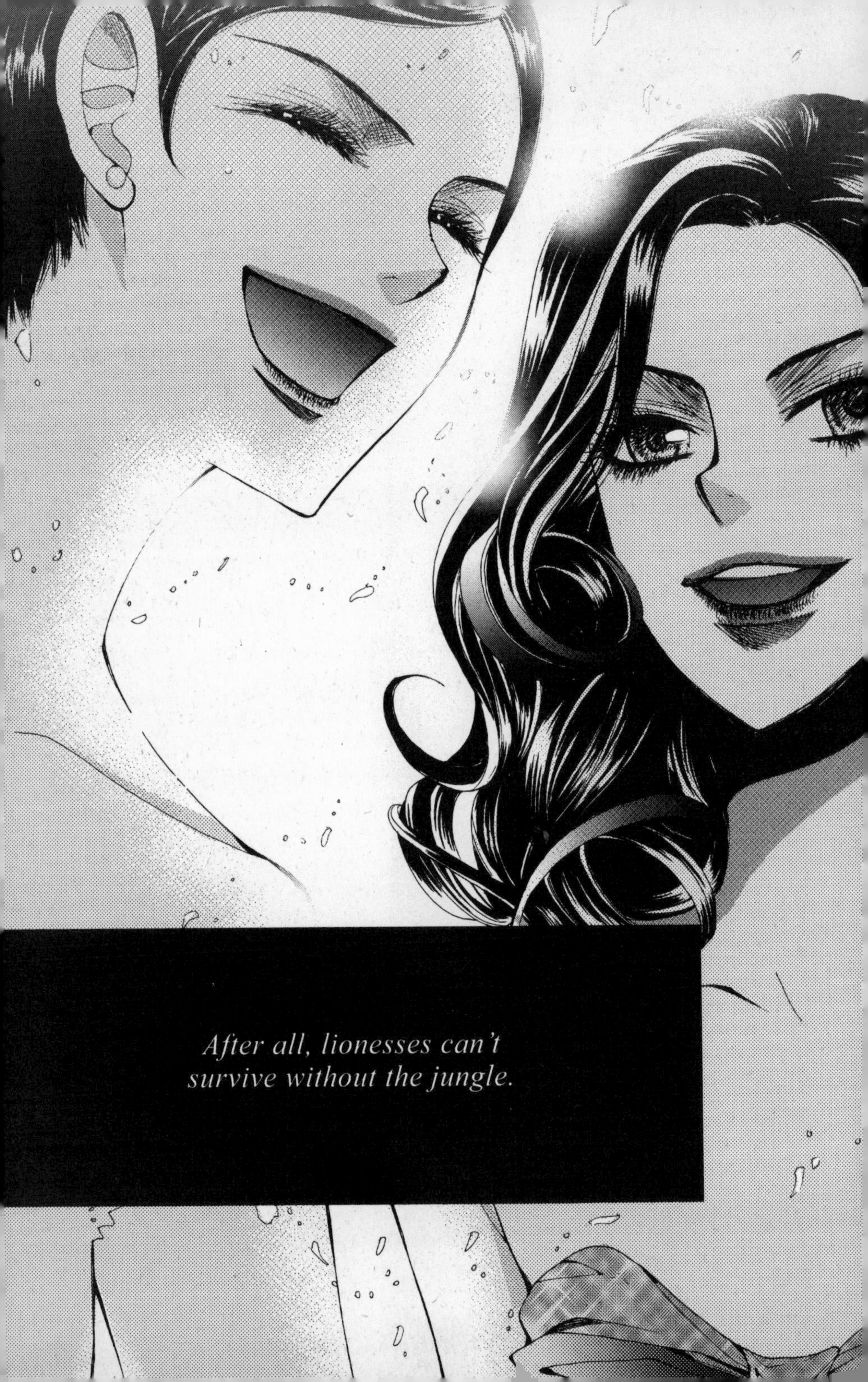
After all, lionesses can't survive without the jungle.

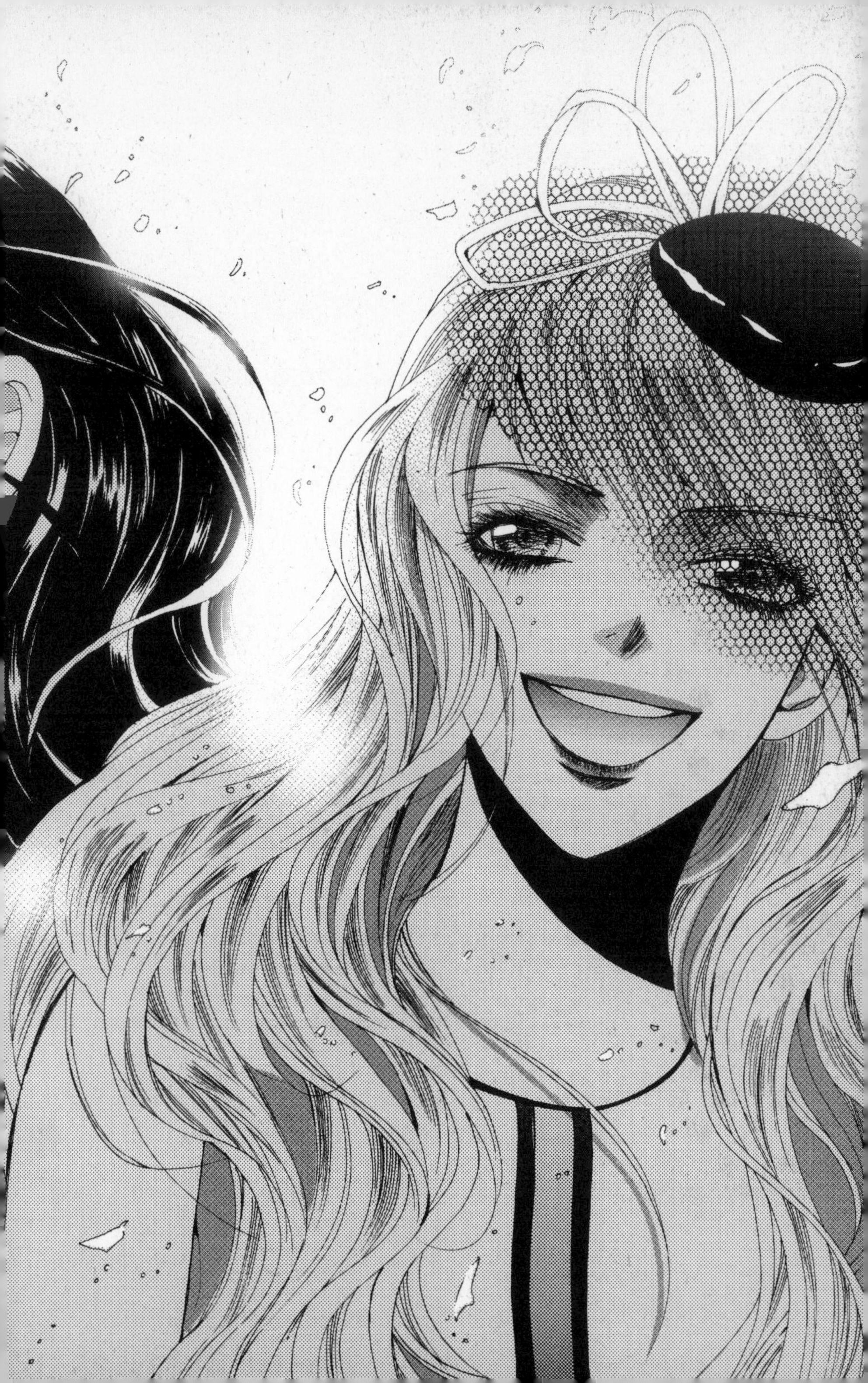

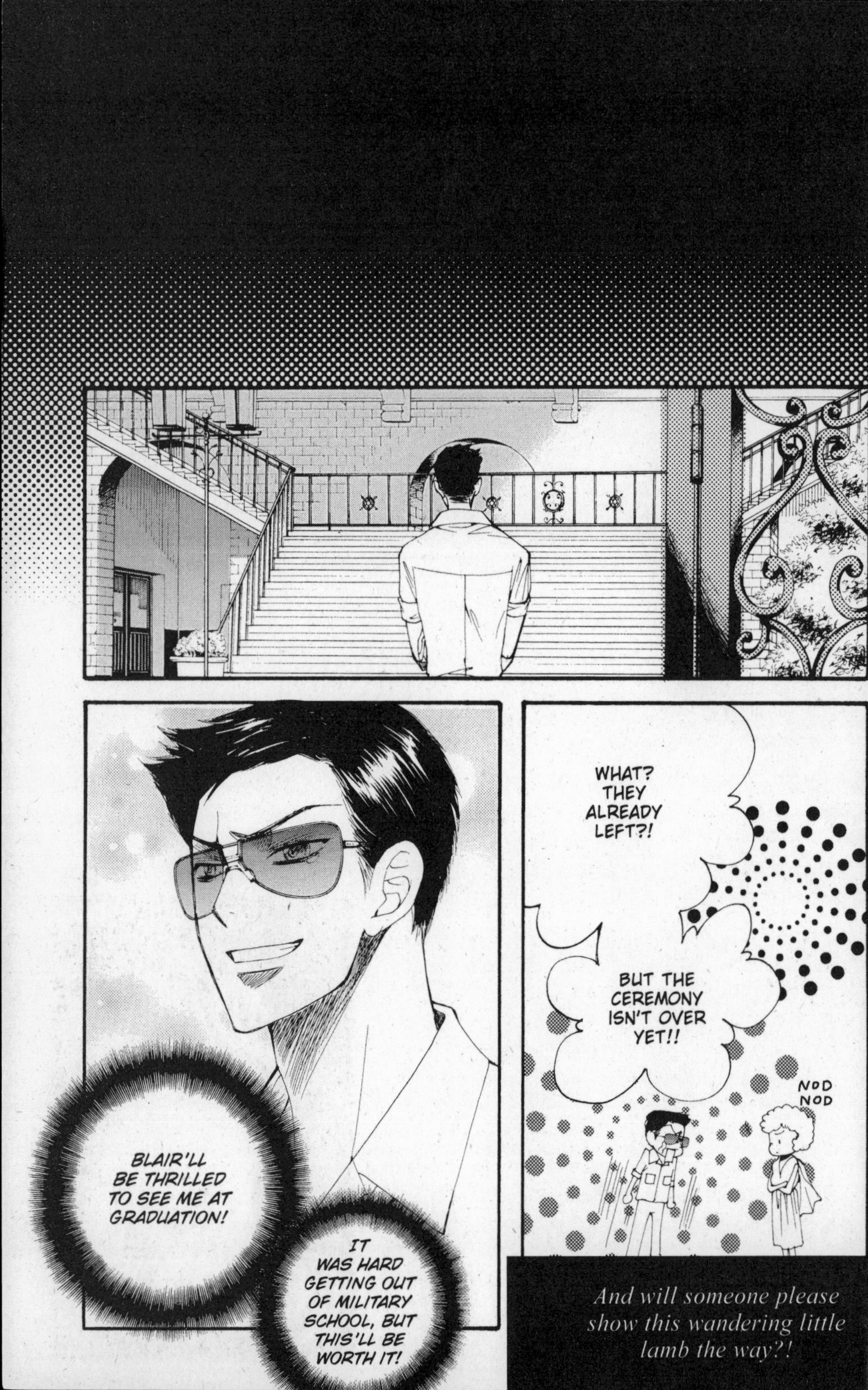
BLAIR'LL BE THRILLED TO SEE ME AT GRADUATION!
IT WAS HARD GETTING OUT OF MILITARY SCHOOL, BUT THIS'LL BE WORTH IT!
WHAT? THEY ALREADY LEFT?!
BUT THE CEREMONY ISN'T OVER YET!!
NOD NOD
And will someone please show this wandering little lamb the way?!

gossip girl
FOR YOUR EYES ONLY

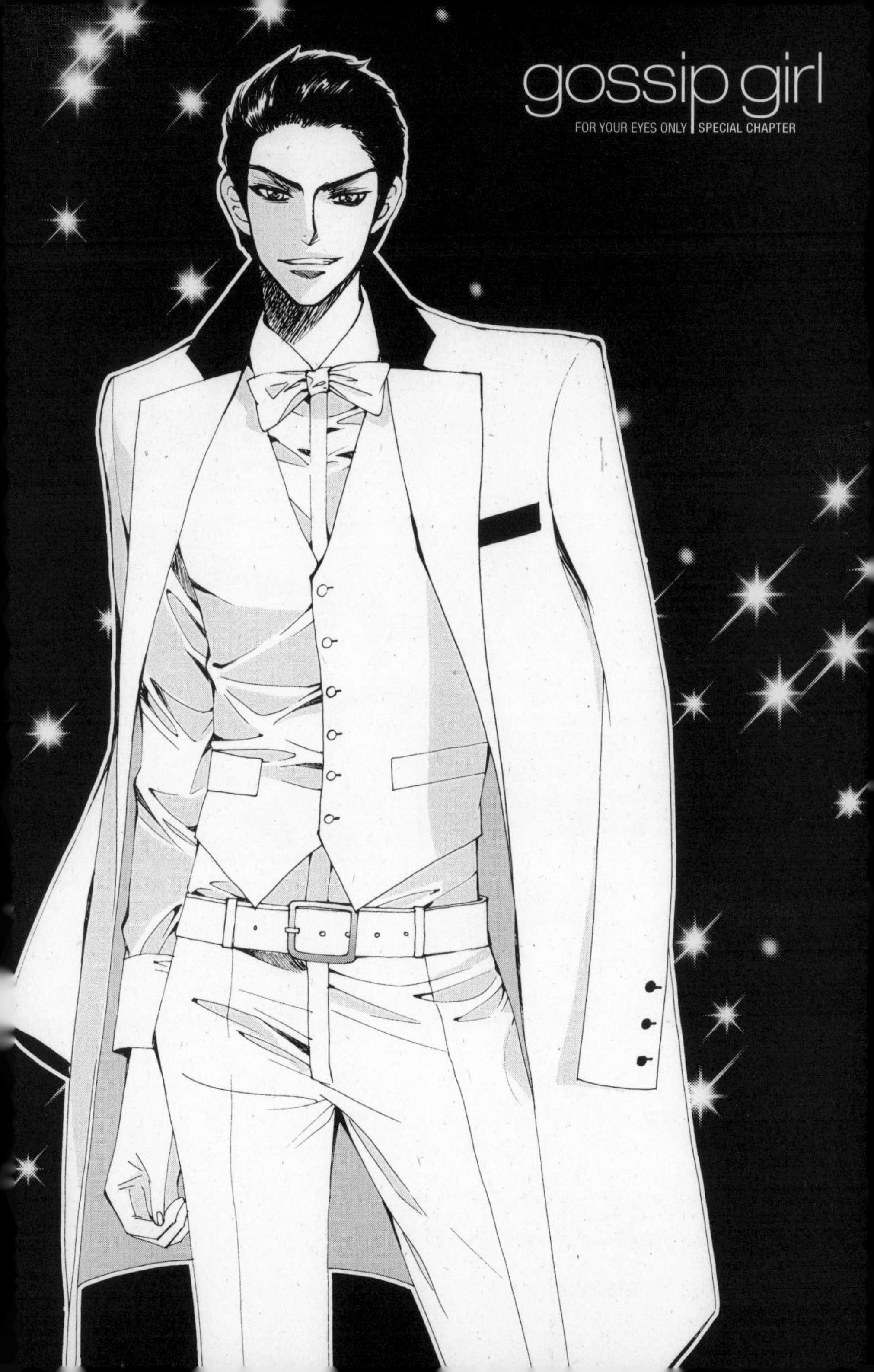
gossip girl
FOR YOUR EYES ONLY | SPECIAL CHAPTER

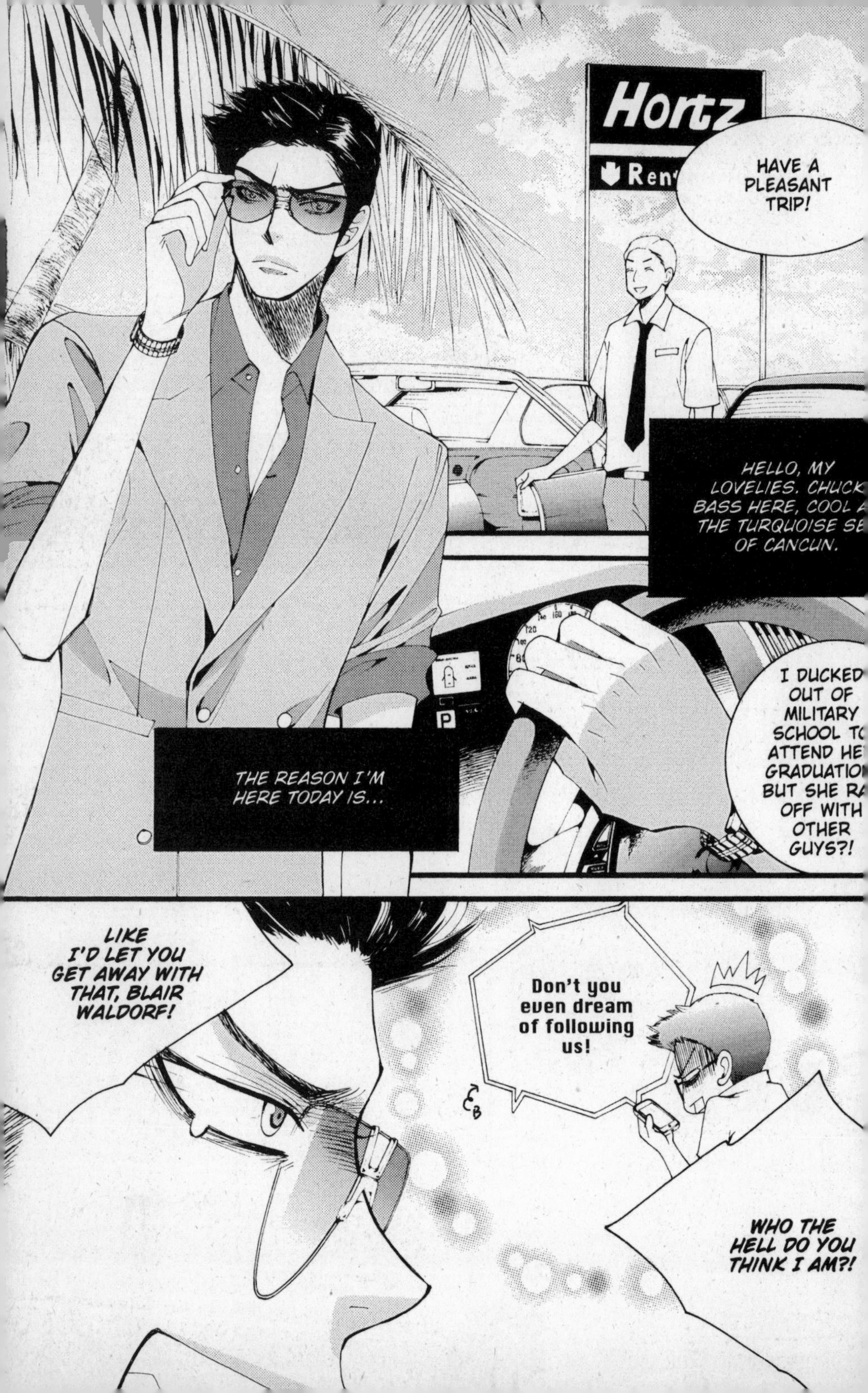
Hortz
HAVE A PLEASANT TRIP!
HELLO, MY LOVELIES. CHUCK BASS HERE, COOL A THE TURQUOISE SE OF CANCUN.
THE REASON I'M HERE TODAY IS...
I DUCKED OUT OF MILITARY SCHOOL T ATTEND HE GRADUATIO BUT SHE RA OFF WITH OTHER GUYS?!
LIKE I'D LET YOU GET AWAY WITH THAT, BLAIR WALDORF!
Don't you even dream of following us!
WHO THE HELL DO YOU THINK I AM?!

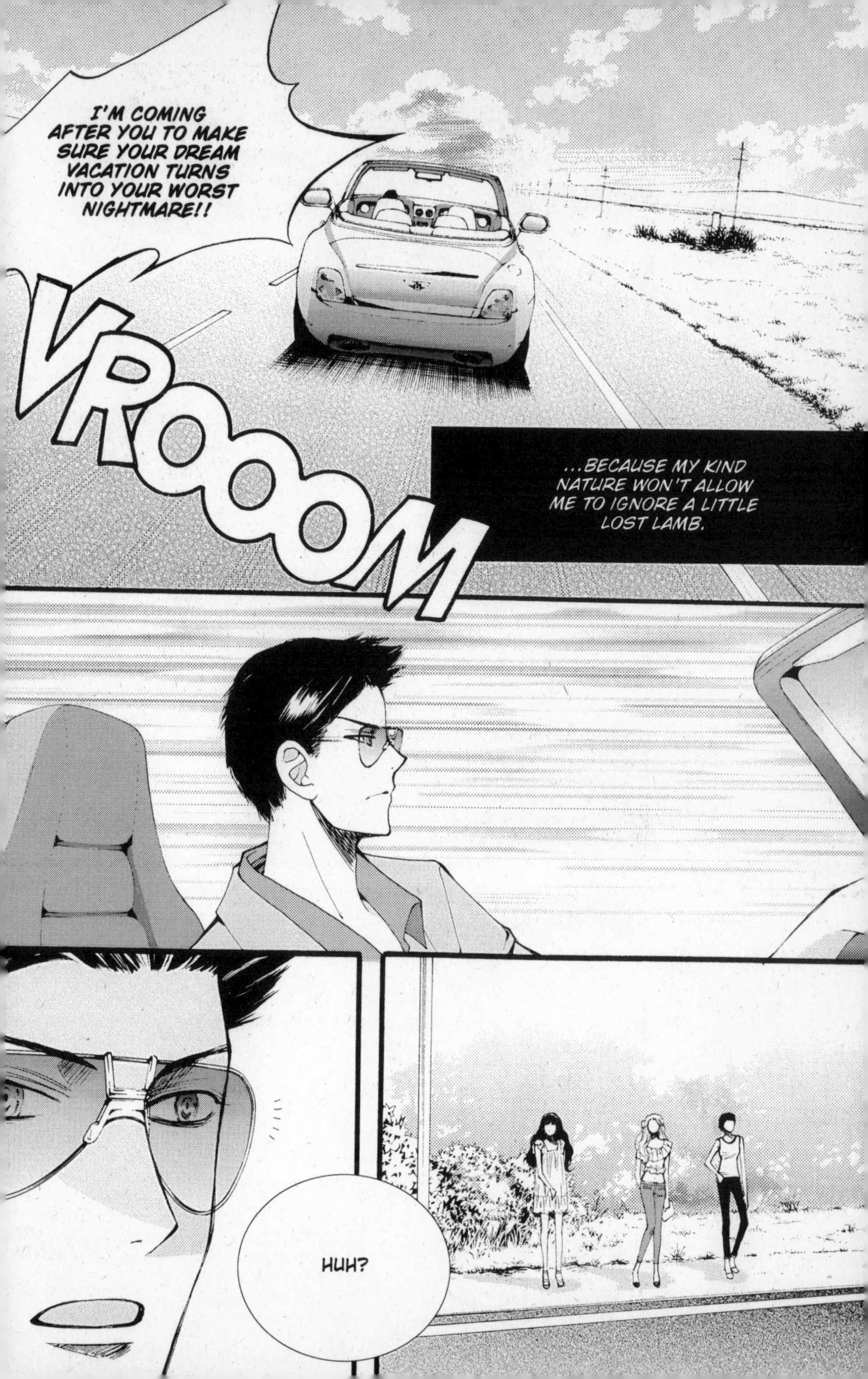
I'M COMING AFTER YOU TO MAKE SURE YOUR DREAM VACATION TURNS INTO YOUR WORST NIGHTMARE!!
VROOOM
...BECAUSE MY KIND NATURE WON'T ALLOW ME TO IGNORE A LITTLE LOST LAMB.
HUH?

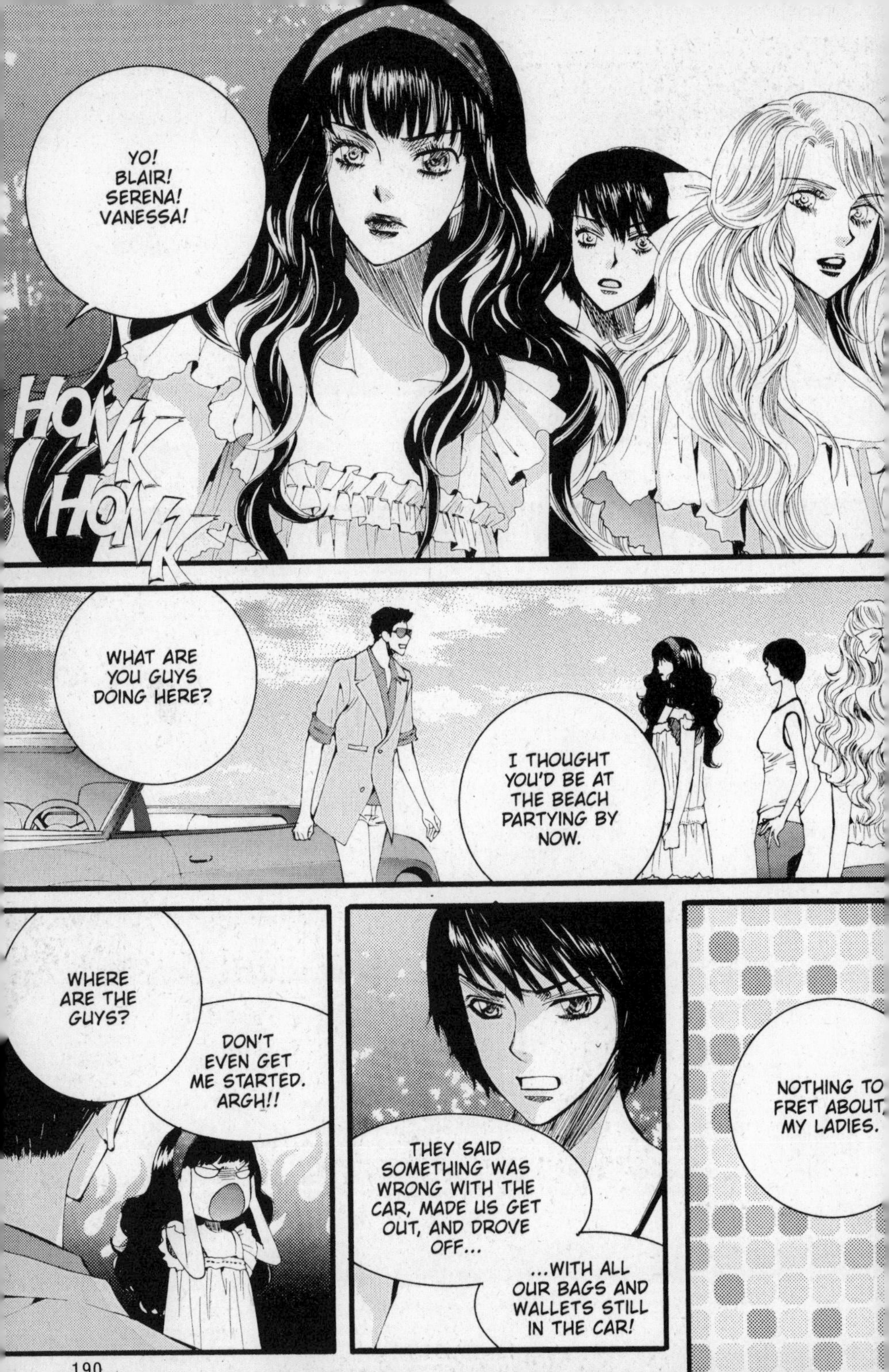
YO! BLAIR! SERENA! VANESSA!
HONK HONK
WHAT ARE YOU GUYS DOING HERE?
I THOUGHT YOU'D BE AT THE BEACH PARTYING BY NOW.
WHERE ARE THE GUYS?
DON'T EVEN GET ME STARTED. ARGH!!
THEY SAID SOMETHING WAS WRONG WITH THE CAR, MADE US GET OUT, AND DROVE OFF...
...WITH ALL OUR BAGS AND WALLETS STILL IN THE CAR!
NOTHING TO FRET ABOUT, MY LADIES.

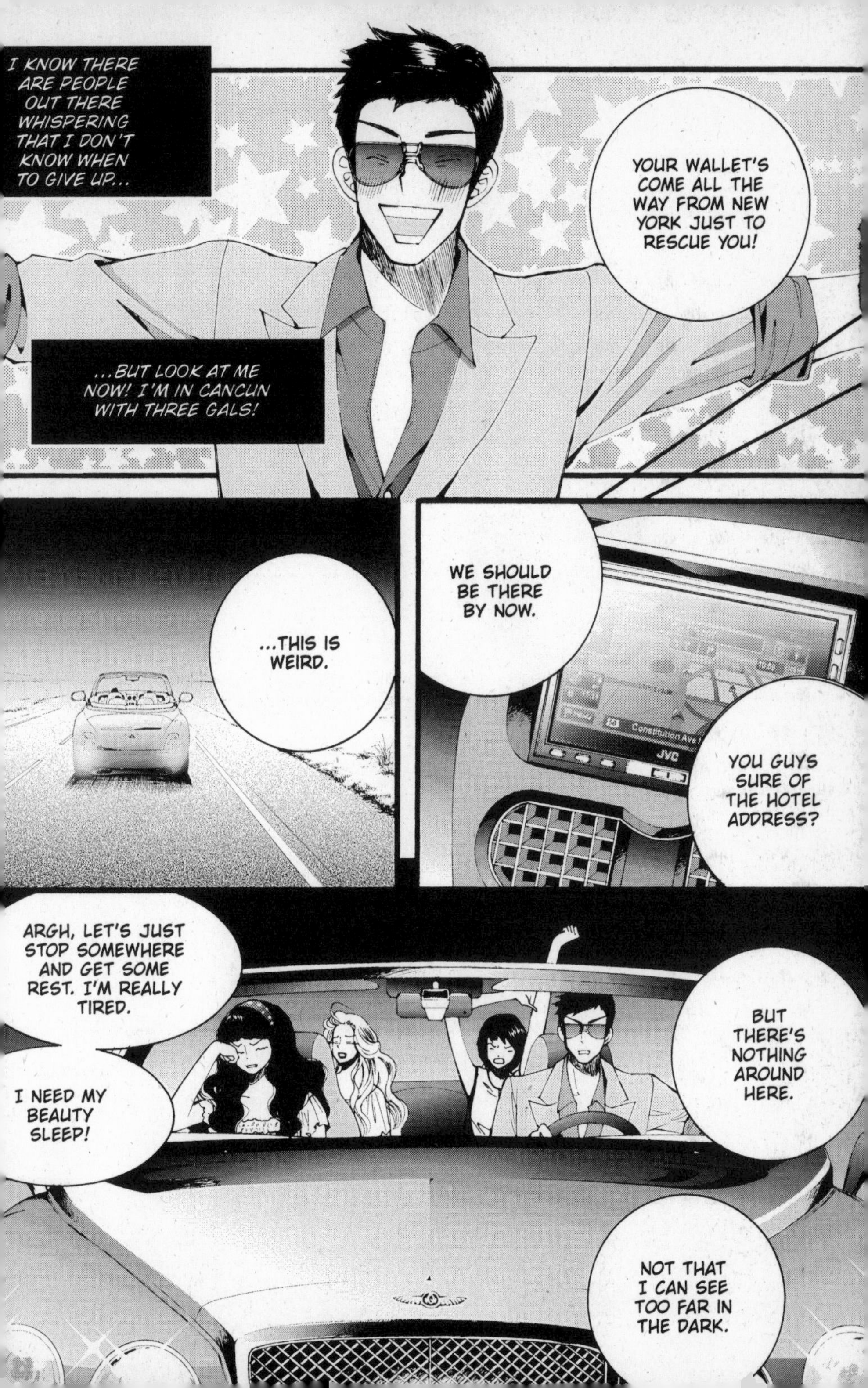
I KNOW THERE ARE PEOPLE OUT THERE WHISPERING THAT I DON'T KNOW WHEN TO GIVE UP...
YOUR WALLET'S COME ALL THE WAY FROM NEW YORK JUST TO RESCUE YOU!
...BUT LOOK AT ME NOW! I'M IN CANCUN WITH THREE GALS!
...THIS IS WEIRD.
WE SHOULD BE THERE BY NOW.
Constitution Ave
JVC
YOU GUYS SURE OF THE HOTEL ADDRESS?
ARGH, LET'S JUST STOP SOMEWHERE AND GET SOME REST. I'M REALLY TIRED.
I NEED MY BEAUTY SLEEP!
BUT THERE'S NOTHING AROUND HERE.
NOT THAT I CAN SEE TOO FAR IN THE DARK.

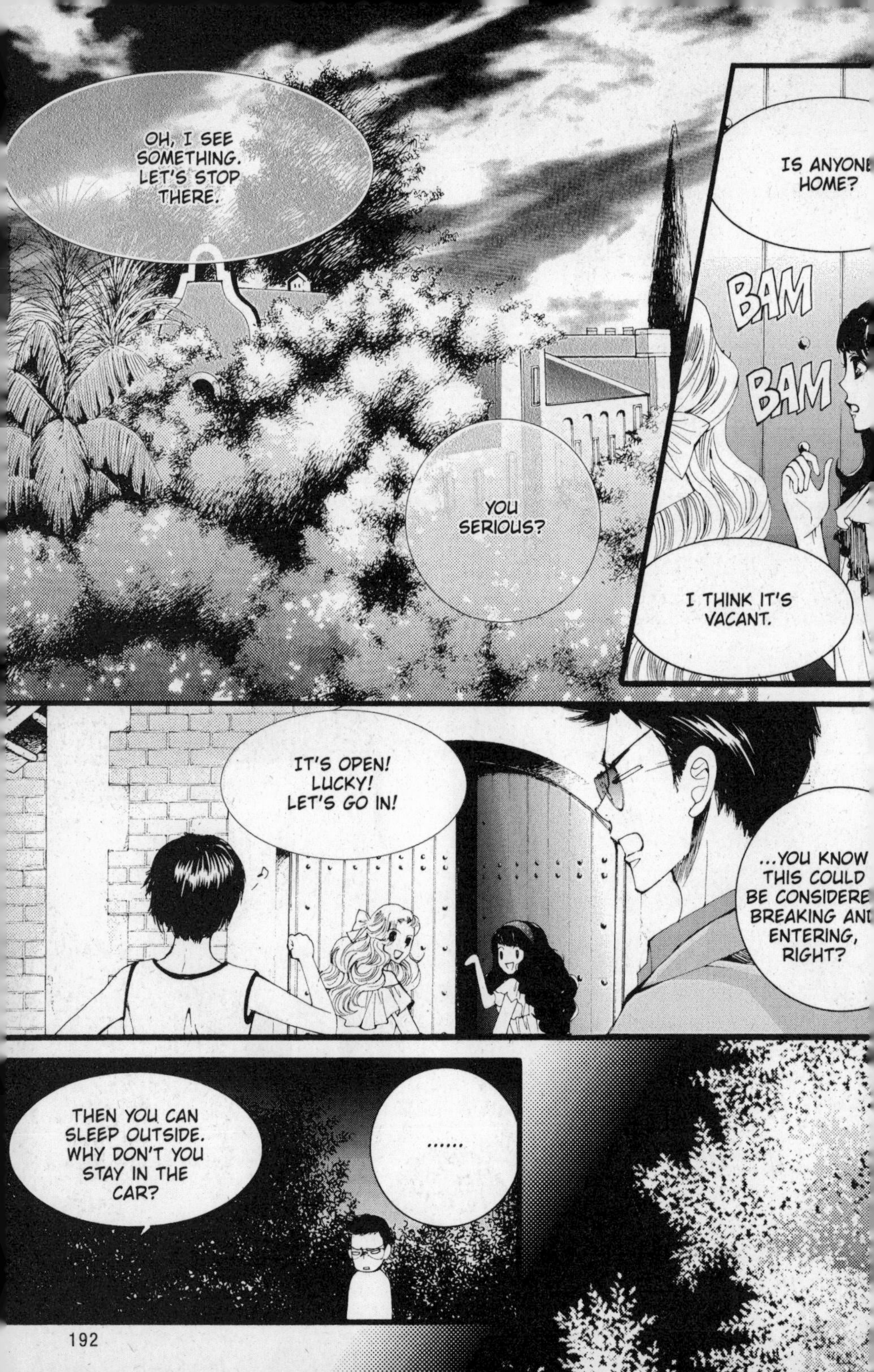
OH, I SEE SOMETHING. LET'S STOP THERE.
YOU SERIOUS?
IS ANYONE HOME?
BAM
BAM
I THINK IT'S VACANT.
IT'S OPEN! LUCKY! LET'S GO IN!
...YOU KNOW THIS COULD BE CONSIDERED BREAKING AND ENTERING, RIGHT?
THEN YOU CAN SLEEP OUTSIDE. WHY DON'T YOU STAY IN THE CAR?
......

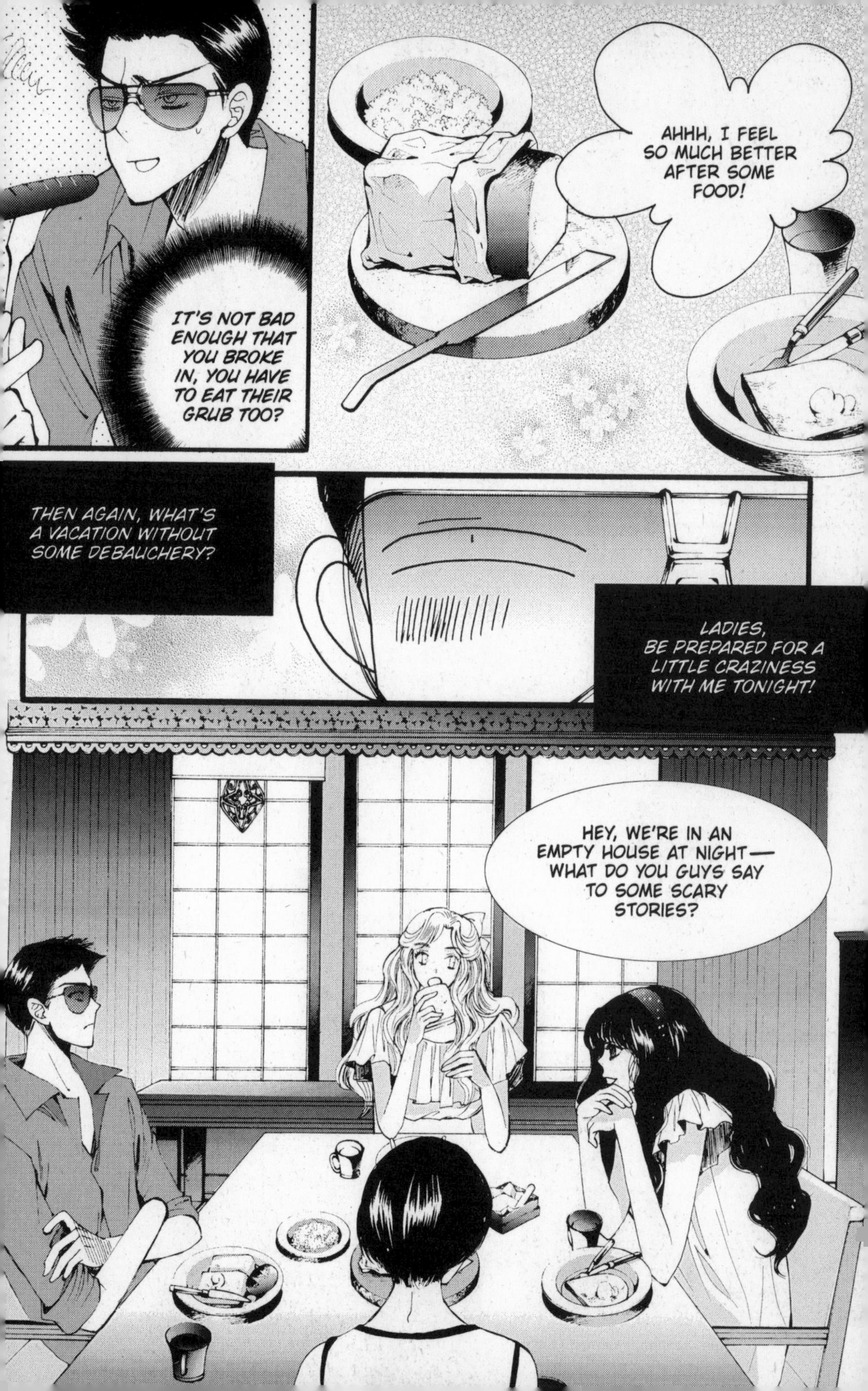
IT'S NOT BAD ENOUGH THAT YOU BROKE IN, YOU HAVE TO EAT THEIR GRUB TOO?
AHHH, I FEEL SO MUCH BETTER AFTER SOME FOOD!
THEN AGAIN, WHAT'S A VACATION WITHOUT SOME DEBAUCHERY?
LADIES, BE PREPARED FOR A LITTLE CRAZINESS WITH ME TONIGHT!
HEY, WE'RE IN AN EMPTY HOUSE AT NIGHT— WHAT DO YOU GUYS SAY TO SOME SCARY STORIES?

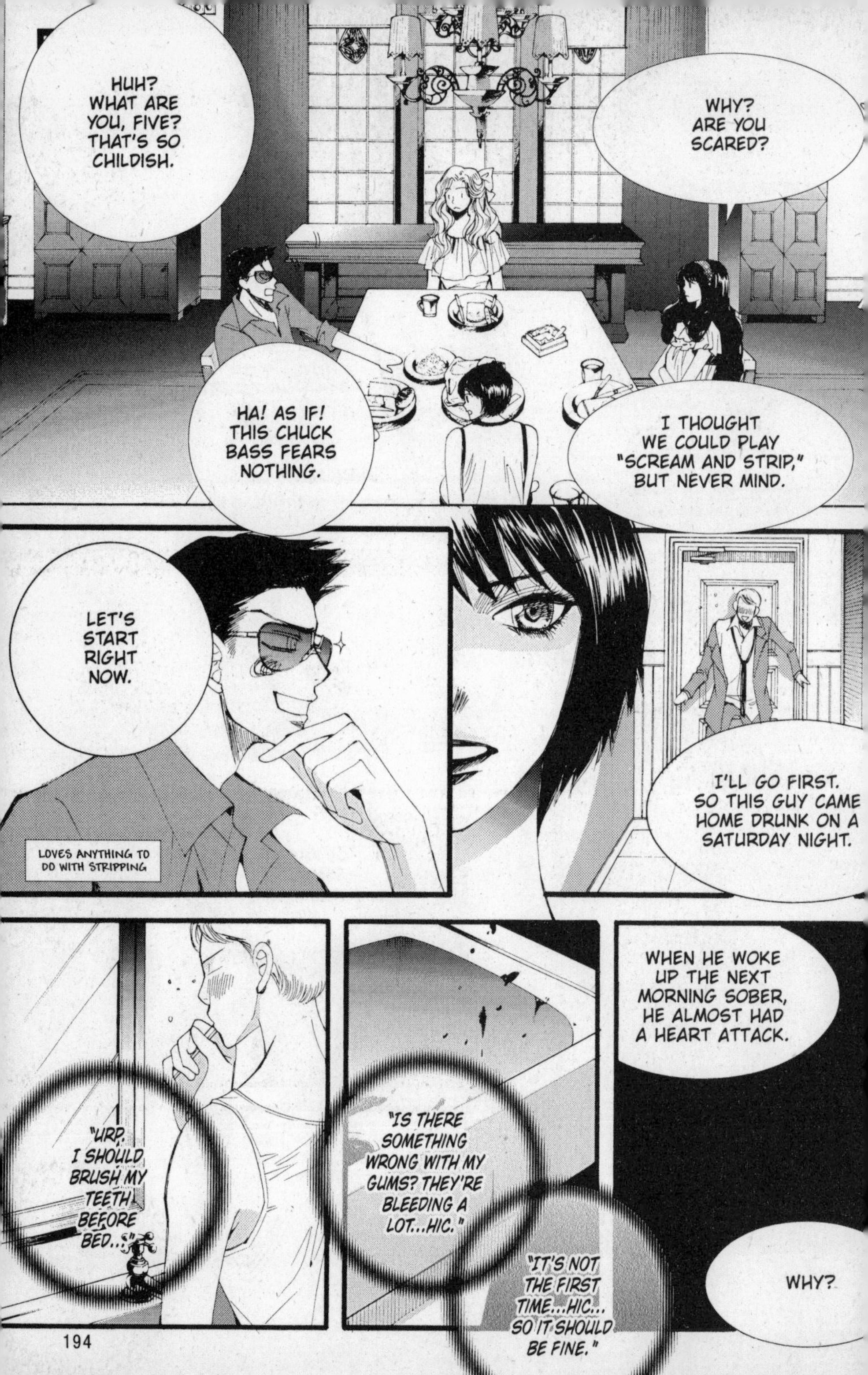
HUH? WHAT ARE YOU, FIVE? THAT'S SO CHILDISH.
WHY? ARE YOU SCARED?
HA! AS IF! THIS CHUCK BASS FEARS NOTHING.
I THOUGHT WE COULD PLAY "SCREAM AND STRIP," BUT NEVER MIND.
LET'S START RIGHT NOW.
LOVES ANYTHING TO DO WITH STRIPPING
I'LL GO FIRST. SO THIS GUY CAME HOME DRUNK ON A SATURDAY NIGHT.
"URP, I SHOULD BRUSH MY TEETH BEFORE BED..."
"IS THERE SOMETHING WRONG WITH MY GUMS? THEY'RE BLEEDING A LOT...HIC."
"IT'S NOT THE FIRST TIME...HIC... SO IT SHOULD BE FINE."
WHEN HE WOKE UP THE NEXT MORNING SOBER, HE ALMOST HAD A HEART ATTACK.
WHY?

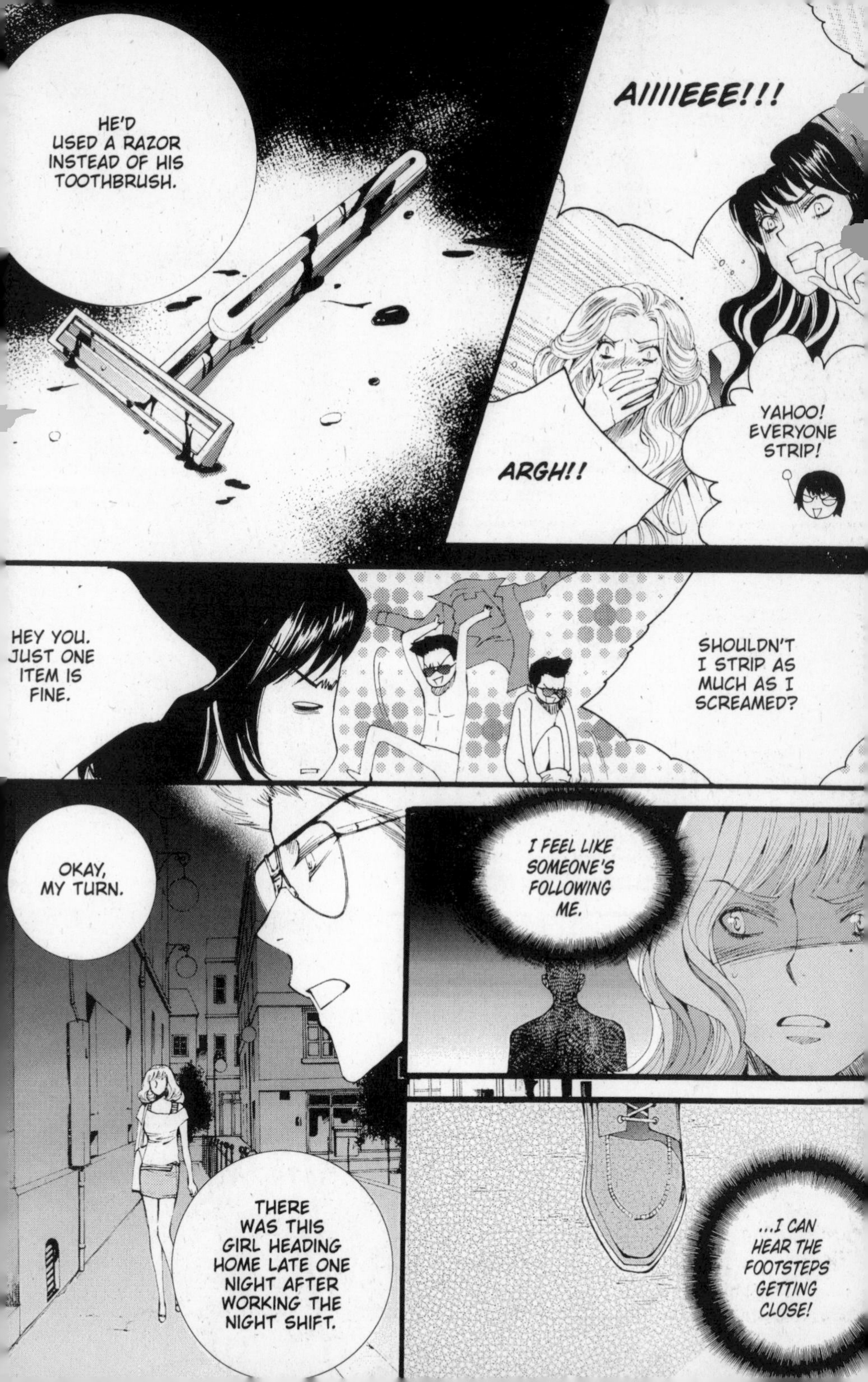
HE'D USED A RAZOR INSTEAD OF HIS TOOTHBRUSH.
AIIIIEEE!!!
ARGH!!
YAHOO! EVERYONE STRIP!
HEY YOU. JUST ONE ITEM IS FINE.
SHOULDN'T I STRIP AS MUCH AS I SCREAMED?
OKAY, MY TURN.
THERE WAS THIS GIRL HEADING HOME LATE ONE NIGHT AFTER WORKING THE NIGHT SHIFT.
I FEEL LIKE SOMEONE'S FOLLOWING ME.
...I CAN HEAR THE FOOTSTEPS GETTING CLOSE!

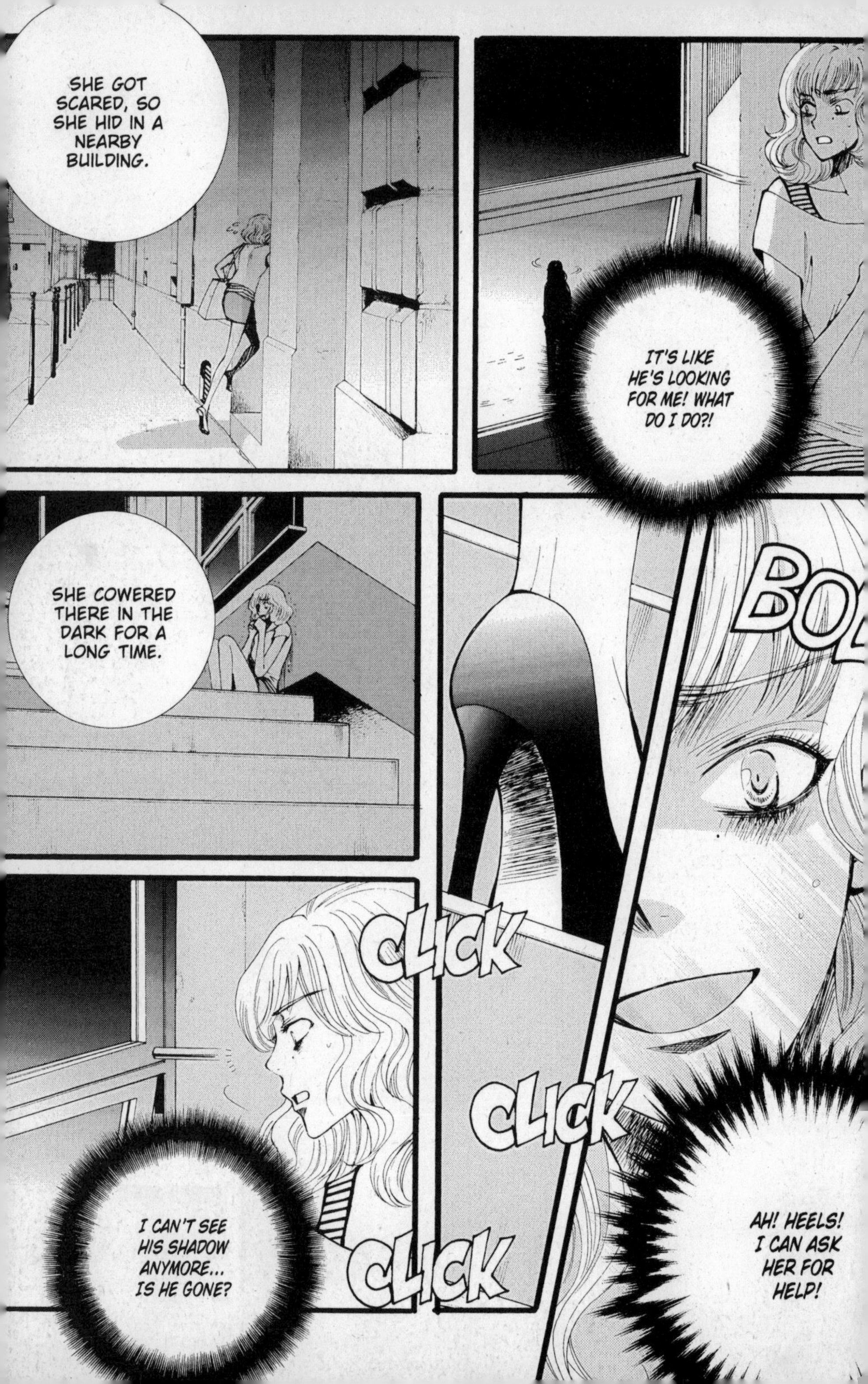
SHE GOT SCARED, SO SHE HID IN A NEARBY BUILDING.
IT'S LIKE HE'S LOOKING FOR ME! WHAT DO I DO?!
SHE COWERED THERE IN THE DARK FOR A LONG TIME.
I CAN'T SEE HIS SHADOW ANYMORE... IS HE GONE?
CLICK
CLICK
CLICK
BO
AH! HEELS! I CAN ASK HER FOR HELP!

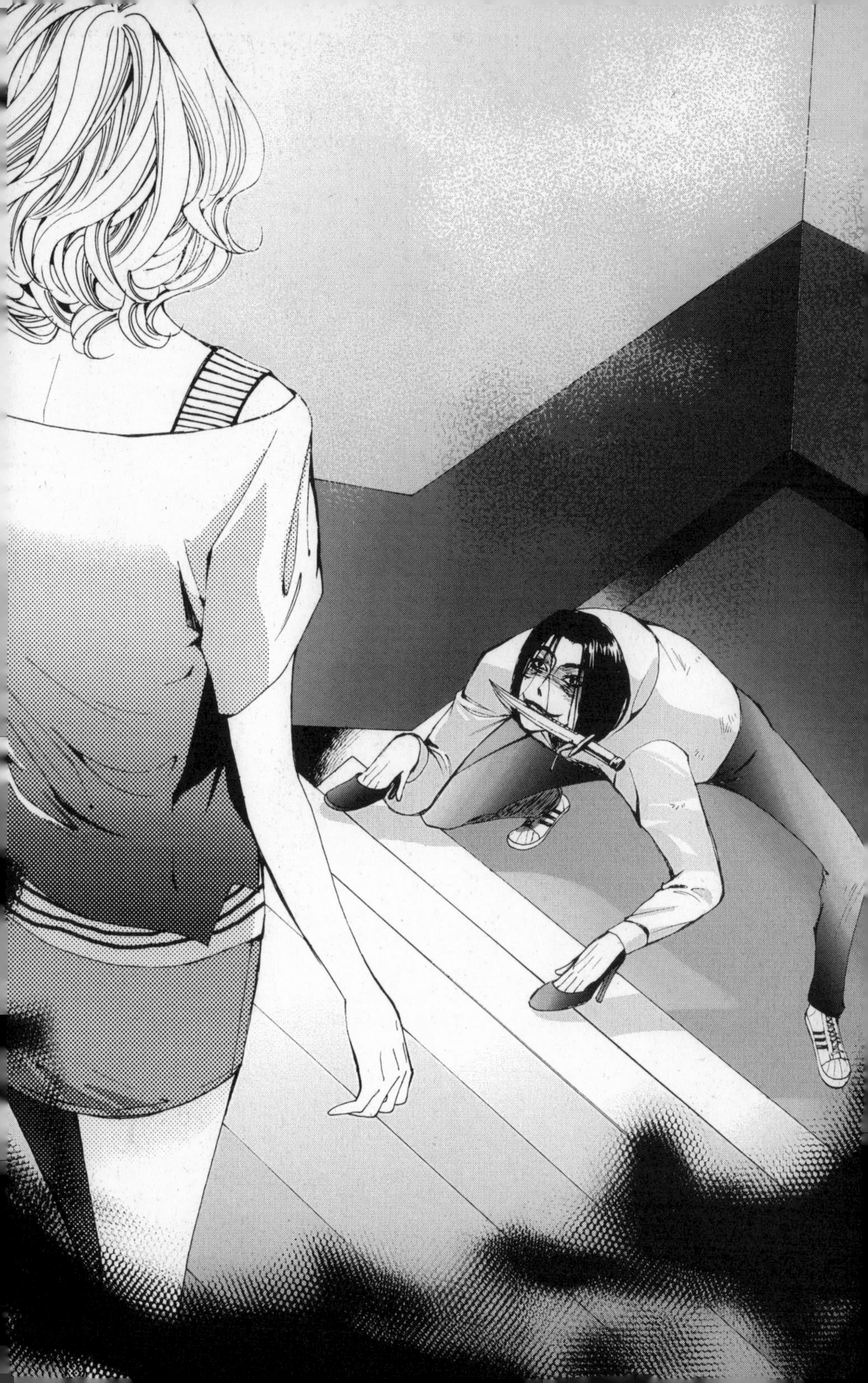

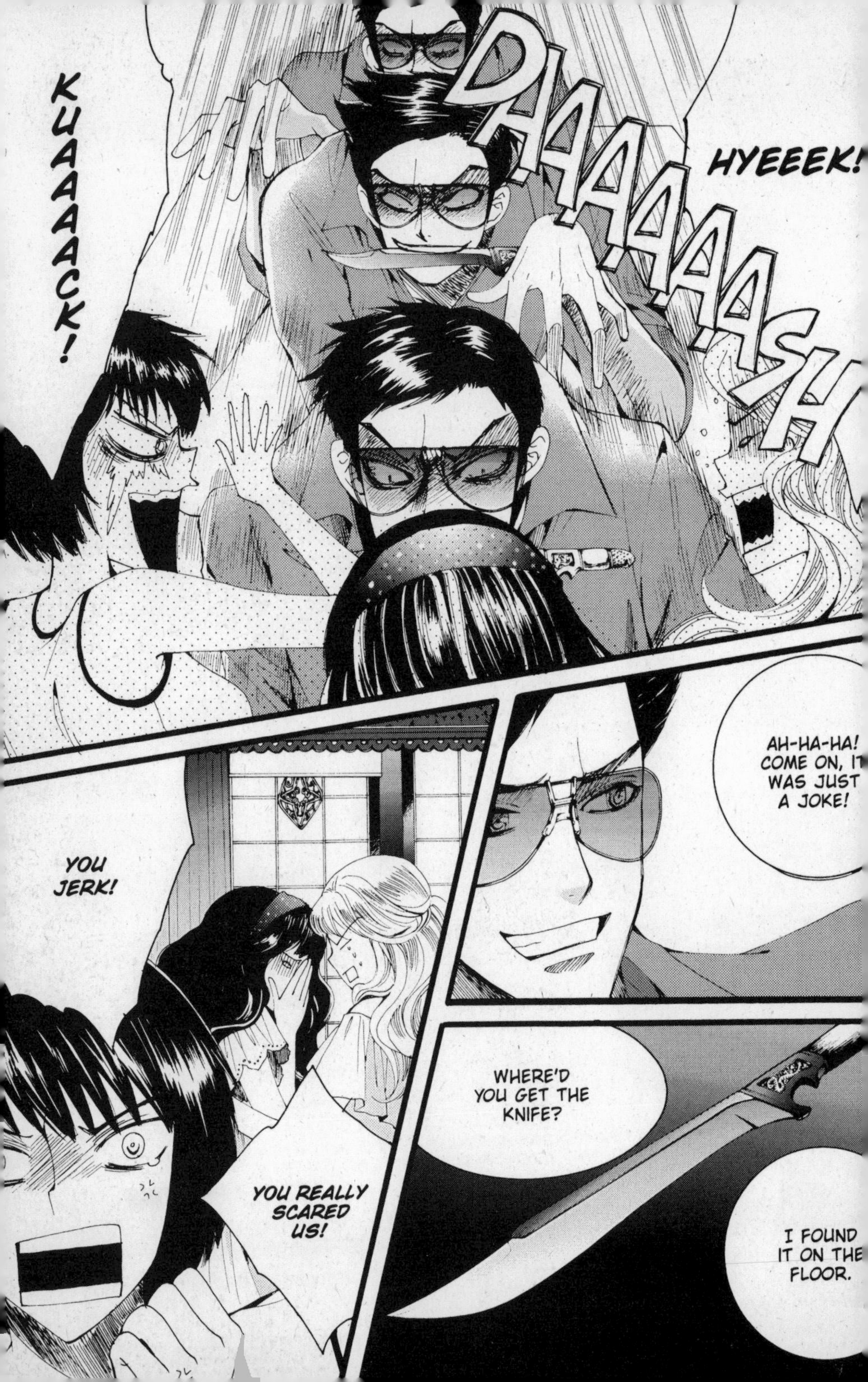
KUAAAACK!
DHAAAAAASH
HYEEEK!
YOU JERK!
YOU REALLY SCARED US!
AH-HA-HA! COME ON, IT WAS JUST A JOKE!
WHERE'D YOU GET THE KNIFE?
I FOUND IT ON THE FLOOR.

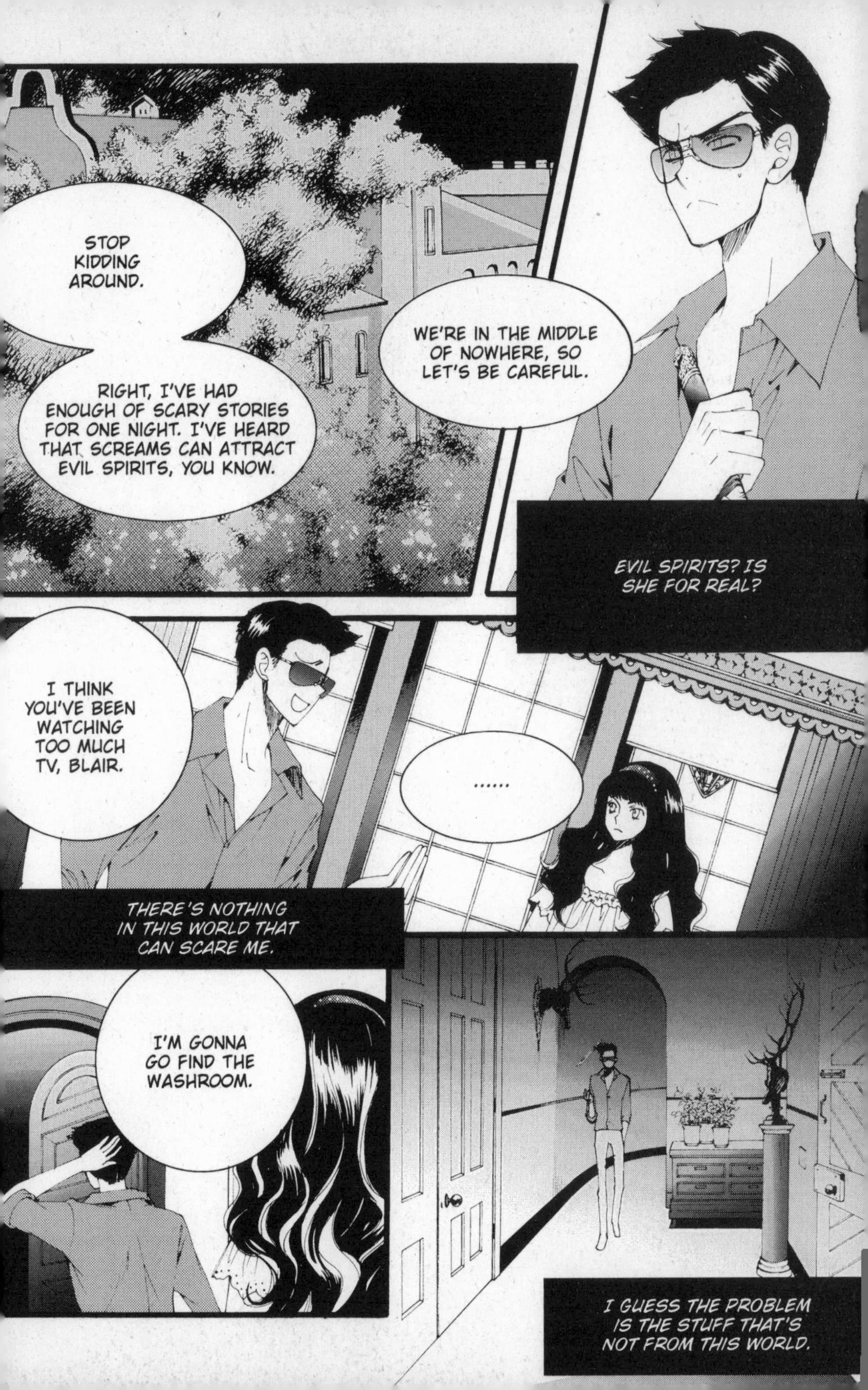
STOP KIDDING AROUND.
RIGHT, I'VE HAD ENOUGH OF SCARY STORIES FOR ONE NIGHT. I'VE HEARD THAT SCREAMS CAN ATTRACT EVIL SPIRITS, YOU KNOW.
WE'RE IN THE MIDDLE OF NOWHERE, SO LET'S BE CAREFUL.
EVIL SPIRITS? IS SHE FOR REAL?
I THINK YOU'VE BEEN WATCHING TOO MUCH TV, BLAIR.
......
THERE'S NOTHING IN THIS WORLD THAT CAN SCARE ME.
I'M GONNA GO FIND THE WASHROOM.
I GUESS THE PROBLEM IS THE STUFF THAT'S NOT FROM THIS WORLD.

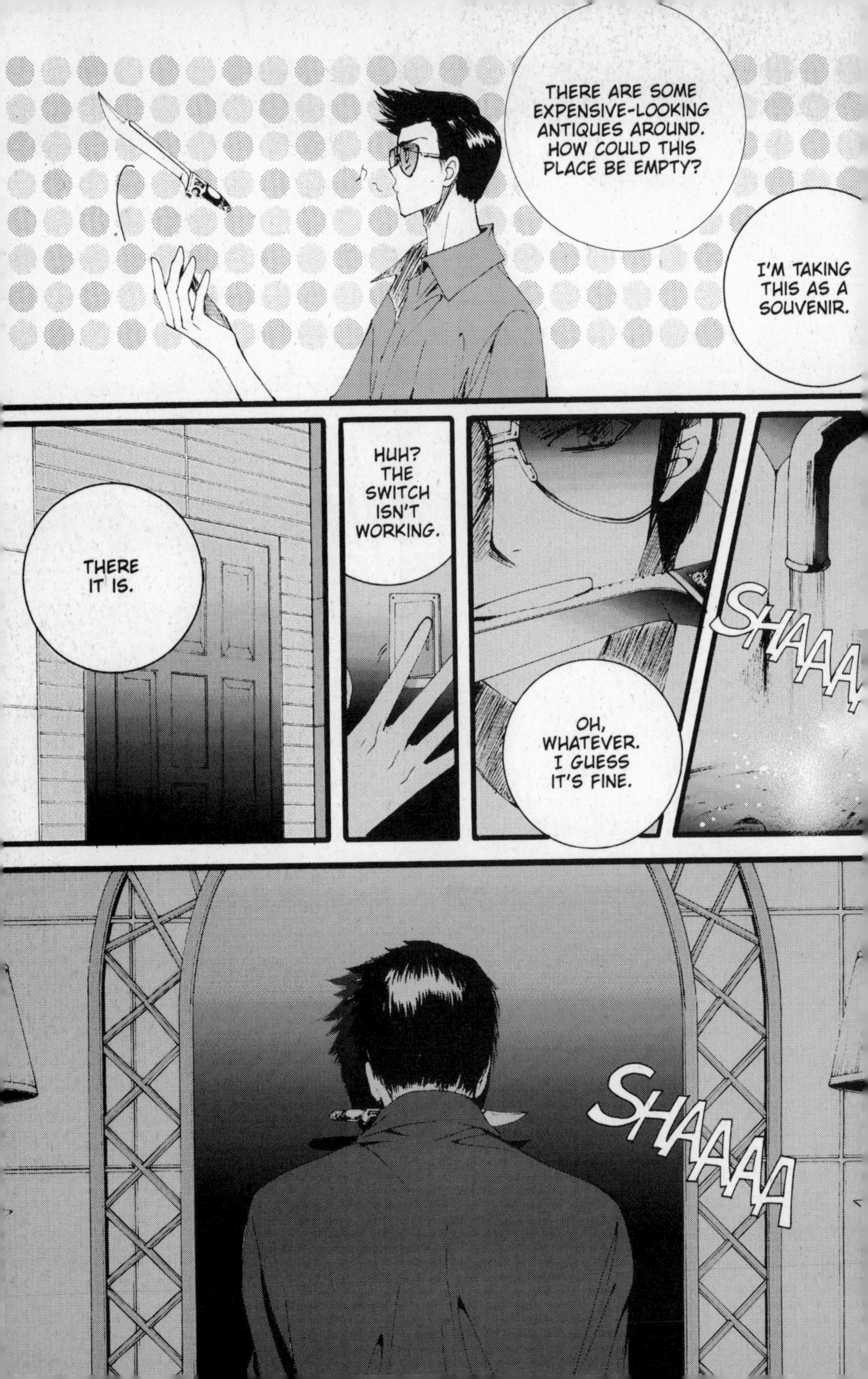
THERE ARE SOME EXPENSIVE-LOOKING ANTIQUES AROUND. HOW COULD THIS PLACE BE EMPTY?
I'M TAKING THIS AS A SOUVENIR.
THERE IT IS.
HUH? THE SWITCH ISN'T WORKING.
OH, WHATEVER. I GUESS IT'S FINE.
SHAAA
SHAAAAA

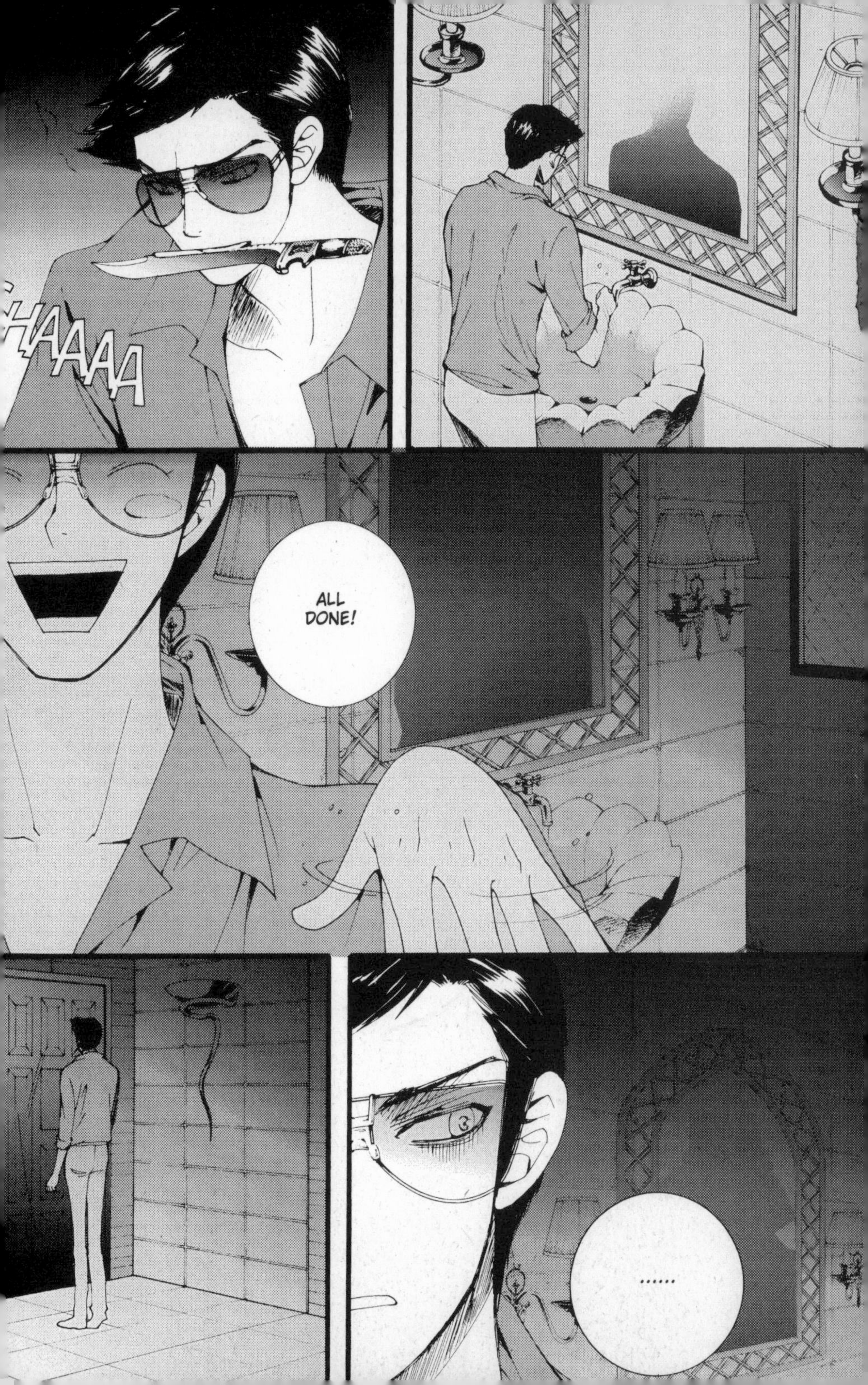
HAAAAA
ALL DONE!
......

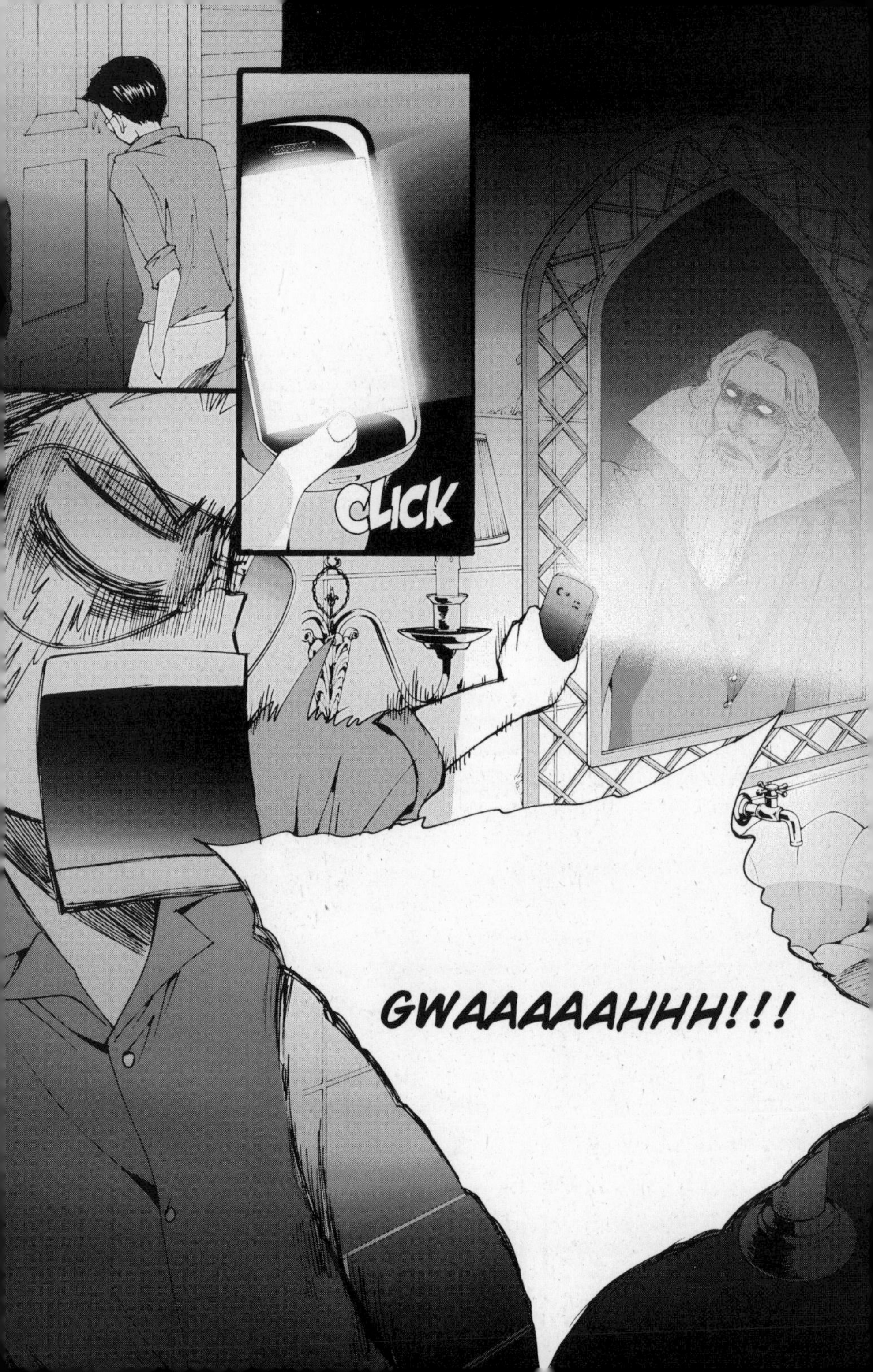
CLICK
GWAAAAAHHH!!!

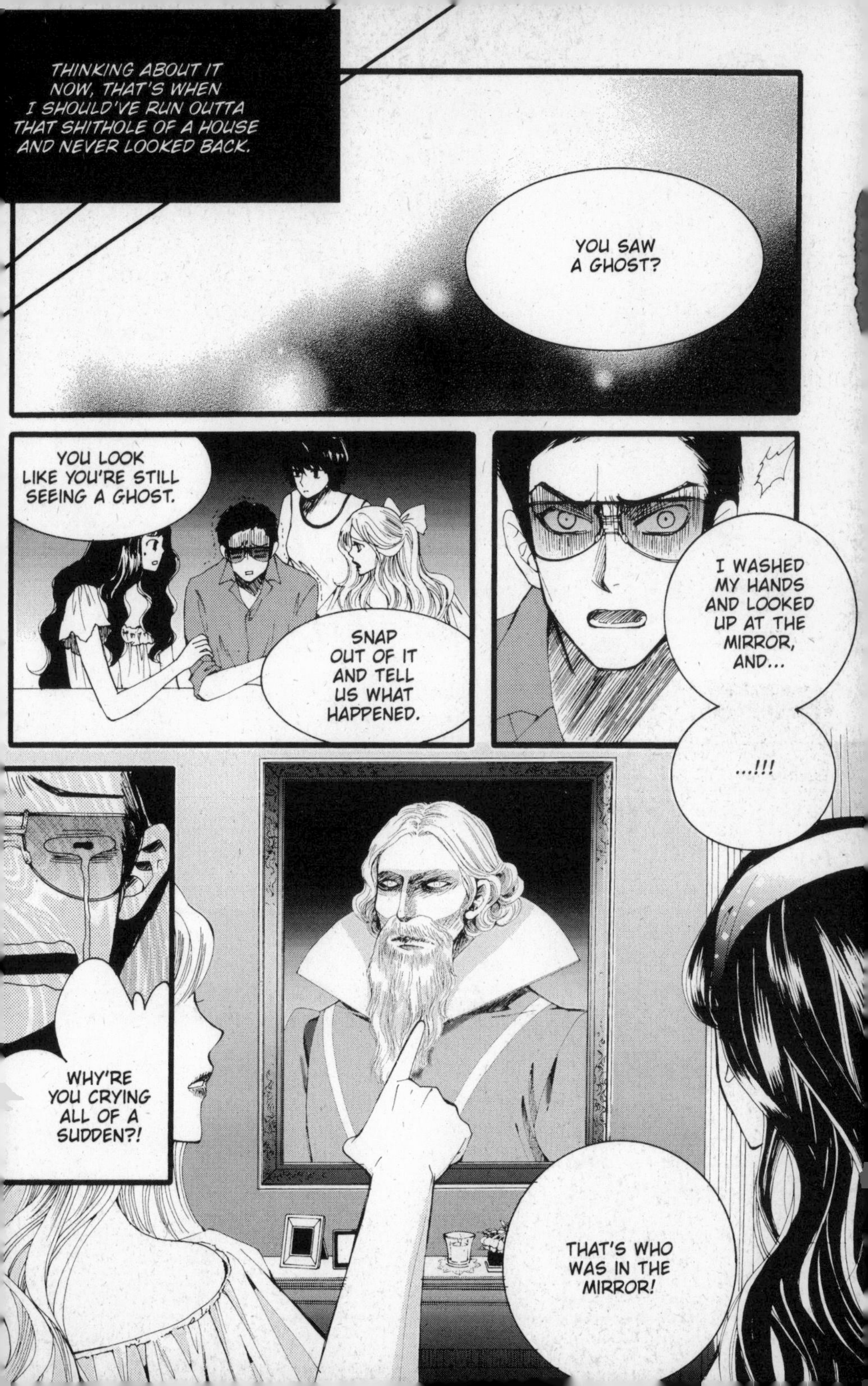
THINKING ABOUT IT NOW, THAT'S WHEN I SHOULD'VE RUN OUTTA THAT SHITHOLE OF A HOUSE AND NEVER LOOKED BACK.
YOU SAW A GHOST?
YOU LOOK LIKE YOU'RE STILL SEEING A GHOST.
SNAP OUT OF IT AND TELL US WHAT HAPPENED.
I WASHED MY HANDS AND LOOKED UP AT THE MIRROR, AND...
...!!!
WHY'RE YOU CRYING ALL OF A SUDDEN?!
THAT'S WHO WAS IN THE MIRROR!

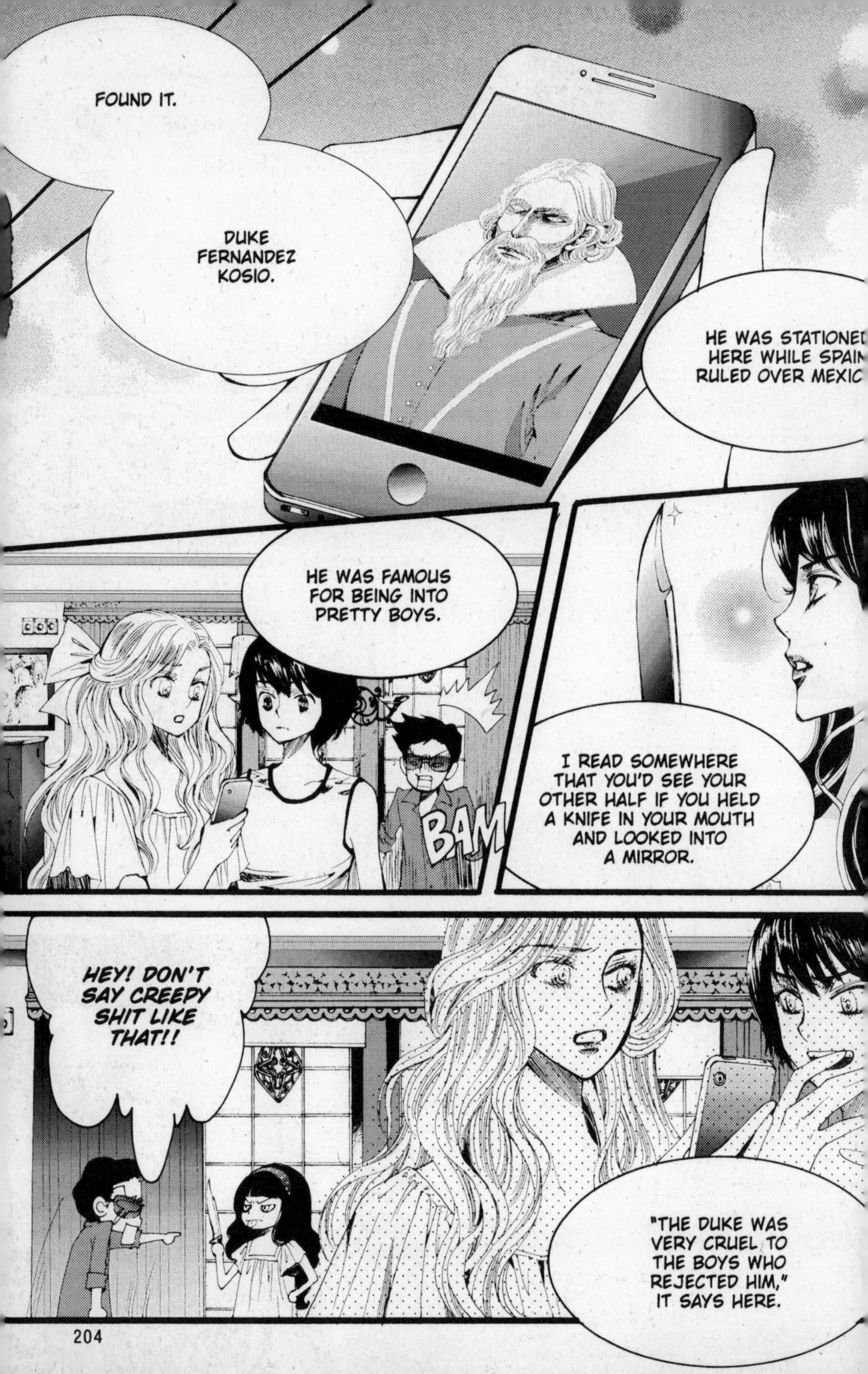
FOUND IT.
DUKE FERNANDEZ KOSIO.
HE WAS STATIONED HERE WHILE SPAIN RULED OVER MEXIC
HE WAS FAMOUS FOR BEING INTO PRETTY BOYS.
BAM
I READ SOMEWHERE THAT YOU'D SEE YOUR OTHER HALF IF YOU HELD A KNIFE IN YOUR MOUTH AND LOOKED INTO A MIRROR.
HEY! DON'T SAY CREEPY SHIT LIKE THAT!!
"THE DUKE WAS VERY CRUEL TO THE BOYS WHO REJECTED HIM," IT SAYS HERE.

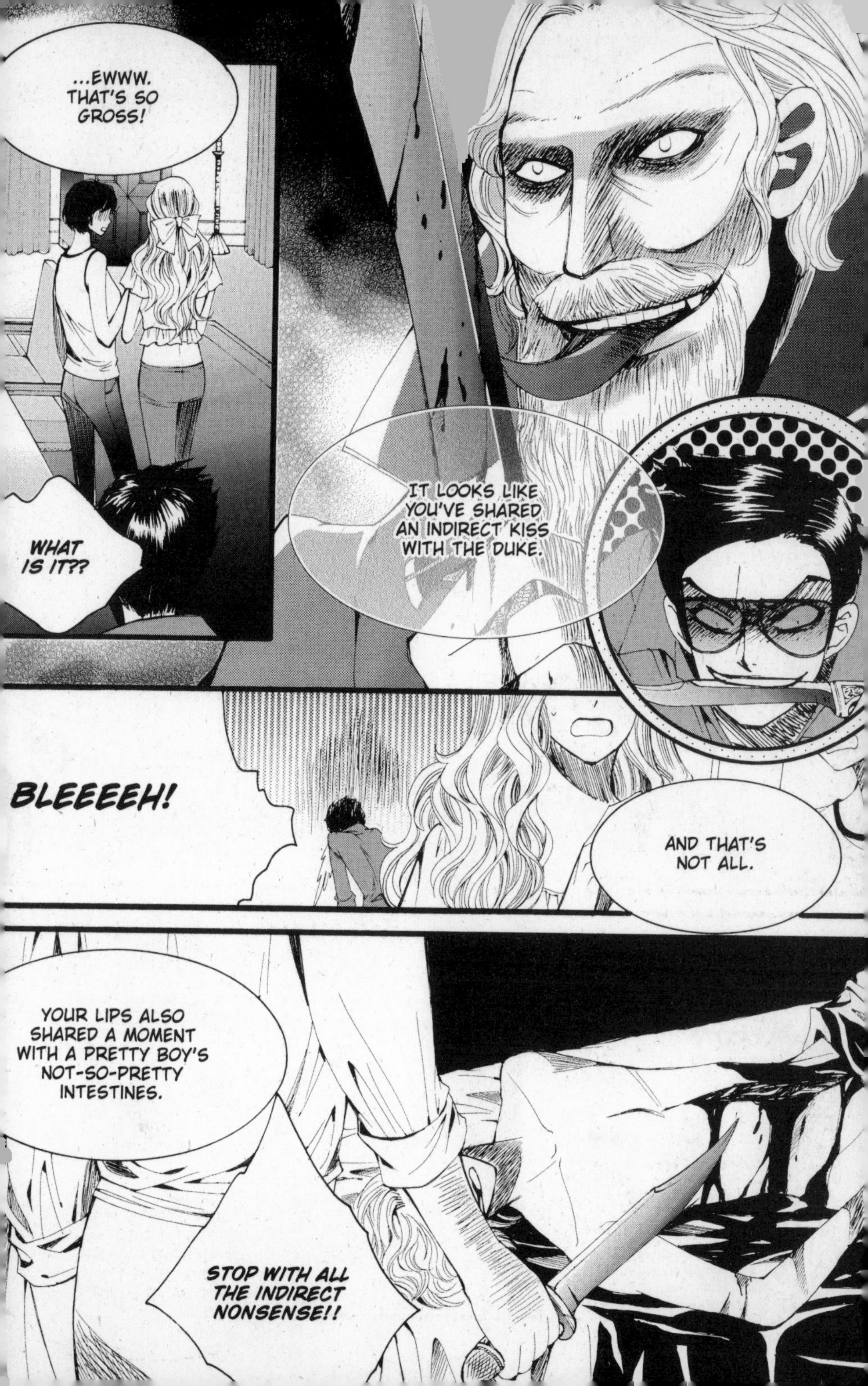
...EWWW. THAT'S SO GROSS!
WHAT IS IT??
IT LOOKS LIKE YOU'VE SHARED AN INDIRECT KISS WITH THE DUKE.
BLEEEEH!
AND THAT'S NOT ALL.
YOUR LIPS ALSO SHARED A MOMENT WITH A PRETTY BOY'S NOT-SO-PRETTY INTESTINES.
STOP WITH ALL THE INDIRECT NONSENSE!!

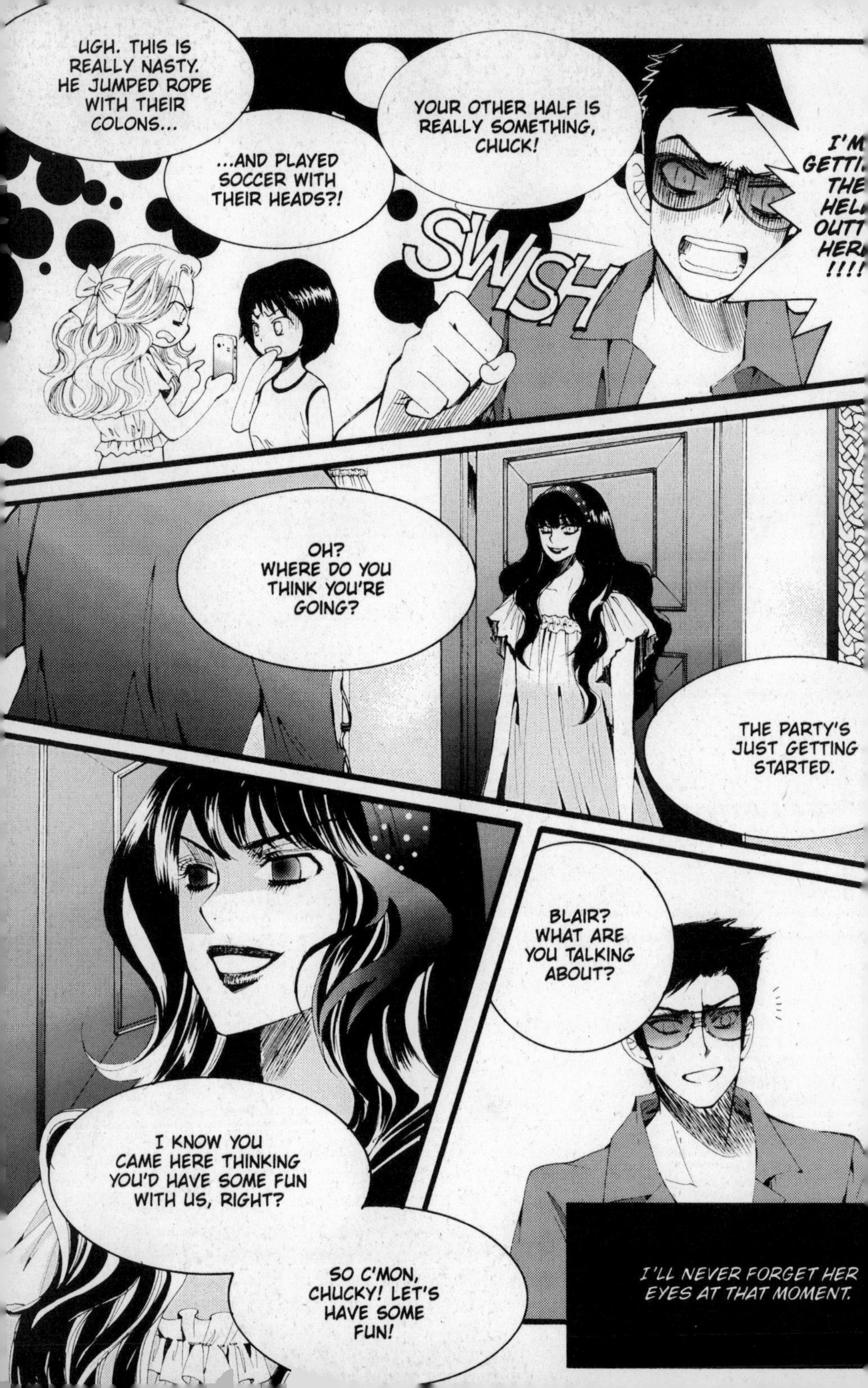
UGH. THIS IS REALLY NASTY. HE JUMPED ROPE WITH THEIR COLONS...
...AND PLAYED SOCCER WITH THEIR HEADS?!
YOUR OTHER HALF IS REALLY SOMETHING, CHUCK!
SWISH
OH? WHERE DO YOU THINK YOU'RE GOING?
THE PARTY'S JUST GETTING STARTED.
I KNOW YOU CAME HERE THINKING YOU'D HAVE SOME FUN WITH US, RIGHT?
SO C'MON, CHUCKY! LET'S HAVE SOME FUN!
BLAIR? WHAT ARE YOU TALKING ABOUT?
I'LL NEVER FORGET HER EYES AT THAT MOMENT.

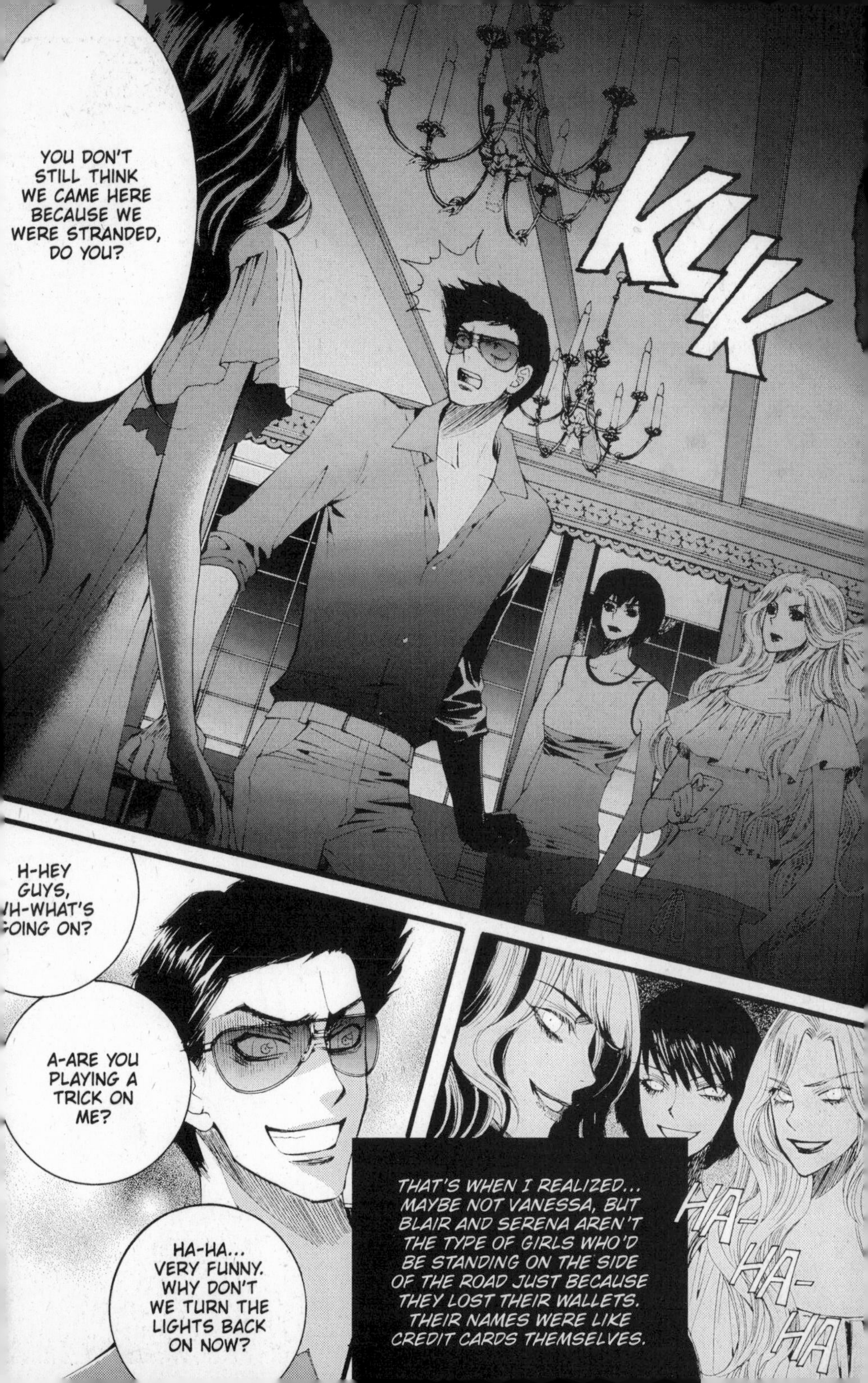
YOU DON'T STILL THINK WE CAME HERE BECAUSE WE WERE STRANDED, DO YOU?
KLIK
H-HEY GUYS, WH-WHAT'S GOING ON?
A-ARE YOU PLAYING A TRICK ON ME?
HA-HA... VERY FUNNY. WHY DON'T WE TURN THE LIGHTS BACK ON NOW?
THAT'S WHEN I REALIZED... MAYBE NOT VANESSA, BUT BLAIR AND SERENA AREN'T THE TYPE OF GIRLS WHO'D BE STANDING ON THE SIDE OF THE ROAD JUST BECAUSE THEY LOST THEIR WALLETS. THEIR NAMES WERE LIKE CREDIT CARDS THEMSELVES.
HA-HA-HA

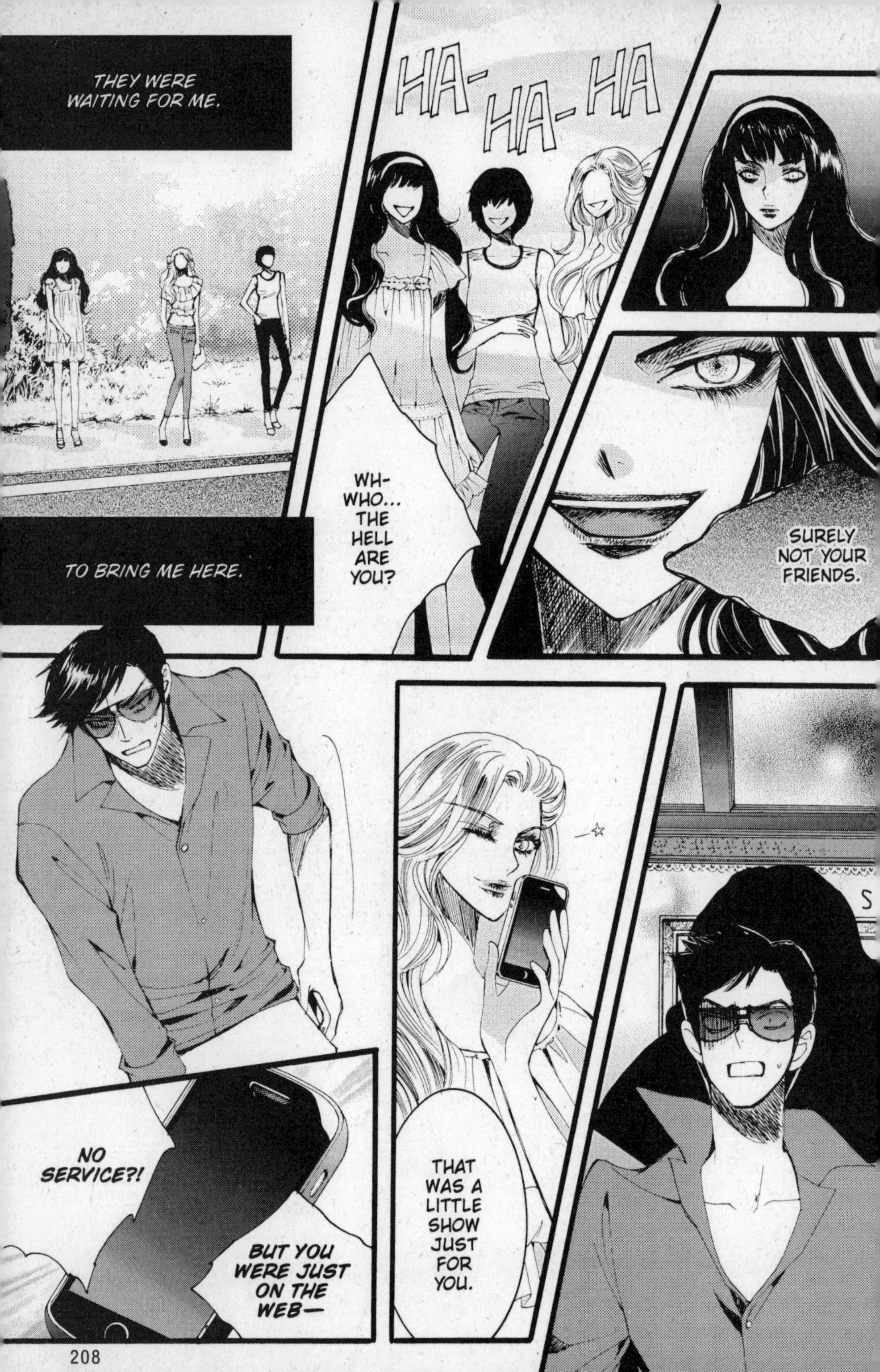
THEY WERE WAITING FOR ME.
TO BRING ME HERE.
HA-HA-HA
WH-WHO... THE HELL ARE YOU?
SURELY NOT YOUR FRIENDS.
NO SERVICE?!
BUT YOU WERE JUST ON THE WEB—
THAT WAS A LITTLE SHOW JUST FOR YOU.

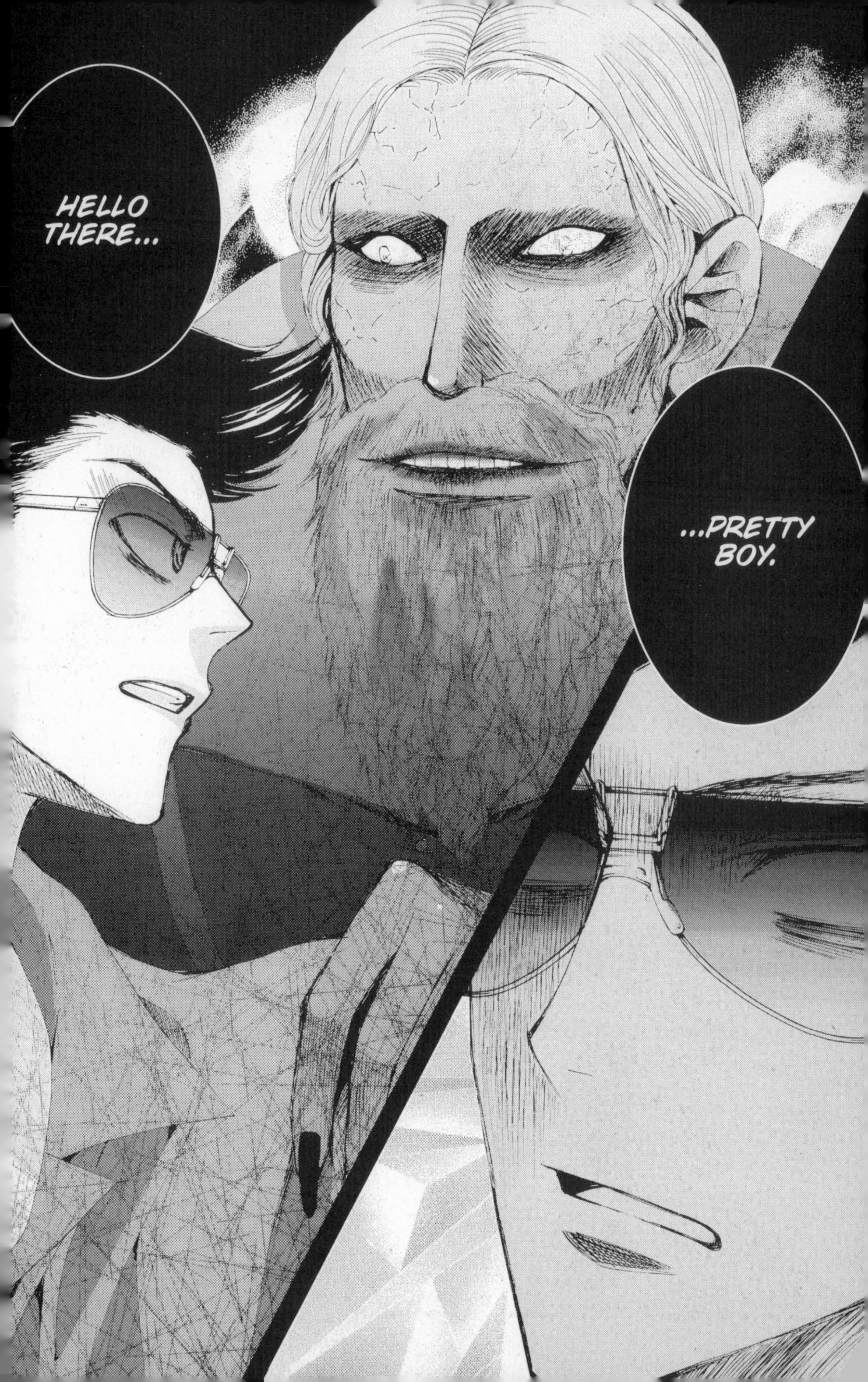
HELLO THERE...
...PRETTY BOY.

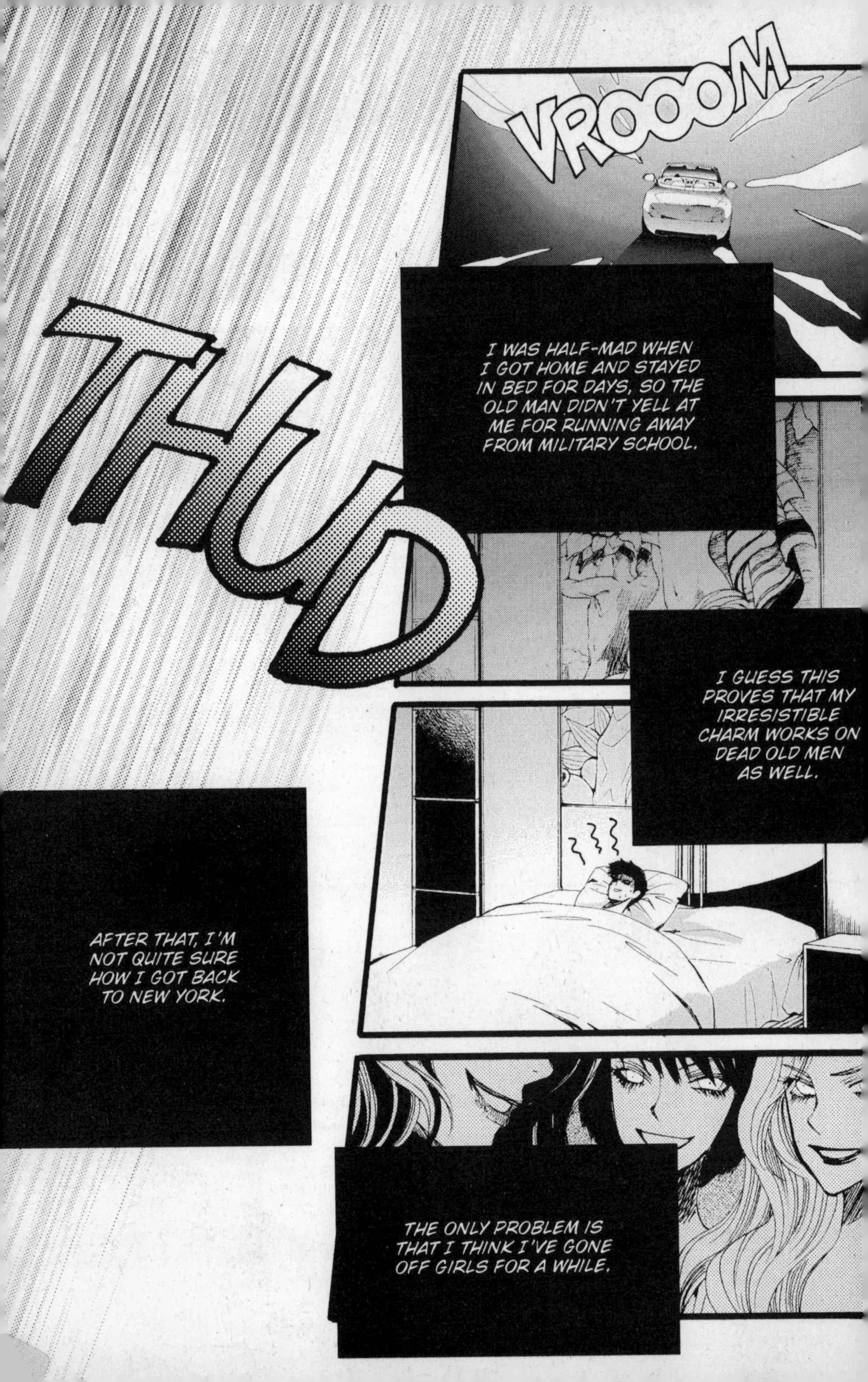
THUD
AFTER THAT, I'M NOT QUITE SURE HOW I GOT BACK TO NEW YORK.
VROOOM
I WAS HALF-MAD WHEN I GOT HOME AND STAYED IN BED FOR DAYS, SO THE OLD MAN DIDN'T YELL AT ME FOR RUNNING AWAY FROM MILITARY SCHOOL.
I GUESS THIS PROVES THAT MY IRRESISTIBLE CHARM WORKS ON DEAD OLD MEN AS WELL.
THE ONLY PROBLEM IS THAT I THINK I'VE GONE OFF GIRLS FOR A WHILE.

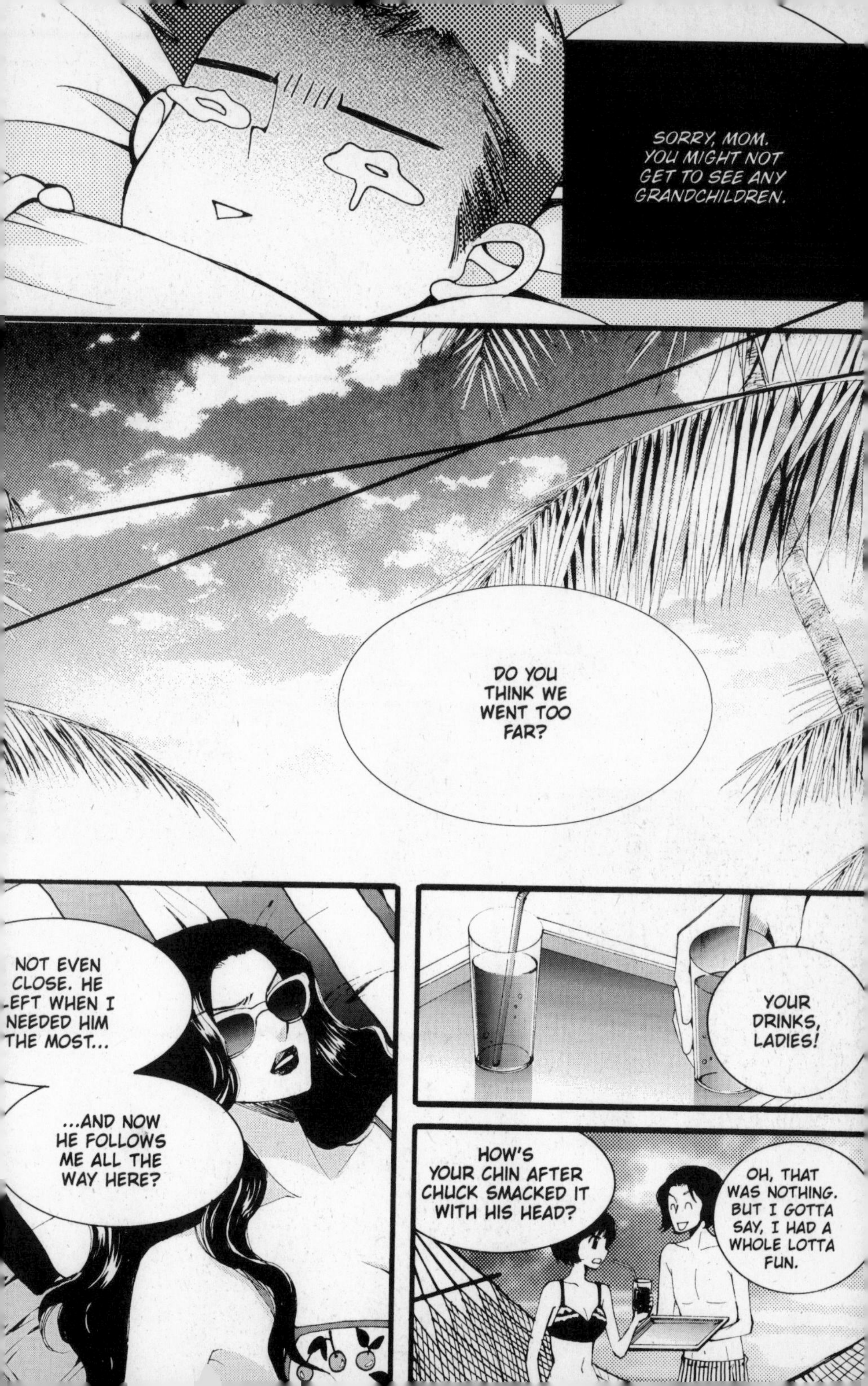

SORRY, MOM. YOU MIGHT NOT GET TO SEE ANY GRANDCHILDREN.
DO YOU THINK WE WENT TOO FAR?
NOT EVEN CLOSE. HE LEFT WHEN I NEEDED HIM THE MOST...
...AND NOW HE FOLLOWS ME ALL THE WAY HERE?
YOUR DRINKS, LADIES!
HOW'S YOUR CHIN AFTER CHUCK SMACKED IT WITH HIS HEAD?
OH, THAT WAS NOTHING. BUT I GOTTA SAY, I HAD A WHOLE LOTTA FUN.

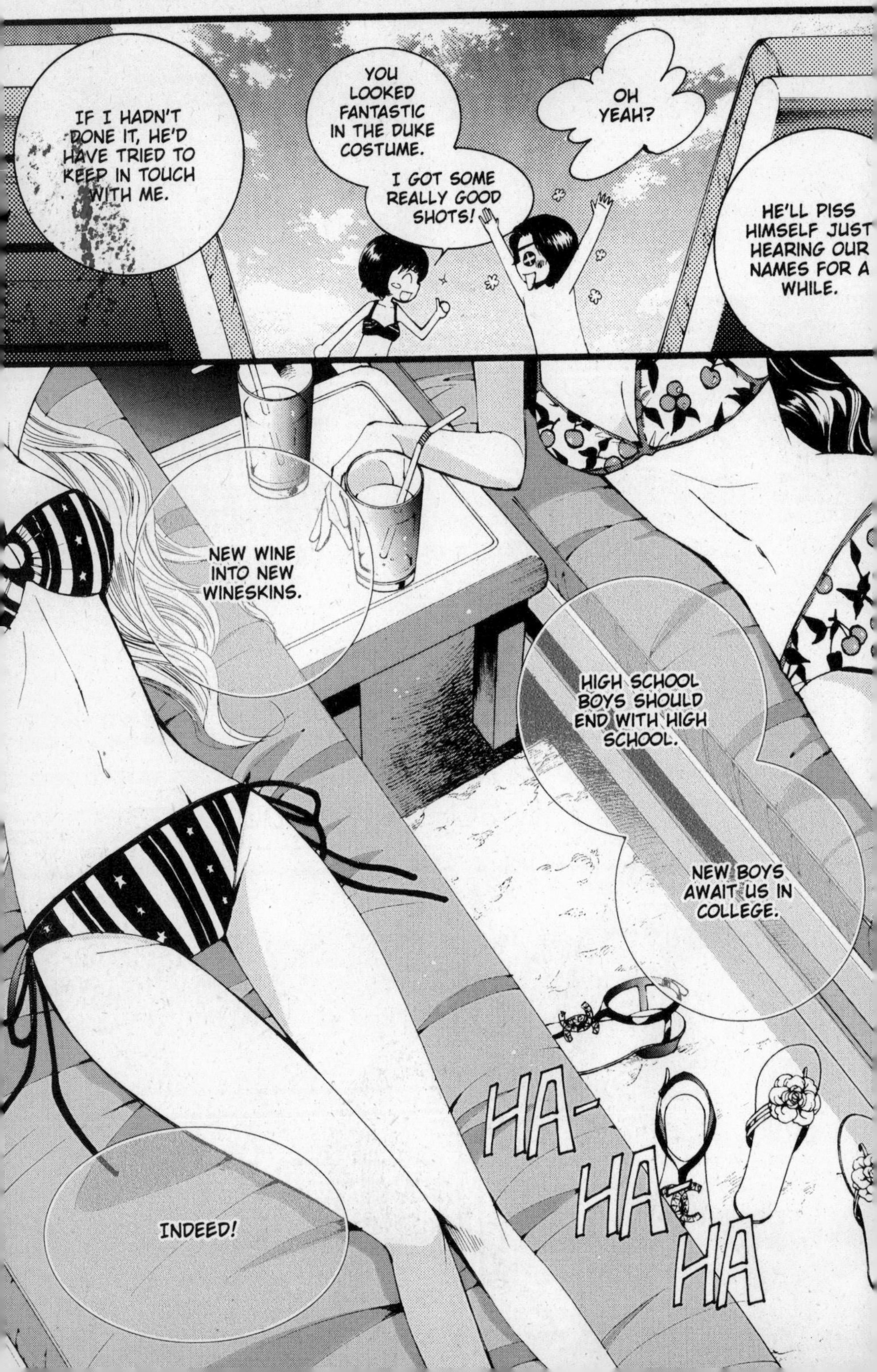
IF I HADN'T DONE IT, HE'D HAVE TRIED TO KEEP IN TOUCH WITH ME.
YOU LOOKED FANTASTIC IN THE DUKE COSTUME.
I GOT SOME REALLY GOOD SHOTS!
OH YEAH?
HE'LL PISS HIMSELF JUST HEARING OUR NAMES FOR A WHILE.
NEW WINE INTO NEW WINESKINS.
HIGH SCHOOL BOYS SHOULD END WITH HIGH SCHOOL.
NEW BOYS AWAIT US IN COLLEGE.
INDEED!
HA-HA-HA